Lean and Green Diet Cookbook 2021

1000+ Healthy & Effortless Recipes and 30-Day Meal Plan to Help You Kill Hunger and Lose Weight Quickly

Wilma Murphy

© Copyright 2021. All rights reserved.

Table of Contents

Introduction

The Lean & Green diet offers a health and fitness lifestyle, incorporating products called "Fuelings." This diet's purpose is "lifelong transformation, one healthy habit at a time," by incorporating healthy practices, engaging with its coaching, and adopting its dietary advice, like Lean & Green products. If you adhere to the Fuelings and replace them every day with a "Lean & Green" meal (one meat, veggie, and balanced fat appetizer), you can remain full and nourished.

What Is Lean & Green Diet?

Lean & Green is a weight loss and maintenance plan that recommends a combination of purchased, refined foods called "Fuelings" and homemade meals. There's no carbs or calories counting. Instead, as part of six-or-so mini-meals every day, followers add water to powdered food or unwrap a cookie. Lean & Green also provides coaches with instructions to help you learn their "Habits of Health" brand. Besides, the strategy advises doing approximately 30 minutes of exercise of mild intensity every day.

What Are You Eating at Lean & Green?

Its 'Fuelings,' that include bars, shakes, cookies, cereal, as well as some savory options, such as soup and mashed potatoes, comprise at least half of any Lean & Green diet. These packaged foods also list the first ingredient as soy protein or whey protein.

The majority of the diet you shop and cook on your own is packed with lean and green foods. This includes:

- 3 servings of broccoli, greens, celery, or cucumbers from non-starchy vegetables.
- 5-7 ounces, such as tuna, chicken, egg whites, turkey, or soy, of cooked lean protein.
- Up to 2 balanced fat meals, such as olive oil, olives, or avocado.

Behind the scenes, some carb curbing also goes on. Since carbohydrates are your main energy source, restricting them sends the body to the best alternative fuel available: to start burning fat, Lean & Green minimizes carbohydrates just enough to consume 80–100 grams a day.

The Benefits of the Lean & Green Diet

Lean & Green diet has so many health benefits. Some of them are as under:

- **It Helps in Weight Loss:** The Lean & Green 5&1 diet plan assists people with weight loss by controlling the serving size of meals and snacks and lowering the number of calories and carbohydrates. The menu reduces the calories of the meal to 800–1000 calories a day and splits them into six regulated food servings. A survey performed for 16 weeks on 198 people reveals that individuals who adopted the Lean & Green diet had a measurable effect on weight loss, obesity levels, and waist height.
- **Less Needed Efforts-Easy to Follow:** As it contains prepared meals from "Fuelings, " the Lean & Green diet plan is easy to execute, and you only need to prepare the meal once a day. Each meal plan, though, comes with demo meal plans that make it much simpler to implement. Besides, this diet encouraged 1–3 "Lean and Greens" meals a day to be prepared, they are easy to produce and have a particular recipe and a shortlist of ingredients.
- **Support in Blood Pressure Control:** The Lean & Green diet plan has the advantage of controlling sufficient blood pressure by encouraging weight loss and less salt consumption. The right study on the Lean & Green diet, however, has not been taken yet, but a 40-week study on 90 persons suffering from obesity, including excess weight disorders, showed substantial improvements in weight and reductions in elevated blood pressure levels.
- **Long-Term Continuing Assistance:** Your diet coaches are available during the year, one of the greatest advantages of adopting the Lean & Green diet. When you are part of the diet plan, they will help manage the weight reduction goals and body maintenance program.

We hope this diet plan works to make the body slim and balanced. It demanded a super simple and less attempted diet plan that has critical impacts on the body. One did not even need to keep away from their cravings for processed food when adopting the Lean & Green diet, as it requires promoting weight loss by consuming pre-packaged low-calorie foods.

Initial Steps

It's all built on our innovative, six-step strategy that will allow you to achieve your personal goals and create your own "Lifelong Optimal Health" foundation.

Those six steps are:

Step 1. Prepare for Your Journey

Your Lean & Green coach will be there for you as you take your first step towards a bigger life to help you see what's possible and to work with you to set the right objectives for yourself. Learning the patterns that lead to "Good Health" begins with maintaining a healthier weight for most individuals. Speak to the trainer about:

- Some queries you have about your journey starting.
- Know the lifestyle program "Habits of Wellness."
- Helping you end the online "Wellness Test."
- Guiding you to set your fitness and wellbeing targets.

Step 2. Achieve A Healthy Weight

The balanced weight is a stimulus for bigger modifications, and the way to get there is the perfect Weight 5&1 Plan®:

- Act to follow our validated Ideal Weight 5&1 Strategy outlined in this guide with your Lean & Green Mentor.
- Note and enjoy each victory and speak with your Lean & Green Coach about possible improvements.
- Participate in our appeals for weekly community assistance.
- Understand your energy management system and take charge of it.

Step 3. Healthy Diet Change

Good eating becomes second nature because you know what a balanced diet looks like. To measure a calorie intake level that preserves your fresh, healthier weight, consult with your Lean & Green coach. Three "Optimum Health Fuels" and three healthy meals are part of our Optimal Health 3&3 Plan®. Please keep loving or matching your favorite Lean & Green fueling, which goes better for your lifestyle. Choose the correct portion sizes and by moving around, begin increasing the overall energy consumption (calories consumed daily). An integral aspect of keeping a healthier weight is also to improve fitness. And don't forget, your mentor, Lean & Green, is still there to assist.

Step 4. Live Healthy Habits

The better habits you integrate into everything you do, the happier you look and sound. These developments are becoming a productive aspect of the routine. Then, in collaboration with your Lean & Green mentor, you can master the "Patterns of Motion and Safe Sleep Patterns, " both to build a room for a bigger life.

Step 5. Optimize Health in Your Age

You've introduced the foundational "Lifestyle Patterns." There are small wins that add up to major ones. You feel better, more optimistic, and there is a rise in the energy levels. You have easily integrated wellness practices into the lifestyle. Optimization is another component of the life transition. Stress management and organizing your life into what matters to you the most. This is when you see that what started as an "Ideal Health" quest will become a strong possibility. When you transition from being the assistant to the coach, your transformation will inspire others. While teaching others the way, you are creating a growing, profitable enterprise. In the Lean & Green culture, you will become a leader.

Step 6. The Ability to Live a Happier, Longer Life

No one can predict how long you will live, but evidence shows that making an overall change in your lifestyle by playing an active role in your decisions and actions, like gaining weight, eating healthy, exercising more, and reducing stress, can help you live a longer, healthier life. For as long as you can, an ideal life means being as safe as you can. After all, your life will become whatever you want it to be, with restored health and energy! "Optimal Wellness" refers to a healthy weight, healthy movement, safe sleep, healthy behaviors, and the ability to improve.

- "Ultra-Wellness" is reaching to you.
- You learn how to create ultimate energy management.
- You learn to safeguard brain development and maintain a balanced body.

Maintenance Phase (Medifast 3&3 Plan)

The Medifast® 5&1 Strategy has helped you get into a good routine of consuming balanced foods for small, regular meals. Medifast® has created the 3&3 Strategy for lifetime weight control and improved fitness to help you preserve all the good work and effort you've done to get fit.

Three plus three is equivalent to six, and that's how many times per day you can have to consume, just as you did on the Medifast® 5&1 Plan:

- Breakfast
- Fueling mid-morning
- Lunch
- Fueling mid-afternoon
- Dinner
- Fueling at night

Depending on your measured maintenance calories, you'll enjoy three smaller "Lean & Green TM"-style meals, plus three (to five) balanced fuels. (The Repair Plan is 3&2—3 meals and two fuels) if the TEE is 200 calories.

Per day, many consumers enjoy two or three Medifast® meals as their balanced fuel. They're a convenient way to supplement your day with compact, nutritious Nutrition per Serving while keeping your calories within range.

Healthy Diet

You will have to consume bananas, low-fat milk products, whole grains, and all vegetables in maintenance, much as you did in change. Here are a few suggestions on what you should choose and what you should stop.

Cereals

1. Pick certain ingredients rather than these foods:
- Whole-grain bread white, processed bread
- Black rice white rice, and white rice
- Whole-wheat pasta, processed pasta from gluten
- Refined wheat whole-grain flour, refined flour
- Whole-grain cereals for breakfast sugary cereals for breakfast

2. Choose foods listed first on the label's ingredient list of whole oats, whole rye, or whole wheat.

3. Look for bread in each slice of at least 3 grams of fiber.

4. Be careful of multi-grain, 100% wheat, stone ground, or bran foods. They are not necessarily whole-grain goods.

5. Pick foods with fewer calories, fats, or oils added.

Examples of a serving with one grain:

- 1 cup of cereal unsweetened
- 1/2 cup of cooked cereal
- 1/3 to 1/2 cup of cooked brown rice
- 1/2 cup of whole-wheat pasta cooked
- 1 whole-grain slice of bread

Dairy Products

1. Pick certain ingredients, rather than these foods:
- Skim, or 1% milk, 2% milk/whole milk
- Whole-milk yogurt tat-free/low-fat yogurt
- Often choose milk and yogurt that are fat-free or low-fat. There is extra sugar in sweetened milk products (which raises calories), so be careful when eating them. Choose yogurt, which is sugar-free.

2. Examples of one serving of milk:
- 1 cup of milk (skim, low-fat 1 percent, or 2 percent)

- 1 cup of low-fat or fat-free soy milk
- 1 cup (low-fat or fat-free) buttermilk
- 1/2 cup of milk evaporated(fat-free)
- 1/2 cup to 1 cup (fat-free or low-fat) yogurt

(Meat/Meat Substitutes) Protein

1. Pick certain ingredients rather than these foods.
2. Boneless, skinless chicken breast with flesh on the chicken thighs.
3. Lean ground beef (70-80 percent lean) standard ground beef (85-99 percent lean).
4. Deep-fried meat cooked, roasted, or broiled meat deep-fried meat.
5. Pick lean beef and pork cuts, such as loin and round cuts.
6. Choose skinless poultry, rather than fry, toast, broil, poach, or barbecue.
7. The leanest poultry options are boneless, skinless chicken breasts, and turkey cutlets.
8. Eat at least two servings of omega-3-fatty acid-rich fish per week, such as salmon, trout, albacore tuna, mackerel, or herring.
9. Choose soybean or textured vegetable protein, legume-type beans, egg whites, egg substitutes, or low-fat cheeses for meat substitutes.
10. There is high cholesterol in the liver and other organ meats, so use it sparingly.
11. Added sodium is present in cooked foods such as pork, sausages, and deli meats. Wherever practicable, select fresh cuts of meat instead of being frozen.
12. Skinless (white meat preferred) chicken or turkey.
13. Whitefish (cod, flounder, haddock, halibut, or trout, fresh or frozen).
14. Tuna (in water new or canned).
15. Salmon (smoked, raw, or canned).
16. Shellfish (clams, net crabs, lobster, scallops, shrimp, or shellfish imitations).
17. Duck, venison, elephant, or ostrich
18. 14 or comparable egg whites (2 cups of egg substitute).
19. 1 cup (1 percent low-fat or fat-free) cottage cheese.
20. 4 oz. cheese (low-fat or free of fat).
21. Processed sandwich meat (turkey, roast beef or ham) with one gram of fat or less per ounce.
22. USDA Pick or Option grades of fat-trimmed lean beef, such as the oval, sirloin, and flank steak, tenderloin, roast rib, chuck, or rump, steak (T-bone, porterhouse).
23. Lamb: roasting, slicing, or leg.
24. Veal: roast or lean chop.
25. 1 cup(cooked) of beans or lentils.

Vegetables & Fruits

1. Serve at least two fruit servings a day (1 serving = 1 medium-sized slice of fruit or ½ cup of cubed fruit or berries) and three servings of vegetables (1 serving = ½ cup of cooked or fresh vegetables or 1 cup of raw salad).
2. If you feel really hungry, go ahead and add more vegetables to your
3. You will get added fiber and nutrients to your daily meal schedule for a minimum intake of calories.
4. Without any added Fat or sauce, use fresh, frozen, or canned fruits or vegetables.
5. Enjoy all vegetables, including those with higher carbohydrates, such as maize, peas, tomatoes, and sprouts from Brussels.
6. It is safe for all vegetables. They have fiber that makes you full up, are low in calories, and vitamins and minerals are filled with them.
7. To get various nutrients, pick a range of colors.

Fats

1. Choose these foods, rather than these foods
- Trans-fat-free butter margarine

- Palm, palm kernel (canola and soybean oil), or coconut oil oils rich in omega-3s
- Strong shortening of peanut oil or olive oil
- Tiny quantities of chocolate and high-calorie nuts and sweets with seeds

Examples of one serving of fat:

- Choices with monounsaturated fat
- 1 teaspoon of olive oil or canola oil
- 8 large black olives
- 1/8 of avocado
- 1/2 tablespoon of peanut butter
- 6 almonds or mixed nuts
- 10 peanuts
- 1 tablespoon of sesame seeds
- 10 large pimento-stuffed green olives
- Polyunsaturated choices for fat
- 2 tablespoons of low-fat dressing

2. Without any added fat or sauce, use fresh, frozen, or canned fruits or vegetables.

Enjoy all vegetables, including those with higher carbohydrates, such as maize, peas, tomatoes, and Brussels sprouts.

All vegetables are healthy. They have fiber that makes you full up, are low in calories, and vitamins and minerals are filled with them.

3. To get different nutrients, choose a variety of colors.

- 1 teaspoon of normal mayonnaise
- 1 tablespoon of mayonnaise with low fat
- 2 whole walnuts or 4 halves of walnut
- 2 teaspoon of Miracle Whip® salad dressing
- 1 tablespoon of Miracle Whip® reduced-fat
- 1 tablespoon of heat flower seeds or pumpkin seeds
- 1 teaspoon of trans-fat-free margarine

Saturated fat choices:

- 2 tablespoons of cream (or half-and-half)
- 1 teaspoon of butter
- 1 tablespoon of cream cheese
- 2 tablespoons of sour cream
- 3 tablespoon of reduced-fat cheese cream
- 1 slice bacon

Food to Have

The only foods approved on the Lean & Green 5&1 Schedule are Lean & Green Fuelings and one "Lean and Green Meal" per day.

Many of these meals consist of lean meats, healthy fats, low-carb vegetables, and two fatty fish servings a week. Some low-carb condiments and drinks are also approved in limited quantities.

In your daily Lean and Green meal, foods allowed include:

- Meat: chicken, turkey, lean beef, game meat, lamb, tenderloin or pork chop, ground beef (at least 85% lean)
- Halibut, trout, salmon, tuna, lobster, crab, shrimp, and scallops: seafood and shellfish
- Eggs: whole eggs, white eggs, beaters for eggs
- Soy goods: just tofu
- Vegetable oils: canola, walnuts, flaxseed, and olive oil

- Such balanced fats: low carb salad dressings, olives, reduced-fat margarine, almonds, walnuts, pistachios, avocado
- Spinach, celery, cucumbers, mushrooms, cabbage, cauliflower, eggplant, zucchini, broccoli, tomatoes, spaghetti squash, jicama, low carb vegetables: collard greens
- Sugar-free snacks: gum, gelatin, popsicles, gum, mint
- Sugar-free drinks: water, almond milk that is not sweetened, tea, coffee
- Condiments and seasonings: dried herbs, spices, salt, lemon juice, lime juice, yellow mustard, soy sauce, salsa, sugar-free syrup, sweeteners for zero calories, 1/2 teaspoon ketchup only, cocktail sauce, or barbecue sauce.
- On the Lean & Green 5&1 plan, homemade meals contain more lean Proteins and low carb vegetables, plus a few good fats. Low carb drinks such as water, unsweetened almond milk, coffee, and tea are permitted only.

Food to Avoid

Any carb-containing foods and drinks are excluded when on the 5&1 Plan, except carbohydrates in the pre-packaged Lean & Green fuels. There are also limits on such fats, as are all fried foods.

Foods to stop include: unless included in the fuels:

- Fried foods: beef, fish, mollusks, vegetables, pastry-like sweets
- White bread, noodles, biscuits, pancakes, tortillas, crackers, white rice, cookies, desserts, baked goods: processed grains
- Some fats: butter, palm oil, shortening solids
- All-fat milk products: milk, cheese, yogurt
- Alcohol: all forms
- Sweetened beverages with sugar: beer, fruit punch, sports drinks, energy drinks, sweet tea
- While on the 5&1 Schedule, the following foods are off-limits but brought in after the 6-week transition process and approved during the 3&3 Plan:
- Fruit: any new fruit
- Low fat or fat-free milk products: yogurt, milk, cheese
- Whole grains: whole grain bread, morning cereal rich in fiber, brown rice, whole-wheat pasta
- Legumes: peas, rice, lentils, soya beans
- Vegetables with starch: sweet potatoes, white potatoes, rice, peas.

You're especially urged to eat berries over other fruits during the transformation process and 3&3 Program, as they are lower in carbs.

Chapter 1: Breakfast Recipes

In this chapter, we are going to give you some delicious and mouthwatering recipes on Octavia Breakfast recipes.

Muffin Pan Frittatas

(Ready in 35 Minutes, Serve 1, Difficulty: Normal)

Nutrition per Serving:

Calories 319, Protein 6.1 g, Carbohydrates 1.5 g, Fat 7 g, Cholesterol 103.7mg, Sodium 146.5mg.

Ingredients:

- Cooking spray
- 1 tablespoon of olive oil
- 1 cup of chopped fresh asparagus
- ¼ cup of chopped green bell pepper
- 2 tablespoons of chopped red onion
- 6 eggs
- ½ cup of milk
- ¼ teaspoon of salt
- ⅛ teaspoon of ground black pepper
- 1 cup of shredded cheddar cheese

Instructions:

1. In a medium-hot saucepan, heat the olive oil, cook and stir the asparagus, green bell pepper, and onion in the hot oil until softened, for 5-10 minutes.

2. In a bowl, combine the eggs, milk, salt, and black pepper. Mix the egg mixture with the cooked vegetables and cheddar cheese. Spoon a mixture of around 1/4 cup into each muffin cup.

3. Bake in the preheated oven for about 20 minutes until the frittatas are set in the middle and lightly browned.

Asparagus Soldiers with A Soft-Boiled Egg

(Ready in 15 Minutes, Serve 6, Difficulty: Easy)

Nutrition per Serving:

Calories 186, Protein 12 g, Carbohydrates 12 g, Fat 10 g, Saturates 2 g, Sugars 0 g, Fiber 2 g, Salt 0.72 g.

Ingredients:

- 1 tablespoon of olive oil
- 50 g of fine dry breadcrumbs
- 1 pinch each chili and paprika
- 16-20 asparagus spears
- 4 eggs

Instructions:

1. In a skillet, heat the oil, add the breadcrumbs, and then fry until golden and crisp.

2. Season with spices and flaky sea salt, then leave to cool.

3. In a large pan of boiling salted water, cook the asparagus until tender for 3-5 minutes.

4. Boil the eggs at the same time for 3-4 minutes.

5. On a plate, placed each egg in an egg cup.

6. Drain and divide the asparagus between plates.

7. Scatter and serve over the crumbs.

No-Cook Overnight Oatmeal

(Ready in 8 Hours and 5 Minutes, Serve 4, and Difficulty: Easy)

Nutrition per Serving:

Calories 279, Protein 9.5 g, Carbohydrates 41.1 g, Fat 9.6 g, Cholesterol 17.8mg, Sodium 69.2mg.

Ingredients:

- ⅓ cup of milk
- ¼ cup of rolled oats
- ¼ cup of Greek yogurt
- 2 teaspoons of chia seeds
- 2 teaspoons of honey
- 1 teaspoon of ground cinnamon
- ¼ cup of fresh blueberries

Instructions:

1. In a 1/2-pint jar with a lid, mix milk, peas, Greek yogurt, chia seeds, sugar, cinnamon, cover, and shake until mixed.

2. Remove the cover and fold the blueberries together. Cover the jar with a cap.

3. Refrigerate the oatmeal overnight for 8 hours.

Honey Nut Crunch Pears

(Ready in 20 Minutes, Serve 6, Difficulty: Normal)

Nutrition per Serving:

Calories 179, Protein 3 g, Carbohydrates 31 g, Fat 6 g, Saturates 0 g, Sugars 21 g, Fiber 4 g, Salt 0.37 g.

Ingredients:

- 4 ripe pears
- 1 knob of butter
- ½ teaspoon of mixed spice
- 2 tablespoons of clear honey
- 50 g of cornflake
- 25 g of toasted flaked almond

Instructions:

1. Heat oven to 200 degrees Celsius (392 F)/ventilator 180/gas 6. Cut out the core, cut the pears in ½ lengthwise, then top with a tiny butter knob and a sprinkling of mixed spice.

2. Put the pears in a shallow baking dish, then roast for 5 minutes before they start to soften.

3. Meanwhile, in a large microwave bowl, heat the honey and another knob of butter for 30 sec. Toss the cornflakes & nuts.

4. Take the pears out of the oven and then add the cornflake mix to the top. Cook for another minute or before a dark golden color takes over the cornflakes.

5. Allow to cool for a few minutes, then serve warm with ice cream (the cornflakes crisp up again when they cool).

Green Lentils and Rice Assyrian Style

(Ready in 40 Minutes, Serve 8, Difficulty: Normal)

Nutrition per Serving:

Calories 123, Protein 8.2 g, Carbohydrates 34.6 g, Fat 7.3 g, Cholesterol 0mg, Sodium 222.1mg.

Ingredients:

* 1 cup of dry green lentils
* 2 cups of water
* 4 tablespoons of divided olive oil
* 1 cup of basmati rice
* 1 large of onion, chopped
* ¾ teaspoon salt, or to taste

Instructions:

1. Place the lentils in a pan and cover them with water.

2. Bring to a rolling boil over high heat for 5 minutes, and then cover and remove it from the heat.

3. Meanwhile, in cold water, rinse the rice until the water is clean.

4. Over medium heat, heat 2 tablespoons of olive or vegetable oil in a skillet. For around 1 minute, whisk in the rice until the grains turn opaque and white, then add the lentils and water.

5. Carry the rice mixture to a simmer, then cover and reduce the heat for 5 minutes to medium-low. Stir once, then cover and further reduce the heat to a minimum.

6. Continue cooking, sealed, until the rice is soft, about 15 more minutes (do not remove the lid!).

7. Meanwhile, over medium heat, heat the remaining 2 tablespoons of oil in the skillet. Stir in the onion, and cook and stir for around 5 minutes until the onion is soft and translucent.

8. Reduce heat to medium-low and continue cooking and stirring, 15-20 minutes more until the onion is very soft and dark brown.

8. Stir in the caramelized onion when the rice is ready and season with salt.

Cranberry & Raspberry Smoothie

(Ready in 5 Minutes, Serve 6, Difficulty: Easy)

Nutrition per Serving:

Calories 100, Protein 4 g, Carbohydrates 17 g, Fat 2 g, Saturates 1 g, Sugars 17 g, Fiber 1 g, Salt 0.16 g.

Ingredients:

* 200ml of cranberry juice
* 176 g of frozen defrosted raspberry
* 100ml of milk
* 200ml of natural yogurt
* 1 tablespoon of caster sugar, or to taste
* Mint sprigs, to serve

Ingredients:

1. In a blender, put all the ingredients and process until smooth.

2. Pour into glasses and serve with new mint coating.

Creamy Yogurt Porridge

(Ready in 10 Minutes, Serve 6, Difficulty: Easy)

Nutrition per Serving:

Calories 184, Protein 13 g, Carbohydrates 26 g, Fat 2 g, Saturates 0 g, Sugars 13 g, Fiber 3 g, Salt 0.4 g.

Ingredients:

* 3 tablespoons(25 g) of porridge oat
* 1 pot (150 g) of 0% fat probiotic yogurt

Instructions:

1. In a shallow non-stick cup, combine 200ml of water and mix in the porridge oats.

2. Cook over low heat until bubbling and thickened. (To make in a microwave, use a deep container to prevent spillage as the mixture will rise as it cooks, and cook for 3 minutes on high.)

3. Stir in yogurt, or swirl in 1/2 and top with the rest.

4. Serve plain or with 1 of our toppings.

Banana pancakes

(Ready in 40 Minutes, Serve 4, Difficulty: Normal)

Nutrition per Serving:

Calories 243, Protein 9 g, Carbohydrates 15 g, Fat 15 g, Saturates 2 g, Sugars 14 g, Fiber 4 g, Salt 0.3 g.

Ingredients:

* 1 large banana
* 2 medium eggs, beaten
* 1 pinch of baking powder (Gluten-free if coeliac)

- 1 splash of vanilla extract
- 1 teaspoon of oil
- 25 g of roughly chopped pecans
- 125 g of raspberries

Instructions:

1. Mash one large banana with a fork in a bowl until it resembles a dense paste.

2. Stir in 2 beaten eggs, a pinch of baking powder, and a splash of vanilla extract (Gluten-free if coeliac).

3. Over medium heat, heat a large non-stick frying pan or pancake pan and spray with 1/2 teaspoon of oil.

4. Spoon 2 pancakes into the pan with ½ the flour, cook each side for 1-2 minutes, then tip them onto a plate.

5. With another 1/2 teaspoon of oil and the remaining batter, repeat the process.

6. Use the 25 g of roughly chopped pecans and 125 g of raspberries to top the pancakes.

Perfect Porridge
(Ready in 15 Minutes, Serve 6, Difficulty: Easy)
Nutrition per Serving:

Calories 317, Protein 10, Carbohydrates 25 g, Fat 5 g, Saturates 2 g, Sugars 0 g, Fiber 3 g, Salt 0.24 g.

Ingredients:
- 50 g of porridge oats
- 350ml of milk or water, or a mixture of the 2

To Serve:
- Greek yogurt thinned with a little milk and clear honey

Instructions:

1. In a saucepan, add 50 g of porridge oats, pour in 350ml of milk or water, and sprinkle with a pinch of salt.

2. Bring to a boil and cook for 5 minutes, stirring from time to time and carefully watching that the pan's bottom does not stick.

2. Or you can try a microwave with this: in a large microwave-proof dish, mix the porridge oats, water or milk, and a pinch of salt, then microwave for 5 minutes on strong, stirring halfway through. Until eating, please leave it to stand for 2 minutes.

3. Spoon Greek yogurt, diluted with a little cream on top, and drizzle with sugar.

4. Pour into cups to serve.

Virginia's Tuna Salad
(Ready in 10 Minutes, Serve 2, Difficulty: Easy)
Nutrition per Serving:

Calories 121, Protein 9.9 g, Carbohydrates 3.9 g, Fat 9.8 g, Cholesterol 59.9mg, Sodium 167.5mg.

Ingredients:
- 1 egg
- 1(5 ounces) can of tuna, drained and flaked
- 3 tablespoons of mayonnaise
- 2 stalks of celery, chopped
- 2 tablespoons of sweet pickle relish
- 1 pinch of ground black pepper

Instructions:

1. Put the egg in a saucepan and cover it with cold water.

2. Bring the water to a boil and remove it from the heat instantly.

3. Cover the egg and allow it rest for 10-12 minutes in hot water. Remove from the hot water and chill for about 5 minutes. Peel and chop into bite-sized bits.

4. Mix the tuna and mayonnaise in a medium dish. Mix the egg, celery, sauce, and black pepper.

Porridge with Blueberry Compote
(Ready in 40 Minutes, Serve 6, Difficulty: Normal)
Nutrition per Serving:

Calories: 215, Protein 13 g, Carbohydrates 54 g, Fat 6 g, Saturated 2.8 g, Sodium 200mg, Sugars 22 g

Ingredients:
- 6 tablespoons of porridge oats
- Just under ½ x 200ml tub 0% fat Greek-style yogurt
- ½ x 350 g of pack frozen blueberries
- 1 teaspoon of honey(optional)

Instructions:

1. Put the oats with 400 ml of water in a non-stick pan and cook overheat, occasionally stirring, until thickened, for around 2 minutes. Remove and combine a third of the yogurt from the heat.

2. Meanwhile, if using and gently poaching until the blueberries have thawed and are tender, while still keeping their form, tip the blueberries into a pan with 1 tablespoon of water and the honey.

3. Spoon the porridge into bowls, top the blueberries with the remaining yogurt, and spoon over.

Kale, Tomato & Poached Egg on Toast
(Ready in 40 Minutes, Serve 3, Difficulty: Normal)
Nutrition per Serving:

Calories 251, Protein 15 g, Carbohydrates 18 g, Fat 12 g, Saturates 3 g, Sugars 2 g, Fiber 3 g, Salt 0.8 g.

Ingredients:

- 2 teaspoon of oil
- 100 g of ready-chopped kale
- 1 clove of garlic, crushed
- ½ teaspoon of chili flakes
- 2 large eggs
- 2 slices of multigrain bread
- 50 g of halved cherry tomatoes
- 15 g of crumbled feta

Instructions:

1. Adjust the heat so that a wide water pan is brought to a boil.

2. Heat the oil over medium-hot heat in a frying pan and add the kale, garlic, and chili flakes.

3. Cook for 4 minutes, stirring regularly until the kale starts to crisp and wilts to 1/2 its size. Set aside.

4. Water rises to a rolling boil, and the eggs are poached for 2 minutes. Toast the bread.

5. With a slotted spoon, remove the poached eggs and cover each slice of toast with half of the kale, the egg, the cherry tomatoes, and the feta.

High-Fiber Muesli

(Ready in 5 Minutes, Serve 18, Difficulty: Normal)

Nutrition per Serving:

Calories 124, Protein 4 g, Carbs 23 g, Fat 3 g, Saturates 0 g, Sugars 0 g, Fiber 3 g, Salt 0.16 g.

Ingredients:

- 300 g of jumbo oats
- 100 g of All-Bran®
- 25 g of wheat germ
- 100 g of dark raisins
- 140 g of ready-to-eat snipped into chunks apricots
- 50 g of golden linseed

Instructions:

1. In a large bowl, combine everything. It would help if you placed it in an air-tight jar for up to 2 months.

2. Pour a lot of chilled milk over when you're about to serve and let it soak for a couple of minutes.

Fig, Nut & Seed Bread with Ricotta & Fruit

(Ready in 2 Hours and 45 Minutes, Serve 16, and Difficulty: Normal)

Nutrition per Serving:

Calories 249, Protein 10 g, Carbohydrates 30 g, Fat 10 g, Saturates 3 g, Sugars 20 g, Fiber 6 g, Salt 0.3 g.

Ingredients:

- 400ml of hot strong black tea
- 100 g of dried fig, hard stalks removed, thinly sliced
- 140 g of sultana scones
- 50 g of porridge oat
- 200 g of self-raising whole meal flour
- 1 teaspoon of baking powder
- 100 g of mixed nuts (almonds, walnuts, Brazils, hazelnuts)
- 1 tablespoon of golden linseed
- 1 tablespoon of sesame seeds, plus 2 teaspoons to sprinkle
- 25 g of pumpkin seed
- 1 large egg
- 25 g of ricotta per person
- 1 orange or green apple, thickly sliced, per person

For Topping:

- 50 g of mixed nuts

Instructions:

1. Heat oven to 170 degrees Celsius (338 F)/fan 150 degrees Celsius/gas 3½. Pour the tea into a large bowl and stir in the figs, sultanas, and oats. Set aside to soak.

2. Meanwhile, line 1 kg loaf tin with baking parchment on the base and bottom.

3. Mix the rice, baking soda, nuts, and seeds. In the cooled fruit mixture, beat the egg and then stir the dried ingredients into the liquid one. With the additional nuts and sesame seeds, dump into the tin, then level the surface and disperse.

4. Bake for 1 hour, then cover the top with foil and bake until a skewer inserted into the loaf center comes out clean for 15 more minutes.

5. To cool, remove from the tin but keep the parchment on until cold. Spread with ricotta, split into pieces, and serve with berries.

6. Store in the refrigerator for one month, or freeze into slices.

Eggy Spelt Bread with Orange Cheese & Raspberries

(Ready in 20 Minutes, Serve 2, Difficulty: Normal)

Nutrition per Serving:

Calories 197, Protein 14 g, Carbohydrates 12 g, Fat 10 g, Saturates 3 g, Sugars 4 g, Fiber 2 g, Salt 0.6 g.

Ingredients:

- 2 medium eggs
- 2 tablespoons of orange juice
- 2 slices of spelt bread, halved

- 50 g of low-fat cottage cheese
- 1 teaspoon of orange zest
- 1 teaspoon of rapeseed oil
- 50 g of raspberries
- Clear honey, to serve (optional)

Instructions:

1. In a bowl wide enough to fit the bread in it, beat the eggs and orange juice. Soak the bread in the eggs and milk for 2 minutes or so, rotating halfway through.

2. Meanwhile, blend the cheese and orange zest in a shallow bowl. Put the rapeseed oil over high heat in a non-stick frying pan. Add the eggy bread when heated.

3. Leave to cook untouched for a few minutes, then flip and cook for another 1-2 minutes on the other side.

3. Divide the bread into 2 pans, dollop up the cheese, followed, if you prefer, by the raspberries and honey.

Peanut Butter Banana Smoothie

(Ready in 5 Minutes, Serve 4, Difficulty: Easy)

Nutrition per Serving:

Calories 133, Protein 12.8 g, Carbohydrates 34.1 g, Fat 18.8 g, Cholesterol 9.8mg, Sodium 202.8mg.

Ingredients:

- 2 bananas, broken into chunks
- 2 cups of milk
- ½ cup of peanut butter
- 2 tablespoons of honey, or to taste
- 2 cups of ice cubes

Instructions:

Place the banana, peanut butter, honey, milk, and ice cubes in a blender and blend for about 30 seconds until smooth.

Yummy Veggie Omelet

(Ready in 15 Minutes, Serve 6, Difficulty: Normal)

Nutrition per Serving:

Calories 386, Protein 21.7 g, Carbohydrates 9.1 g, Fat 29.8 g, Cholesterol 429.8mg, Sodium 1157.8mg.

Ingredients:

- 2 tablespoons of butter
- 1 small onion, chopped
- 1 green bell pepper, chopped
- 4 eggs
- 2 tablespoons of milk
- ¾ teaspoon of salt
- ⅛ teaspoon of freshly ground black pepper
- 2 ounces of shredded Swiss cheese

Instructions:

1. In a medium skillet over medium pressure, melt one tablespoon of butter. Place the bell pepper and onion inside the skillet. Cook for 4-5 minutes, stirring regularly until the vegetables are smooth.

2. Then beat the eggs with the milk, 1/2 teaspoon of salt and pepper while the vegetables are frying.

3. In a small bowl, shred the cheese and set it aside.

4. Remove the vegetables from the heat, sprinkle the remaining 1/4 teaspoon of salt over them, and transfer them to another bowl.

5. Over medium heat, melt the remaining one tablespoon butter (in the skillet just used to cook the vegetables).

6. Coat the butter with the skillet. Add the egg mixture when the butter is bubbly and cook the egg for 2 minutes or before the eggs begin to set on the pan's bottom. Using a spatula to gently lift the omelet's edges and let the uncooked portion of the eggs flow toward the edges, and cook.

7. Continue to cook for 2-3 minutes or until the omelet center begins to look dry.

8. Sprinkle the cheese over the omelet and spoon into the middle of the omelet with the vegetable mixture.

9. Fold one edge of the omelet carefully over the vegetables using a spatula. For another 2 minutes or until the cheese melts to your perfect consistency, let the omelet cook.

10. Slide the omelet onto a plate and out of the skillet.

11. Break and serve in 2.

Pumpkin Parfait

(Ready in 1 Hour, Serve 6, Difficulty: Easy)

Nutrition per Serving:

Calories 117, Protein 4.9 g, Carbohydrates 12.7 g, Fat 0.2 g, Cholesterol 2.5mg, Sodium 260.6mg.

Ingredients:

- 1 cup of pumpkin puree
- 1(1 ounce) of package instant sugar-free vanilla pudding mix
- 1 teaspoon of pumpkin pie spice
- 1 cup of evaporated skim milk
- 1 cup of skim milk

Instructions:

1. Combine the vanilla pudding paste, pumpkin puree, pumpkin pie spice, evaporated milk, and condensed milk in a mixing bowl.

2. Mix until gentle, put in perfect glasses, and chill until set.

Ham, Mushroom & Spinach Frittata

(Ready in 20 Minutes, Serve 4, Difficulty: Normal)

Nutrition per Serving:

Calories 226, Protein 22 g, Carbs 0 g, Fat 15 g, Saturates 5 g, Sugars 0 g, Fiber 1 g, Salt 1.1 g.

Ingredients:

- 1 teaspoon of oil
- 80 g of chestnut mushrooms, sliced
- 50 g of diced ham
- 80 g of bag spinach
- 4 medium eggs, beaten
- 1 tablespoon of grated cheddar cheese

Instructions:

1. Heat the grill to its maximum setting.

2. Over medium-high pressure, heat the oil in an oven-safe frying pan. Tip in the mushrooms and fry until mostly softened, for 2 minutes.

3. Stir in the ham and spinach, and simmer until the spinach has wilted for another 1 min.

4. Season well with black pepper and a pinch of salt.

5. Reduce the heat and pour the eggs over them. Cook for 3 minutes undisturbed until the eggs are mostly complete.

6. Sprinkle over the cheddar cheese and place it for 2 minutes under the grill.

7. Serve cold or hot.

Blueberry and Banana Steel Cut Oats

(Ready in 5 Hours and 10 Minutes, Serve 6, and Difficulty: Normal)

Nutrition per Serving:

Calories 131, Protein 6.8 g, Carbohydrates 64.6 g, Fat 4.3 g, Cholesterol 0mg, Sodium 230.8mg.

Ingredients:

- 2 cups of water
- 2 cups of almond milk
- 2 cups of blueberries
- 2 ripe bananas, mashed
- 1 cup of steely cut oats
- 2 tablespoons of honey
- 2 teaspoons of vanilla extract
- 1 teaspoon of ground cinnamon
- ¼ teaspoon of salt

Instructions:

1. Stir water, almond milk, oats, honey, vanilla extract, blueberries, bananas, cinnamon, and salt together in the crock of a slow cooker.

2. Cook on low heat for 5-8 hours.

Cardamom & Peach Quinoa Porridge

(Ready in 40 Minutes, Serve 4, Difficulty: Normal)

Nutrition per Serving:

Calories 231, Protein 8 g, Carbohydrates 37 g, Fat 4 g, Saturates 1 g, Sugars 10 g, Fiber 6 g, Salt 0.2 g.

Ingredients:

- 75 g of quinoa
- 25 g of porridge oats
- 4 cardamom pods
- 250ml of unsweetened almond milk
- 2 ripe peaches, cut into slices
- 1 teaspoon of maple syrup

Instructions:

1. In a shallow saucepan, combine 250ml of water and 100ml of almond milk to the quinoa, oatmeal, and cardamom pods. Bring to a boil, then simmer gently, stirring regularly, for 15 minutes.

2. Pour in the remaining almond milk and cook until smooth for an additional 5 minutes.

3. Remove the pods of cardamom, spoon them into bowls or pots, then add the peaches and maple syrup to the end.

Creamy Mustard Mushrooms on Toast with A Glass of Juice

(Ready in 15 Minutes, Serve 6, Difficulty: Easy)

Nutrition per Serving:

Calories 220, Protein 13 g, Carbohydrates 28 g, Fat 7 g, Saturates 2 g, Sugars 16 g, Fiber 4 g, Salt 0.1 g.

Ingredients:

- 1 slice of wholemeal bread
- 1 ½ tablespoon of light cheese cream
- 1 teaspoon of rapeseed oil
- 3 handfuls of sliced, small flat mushrooms
- 2 tablespoons skimmed milk
- ¼ teaspoon of wholegrain mustard
- 1 tablespoon of snipped chives
- 150ml of orange juice freshly squeezed or from a carton

Instructions:

1. Toast the bread, then sprinkle (do not use butter) with a little cheese.

2. Meanwhile, in a non-stick skillet, heat the oil and cook the mushrooms, stirring regularly, until they are softened. Spoon in cream, extra cheese, and mustard.

3. Until coated, stir well. Cover with chives.

4. Serve with the juice on the bread.

Hash Browns with Mustard & Smoked Salmon

(Ready in 20 Minutes, Serve 4, Difficulty: Normal)

Nutrition per Serving:

Calories 129, Protein 9 g, Carbohydrates 18 g, Fat 6 g, Saturates 2 g, Sugars 1 g, Fiber 1 g, Salt 1.61 g.

Ingredients:

- 1 large potato (about350 g/12 ounces), washed
- 1 tablespoon of plain flour
- 1 tablespoon of wholegrain mustard or horseradish sauce
- 1 tablespoon of sunflower oil
- 4 slices of smoked salmon
- 1 knob of butter

To Serve:

- Soured cream or crème Fraiche
- Chives

Instructions:

1. On a clean tea towel, grate the unpeeled potato. Bring up the towel edges, and squeeze over the sink to clear the potatoes from any excess water. Place the flour and the mustard or horseradish in a bowl. Season well and combine.

2. Divide the mixture into 8 spheres, then with your hands, flatten it.

3. With the butter and oil, heat a large frying pan, then add the potatoes to the pan.

4. Cook on each side for 2-3 minutes, over medium heat, until golden.

5. On each serving plate, stack a few hash browns and finish with a slice of smoked salmon, a dollop of soaked cream or crème Fraiche, and some chives to serve.

English Muffins

(Ready in 2 Hours and 15 Minutes, Serve 18, and Difficulty: Normal)

Nutrition per Serving:

Calories 190, Protein 4.9 g, Carbohydrates 34 g, Fat 3.5 g, Cholesterol 1.1mg, Sodium 136.2mg.

Ingredients:

- 1 cup of milk
- 2 tablespoons of white sugar
- 1(25 ounces) package of active dry yeast
- 1 cup of warm water (110 degrees Fahrenheit /45 degrees Celsius)
- ¼ cup of melted shortening
- 6 cups of all-purpose flour
- 1 teaspoon of salt

Instructions:

1. In a small saucepan, heat the milk until it bubbles, then remove it from the heat. Combine the sugar, stirring until dissolved. Allow it to cool until lukewarm. Dissolve the yeast in warm water in a small bowl. Let it stand for around 10 minutes before creamy.

2. Combine the milk, yeast mixture, shortening, and 3 cups of flour in a large dish. Beat until smooth. Add the salt and the rest of the flour, or add enough to make the dough fluffy. Knead. Place it in a greased bowl and cover it, then let it rise.

3. Roll out to a thickness of about 1/2 inch. Using a biscuit knife, a drinking glass, or an empty tuna can cut rounds. Sprinkle the cornmeal with waxed paper and set the rounds on this to rise. Dust the tops of muffin with cornmeal. Cover it and let it rise for ½ hour.

4. Cook the muffins on the griddle for around 10 minutes over medium heat on either side. Store the baked muffins in a warm oven until they're all finished. Allow it to cool and put it in a plastic bag for storage. To use, split and toast great with orange butter, or cream cheese and jam.

Skinny Pepper, Tomato & Ham Omelet

(Ready in 15 Minutes, Serve 6, Difficulty: Normal)

Nutrition per Serving:

Calories 206, Protein 21 g, Carbohydrates 5 g, Fat 12 g, Saturates 3 g, Sugars 5 g, Fiber 1 g, Salt 1.21 g.

Ingredients:

- 2 whole eggs
- 3 egg whites
- 1 teaspoon of olive oil
- 1 red pepper, deseeded and finely chopped
- 2 spring onions, white and green parts kept separate and finely chopped
- Few slices of wafer-thin extra-lean ham, shredded
- 25 g of reduced-fat mature cheddar cheese

To Serve (optional):

- Wholemeal toast
- 1-2 chopped fresh tomatoes

Ingredients:

1. Mix some seasoning with the eggs and egg whites and put aside.

2. Heat the oil and cook the pepper for 3-4 minutes in a medium non-stick frying pan.

3. Throw the spring onions In the white parts and cook for a further 1 minute.

4. Pour in the eggs and cook until almost completely set, over medium heat.

5. Sprinkle on the ham and cheese and continue to cook until just put in the middle, or if you like it more done, flash it under a hot grill.

6. Serve with the green portion of the spring onion scattered on top, the sliced tomato, and some wholemeal toast straight from the pan.

Banana Yogurt Pots

(Ready in 30 Minutes, Serve 6, Difficulty: Easy)

Nutrition per Serving:

Calories 230, Protein 7 g, Carbohydrates 40 g, Fat 6 g, Saturates 1 g, Sugars 39 g, Fiber 1 g, Salt 0.23 g.

Ingredients:

- 1 (x-side) tub of thick yogurt
- 3-4 bananas, cut into chunks
- 4 tablespoons of sort dark brown sugar
- 25 g of toasted and chopped walnuts

Instructions:

1. Dollop approximately 1 tablespoon of yogurt into 4 little glasses at the bottom.

2. Add the banana layer and some more yogurt. Until the glasses are full, repeat the layers.

3. Scatter over the sugar and nuts and leave for 20 minutes in the refrigerator before the sugar has dissolved.

Baked Eggs Brunch

(Ready in 40 Minutes, Serve 4, Difficulty: Normal)

Nutrition per Serving:

Calories 210, Protein 12 g, Carbohydrates 10 g, Fat 13 g, Saturates 3 g, Sugars 7 g, Fiber 5 g, Salt 0.5 g.

Ingredients:

- 2 tablespoons of olive oil
- 2 leeks, thinly sliced
- 2 onions, thinly sliced
- 2 (100 g each) bags of baby spinach leaves
- Handful fresh wholemeal breadcrumbs
- 25 g of finely grated parmesan (or vegetarian alternative)
- 4 heat dried tomatoes, chopped
- 4 medium eggs

Instructions:

1. Heat oven to 200 degrees Celsius (392 F)/fan 180 degrees Celsius/gas 6. In a skillet, heat the oil and combine the leeks, onions, and seasoning it.

2. Cook until smooth and begin to caramelize for 15-20 minutes.

3. Meanwhile, place the spinach in a colander and pour a hot water kettle over it. Squeeze out as much liquid as possible while it is cold enough to handle. Mix the breadcrumbs and butter.

4. Arrange the leek and onion mixture between 4 ovenproof bowls, then scatter with the spinach and the sliced tomato. In the center of each dish, make a well and crack an egg in it. Season with the cheese crumbs and sprinkle.

5 Place the dishes on a baking tray and cook for 12-15 minutes until the whites are fixed and the yolks are cooked to your preference.

Waffled Falafel

(Ready in 30 Minutes, Serve 6, Difficulty: Easy)

Nutrition per Serving:

Calories 210, Protein 10 g, Carbohydrates 38.7 g, Fat 2.1 g, Cholesterol 0mg, Sodium 1470.7mg.

Ingredients:

- Cooking spray
- 2(15 ounces) cans of garbanzo beans(chickpeas), drained and rinsed
- 1 medium onion, chopped
- 2 large egg whites
- ¼ cup of chopped fresh cilantro
- ¼ cup of chopped fresh parsley
- 3 cloves of roasted garlic, or to taste
- 1 ½ tablespoon of all-purpose flour
- 2 teaspoons of ground cumin
- 1 ¾ teaspoon of salt
- 1 teaspoon of ground coriander
- ¼ teaspoon of ground black pepper
- ¼ teaspoon of cayenne pepper
- 1 pinch of ground cardamom

Instructions:

1. Preheat a waffle iron according to directions from the maker. Spray the waffle iron inside with the cooking spray.

2. Cook the garbanzo beans until coarsely sliced in a food processor. Add the garbanzo beans to the onion, garlic, rice, egg whites, cilantro, parsley, cinnamon, cilantro, cayenne pepper, black pepper, and cardamom. Pulse, sometimes scraping down the sides of the dish, until a coarse meal resembles falafel batter. In a bowl, add the batter and stir with a fork.

3. Spoon onto each part of the preheated waffle iron around 1/4 cup of falafel batter.

4. Cook until it is browned uniformly, about 5 minutes. Repeat for the batter that remains.

Avocado Toast with Egg

(Ready in 10 Minutes, Serve 4, Difficulty: Easy)

Nutrition per Serving:

Calories 230, Protein 11.9 g, Carbohydrates 20.8 g, Fat 22.9 g, Cholesterol 191.4mg, Sodium 360.9mg.

Ingredients:

- 1 teaspoon of butter
- 2 eggs
- 2 slices of multigrain bread
- 1 ripe avocado, pitted, peeled
- 1 teaspoon of lemon juice, or to taste
- 1 pinch of cayenne pepper
- Sea salt, to taste
- Ground black pepper, to taste

Instructions:

1. Melt butter over medium-low heat in a skillet. Crack the side of the egg by the side in the skillet and cook for 2-3 minutes, until the eggs on the bottom layer are white and solid enough to flip-flop the shells, attempt not to break the yolk, and cook for 2-5 more minutes before the egg achieves the ideal density.

2. In the meantime, toast slices of bread to the perfect doneness for 3-5 minutes.

3. In a dish, stir in the avocado, cayenne pepper, lemon juice, and sea salt. Spread the combination of avocado over the bread. Place the fried egg on top and season with sea salt and pepper.

Zucchini Pancakes

(Ready in 20 Minutes, Serve 6, Difficulty: Easy)

Nutrition per Serving:

Calories 236, Protein 9.6 g, Carbohydrates 22.2 g, Fat 26.9 g, Cholesterol 216.5mg, Sodium 936.9mg.

Ingredients:

- 4 eggs
- 2 cups of grated zucchini
- ¾ cup of all-purpose flour
- ½ teaspoon of white sugar
- ½ teaspoon of salt
- 3 tablespoons of olive oil
- 4 teaspoons of baking powder
- ¼ cup of butter, melted

Instructions:

1. Preheat the grill to 425-450 degrees Fahrenheit (218-225 degrees Celsius).

2. Beat the eggs in a large mixing bowl, add the shredded zucchini and mix well with a fork. To mix well, salt, add flour, sugar, and vegetable oil and stir.

3. Finally, combine the baking powder and use a large spoon to blend properly. The consistency of the batter should be like whipping heavy cream.

4. For each pancake, spoon the batter over a hot grill (about 2 tablespoons). Cook for about 2 minutes before no more bubbles form in the pancake, turn over and cook for 2 minutes longer.

5. Rub with melted butter on the pancakes and serve immediately.

Blueberry Muffins

(Ready in 30 Minutes, Serve 1, Difficulty: Normal)

Nutrition per Serving:

Calories 206, Protein 5 g, Carbohydrates 36 g, Fat 6 g, Saturates 1 g, Sugars 16 g, Fiber 2 g, Salt 0.43 g.

Ingredients:

- 5 tablespoons of rapeseed oil
- 225 g of self-rising flour
- 115 g of whole meal flour
- 2 teaspoons of baking powder
- Zest of ½ lemon
- 1 teaspoon of lemon juice
- 85 g of golden caster sugar
- 50 g of light muscovado sugar
- 1 small (about 85 g peeled weight) very ripe banana with black skin
- 1 egg
- 284ml of pot buttermilk
- 225 g of fresh blueberries

Instructions:

1. Heat oven to 200 degrees Celsius (392 F)/180 degrees Celsius fan/gas 6. To lightly oil a 12-hole muffin pan, use 1 teaspoon of oil to (or use paper cases).

2. For the baking powder and lemon zest, combine all flours. Reserve 1 tablespoon of caster sugar. Stir the remainder into the flour with the muscovado sugar, then the caster sugar.

3. Mash well with the banana. Beat the egg in a separate dish, then whisk in the banana, buttermilk, and oil.

4. Stir very lightly into the flour mix using a broad metal spoon, enough to blend. Over-mixing can make things difficult for muffins.

5. Toss the blueberries in and allow the spoon only a few turns to stir them in gently without crushing.

3. Spoon the mixture into the tin, and it should be really deep in each hole. Bake until lifted and golden, for 20-25 minutes.

4. With the lemon juice, combine the reserved caster sugar. Remove from the oven when the muffins are cooked, then broach with the sugar and lemon mixture while still sweet.

5. Loosen each muffin's edges gently with a knife, then leave to cool for 15 minutes in the tin, as they are very fragile when heated.

6. Remove to the wire rack. Best eaten on the day of preparation, but can last for up to 2 days.

Chia Seed Pudding

(Ready in 10 Minutes, Serve 6, Difficulty: Normal)

Nutrition per Serving:

Calories 312, Protein 7.1 g, Carbohydrates 38.2 g, Fat 7.9 g, Cholesterol 1mg, Sodium 158.9mg.

Ingredients:

*   1 cup of unsweetened vanilla-flavored almond milk
*   1 cup of vanilla fat-free yogurt
*   2 tablespoons of pure maple syrup
*   1 teaspoon of pure vanilla extract
*   ⅛ teaspoon of salt
*   ¼ cup of chia seeds
*   1-pint of strawberries, hulled and chopped
*   4 teaspoons of pure maple syrup
*   ¼ cup of toasted almonds

Instructions:

1. In a cup, whisk together almond milk, tofu, 2 teaspoons maple syrup, vanilla, and salt until combined, add chia seeds, whisk to combine, and let the chia seeds soak for 30 minutes.

2. To reallocate seeds that have settled throughout the mixture, stir the chia seed mixture. Cover the bowl with plastic wrap and chill overnight for 8 hours.

3. Sprinkle 4 teaspoons of maple syrup in a bowl over the strawberries, stir to cover. Add strawberries with almonds, stir.

4. Spoon the mixture of chia seeds into four containers, each with a part of the strawberry mixture.

Banana & Almond Butter Toast

(Ready in 10 Minutes, Serve 4, Difficulty: Normal)

Nutrition per Serving:

Calories 280, Protein 6 g, Carbohydrates 44 g, Fat 11 g, Saturated Fat 1 g, Mono Fat 7 g, Poly Fat 2.5 g, Fiber 5 g, Cholesterol 0mg, Sodium 260mg.

Ingredients:

*   1 tablespoon of almond butter
*   1 slice of rye bread, toasted
*   1 banana, sliced

Instructions:

1. Spread almond butter on toast.

2. Top with banana slices.

Baked Salmon & Eggs

(Ready in 20 Minutes, Serve 6, Difficulty: Normal)

Nutrition per Servings:

Calories 238, Protein 15 g, Carbohydrates 22 g, Fat 10 g, Saturates 4 g, Sugars 1 g, Fiber 1 g, Salt 2 g.

Ingredients:

*   6 crusty white rolls
*   25 g of melted butter
*   6 slices of smoked salmon gravlax
*   6 medium eggs
*   A few snipped of chives

Instructions:

1. Heat oven to 180 degrees Celsius (356 F)/fan 160 degrees Celsius/gas 4.

2. Cut the top of each roll-off, then gently cut the bread's interior until an opening is wide enough to suit a slice of salmon and an egg. Arrange the rolls on a baking dish, with the tops reserved.

2. Using a little melted butter to brush the rolls' inside and sides, arrange a salmon slice inside each. Crack each 1 with an egg and season. Bake until the eggs are cooked to your taste or for 10-15 minutes. With snipped chives, disperse.

3. Brush the tops with the remaining butter, split them into troops, and dip them into shells.

Spiced Sweet Roasted Red Pepper Hummus

(Ready in 1 Hour and 15 Minutes, Serve 8, Difficulty: Hard)

Nutrition per Serving:

Calories 216, Protein 2.5 g, Carbohydrates 9.6 g, Fat 2.2 g, Cholesterol 0mg, Sodium 370.3mg.

Ingredients:

*   1(15 ounces) can of garbanzo beans, drained
*   1(4 ounces) of jar roasted red peppers
*   3 tablespoons of lemon juice
*   1 ½ tablespoon of tahini
*   1 clove of garlic, minced
*   ½ teaspoon of ground cumin
*   ½ teaspoon of cayenne pepper
*   ¼ teaspoon of salt
*   1 tablespoon of chopped fresh parsley

Instructions:

1. Purée the chickpeas, tahini, garlic, red peppers, lemon juice, cayenne, and salt in an electronic blender or food processor.

2. Process until the mixture is fairly smooth and somewhat fluffy, using long pulses. Make sure to scrape the mixture off the sides of the food processor or blender in between pulses. In a serving dish, switch and refrigerate for at least 1 hour.

3. Until serving, brush the hummus with chopped parsley.

Welsh Rarebit Muffins

(Ready in 30 Minutes, Serve 1, Difficulty: Normal)

Nutrition per Serving:

Calories 189, Protein 19 g, Carbohydrates 6 g, Fat 11 g, Saturates 4 g, Sugars 1 g, Fiber 1 g, Salt 0.79 g.

Ingredients:

- 225 g of self-rising flour
- 50 g of plain flour
- 1 teaspoon of baking powder
- ½ level teaspoon of bicarbonate of soda
- ¼ teaspoon of salt
- ½ level teaspoon of mustard powder
- 100 g of strong cheese, half grated and half cubed
- 6 tablespoon of vegetable oil
- 150 g of Greek yogurt
- 125ml of milk
- 1 egg
- 1 tablespoon of Worcestershire sauce

Instructions:

1. Heat oven to 200 C(392 F)/ventilator 180C/gas 6.

2. In a cup, combine the self-raising and plain flour, baking powder, baking soda, salt, and mustard powder.

3. Mix the cheese, grease, yogurt, and sugar, egg, and Worcestershire sauce in a separate bowl.

4. Combine all the ingredients in the muffin tin and divide between the muffin cases.

5. Place for 20-25 minutes in the oven until golden. On a shelf, remove and cool slightly.

6. What you need: ask the children to help prepare everything, weighing scales, measurement bottle, fork, 2 mixing bowls, 12 paper muffin cases, muffin box, cheese grater, sharp knife, cooling rack, and tablespoon.

Spicy Moroccan Eggs

(Ready in 40 Minutes, Serve 4, Difficulty: Normal)

Nutrition per Serving:

Calories 269, Protein 16 g, Carbohydrates 22 g, Fat 10 g, Saturates 2 g, Sugars 11 g, Fiber 8 g, Salt 1 g.

Ingredients:

- 2 teaspoons of rapeseed oil
- 1 large onion, halved and thinly sliced
- 3 cloves of garlic, sliced
- 1 tablespoon of rose harissa
- 1 teaspoon of ground coriander
- 150ml of vegetable stock
- 400 g of can chickpea
- 2 (400 g) cans of cherry tomatoes
- 2 courgettes, finely diced
- 200 g bag baby spinach
- 4 tablespoons of chopped coriander
- 4 large eggs

Instructions:

1. In a big deep-frying pan, heat the oil and fry the onion and garlic for around 8 minutes, stirring from time to time, until the onion and garlic turn golden.

2. Add the harissa and ground coriander, mix well and then dump the liquid into the stock and chickpeas.

3. To thicken the stock a bit, cover and boil for 5 minutes, then mash around one-third of the chickpeas.

4. Put the tomatoes and courgettes in the pan and cook gently until the courgettes are soft, for 10 minutes. Fold the spinach into the pan such that it wilts.

5. In the mixture, stir in the minced cilantro, make 4 hollows, and split into the shells.

6. Cover and cook for 2 minutes, then take off the heat and allow 2 minutes before serving to settle.

Easy Apple Strudel

(Ready in 1 Hour and 10 Minutes, Serve 6, Difficulty: Easy)

Nutrition per Serving:

Calories 230, Protein 5.6 g, Carbohydrates 87.9 g, Fat 16.5 g, Cholesterol 31.8mg, Sodium 130.3mg.

Ingredients:

- 1 Granny Smith apple, peeled, cored and coarsely shredded
- 3 Granny Smith apples, peeled, cored and sliced
- 1 cup of brown sugar
- 1 cup of golden raisins

- 1 sheet of frozen puff pastry, thawed
- 1 egg
- ¼ cup of milk

Instructions:

1. Preheat the oven to 400 degrees Fahrenheit (200 degrees Celsius). Line the parchment paper with a baking sheet.

2. Place the apples in a big bowl. Stir in brown sugar, set aside, and add golden raisins. Place the puff pastry on the baking sheet. For a rolling pin, roll gently.

3. Arrange the apple filling lengthwise down the center of the pastry. Fold the pastry over the mixture lengthwise. Use a bit of water on your fingertips to seal the pastry's sides and rub the pastry edges together.

4. Whisk together the egg and the milk, and brush the pastry on top.

5. Bake for 35-40 minutes in a preheated oven, or until golden brown.

Avocado Toast with Smoked Salmon

Nutrition per Serving:

Calories: 280, Protein: 15 g, Total Fat: 14 g, Saturated Fat: 2 g, Trans Fat: 0 g, Unsaturated Fat: 10 g, Cholesterol: 10mg, Fiber: 9 g.

(Ready in 15 Minutes, Serve 4, Difficulty: Easy)

Ingredients:

- 1 large slice of whole grain bread
- ½ avocado
- 1/16 teaspoon of kosher salt
- 3 thin slices of tomato
- ¼ cup of loosely packed baby spinach
- 1.5 ounces of thinly sliced smoked salmon
- 1 teaspoon of thinly sliced green onions (green part only)
- ½ teaspoon of capers

Instructions:

1. Toast the bread gently.

2. Arrange the avocado slices on the warm toast in a thin layer and brush evenly with salt.

3. Top avocado with tomato, then spinach, then smoked salmon. Sprinkle green onions and capers on top and serve immediately.

Breakfast Smoothie

(Ready in 10 Minutes, Serve 6, Difficulty: Easy)

Nutrition per Serving:

Calories 212, Protein 2 g, Carbohydrates 25 g, Fat 10 g, Saturates 0.1 g, Sugars 24 g, Fiber 5 g, Salt 0.01 g.

Ingredients:

- 1 small ripe banana
- About 140 g of blackberries, blueberries, raspberries, or strawberries (or use a mix)
- Apple juice or mineral water (Optional)

To Serve:

- Runny honey
- Blackberries, blueberries, raspberries, or strawberries

Instructions:

1. In your blender or food processor, slice the banana and add the berries of your choice.

2. Whizz until smooth. Pour in juice or water with the blades whirring to build the consistency you need.

3. Toss on top of a few additional bananas, drizzle with honey and berries, then serve.

Vegan Banana Muffins

(Ready in 30 Minutes, Serve 12, Difficulty: Easy)

Nutrition per serving:

Calories218, Protein 3 g, Carbohydrate 32 g, Fat 10 g, Sodium 253mg.

Ingredients:

- 3-4 very ripe bananas
- 1/4 cup of oil (or softened vegan margarine)
- 1 cup of organic granulated sugar
- 2 cups of all-purpose flour
- 1 teaspoon of salt
- 1 teaspoon of baking soda
- 1 cup of chopped walnuts (optional)

For Topping:

- 2 tablespoons of organic sugar (such as demerara, optional)

Instructions:

1. Gather all the ingredients.

2. Turn the oven to 182 degree Celsius (360 degrees Fahrenheit), produce a 12-cup muffin tin with liners, or coat it with a light spray.

3. Mash the bananas into a large bowl with a fork softly.

4. Add margarine and sugar to the oil or vegan, mix to create.

5. Combine the meal, salt, and baking soda into a separate bowl until it is well mixed. Into the banana mixture, add the meal mixture, and mix well. Do not even over mix. The batter would be thick.

6. Now is the time for you to ply them carefully if you use the walnuts. Alternatively, before baking, you can sprinkle it on top of every single muffin.

7. Put the batter carefully in the muffin tins and fill them approximately 2/3 complete. Sprinkle with organic sugar just before baking if desired.

8. For about 25 minutes, bake the muffins or clean the toothpick. Let it cool a few minutes and relax for longer storage while still warm or cool.

9. Enjoy.

Personal Portobello Pizza

(Ready in 40 Minutes, Serve 4, Difficulty: Normal)

Nutrition per Serving:

Calories 223, Protein 18.8 g, Carbohydrates 10.6 g, Fat 13.6 g, Cholesterol 44.9mg, Sodium 589.9mg.

Ingredients:
- 1 large Portobello mushroom, stem removed
- 1 tablespoon of spaghetti sauce
- ½ cup of mozzarella cheese
- ½ tablespoon of sliced black olives
- 4 slices of pepperoni sausage
- 1 clove of garlic, chopped

Instructions:

1. Preheat the furnace to 375 degrees Fahrenheit (190 degrees Celsius).

2. Place the mushroom on a baking sheet, and bake in the preheated oven for 5 minutes. Remove from the oven and spread the spaghetti sauce in the p cup of a cap. Place the cheese, olives, pepperoni, and garlic on top.

3. Bake for 20 minutes, or until the cheese is golden and melted.

Yogurt Parfait

(Ready in 10 Minutes, Serve 1, Difficulty: Easy)

Nutrition per Serving:

Calories 121, Protein 21.4 g, Carbohydrates 68.2 g, Fat 17.8 g, Cholesterol 12.3mg, Sodium 177.1mg.

Ingredients:
- 2 cups of vanilla yogurt
- 1 cup of granola
- 8 blackberries

Instructions:

1. Layer 1 cup of yogurt, 1/2 cup of granola, and 4 blackberries into a big glass.

2. Place layers to repeat.

Power Oatmeal

(Ready in 25 Minutes, Serve 2, Difficulty: Easy)

Nutrition per Serving:

Calories 102, Protein 9.5 g, Carbohydrates 27.4 g, Fat 11.4 g, Cholesterol 10.5mg, Sodium 81.7mg.

Ingredients:
- 2 tablespoons of peanut butter
- 1 cup of quick cooking oats
- 1 cup of milk
- ½ cup of Greek yogurt
- 1 banana, mashed
- 3 tablespoons of flax seed meal
- 2 tablespoons of peanut butter

Instructions:

1. In a bowl, whisk together the oats, sugar, cream, flaxseed meal, banana, and peanut butter.

2. Refrigerate until set, for 15 minutes.

Chocolate Chip Vegan Muffins

(Ready in 30 Minutes, Serve 15, Difficulty: Normal)

Nutrition per Serving:

Calories 176, Protein 5.6 g, Carbohydrate 44.1 g, Fat 10 g, Cholesterol 0mg, Sodium 222.4mg, Sugars 22 g,

Ingredients:
- 1 cup of flour (such as all-purpose, whole wheat, pastry flour, or a gluten-free 1–1 substitute)
- 1/2 teaspoon of baking soda
- 1 teaspoon of baking powder
- 1 pinch of salt
- 1/2 teaspoon of cinnamon
- 1/4 cup of maple syrup
- 1/2 cup of almond milk
- 3 tablespoons of nut butter (such as peanut or almond butter)
- 1 teaspoon of vanilla extract
- 1 medium banana, mashed
- 1/2 cup of non-dairy chocolate chips (such as mini chocolate chips)

Instructions:

1. Preheat the oven to 350 degrees Fahrenheit. Spread the muffin tin.

2. Mix flour, soda, baking powder, salt and cinnamon together. Mix together.

3. Add the milk, butter, maple syrup, vanilla essence and banana mashed.

4. Stir well together. Stir well.

5. Mix the chocolate chips carefully.

6. Spread the mixture evenly into the six muffins.

7. If desired, add more chocolate chips.

8. Bake in the oven, or gold brown for 20-25 minutes.

9. Refrigerate and enjoy.

Pumpkin Spice Protein Drink

(Ready in 10 Minutes, Serve 6, Difficulty: Easy)

Nutrition per Serving:

Calories 280, Protein 22 g, Carbohydrates 45.6 g, Fat 3 g, Cholesterol 6.3mg, Sodium 191.8mg.

Ingredients:

- 2 bananas, sliced and frozen
- ½ cup of canned pumpkin
- 2 dates, pitted
- 1 scoop of vanilla protein powder
- ½ teaspoon of vanilla extract
- 1 pinch of ground nutmeg
- 1 pinch of ground cinnamon
- 1 pinch of ground cloves
- 1 pinch of ground ginger

Instructions:

Blend almond milk, pumpkin, bananas, dates, protein powder, cinnamon, cloves, vanilla extract, and nutmeg in a blender, and ginger together until smooth.

Vegan Protein Pancakes with Blueberries

(Ready in 30 Minutes, Serve 8, Difficulty: Normal)

Nutrition per Serving:

Calories 210, Protein 18.9 g, Carbohydrates 4.5 g, Fat 1 g, Cholesterol 6.3mg, Sodium 271.9mg.

Ingredients:

- 4 scoops of vanilla protein powder
- 1 cup of almond milk
- 1 teaspoon of vanilla extract (Optional)
- 2(1 gram) packets of stevia powder (Optional)
- ½ teaspoon of salt (Optional)
- Non-stick cooking spray
- 50 fresh blueberries
- ¼ cup of water

Instructions:

1. In a medium bowl, gradually add the protein powder to the almond milk and whisk to combine. Add the vanilla paste, salt, and stevia powder.

2. Over low pressure, heat a skillet and spray with non-stick spray. In a round, pour in a little batter and let cook until set, for around 2 minutes. Flip and cook, on the other hand, for 2 minutes. Transfer to a dish. Repeat for the batter that remains.

3. Place it in a mug with blueberries and water. Heat in the microwave, stirring and mashing the berries at intervals of 30 seconds, until smooth and syrupy, around 2 minutes in total.

4. Pour over the pancakes with sugar.

Spinach, Avocado, and Mango Smoothie

(Ready in 5 Minutes, Serve 4, Difficulty: Easy)

Nutrition per Serving:

Calories 127, Protein 3.3 g, Carbohydrates 38.2 g, Fat 15.1 g, Cholesterol 0mg, Sodium 40.9mg.

Ingredients:

- 1 cup of firmly packed spinach leaves
- ½ cup of frozen mango chunks
- ½ avocado, diced
- 1 tablespoon of powdered lemonade mix
- 1 packet of Stevia sugar substitute
- ¾ cup of cold water

Instructions:

Combine spinach, mango, sugar substitute, avocado, powdered lemonade mix, and water in a blender, blend until thick and frothy.

Cranberry-Walnut Quinoa (Oil Free)

(Ready in 10 Minutes, Serve 4, Difficulty: Easy)

Nutrition per Serving:

Calories 311, Protein 13, Carbohydrates 34, Fat 29 g, Fiber 2.52g.

Ingredients:

- 2 cups water
- 2 cups dried cranberries
- 1 cup quinoa
- 1 cup chopped walnuts
- 1 cup sunflower seeds
- ½ tablespoon cinnamon

Instructions:

1. Wash Quinoa.

2. In a pressure cooker, bring the quinoa, water, and salt in.

3. Get the lid closed.

4. Click 'manual,' then cook on high pressure for 10 minutes.

5. "Hit "cancel" and quick-release when the timer beeps.

6. OPEN the cooker when the pressure is gone.

7. Combine the dried cranberries, almonds, peas, cinnamon, and sweetener.

8. Serve as well as enjoy!

Southwest Breakfast Burritos

(Ready in 1 Hour and 5 Minutes, Serve 20, Difficulty: Normal)

Nutrition per Serving:

Calories 296, Protein 11.7 g, Carbohydrates 19.4 g, Fat 18.8 g, Cholesterol 139.6mg, Sodium 706.6mg.

Ingredients:

- 12 eggs
- ⅔ cup of milk
- ½ teaspoon of salt
- 2 tablespoons of butter
- 453 g bulk of pork sausage
- 2 tablespoons of minced garlic
- ½ red onion, diced
- 1 tomato, diced
- ¼ cup of chopped fresh cilantro
- 1(3.5 ounces) can of diced jalapenos (Optional)
- 1(1 ounce) package of taco seasoning
- 1 ½ cup of shredded cheddar cheese
- 20(6 inches) flour tortillas

Instructions:

1. In a large bowl, whisk together the eggs, milk, and salt.

2. Heat butter over a medium-high in a large skillet. Pour in the mixture of eggs, cook and stir until the eggs are fully set for around five minutes. The cooked eggs should be chopped and put in a large bowl. Set aside.

3. Over medium heat, heat a large skillet and stir in the sausage and garlic up for 5 minutes, cook and stir, then add the onion. Unless the sausage is crumbly, evenly browned, and no longer green, continue cooking and stirring. Drain some extra grease and discard it.

4. Combine the eggs, onion, cilantro, jalapeno, and taco seasoning with the sausage. Allow the mixture to cool down to room temperature and add the cheddar cheese to the mixture.

5. On the work surface, put a tortilla, then spoon some of the fillings halfway between the bottom edge and the tortilla core. Flatten the filling with the back of a spoon into a rectangular shape.

6. Tightly fold the tortilla's bottom over the filling, then fold the left and right sides together. Roll the burrito, making a tight cylinder, up to the top edge. With the remaining ingredients, repeat.

7. Cover individual burritos tightly with plastic wrap and freeze until they are ready for serving. Heat until hot, for 3-4 minutes, in the microwave, before serving.

Banana-Amaranth Porridge (Oil Free)

(Ready in 13 Minutes, Serve 4, Difficulty: Easy)

Nutrition per Serving:

Calories 271, Protein 8 g, Carbohydrates 17 g, Fat 6 g, Fiber 3.25g.

Ingredients:

- 2 ½ cups unsweetened almond milk
- 1 cup amaranth
- 2 sliced bananas
- Dash of cinnamon

Instructions:

1. In your pressure cooker, blend the amaranth, milk, and bananas.

2. Seal the lid.

3. Pick 'manual,' and cook for just 3 minutes at high speed.

4. Hit "cancel" as time is up and wait for the weight to come down independently.

5. You should serve the porridge with cinnamon when all of the pressure is gone.

Pumpkin Spice Muffins

(Ready in 15 Minutes, Serve 12, Difficulty: Easy)

Nutrition per Serving:

Calories 160, Protein 5 g, Total Fat 0.5 g, Sodium 260mg, Potassium 360mg.

Ingredients:

- 1(18.25 ounces) package of spice cake mix
- 1(15 ounces) can of pumpkin puree
- 1-ounce of cinnamon chips
- 1 cup of chopped pecans

Instructions:

1. Preheat the oven to a maximum of 375 degrees Fahrenheit (190 degrees Celsius).

2. Line 18 liners of muffin cups.

3. In a bowl, combine spice cake mixture and pumpkin puree with cinnamon chips until they are fully moistened, stir and add nuts. Spoon the batter with about 2/3-full in prepared muffin cups.

4. Bake in the preheated oven until 25-30 minutes until the toothpick inserted into the center is clean. Cool on a wire rack for 10 minutes before serving.

Chai-Spiced Oatmeal with Mango

(Ready in 13 Minutes, Serve 2-3, Difficulty: Easy)

Nutrition per Serving:

Calories 236, Protein 6 g, Carbohydrates 10 g, Fat 4 g, Fiber 5.5 g.

Ingredients:

* 3 cups water
* 1 cup steel-cut oats
* ½ teaspoon vanilla
* Dash of cinnamon
* Dash of ginger
* Dash of cloves
* Dash of cardamom
* Dash of salt
* ½ mango, cut into pieces

Instructions:

1. In the pressure cooker, mix the water with the oats.

2. Get the cover closed.

3. Click 'manual,' then cook on high pressure for 3 minutes.

4. Hit "cancel" as the beeper rings, then wait for the energy to come down naturally.

5. Place the lid open and stir well.

6. Season and taste.

7. Divide and add sliced mango into even servings.

Carrot Apple Muffins

(Ready in 45 Minutes, Serve 12, Difficulty: Normal)

Nutrition per Serving:

Calories: 203, Carbohydrates: 30 g, Protein: 3.5 g, Fat: 8.5 g, Saturated Fat: 1 g, Trans Fat: 0 g, Cholesterol: 0 mg, Sodium: 255 mg, Fiber: 3.5 g, Sugar: 14 g.

Ingredients:

* 1 1/2 batches of flax eggs
* 1/4 cup of olive oil
* 1/3 cup of very ripe mashed banana
* 1/4 cup of agave nectar or maple syrup (or honey if not vegan)
* 1/2 cup of unsweetened applesauce (or finely grated apple)
* 1/2 cup of brown sugar (or muscovado)
* 1/2 teaspoon of sea salt
* 1 1/2 teaspoon of baking soda
* 1/2 teaspoon of ground cinnamon
* 1/2 cup of plain almond milk(unsweetened)
* 1 heaping cup of grated packed carrot
* 2/3 cup of gluten-free rolled oats
* 1/2 cup of almond meal
* 1 heaping cup of gluten-free flour blend

For Topping:

* 1/4 cup of raw walnuts, chopped

Instructions:

1. In a large bowl, prepare flax eggs and preheat oven to 375 degrees Fahrenheit (190 degrees Celsius).

2. Prepare muffin tin with liners.

3. Add mashed banana, agave rather than maple jar to flax eggs, olive oil and whisk.

4. Then add applesauce and brown sugar to the mixture, baking soda, salt and cinnamon.

5. Stir and add almond milk.

6. Add carrot and mix.

7. Stir in a gluten-free blend of oats, almond meal and oats.

8. Divide evenly between 12 muffin tins and fill them with shredded walnuts(adjustable).

9. Bake for 32-36 minutes, just until the center gets clean with a deep golden-brown toothpick inserted.

10. Remove from the oven and allow 15 minutes to put in the saucepan. Then flip on the sides in the pot to make it cool.

11.They tend to stick to the wrappers if you try unwrapping them too quickly.

12. Store fresh once cooled in a covered bag or container at room temp. Freeze to stay fresh after that.

Avocado Toast

(Ready in 15 Minutes, Serve 4, Difficulty: Easy)

Nutrition per Serving:

Calories 170, Protein 4.9 g, Carbohydrates 16.8 g, Fat 10.1 g, Cholesterol 0mg, Sodium 429.6mg.

Ingredients:

* 4 slices of whole-grain bread
* 1 avocado, halved and pitted
* 2 tablespoons of chopped fresh parsley
* 1 ½ teaspoons of extra-virgin olive oil
* ½ lemon, juiced
* ½ teaspoon of salt
* ½ teaspoon of ground black pepper
* ½ teaspoon of onion powder
* ½ teaspoon of garlic powder

Instructions:

1. Toast bread in an oven with a toaster.

2. Scoop out a cup of avocado. Using a potato masher to blend the parsley, onion powder, lemon juice, olive oil, salt, pepper, and garlic powder.

3. Spread the mixture of avocado into each toast piece.

Low Carb Zucchini Fries

(Ready in 37 Minutes, Serve 6, Difficulty: Normal)

Nutrition per Serving:

Calories 298, Protein 8.9 g, Carbohydrates 4.5 g, Fat 5.4 g, Cholesterol 67.9mg, Sodium 1292.6mg.

Ingredients:

* 2 zucchinis
* 1 tablespoon of salt
* 2 eggs
* ½ cup of ground almonds
* ½ cup of grated parmesan cheese
* ½ teaspoon of dried Italian herb seasoning, or to taste

Instructions:

1. Preheat the oven to 425 degrees Fahrenheit (218 degrees Celsius). Line the parchment paper with a baking sheet.

2. Cut the zucchini into a length of 3 inches, then cut each slice into 9 fries. Place the zucchini fries and sprinkle them with salt in a colander. To remove excess liquid, let the zucchini parts drain for at least 1 hour.

3. In a small cup, beat the eggs. In a second shallow bowl, combine the nuts, the parmesan cheese, and the Italian seasoning. Rinse the salt from the zucchini with paper towels and pat it dry.

4. Dip each piece of zucchini into the beaten egg and roll in the almond coating. On a lined baking sheet, put the coated fries.

5. Bake until the zucchini is tender in the preheated oven and the coating is crisp and browned, about 25 minutes, turning halfway through cooking time.

Soy Yogurt (Oil Free)

(Ready in 12 hours to make + 6 hours chilling before eating, Serve 1, Difficulty: Easy)

Nutrition per Serving:

Calories 55, Protein 4 g, Carbohydrate 5 g, Fat 2g, Fiber 5g.

Ingredients:

* 2 quarts of soy milk
* 1 packet of vegan yogurt culture

Instructions:

1. Mix the milk culture and the yogurt culture.

2. Pour your pressure cooker into a heatproof tub that you know suits in. Keep the lids off.

3. Put the cooker back. You don't have to add more water to the pot, so the pressure does not raise!

4. Close the lid and click the "yogurt." For a dense, smooth yogurt of professional consistency, change the time to 12 hours.

5. When the time is up, go about your business and then pull out the yogurt.

6. Put the lids on the containers and position them for at least 6 hours in the refrigerator.

7. Sweetened with vanilla, honey, jelly, fruit, and so on, the yogurt would be very tangy!

Salmon Wraps

(Ready in 10 Minutes, Serve 2, Difficulty: Easy)

Nutrition per Serving:

Calories 116, Protein 2.5 g, Carbohydrates 3.7 g, Fat 4 g, Cholesterol 11.9mg, Sodium 112mg.

Ingredients:

* 1(8 ounces) package of softened cheese cream
* 2 tablespoons of chopped fresh dill
* 2 tablespoons of chopped fresh chives
* 1 tablespoon of lemon juice
* 3(8 inches) flour tortillas
* 6 slices of smoked salmon

Instructions:

1. In a cup, mix the dill, chives, cream cheese, and lemon juice.

2. Spread over 1/3 of each tortilla with cream cheese. Using a dab of cream cheese to lay 2 salmon slices on top, roll tightly and seal the sides.

3. Cut each roll into segments of 1 inch.

Chapter 2: Snacks Recipes

In this chapter, we are going to give you some delicious and mouthwatering recipes on Octavia Snacks recipes.

White Chocolate Snack Mix

(Ready in 10 Minutes, Serve 40, Difficulty: Normal)

Nutrition per Serving:

Calories 240, Protein 4.5 g, Carbohydrates 18.3 g, Fat 12.7 g, Cholesterol 4.7mg, Sodium 262.3mg.

Ingredients:

- 1(10 ounces) package of mini twist pretzels
- 5 cups of toasted oat cereal
- 5 cups of crispy corn cereal squares
- 2 cups of salted peanuts
- 1(14 ounces) package of candy-coated milk chocolate pieces
- 2(11 ounces) packages of white chocolate chips
- 3 tablespoons of vegetable oil

Instructions:

1. With waxed paper or parchment, line 3 baking sheets. Set aside.

2. Combine mini pretzels, toasted oat cereal, crispy squares of corn cereal, salted peanuts, and candy-coated chocolate bits in a large bowl. Set aside.

3. Heat chips and oil in a microwave-safe bowl over medium-high heat for 2 minutes, stirring once.

5. Microwave for 10 seconds on high, stirring until smooth. Pour over the mixture of cereal and combine properly.

6. Spread over ready-made baking sheets. Cool, and break apart.

7. Store in an airtight jar.

Feta Stuffed Jalapenos

(Ready in 20 Minutes, Serve 1, Difficulty: Normal)

Nutrition per Serving:

Calories 147, Protein 1.5 g, Carbohydrates 4.1 g, Fat 5.8 g, Cholesterol 4.4mg, Sodium 50.6mg.

Ingredients:

- 12 red jalapeno peppers, tops and seeds removed
- ¼ cup of olive oil
- ⅛ cup of distilled white vinegar
- 5 tablespoons of feta cheese
- 1 tablespoon of cheese cream

Instructions:

1. In a pot, put the peppers and add in the olive oil and vinegar. Insert more of each if there is no covering for the peppers. Allow for about 4 hours to marinate.

2. The oven should be preheated to 325 degrees Fahrenheit (165 degrees Celsius). On a baking sheet, place the marinated peppers.

3. Bake for 15-20 minutes, until soft but not browned. Left to calm aside. Mix the feta cheese and the cheese cream in a little tub. Spoon some of the cheese mixtures into each one while the peppers are cool and serve.

4. For packaging, keep a little bit of olive or vegetable oil in a sealed jar.

Salt and Pepper Skillet Fries

(Ready in 25 Minutes, Serve 6, Difficulty: Normal)

Nutrition per Serving:

Calories 128, Protein 5.6 g, Carbohydrates 48.4 g, Fat 8 g, Cholesterol 2.7mg, Sodium 134mg.

Ingredients:

- 2 tablespoons of olive oil
- 1 teaspoon of butter
- 3 large potatoes, sliced lengthwise into 1/2-inch circles and cut into 1/2-inch strips
- ¼ teaspoon of coarse sea salt
- ¼ teaspoon of cracked black pepper

Instructions:

1. Heat the olive oil and butter over medium heat in a skillet. In the hot oil-butter, cook and mix the potato strips until browned on all sides, for about 20-25 minutes.

2. Move the fries to a plate lined with paper towels and season with salt and pepper.

Baked Kale Chips

(Ready in 20 Minutes, Serve 6, Difficulty: Normal)

Nutrition per Serving:

Calories 58, Protein 2.5 g, Carbohydrates 7.6 g, Fat 2.8 g, Cholesterol mg, Sodium 185.1mg.

Ingredients:

- 1 bunch of kale
- 1 tablespoon of olive oil
- 1 teaspoon of seasoned salt

Instructions:

1. Preheat the oven to 350 degrees Fahrenheit (176 degrees Celsius). Cover a baking sheet of parchment paper that is not insulated.

2. Cut the leaves carefully from the thick stems with a knife or kitchen shears and break them into bite-size pieces.

3. Clean and dry the kale properly with a salad spinner. Scatter the olive oil on the kale, then sprinkle it with seasoning salt.

3. Bake for 10-15 minutes, until the sides are brown but not charred.

WWII Oatmeal Molasses Cookies

(Ready in 30 Minutes, Serve 48, Difficulty: Normal)

Nutrition per Serving:

Calories 97, Protein 1.4 g, Carbohydrates 13.5 g, Fat 4.4 g, Cholesterol 7.8mg, Sodium 94.8mg.

Ingredients:

- 2 cups of all-purpose flour
- 2 cups of oatmeal
- 1 teaspoon of baking soda
- 1 teaspoon of baking powder
- 1 teaspoon of salt
- 1 cup of sugar
- ¾ cup of shortening
- 2 eggs, beaten
- 5 tablespoons of light molasses
- 2 teaspoons of vanilla extract
- ½ cup of chopped walnuts (optional)
- ½ cup of raisins (optional)

Instructions:

1. Preheat the oven to 350 degrees Fahrenheit (176 degrees Celsius).

2. Stir the rice, oatmeal, baking soda, baking powder, and salt together in a large bowl.

3. Beat the sugar in another large bowl until smooth and fluffy, and add in the beaten whites, molasses, and vanilla.

4. Mix in the dry ingredients steadily. Stir in the raisins and walnuts. Drop by teaspoonful onto ungreased baking sheets.

5. Bake for 10-12 minutes or until browned slightly. Allow cookies to chill for 5 minutes on a baking sheet before transferring to a wire rack to cool entirely.

Mexican Jicama Snack

(Ready in 10 Minutes, Serve 6, Difficulty: Normal)

Nutrition per Serving:

Calories 118, Protein 1.7 g, Carbohydrates 19.6 g, Fat 0.4 g, Cholesterol 0mg, Sodium 8.7mg.

Ingredients:

- 1 large of jicama

- 2 lime, juiced
- 1 tablespoon of crushed red pepper, or to taste

Instructions:

1. Peel and cut the jicama into French fry-sized parts.

2. Mix lime juice & cayenne pepper in a medium bowl and toss to cover.

3. Serve.

Breaded Chicken Fingers

(Ready in 4 hrs. 10 Minutes, Serve 8, and Difficulty: Normal)

Nutrition per Serving:

Calories 346, Protein 25.4 g, Carbohydrates 14.6 g, Fat 15.7 g, Cholesterol 78.6mg, Sodium 703.7mg.

Ingredients:

- 6 skinless, boneless chicken breast halves, cut into 1/2-inch strips
- 1 egg, beaten
- 1 cup of buttermilk
- 1 ½ teaspoon of garlic powder
- 1 cup of all-purpose flour
- 1 cup of seasoned bread crumbs
- 1 teaspoon of salt
- 1 teaspoon of baking powder

For Drying:

- 1 quart of oil

Instructions:

1. Place the strips of chicken into a large, resealable plastic bag.

2. Blend the egg, buttermilk, and garlic powder in a shallow bowl. Pour the mixture and the chicken into a bag. Seal and chill for 2-4 hours.

3. Mix the bread crumbs, flour, salt, and baking powder in another big, resealable plastic container.

4. Remove the chicken from the fridge and drain, discarding the mixture of buttermilk. Place the chicken in a bag with the flour mixture. Seal and shake to coat.

5. In a large, heavy skillet, heat the oil to 375 degrees F (190 degrees Celsius).

6. Place the coated chicken carefully in the hot oil. Fry until the juices are golden brown and clear.

7. Drain on paper towels.

Salt and Pepper Skillet Fries

(Ready in 25 Minutes, Serve 6, Difficulty: Normal)

Nutrition per Serving:

Calories 228, Protein 5.6 g, Carbohydrates 48.4 g, Fat 8 g, Cholesterol 2.7mg, Sodium 134mg.

Ingredients:

- 2 tablespoons of olive oil
- 1 teaspoon of butter
- 3 large potatoes, sliced lengthwise into ½-inch circles and cut into ½-inch strips
- ¼ teaspoon of coarse sea salt
- ¼ teaspoon of cracked black pepper

Instructions:

1. Heat the olive oil and butter over medium heat in a skillet. In the heated oil-butter, cook and mix the potato strips until browned on all sides, for about 20-25 minutes.

2. Transfer the fries to a plate lined with paper towels and season with salt and pepper.

Kettle Corn

(Ready in 15 Minutes, Serve 4, Difficulty: Normal)

Nutrition per Serving:

Calories 209, Protein 2.4 g, Carbohydrates 24.8 g, Fat 11.9 g, Sodium 0.6mg.

Ingredients:

- ¼ cup of vegetable oil
- ¼ cup of white sugar
- ½ cup of unlopped popcorn kernels

Instructions:

1. Heat the vegetable oil in a big pot over a medium bowl. Stir in the popcorn and sugar until they have warmed up. To prevent the sugar from smoking, cover, shake the pot continuously before the popping has slowed to once, every 2-3 seconds.

2. Remove the pot from the heat and start shaking for a couple of minutes before the popping has stopped. Pour into a large bowl and allow to cool, frequently mixing to break up large clumps.

Vanilla Popcorn

(Ready in 20 Minutes, Serve 1, Difficulty: Normal)

Nutrition per Serving:

Calories 90, Protein 1.2 g, Carbohydrates 9.1 g, Fat 5.7 g, Cholesterol 4.1mg, Sodium 50mg.

Ingredients:

- ¼ cup of corn oil
- 1(4 inches) vanilla bean, split lengthwise
- ¾ cup of unpopped popcorn
- 1 tablespoon of superfine sugar
- Salt, to taste
- 2 tablespoons of butter, melted

Instructions:

1. Heat the corn oil for a minute in a large pot over medium-high or high heat.

2. To the oil, add one kernel of popcorn. Pour in the remaining popcorn as well as the vanilla bean as the kernel bursts. Place the pot with a lid and shake softly until the corn begins to pop, then shake vigorously until the popping subsides.

3. Remove from the heat, and dump it into a big tub. Strip the corn from the vanilla beans. Scrape the vanilla bean seeds together and combine them with the honey.

4. Stir in the corn with sugar, salt, and melted butter until evenly coated.

5. Serve and eat.

Parmesan Thyme Crisps

(Ready in 30 Minutes, Serve 1, Difficulty: Normal)

Nutrition per Serving:

Calories 216, Protein 5.8 g, Carbohydrates 0.7 g, Fat 4.3 g, Cholesterol 13.3mg, Sodium 231.2mg.

Ingredients:

- 8 ounces of fresh-grated parmesan cheese
- 4 teaspoons of fresh thyme leaves

Instructions:

1. Preheat the oven to 300 degrees Fahrenheit (150 degrees Celsius). Line 2 parchment paper baking sheets.

2. In a bowl, mix the parmesan cheese with the thyme leaves. Into the lined baking sheets, drop heaping teaspoonfuls of the mixture, spacing them 2 inches apart. To compress them into 2-inch circles, press lightly with your fingertips.

3. Bake in the preheated oven for 8-10 minutes, until well browned and crispy. Cool slowly, around 2 minutes, on the baking sheets. With a spatula, loosen the edges and cut the parchment paper.

4. Move to wire racks and let cool completely, around 10 minutes, until firm.

Ranch Oyster Crackers

Nutrition per Serving:

Calories 137, Protein 1.9 g, Carbohydrates 16.2 g, Fat 7 g, Cholesterol 0mg, Sodium 558.2mg.

(Ready in 25 Minutes, Serve 20, Difficulty: Normal)

Ingredients:

- 1(1 ounce) package of ranch-style dressing mix
- ½ teaspoon of dried dill weed
- ¼ cup of vegetable oil
- ¼ teaspoon of lemon pepper
- ¼ teaspoon of garlic powder
- 5 cups of oyster crackers

Instructions:

1. Preheat the oven to 250 degrees Fahrenheit (120 degrees Celsius).

2. Combine the dill weed, dressing mix, olive oil, lemon pepper, and garlic powder in a large cup. Add oyster crackers and coat with a toss. Evenly placed on a baking dish.

3. Bake in the preheated oven for 15-20 minutes, gently stirring after 10 minutes. Take it out of the oven and let it cool before eating.

Fruit Leather

(Ready in 6 Hours and 10 Minutes, Serve 16, and Difficulty: Normal)

Nutrition per Serving:

Calories 90, Protein 0.3 g, Carbohydrates 13.5 g, Fat 0.1 g, Cholesterol mg, Sodium 0.8mg.

Ingredients:

* 1 cup of sugar
* ¼ cup of lemon juice
* 4 cups of peeled, cored, and chopped apple
* 4 cups of peeled, cored, and chopped pears

Instructions:

1. Preheat the oven to a temperature of 150 degrees Fahrenheit (65 degrees Celsius). Cover a baking sheet with a sheet of parchment paper or plastic wrap.

2. Combine the sugar, apple, lemon juice, and pear in a blender's container. Cover and blend until smooth. Spread on the prepared pan evenly. Place the pan on the oven's top rack.

3. Bake for 5-6 hours, keeping the door to the oven partway open. When the surface is not tackier, and you may tear it like leather, the fruit is dry.

4. Roll up the plastic wrap and store it in an airtight bag.

Healthier Bran Muffins

(Ready in 40 Minutes, Serve 1, Difficulty: Normal)

Nutrition per Serving:

Calories 197, Protein 3.3 g, Carbohydrates 17.3 g Fat 1.9 g, Cholesterol mg, Sodium 271mg.

Ingredients:

* ½ teaspoon of salt
* 2 tablespoons of packed brown sugar
* 1 ¼ cup of all-purpose flour
* 1 tablespoon of baking powder
* 1 ½ cup of whole bran cereal
* 1 ½ cup of vanilla soy milk
* 1 tablespoon of olive oil
* 2 egg whites

Instructions:

1. Preheat the oven to 400 degrees Fahrenheit (204 degrees Celsius).

2. In a large bowl, sift the sugar, flour, salt, and baking powder together.

3. Combine the bran cereal and soy milk in a separate bowl and leave to rest for 5 minutes before stirring in the olive oil and egg whites.

4-Fold in the warm, dry ingredients. Spoon the batter into cups of muffins.

5. Bake in a preheated oven for around 20 minutes, until lightly browned.

Grilled Bell Peppers with Goat Cheese

(Ready in 20 Minutes, Serve 6, Difficulty: Normal)

Nutrition per Serving:

Calories 219, Protein 2.9 g, Carbohydrates 2.5 g, Fat 8.1 g, Cholesterol 9.2mg, Sodium 292.3mg.

Ingredients:

* 1 clove of garlic, minced
* 2 tablespoons of olive oil
* ½ cup of goat cheese
* 1 tablespoon of lemon pepper seasoning

Instructions:

1. Core and seed the peppers of the bell. Break each of them into 6 wedges and put them in a resalable bag of plastic Add the garlic and add the olive oil to drizzle. Toss, seal, and set aside for at least 20 minutes to marinate.

2. Preheat a medium-hot outside barbecue and gently grease the grill. In a shallow cup, whisk together the goat cheese with lemon pepper seasoning, and set aside.

3. Cook the peppers until lightly charred, around 3 minutes, on the preheated grill, skin-side-up. Flip over the peppers and spill the cheese carefully onto each pepper. Cover the barbecue lid and cook for 2-3 minutes, before the bottoms are gently charred and even the cheese is warm.

Grilled Pineapple Slices

(Ready in 10 Minutes, Serve 8, Difficulty: Easy)

Nutrition per Serving:

Calories 219, Protein 0.5 g, Carbohydrates 10.4 g, Fat 1.6 g, Cholesterol mg, Sodium 1.6mg.

Ingredients:

* 1 fresh pineapple, peeled, cored and cut into rings
* ¼ cup of canned coconut milk
* ½ cup of cinnamon sugar

Instructions:

1. Preheat a grill on medium heat. Oil the grill lightly when the grill is hot.

2. Place the cinnamon sugar and coconut milk in a separate bowl. Dip the pineapple slices into the coconut milk, then cover them with cinnamon sugar.

3. Grill the slices on each side for 6 minutes. Remove and serve on plates.

Mini Pumpkin Butterscotch Muffins

(Ready in 30 Minutes, Serve 48, Difficulty: Normal)

Nutrition per Serving:

Calories 217, Protein 0.8 g, Carbohydrates 10.5 g, Fat 3.2 g, Cholesterol 12.8mg, Sodium 86.3mg

Ingredients:

- 1 ¾ cups of all-purpose flour
- ½ cup of brown sugar
- ½ cup of white sugar
- 1 teaspoon of ground cinnamon
- ½ teaspoon of ground ginger
- ½ teaspoon of ground nutmeg
- 1 teaspoon of baking soda
- ¼ teaspoon of baking powder
- ½ teaspoon of salt
- 2 eggs
- ½ cup of melted butter
- 1 cup of canned pumpkin
- 1(6 ounces) package of butterscotch chips

Instructions:

1. Preheat the oven to 350 degrees Fahrenheit (176 degrees Celsius).

2. Grease a mini-muffin pan with a cooking spray.

3. In a large bowl, sift together the brown sugar, flour, cinnamon, ginger, white sugar, baking soda, nutmeg, baking powder, and salt.

4. In a separate dish, whisk the eggs, sugar, and pumpkin together. Mix a mixture of flour with a mixture of eggs. Stir in the butterscotch chips and pour about ¾ full into each cup of the muffin tin.

3. Bake in a preheated oven for 10-12 minutes, until the toothpick inserted in the middle of the muffin comes out clean.

Coconut and Chocolate Rice Crispiest

(Ready in 30 Minutes, Serve 2, Difficulty: Normal)

Nutrition per Serving:

Calories 119, Protein 0.7 g, Carbohydrates 17.6 g, Fat 2.5 g, Cholesterol 5.1mg, Sodium 80.7mg

Ingredients:

- ¼ cup of butter

- 1(10 ounces) package of large marshmallows
- 5 cups of chocolate-flavored crispy rice cereal
- 1/3 cup of sweetened flaked coconut

Instructions:

1. Grease a 9x13-inch pan. Melt butter over medium-low heat in a large saucepan. Add the marshmallows and stir until they are smooth and warm. Remove from the heat.

2. To coat, stir the marshmallow mixture quickly into the cereal and coconut. Use the back of a buttered spoon to press into the prepared plate until cutting into squares.

3. Cool completely, and then serve.

No-Bake Energy Bites

(Ready in 30 Minutes, Serve 2, Difficulty: Normal)

Nutrition per Serving:

Calories 219, Protein 2.5 g, Carbohydrates 10.6 g, Fat 5.3 g, Cholesterol 0mg, Sodium 27.9mg.

Ingredients:

- 1 cup of rolled oats
- ½ cup of mini semi-sweet chocolate chips
- ½ cup of ground flax seed
- ½ cup of crunchy peanut butter
- ⅓ cup of honey
- 1 teaspoon of vanilla extract

Instructions:

1. In a bowl, mix oats, flax seeds, chocolate chips, peanut butter, sugar, and vanilla extract, and use your hands to shape balls.

2. On a baking sheet, place energy bites and freeze once set, nearly for 1 hour.

Baked Oatmeal Breakfast Bars

(Ready in 1 Hour and 5 Minutes, Serve 8, Difficulty: Normal)

Nutrition per Serving:

Calories 118, Protein 5.3 g, Carbohydrates 16.2 g, Fat 6.7 g, Cholesterol 48.9mg, Sodium 270.6mg

Ingredients:

- 2 cups of old-fashioned rolled oats
- ⅓ cup of packed brown sugar
- 1 tablespoon of white sugar
- 1 ½ teaspoon of baking powder
- ½ teaspoon of salt
- ½ teaspoon of ground cinnamon
- 1 cup of milk
- 2 eggs
- 2 tablespoons of canola oil

- 1 teaspoon of vanilla extract

Instructions:

1. Preheat the oven to 350 degrees Fahrenheit (176 degrees Celsius). Grease an 8-inch square pan.

2. In a bowl, add the oatmeal, baking powder, brown sugar, white sugar, salt, and cinnamon. In a separate bowl, whisk together the milk, canola oil, eggs, and vanilla extract.

3. Stir the egg mixture into the oat mixture until well mixed, set aside for around 20 minutes until the flavors blend. Spread the blended oats into the prepared square pan.

4. Bake in the preheated oven for around 30 minutes, until the sides are golden brown.

Coconut Cream Pops

(Ready in 10 Minutes, Serve 10, Difficulty: Normal)

Nutrition per Serving:

Calories 90, Protein 3 g, Carbohydrates 11 g, Fat 3.5 g, Sodium 44.5mg.

Ingredients:

- 1(12 fluid ounces) can of fat-free evaporated milk
- 1(13.5 ounces) can of light coconut milk
- ½ cup of confectioners' sugar
- 2 teaspoons of coconut extract
- Ground cinnamon, to taste

Instructions:

1. Whisk together the evaporated milk, coconut milk, confectioners' sugar, coconut extract, and ground cinnamon.

2. Pour into freezer pop molds, and freeze them until they are solid.

Alabama Fire Crackers

(Ready in 2-3 Hours, Serve 30, Difficulty: Normal)

Nutrition per Serving:

Calories 218, Protein 1.2 g, Carbohydrates 12.5 g, Fat 13.9 g, Cholesterol 0mg, Sodium 320.2mg.

Ingredients:

- 1 ⅔ cup of vegetable oil
- 1 teaspoon of garlic powder
- 1 teaspoon of onion powder
- ½ teaspoon of black pepper
- 2(1 ounce) envelopes of ranch dressing mix
- 3 tablespoons of crushed red pepper flakes
- 1(16.5 ounces) package of multigrain saltine crackers

Instructions:

1. In a 2-gallon plastic zipper container, place the vegetable oil, garlic powder, black pepper, onion powder, ranch dressing blend, and crushed red pepper flakes.

2. To mix the oil and spices thoroughly, close the bag and smooch between your hands. To cover the crackers with the spice blend, put the crackers in the bag, seal, and turn it over.

3. Let the bag sit for 1 hour or so, then turn it over again. Repeat some more times and allow the bag to sit overnight till the crackers are well-coated with the spice mix.

4. Remove and serve the crackers.

Salmon Deviled Eggs with Homemade Mayonnaise

(Ready in 30 Minutes, Serve 2, Difficulty: Normal)

Nutrition per Serving:

Calories 119, Protein 5.1 g, Carbohydrates 0.7 g, Fat 7.9 g, Cholesterol 113.2mg, Sodium 61.4mg.

Ingredients:

- 2 egg yolks, room temperature
- 1 clove of garlic, pressed
- ½ cup of vegetable oil
- 1 pinch of salt
- Pepper, to taste
- 2 tablespoons of red-wine vinegar, or to taste
- 12 eggs
- 1 shallot, minced
- 1(6 ounces) can of salmon, drained and flaked
- 1 pinch of salt and pepper, or to taste

Instructions:

1. Beat the egg yolks in a medium bowl with an electric mixer or hand blender to make the mayonnaise. Slowly blend 1 tablespoon at a time into the oil while continuously mixing. Continue to add oil until it is a little smoother than regular mayonnaise.

2. Pierce the clove of garlic and whisk in the mixture before it releases its juice. Season with salt and pepper and cut the garlic. Mix 1 teaspoon at a time with the red wine vinegar. Go slow. This will make the mayonnaise a little thinner.

3. In a large pot, place the eggs with enough water to cover them. Bring to a boil and simmer for 10 minutes. Remove from the heat, drain, and cool.

4. Peel off the shells and cut the eggs lengthwise in halves. Remove the yolks, then place the yolks in a medium bowl. On a serving plate, put the egg whites.

5. Add the shallot, trout, 1/2 cup of mayonnaise, salt, and pepper to the yolks. Mix until completely

combined. Stir in more mayonnaise if the mixture is dry.

6. Spoon into the egg white halves and cool or serve.

Annie's Fruit Salsa and Cinnamon Chips

(Ready in 25 Minutes, Serve 10, Difficulty: Normal)

Nutrition per Serving:

Calories 131, Protein 6.8 g, Carbohydrates 59 g, Fat 5.9 g, Cholesterol 0mg, Sodium 461.7mg.

Ingredients:

- 2 kiwis, peeled and diced
- 2 Golden Delicious apples, peeled, cored, and diced
- 8 ounces of raspberries
- 453 g of strawberries
- 2 tablespoons of white sugar
- 1 tablespoon of brown sugar
- 3 tablespoons of fruit preserves, any flavor
- 10(10 inches) flour tortillas
- Butter flavored cooking spray
- 2 tablespoons of cinnamon sugar

Instructions:

1. In a large bowl, combine the kiwis, golden sweet apples, raspberries, bananas, white sugar, brown sugar, and fruit preserves deeply. Cover and chill for at least 15 minutes in the refrigerator.

2. Preheat the oven to 350 degrees Fahrenheit (176 degrees Celsius).

3. Coat one side of each flour tortilla with a cooking spray flavored with butter. Cut into wedges and arrange on a wide baking sheet in one single layer.

4. Sprinkle the wedges with the quantity of cinnamon sugar desired. Spray again with cooking spray.

5. Bake for 8-10 minutes in a preheated oven. Repeat for any tortilla wedges that remain. Allow it to cool for about 15 minutes.

6. Serve with a mixture of chilled fruit.

Porcini Mushroom Pate

Nutrition per Serving:

Calories 569, Protein 20 g, Fat 29 g, Saturated Fat 4.6 g, Trans Fat 0 g, Cholesterol 53mg, Sodium 1497mg, Sugars 4.8 g.

(Ready in 2 hours, 21 minutes, Serve 6-8, Difficulty: Hard)

Ingredients:

- 453 g sliced fresh Cremini mushrooms
- 30 grams rinsed dry porcini mushrooms
- 1 cup boiling water
- ¼ cup dry white wine
- 1 bay leaf
- 1 sliced shallot
- 2 tablespoons olive oil
- 1 ½ teaspoons salt
- ½ teaspoon white pepper

Instructions:

1. In a bowl, put the dried porcini mushrooms and pour over the boiling water.

2. For now, cover and put aside.

3. In your pressure cooker, boil one tablespoon of oil.

4. When the shallot is hot, cook until it is tender.

5. Add the Cremini and cook until the mushrooms have become golden.

6. For the wine, deglaze it and let it evaporate.

7. Pour the porcini mushrooms and their water together.

8. Add salt, pepper, and bay leaf to the mixture.

9. Cover the lid and seal it.

10. Pick the "manual" and cook for 10 minutes at high speed.

11. "Hit "cancel" and quick-release when the timer beeps.

12. Before adding the last tablespoon of oil, pick out the bay leaf.

13. Mixture of purée until smooth.

14. Before feeding, refrigerate in a closed jar for at least 2 hours.

Potato Chips

(Ready in 10 Minutes, Serve 2, Difficulty: Normal)

Nutrition per Serving:

Calories 80, Protein 1.2 g, Carbohydrates 11.6 g, Fat 3.5 g, Sodium 294.5mg, Cholesterol mg.

Ingredients:

- 1 tablespoon of vegetable oil
- 1 potato, sliced paper-thin (Peeling is optional)
- ½ teaspoon of salt, or to taste

Instructions:

1. Through a plastic bag, pour vegetable oil (a produce bag works well). Add the slices of potatoes and shake to coat.

2. Lightly coat a large dinner plate with oil or cooking spray. Arrange the potato slices on the large plate in a single layer.

3. Cook for 3-5 minutes, or until gently browned in the microwave (if they are not browned, they will

not become crisp). Depending on the microwave's power, time can vary.

4. Take the chips off the plate and toss them with salt (or other seasonings). Let it cool. Repeat the procedure with the remaining slices of potatoes. No need to continue to oil the plate.

Donut Muffins

(Ready in 30 Minutes, Serve 2, Difficulty: Normal)

Nutrition per Serving:

Calories 188, Protein 0.8 g, Carbohydrates 12.8 g, Fat 3.9 g, Cholesterol 0.4mg, Sodium 66.3mg.

Ingredients:

* ½ cup of white sugar
* ¼ cup of melted margarine
* ¾ teaspoon of ground nutmeg
* ½ cup of milk
* 1 teaspoon of baking powder
* 1 cup of all-purpose flour
* ¼ cup of margarine, melted
* ½ cup of white sugar
* 1 teaspoon of ground cinnamon

Instructions:

1. Preheat the oven to 375°Fahrenheit (190 degrees Celsius).

2. Grease 24 cups of mini-muffins.

2. In a large bowl, blend 1/4 cup margarine, 1/2 cup sugar, and nutmeg. Stir in the egg, then whisk in the baking powder and the flour until just mixed. Fill up about half the prepared mini muffin cups.

3. Bake until the tops are lightly brown, for 15 to 20 minutes, in the preheated oven.

4. Place 1/4 cup of melted margarine in a bowl when the muffins are baking. Mix 1/2 cup of sugar with the cinnamon in a separate bowl.

5. Remove the muffins from their cups, add the melted margarine to each muffin, and roll in the cinnamon-sugar mixture.

6. Allow it to cool and serve.

Extra Easy Hummus

(Ready in 10 Minutes, Serve 2, Difficulty: Easy)

Nutrition per Serving:

Calories 118, Protein 3.7 g, Carbohydrates 16.5 g, Fat 4.4 g, Cholesterol 0mg, Sodium 501.9mg.

Ingredients:

* 1(15 ounces) can of garbanzo beans, drained and liquid reserved
* 1 clove of garlic, crushed
* 2 teaspoons of ground cumin
* ½ teaspoon of salt
* 1 tablespoon of olive oil

Instructions:

1. Mix the garbanzo beans, salt, garlic, and olive oil in a blender or food processor. Blend at a low level, adding the reserved bean liquid gradually.

2. Until they obtain the required consistency.

Dirty Diapers

(Ready in 30 Minutes, Serve 3, Difficulty: Normal)

Nutrition per Serving:

Calories 90, Protein 4.8 g, Carbohydrates 4 g, Fat 5.9 g, Cholesterol 16.1mg, Sodium 210.8mg.

Ingredients:

* 453 g of ground beef
* 1 small onion, finely chopped
* 1(10 ounces) can of refrigerated crescent roll dough
* 8 slices of cheddar cheese
* 32 slices of dill pickle

Instructions:

1. The oven should be preheated to 350 degrees Fahrenheit (176 degrees Celsius).

2. Place the ground beef over a medium-high in a skillet. Cook until it is no longer pink, stirring to crumble. In the pan, add the onion, roast, and stir until tender. Drain out the grease.

3. Unroll the dough from the crescent roll on a clean surface. To make two smaller triangles, separate the triangles and then cut each one in ½ diagonally.

4. Stack the cheese slices and cut them into 4 triangles diagonally. Place 1 cheese triangle on each dough triangle. Spoon over the cheese with about a tablespoon of ground beef and then finish with a slice of pickle.

5. Like a diaper, fold the dough's points into the middle and put them on a baking sheet.

6. Bake in the preheated oven for 10-15 minutes, until golden brown.

Fried Farfalle Chips

(Ready in 20 Minutes, Serve 1, Difficulty: Normal)

Nutrition per Serving:

Calories 269, Protein 1.3 g, Carbohydrates 5 g, Fat 5.1 g, Cholesterol 0.7mg, Sodium 15.4mg.

Ingredients:

* 2 cups of bow tie pasta
* 4 tablespoons of vegetable oil
* 2 tablespoons of grated parmesan cheese

- 1 teaspoon of chili powder
- 1 teaspoon of garlic powder
- 1 teaspoon of dry mustard

Instructions:

1. To a boil, bring a large pot of mildly salted water. Add the pasta and cook for 8-10 minutes or until al dente, drain and rinse the pasta under cold water. The pasta should be thoroughly drained from the water.

2. Heat the oil to 375 degrees Fahrenheit (190 degrees Celsius) in a large skillet and fry around 1 cup of pasta at a time until golden. Drain on towels.

3. Combine the parmesan, chili powder, garlic powder, and dried mustard in a large bowl. Toss the drained pasta with it.

4. Serve.

Prosciutto e Malone (Italian Ham and Melon)

(Ready in 15 Minutes, Serve 6, Difficulty: Normal)

Nutrition per Serving:

Calories 99, Protein 3.9 g, Carbohydrates 11.3 g, Fat 4.8 g, Sodium 296.4mg, Cholesterol 12.5mg.

Ingredients:

- 1 cantaloupe, seeded and cut into 8 wedges
- 8 thin slices of prosciutto

Instructions:

1. Remove the tissue from the cantaloupe's rind.

2. Wrap a slice of ham for each piece of cantaloupe.

3. Serve it cold.

Spicy Pretzels

(Ready in 15 Minutes, Serve 10, Difficulty: Normal)

Nutrition per Serving:

Calories 316, Protein 0.3 g, Carbohydrates 3.4 g, Fat 16.5 g, Cholesterol 0mg, Sodium 552.6mg.

Ingredients:

- 1 teaspoon of ground cayenne pepper
- 1 teaspoon of lemon pepper
- 1 ½ teaspoon of garlic salt
- 1(1 ounce) package of dry ranch-style dressing mix
- ¾ cup of vegetable oil
- 1 ½ (15 ounces) package of mini pretzels

Instructions:

1. In a shallow bowl, mix the cayenne pepper, ranch-style dressing mix, lemon pepper, garlic salt, and vegetable oil.

2. Place the pretzels in a plastic bag that is wide and sealable.

3. Pour the mixture out of the tub. Shake well. Allow the pretzels to marinate for around 2 hours in the mixture before eating.

4. Shake occasionally to preserve the coating.

Baked Tortilla Chips

(Ready in 20 Minutes, Serve 6, Difficulty: Normal)

Nutrition per Serving:

Calories 147, Protein 3.3 g, Carbohydrates 26 g, Fat 4.1 g, Sodium 418mg.

Ingredients:

- 1(12 ounces) package of corn tortillas
- 1 tablespoon of vegetable oil
- 3 tablespoons of lime juice
- 1 teaspoon of ground cumin
- 1 teaspoon of chili powder
- 1 teaspoon of salt

Instructions:

1. Preheat the oven to 350 degrees Fahrenheit (176 degrees Celsius).

2. Break each tortilla into wedges of 8 chip sizes and place the wedges on a cookie sheet in a single layer.

3. Combine oil and lime juice in a mister. Mix well and spray until mildly moist with each tortilla wedge.

4. In a small dish, mix the chili powder, salt, and brush on the chips.

5. Bake for about 7 minutes. Rotate the pan and bake until the chips are crispy but not too brown, or for another 8 minutes.

6. Serve with garnishes, salsas, or guacamole.

Chex® Muddy Buddies

(Ready in 25 Minutes, Serve 18, Difficulty: Normal)

Nutrition per Serving:

Calories 206, Protein 3.2 g, Carbohydrates 30.7 g, Fat 9 g, Cholesterol 6.8mg, Sodium 192.2mg.

Ingredients:

- 9 cups of Rice Chex®, Corn Chex®, or Chocolate Chex® cereal (or combination)
- 1 cup of semisweet chocolate chips
- ½ cup of peanut butter
- ¼ cup of butter or margarine
- 1 teaspoon of vanilla
- 1 ½ cup of powdered sugar

Instructions:

1. Measure the cereal in a large bowl and put it aside.

2. Microwave peanut butter, chocolate chips, and butter uncovered on high for 1 minute, in 1-quart microwaveable bowl and stir.

3. Microwave for 30 seconds longer or before it is possible to smoothly stir the mixture. Stir in the vanilla Pour over the cereal mixture, stirring until evenly coated. Pour in a plastic container with 2-gallon resalable food-storage.

4. Add sugar powder. Shake until well coated. Seal the container. Spread to cool on waxed parchment.

5. Store in a refrigerator in airtight packages.

Pecan Snack

(Ready in 1hr. 20 Minutes, Serve 4, Difficulty: Normal)

Nutrition per Serving:

Calories 117, Protein 1.4 g, Carbohydrates 6.7 g, Fat 10.2 g, Cholesterol 0mg, Sodium 74.4mg.

Ingredients:

- 1 egg white
- 1 tablespoon of water
- 453 g of pecans
- ¾ cup of white sugar
- 1 teaspoon of ground cinnamon
- 1 teaspoon of salt

Instructions:

1. Preheat the oven to 250 degrees Fahrenheit (120 degrees Celsius).

2. Beat the white egg with water in a large bowl until frothy. Stir in the pecans and coat with the mixture. Combine sugar, cinnamon, and salt and stir into pecan mixture. Spread on a baking sheet.

3. Bake for 1 hour in a preheated oven, stirring every 15 minutes.

4. Place in an airtight jar.

Fresh Applesauce

(Ready in 25 Minutes, Serve 8, Difficulty: Normal)

Nutrition per Serving:

Calories 186, Protein 0.5 g, Carbohydrates 48.6 g, Fat 0.3 g, Cholesterol 0mg, Sodium 4.8mg.

Ingredients:

- 4 apples, peeled, cored and chopped
- 3 cups of water
- 1 cup of white sugar
- 1 tablespoon of lemon juice

Instructions:

1. In a large saucepan, put the apples and barely cover them with water. Simmer until the apples are soft, for around 15-20 minutes, over medium-low heat.

2. Run the cooked apples through a blender or food mill. Stir in the lemon juice and honey. Cook for approximately 3-5 minutes over medium heat.

Sweet, Salty, Spicy Party Nuts

(Ready in 30 Minutes, Serve 16, Difficulty: Normal)

Nutrition per Serving:

Calories 219, Protein 4.8 g, Carbohydrates 12.7 g, Fat 18.1 g, Cholesterol 1.9mg, Sodium 205.7mg.

Ingredients:

- Cooking spray
- 1 cup of untoasted walnut halves
- 1 cup of untoasted pecan halves
- 1 cup of unsalted, dry-roasted almonds
- 1 cup of unsalted, dry-roasted cashews
- 1 teaspoon of salt
- ½ teaspoon of fresh-ground black pepper
- ¼ teaspoon of ground cumin
- ¼ teaspoon of cayenne pepper
- ½ cup of white sugar
- ¼ cup of water
- 1 tablespoon of butter.

Instructions:

1. Preheat the oven to 350 degrees Fahrenheit (176 degrees Celsius). Cover the baking sheet with an aluminum foil and lightly coat it with a cooking spray.

2. In a large bowl, combine the walnut halves, almonds, pecan halves, and cashews. To coat, add cinnamon, black pepper, and cayenne pepper.

3. In a small saucepan over medium heat, heat the sugar, water, and butter until the butter is melted. Remove from the heat and simmer for 1 minute. Pour the butter mixture slowly over the nut bowl and stir to coat.

4. Move the nuts to the baking sheet that has been prepared and spread into a single layer.

5. Bake the nuts for 10 minutes in a preheated oven. Stir in the nuts until each nut is filled with warm syrup. Spread into a single layer, return to the oven and bake for around 6 minutes, until the nuts are sticky and roasted.

6. Before serving, allow it to cool.

Caramel Snack Mix

(Ready in 1 Hour and 30 Minutes, Serve 20, Difficulty: Normal)

Nutrition per Serving:

Calories 226, Protein 3.4 g, Carbohydrates 36.9 g, Fat 12.6 g, Cholesterol 12.2mg, Sodium 182.6mg.

Ingredients:

- ½ cup of butter
- ¾ cup of white-corn syrup
- 1 cup of packed brown sugar
- 1 cup of chopped pecans
- 1 cup of almonds
- 1(12 ounces) package of crispy corn and rice cereal

Instructions:

1. Preheat the oven to 275 degrees Fahrenheit (135 degrees Celsius). Spray a large roasting pan with a non-stick cooking spray.

2. Mix the white corn syrup, butter, and brown sugar in a medium-sized, microwave-proof bowl. In a microwave, place the mixture and cook for 2 minutes, or until the butter melts.

3. In the prepared roasting pan, put the cereal, pecans, and almonds. Pour the molten butter mixture over the nuts and cereal and blend gently until the nuts and cereal are coated.

4. Bake for 1 hour, stirring every 15 minutes.

5. Since the snack mix is cooling, make sure to continue to mix so that the mixture will not harden in one big lump.

Jalapeno Snacks

(Ready in 25 Minutes, Serve 10, Difficulty: Normal)

Nutrition per Serving:

Calories 126, Protein 10.5 g, Carbohydrates 4.5 g, Fat 22.3 g Cholesterol 55mg, Sodium 708.3mg.

Ingredients:

- 1(8 ounces) package of softened cheese cream
- 1 cup of shredded cheddar cheese
- ¼ cup of mayonnaise
- 1(1 ounce) package of dry ranch salad dressing mix
- 1 ½ teaspoon of garlic powder
- 20 large jalapeno peppers, halved and seeded
- 453 g of sliced bacon, cut in half

Instructions:

1. Preheat the oven to a temperature of 400 degrees Fahrenheit (204 degrees Celsius).

2. In a mixing bowl, whisk together the cream cheese, mayonnaise, cheddar cheese, ranch dressing blend, and garlic powder until combined uniformly.

3. Spoon some of the cheese mixtures onto each half of the jalapeno, wrap it with ½ strip of bacon, and protect it with a toothpick. Using a broiler pan to arrange the packed jalapeno halves.

4. Bake in a preheated oven for around 20 minutes before the bacon is no longer pink and starts to brown.

Grandma Olga's Kolacky

(Ready in 1 Hour and 30 Minutes, Serve 7, Difficulty: Normal)

Nutrition per Serving:

Calories 90, Protein 1.1 g, Carbohydrates 14.1 g, Fat 3.5 g, Cholesterol 12.8mg, Sodium 36.3mg.

Ingredients:

- 1 teaspoon of white sugar
- ¼ cup of warm water (100 degrees Fahrenheit/40 degrees Celsius)
- 2(25 ounces) packages of active dry yeast
- 4 cups of sifted all-purpose flour
- 1 cup of softened margarine
- 4 egg yolks
- 1 cup of sour cream
- 3(10 ounces) of jars apricot or another fruit filling (such as Baker® Fine Dessert Filling)

For Dusting:

- ½ cup of confectioners' sugar

Instructions:

1. In a bowl, dissolve the sugar in hot water, then stir in the yeast. Let stand until a creamy coating of yeast emerges, around 5 minutes.

2. Mix the flour and margarine in another bowl until well mixed, and stir in the egg yolks, one at a time. To make a fluffy but not sticky dough, add in the yeast mixture once incorporated, then stir in the sour cream.

3. Break the dough into 6 same-sized bits, cover with a cloth and refrigerate for a minimum of 1 hour.

4. Preheat the oven to 350 degrees Fahrenheit (176 degrees Celsius). Grease sheets for baking or a line of parchment paper.

5. Rolling out one of the dough balls into 6x8-inch a squared, around 1/8-inch thick, operating on a floured work surface. Keep refrigerating the other bits of dough.

6. Cut the rectangle into 12 smaller squares, about 2 inches on 1 side, using a pastry cutter or pizza roller. In the middle of each square, put around 2 teaspoons of fruit filling and fold 2 opposite dough corners to meet in the center.

7. To partly enclose the filling, pinch the corners together. Place the filled Kolacky on baking sheets that have been prepared.

8. Bake in the preheated oven for 20-25 minutes, until the cookies begin to become golden brown.

9. Before removing them onto wire racks to finish cooling, let the baking sheets chill for around 2 minutes. Sprinkle Kolacky confectioners' sugar.

Granola Bars
(Ready in 25 Minutes, Serve 8, Difficulty: Normal)
Nutrition per Serving:
Calories 188, Protein 3.9 g, Carbohydrates 34.4 g, Fat 4.7 g, Cholesterol 0mg, Sodium 70.3mg.
Ingredients:
- Quick, easy granola bars.
- 2 cups of rolled oats
- ½ cup of shredded coconut
- ½ cup of honey
- 2 tablespoons of creamy peanut butter
- 1 teaspoon of vanilla extract
- ⅛ teaspoon of salt
Instructions:
1. Preheat the oven to 325 degrees Fahrenheit (165 degrees Celsius).

2. Grease a 9-inch square baking dish.

3. Evenly spread the oats and coconut around a baking sheet.

4. In a preheated oven, toast the oats and coconut until browned, for around 10 minutes, and transfer to a large mixing bowl.

5. In a saucepan over medium-low heat, mix the sugar, vanilla extract, peanut butter, and salt.

6. Cook, and when soft, stir. Over the oats and coconut, pour the honey mixture, stir to cover. Spread the mixture into the prepared baking dish uniformly.

7. Bake until dried in a preheated oven, for around 15 minutes for crunchy granola bars, less if you want to chew them. Before cutting, cool absolutely.

Snicky Snackies
(Ready in 40 Minutes, Serve 20, Difficulty: Normal)
Nutrition per Serving:
Calories 213, Protein 4.4 g, Carbohydrates 18.2 g, Fat 17 g, Cholesterol 24.4mg, Sodium 468.8mg.
Ingredients:
- 15 ounces of mini twist pretzels
- 2 cups of mixed nuts
- 1 cup of unsalted butter
- 2 cups of packed dark brown sugar
- ½ cup of light corn syrup
- 1 pinch of salt
Instructions:

1. Preheat the oven to 250 degrees Fahrenheit (120 degrees Celsius).

2. Mix the pretzels and nuts in a 9x13-inch baking dish. Set aside.

3. Mix the butter, sugar, corn syrup, and salt in a large saucepan. Stir together until the sugar dissolves, over medium heat.

4. Bring to a boil and cook until very dense and at the point of the 'firm ball'(260 degrees Fahrenheit, 125 degrees Celsius).

5. Remove from the heat, pour over the mixture of mini twist pretzels, and blend it.

6. Bake for 20 minutes in a preheated oven, stirring after 10 minutes.

7. Remove from the oven and spread out on wax paper to cool completely.

Sweet Party Mix
(Ready in 1 Hour and 20 Minutes, Serve 2, Difficulty: Normal)
Nutrition per Serving:
Calories 267, Protein 3 g, Carbohydrates 35.6 g, Fat 13.9 g, Cholesterol 15.3mg, Sodium 176.6mg.
Ingredients:
- 1(12 ounces) package of crispy corn and rice cereal
- 5 ounces of slivered almonds
- 6 ounces of toasted, chopped pecans
- ¾ cup of butter
- ¾ cup of dark corn syrup
- 1 ½ cup of light brown sugar
Instructions:
1. Preheat the oven to 250 degrees Fahrenheit (120 degrees Celsius). Grease a large roasting pan lightly.

2. Mix the crispy corn and rice cereal, the slivered almonds, and the toasted, diced pecans in a large bowl.

3. Melt the butter and blend it with dark corn syrup and light brown sugar in a medium saucepan over medium heat.

4. Pour the mixture over the crispy corn and rice cereal mixture. Stir and shake to coat all the nuts and cereal.

5. In the prepared roasting pan, pour the covered mixture into it. Cook in the preheated oven for 1 hour, stirring evenly after 15 minutes.

6. Cool on wax paper and put in airtight containers.

Baked Tortilla Chips

(Ready in 20 Minutes, Serve 6, Difficulty: Normal)

Nutrition per Serving:

Calories, 147 Protein 3.3 g, Carbohydrates 26 g, Fat 4.1 g, Cholesterol 0mg, Sodium 418mg.

Ingredients:

- 1(12 ounces) package of corn tortillas
- 1 tablespoon of vegetable oil
- 3 tablespoons of lime juice
- 1 teaspoon of ground cumin
- 1 teaspoon of chili powder
- 1 teaspoon of salt

Instructions:

1. Preheat the oven to 350 degrees Fahrenheit (176 degrees Celsius).

2. Cut each tortilla into wedges of 8 chip sizes and place the wedges on a cookie sheet in a single layer.

3. Combine oil and lime juice in a mister. Mix well and spray until mildly moist with each tortilla wedge.

4. In a small bowl, mix the chili powder, salt, and brush on the chips.

5. For around 7 minutes, bake. Rotate the pan and bake till the chips are crisp but not too brown, or for another 8 minutes.

6. Serve with garnishes, salsas, or guacamole.

Microwave Popcorn

(Ready in 5 Minutes, Serve 4, Difficulty: Normal)

Nutrition per Serving:

Calories 137, Protein 4.1 g, Carbohydrates 14.6 g, Fat 3.1 g, Cholesterol 0mg, Sodium 388.6mg.

Ingredients:

- ½ cup of unpopped popcorn
- 1 teaspoon of vegetable oil
- ½ teaspoon of salt, or to taste

Instructions:

1. Mix the unpopped popcorn and oil in a cup or small bowl. Pour the coated corn into a lunch bag of brown paper and sprinkle it with salt. To seal in the ingredients, fold the top of the bag over twice.

2. Cook for 2 ½-3 minutes in the microwave at full power, or before you hear a delay of around 2 seconds between pops.

3. Open the bag cautiously to prevent steam, then pour it into a serving bowl.

Playgroup Granola Bars

(Ready in 40 Minutes, Serve 2, Difficulty: Normal)

Nutrition per Serving:

Calories 216, Protein 2.4 g, Carbohydrates 26.6 g, Fat 5.5 g, Cholesterol 7.8mg, Sodium 79.2mg.

Ingredients:

- 2 cups of rolled oats
- ¾ cup of packed brown sugar
- ½ cup of wheat germ
- ¾ teaspoon of ground cinnamon
- 1 cup of all-purpose flour
- ¾ cup of raisins (Optional)
- ¾ teaspoon of salt
- ½ cup of honey
- 1 egg, beaten
- ½ cup of vegetable oil
- 2 teaspoons of vanilla extract

Instructions:

1. The oven should be preheated to 350 degrees Fahrenheit (176 degrees Celsius). Grease a 9x13 inch baking sheet appropriately.

2. Stir together the oats, cinnamon, brown sugar, wheat germ, starch, raisins, and salt in a large bowl. In the middle, make a well and pour in the sugar, egg, oil, and vanilla. Use your hands to mix properly. Onto the prepared plate, pat the mixture evenly.

3. Bake in the preheated oven for 30-35 minutes, until the bars start to change golden at the edges.

4. Cool for 5 minutes, then, while still warm, cut into bars. Before cutting, do not allow the bars to cool completely, or they will be too hard to cut.

Easy Mini Bagel Pizzas

(Ready in 10 Minutes, Serve 4, Difficulty: Normal)

Nutrition per Serving:

Calories 224, Protein 13.9 g, Carbohydrates 30.3 g, Fat 5.8 g, Cholesterol 32.9mg, Sodium 787.7mg.

Ingredients:

- 8 mini bagels, split
- ¼ cup of pizza sauce
- ⅓ cup of shredded pizza cheese blend
- 16 slices of turkey pepperoni

Instructions:

1. Preheat the oven to 425 degrees Fahrenheit (218 degrees Celsius). Use aluminum foil to cover a baking sheet.

2. Arrange bagels, cut sides up, on a lined baking sheet.

3. Spoon over each ½ of the bagel with a thin layer of pizza sauce and sprinkle with pizza cheese. On each bagel, put 2 pepperoni slices.

4. Bake in a preheated oven for around 6 minutes, until the cheese is melted and the pepperoni is lightly browned.

Spider Deviled Eggs for Halloween

(Ready in 25 Minutes, Serve 1, Difficulty: Normal)

Nutrition per Serving:

Calories 250, Protein 3.2 g, Carbohydrates 0.6 g, Fat 3.9 g, Cholesterol 93.4mg, Sodium 100.7mg.

Ingredients:

* 6 eggs
* 1 tablespoon of mayonnaise
* ¼ teaspoon of Dijon mustard
* Salt and freshly ground pepper, to taste
* 12 black olives
* 1 pinch of paprika (Optional)

Instructions:

1. In a saucepan, put the eggs and cover them with water. Bring to a boil, remove from the heat, and allow the eggs to stand for 15 minutes in hot water.

2. Remove the hot water from the shells, cool them under cold running water, and peel.

3. Break each egg in half lengthwise, remove the yolks, and put the mayonnaise, mustard, salt, and pepper in a bowl with the yolks. Mash the yolks and whisk the mixture until fully mixed and smooth.

4. Fill each egg ½ with the deviled yolk mixture using a spoon, piping bag, or a sturdy plastic bag with a corner cut off.

5. Cut olives in ½ and place ½ on each filled egg as the spider body. Cut the other ½ of the olive into 4 strips. Cut each strip in ½ so that you end up with eight thin pieces of olive for the legs.

6. Arrange 4 olive legs on each side of the body of the spider. Dust with paprika.

Home-style Potato Chips

(Ready in 40 Minutes, Serve 8, Difficulty: Normal)

Nutrition per Serving:

Calories 179, Protein 2.2 g, Carbohydrates 18.6 g, Fat 11.1 g, Cholesterol 0mg, Sodium 2622.6mg.

Ingredients:

* 4 medium potatoes, peeled and paper-thin sliced
* 3 tablespoons of salt

For Deep Frying:

* 1 quart of oil

Instructions:

1. When you slice, put the potato slices into a large bowl of cold water. Drain and clean, then wash the bowl again and add the salt.

2. For at least 30 minutes, let the potatoes soak in the saline water. Drain, then rinse again and drain.

3. Heat the oil to 365 degrees Fahrenheit (185 degrees Celsius). in a deep-fryer

4. In small batches, fry the potato slices. Remove and drain on paper towels when they start turning golden. Continue until all the slices are fried.

5. If needed, season with additional salt.

Sweet Thai Coconut Rice (Oil Free)

(Ready in 23 Minutes, Serve 4, Difficulty: Normal)

Nutrition per Serving:

Calories 269, Protein 4 g, Carbohydrates 20 g, Fat 8g, Fibre 0 g.

Ingredients:

* 1 ½ cups water
* 1 cup Thai sweet rice
* ½ can full-fat coconut milk
* 2 tablespoons sugar
* Dash of salt

Instructions:

1. Mix the pressure cooker with rice and water.

2. Click 'manual' and cook on high pressure for just 3 minutes.

3. Hit "cancel" when the time is up, then wait 10 minutes for a natural release.

4. Meanwhile, in a saucepan, heat the coconut milk, sugar, and salt.

5. Remove it from the heat until the sugar has melted.

6. Mix the coconut milk mixture into your rice when the cooker has removed its strain, and stir.

7. Put the lid back on and allow it to rest for 5-10 minutes without bringing it back under pressure.

8. Serve!

Banana Fritters

(Ready in 20 Minutes, Serve 6, Difficulty: Normal)

Nutrition per Serving:

Calories 208, Protein 7.5 g, Carbohydrates 52.8 g, Fat 19 g, Cholesterol 63.6mg, Sodium 427.3mg.

Ingredients:

* ½ cup of milk
* 2 bananas, mashed
* 2 cups of all-purpose flour

- ½ teaspoon of salt
- 3 teaspoons of baking powder
- 2 eggs, beaten
- 1 tablespoon of melted margarine

For Frying:
- 1 quart of vegetable oil
- ½ cup of confectioners' sugar

Instructions:

1. Combine the milk and bananas in a mixing bowl. Sift the rice, salt, and baking powder together. Mix in the eggs and margarine thoroughly.

2. Heat the oil to 365 degrees Fahrenheit (180 degrees Celsius). in a large skillet

3. Place the mixture carefully in the hot oil and fry until brown. Flip the fritter, and continue browning.

4. Remove the oil from the fritters and drain on towels. Dust the fritters with sugar from confectioners.

5. Serve when warm.

Candied Almonds

(Ready in 15 Minutes, Serve 8, Difficulty: Normal)

Nutrition per Serving:

Calories 230, Protein 7.6 g, Carbohydrates 32.7 g, Fat 18 g, Cholesterol 0mg, Sodium 0.9mg.

Ingredients:
- ½ cup of water
- 1 cup of white sugar
- 1 tablespoon of ground cinnamon
- 2 cups of whole almonds.

Instructions:

1. In a medium-hot saucepan, combine the water, sugar, and cinnamon, bring to a boil and add the almonds.

2. Cook and whisk the mixture until the salt dissolves and the almonds are left with a syrup-like covering.

3. On a baking sheet lined with waxed paper, pour the almonds onto it. Almonds separate using forks.

4. Let it cool for around 15 minutes.

Clam Fritter Snacks

(Ready in 10 Minutes, Serve 4, Difficulty: Normal)

Nutrition per Serving:

Calories 230, Protein 21.6 g, Carbohydrates 22.2 g, Fat 14 g, Cholesterol 93.4mg, Sodium 473.8mg.

Ingredients:
- 1(10 ounces) can of minced clams, drained
- 1 cup of baking mix
- 1 egg, beaten
- 2 tablespoons of vegetable oil

Instructions:

1. Drain the clams. Beat one egg in a medium bowl and stir in the cup of baking mix and the clams.

2. Heat the oil in a medium skillet and fry the clams in pieces until they are golden brown.

3. drain them on a tray lined with paper towels.

No-Bake Energy Balls

(Ready in 35 Minutes, Serve 20, Difficulty: Normal)

Nutrition per Serving:

Calories 211, Protein 3.1 g, Carbohydrates 12.6 g, Fat 6.5 g, Cholesterol 0mg, Sodium 31.8mg.

Ingredients:
- 1 cup of old-fashioned oats
- ½ cup of peanut butter
- ½ cup of ground flax seed
- ½ cup of chocolate chips
- ⅓ cup of honey
- 1 tablespoon of chia seeds (Optional)
- 1 teaspoon of vanilla extract

Instructions:

1. In a cup, combine the oats, ground flax seeds, peanut butter, chocolate chips, sugar, chia seeds, and vanilla extract. Cover and cool the dough for 30 minutes in the refrigerator.

2. Remove the dough from the freezer, roll it into balls, around 1 inch in diameter.

Smoky Lima Beans

(Ready in 1 Hour 10 Minutes, Serve 12, Difficulty: Normal)

Nutrition per Serving:

Calories 213, Protein 16 g, Carbohydrates 14 g, Fat 0.g, Fiber 7g.

Ingredients:
- 12 cups water
- 2 pounds dry large lima beans
- ⅛ cup Colgin liquid smoke
- 1 teaspoon onion powder
- 1 teaspoon garlic powder
- Salt and pepper to taste

Instructions:

1. Before you put your water into the pressure cooker, rinse the beans.

2. Attach the powdered onion and garlic, and close the lid.

3. Hit and switch to 'Bean' for 25 minutes.

4. Wait 5 minutes and then immediately relieve the strain when the time is up.

5. Incorporate salt and solvent smoke.

6. When needed, taste and add more seasonings.

7. Hit "sauté" and get it to a 10-minute boil.

8. Hit "cancel," then.

9. For 20-30 minutes, change back to "sauté" and boil until thickened.

Fava Bean Dip

(Ready in 27 mins, Serve 1 ½ cup, Difficulty: Normal)

Nutrition per Serving:

Calories 315, Protein 15 g, Carbohydrates 13 g, Fat 26 g, Fiber 7 g.

Ingredients:

- 3 cups water
- 2 cups soaked split fava beans
- 2 crushed garlic cloves
- 2 tablespoons veggie oil
- 1 tablespoon olive oil
- 1 zested and juiced lemon
- 2 teaspoons tahini
- 2 teaspoons cumin
- 1 teaspoon harissa
- 1 teaspoon paprika
- Salt to taste

Instructions:

1. Soak the fava beans the night before and drain the fava beans before doing so.

The recipe begins.

2. Preheat your pressure cooker.

3. When hot, add garlic and cook until it becomes golden.

4. Combine the beans, veggie oil, and three cups of water.

5. Close the lid and seal it.

6. Select the "manual" and cook for 12 minutes at high pressure.

7. Hit "cancel" when the time is up and wait 10 minutes before any remaining pressure is quickly released.

8. Drain from the pressure cooker the cooking liquid, leaving approximately 1 cup.

9. Toss the cumin, harissa, and lemon zest with the tahini.

10. Purée until it's smooth.

11. Again, salt and mix.

12. Serve with a drizzle of paprika and olive oil.

Polenta with Herbs (Oil Free)

(Ready in 20 Minutes, Serve 4-6, Difficulty: Easy)

Nutrition per Serving:

Calories 130, Protein 0g, Carbohydrates 3 g, Fat 0, Fibre 2g.

Ingredients:

- 3 cups veggie broth
- 1 cup water
- 1 cup coarse-ground polenta
- 1 large minced onion
- 3 tablespoons fresh, chopped thyme
- 2 tablespoons fresh, chopped Italian parsley
- 1 tablespoon minced garlic
- 1 teaspoon fresh, chopped sage
- Salt and pepper to taste

Instructions:

1. Preheat the cooker and sauté the onion for about a minute to dry.

2. Stir in the minced garlic and simmer for another minute.

3. Along with thyme, parsley, and sage, pour in the broth.

4. Yeah, stir.

5. Sprinkle the pot with the polenta, but do not stir it in.

6. Cover the lid and seal it.

7. Select the "manual" and cook for 5 minutes at high speed.

8. Hit "cancel" when the timer beeps and wait for 10 minutes.

9. Select the bay leaf out there.

10. To smooth it, swirl the polenta using a whisk. Simmer on the "sauté" setting if it's thin until it achieves the consistency you need.

11. Before eating, season with salt and pepper to taste.

Chapter 3: Lunch Recipes

In this chapter, we are going to give you some delicious and mouthwatering recipes on Octavia Lunch recipes.

Quinoa, Couscous, and Beetroot Tikki
(Ready in 35 Minutes, Serve 8, Difficulty: Easy)
Nutrition per Serving:

Calories 329, Protein 2 g, Carbohydrates 15 g Fat 3 g, Sodium 280mg.

Ingredients:

- 1 ½tablespoon oil
- 1 cup quinoa
- 1 medium sized mashed potato
- 1 medium sized beetroot
- ¾ cup shredded spinach
- ½ cup oats
- 1 tablespoon ginger paste
- ½ tablespoon garlic paste

Ingredients:

1. In a bowl, mix the mashed potatoes and add all the ingredients except oil.

2. Combine well before mixing.

3. Take ½ cup of the mixture and turn it into a round ball.

4. To make a tikki, flatten it gently with your hand. Do the same for the rest of the mixture and put it on a plate or baking sheet for 15 minutes.

5.Refrigerate.

6. Heat the oil in the frying pan, and place the tikkis by one by one to ensure the pan is not crowded.

7. Cook for 8-10 minutes, and then turn for the same period to cook the other side. Increase the flame at the end and crisp them up on both ends.

8. Serve along with a little chutney of mint and tamarind.

9. Add some assorted micro-greens to the garnish.

Mom's Sushi Rice

(Ready in 1 Hour and 5 Minutes, Serve 10, Difficulty: Hard)

Nutrition per Serving:

Calories 318, Protein 2.9 g, Carbohydrates 40.7 g, Fat 0.2 g, Cholesterol 0mg, Sodium 296.2mg.

Ingredients:

- 2 ¼ cups of Japanese sushi-style rice
- 1(4 inch) piece of kombu dried kelp
- 3 cups of water
- ¼ cup of rice vinegar
- ¼ cup of white sugar
- 1 ¼ teaspoon of salt

Instructions:

1. Put the rice in a deep, large bowl. Cover the rice with cold water and rub it with your hands until the water turns milky white. Pour the cloudy water out, taking care not to pour the rice out. Repeat 3 or 4 times before the rice can be seen through 3 inches of water.

2. Drain the rice in a fine strainer, then bring it together with kombu and 3 cups of water in a saucepan. Allow it to stand for 30 minutes. Stir together the rice vinegar, sugar, and salt until set aside and dissolved in a small bowl.

3. Cover and over high heat, bring rice to a boil, then reduce heat to low and simmer for 15 minutes. Remove from the heat and allow to stand for 5 minutes, covered.

4. In a bowl, scrape the rice, remove and discard the kombu. Stir in the mixture of vinegar until well incorporated, and no rice lumps remain. Allow cooling at room temperature. Use an electric fan to quickly cool the rice for a shinier appearance.

Watermelon and Strawberry Smoothie
Nutrition per Serving:

Calories 18, Carbohydrates 30 g, Protein 5 g, Fat 6.2 g, Saturated Fat 0.8 g, Trans Fat 0 g, Cholesterol 0mg, Sodium 48mg, Fiber 9 g, Sugar 14 g.

(Ready in 20 Minutes, Serve 6, Difficulty: Easy)
Ingredients:

- 100 g of fresh strawberries
- 1 tablespoon of honey
- 150 g of low-fat yogurt
- 50 g of watermelon, chopped

For Topping:

- ¼ cup of chia seeds

Instructions:

1. In a mixer, combine all the ingredients.

2. Into a glass, pour the mixed smoothie.

3. Garnish with chia seeds.

4. Before eating, blend the chia seeds with the smoothie.

Beaker's Vegetable Barley Soup

(Ready in 1 Hour and 30 Minutes, Serve 8, Difficulty: Hard)
Nutrition per Serving:

Calories 188, Protein 6.9 g, Carbohydrates 37 g, Fat 1.6 g, Cholesterol 0mg, Sodium 968.8mg.

Ingredients:

- 2 quarts of vegetable broth
- 1 cup of uncooked barley
- 2 large carrots, chopped
- 2 stalks of celery, chopped
- 1(14.5 ounces) can of diced tomatoes with juice
- 1 zucchini, chopped
- 1(15 ounces) can of garbanzo beans, drained
- 1 onion, chopped
- 3 bay leaves
- 1 teaspoon of garlic powder
- 1 teaspoon of white sugar
- 1 teaspoon of salt
- ½ teaspoon of ground black pepper
- 1 teaspoon of dried parsley
- 1 teaspoon of curry powder
- 1 teaspoon of paprika
- 1 teaspoon of Worcestershire sauce

Instructions:

1. In a large pot, pour the vegetable broth into it. Add the barley, celery, carrots, tomatoes, zucchini, onion, garbanzo beans, and bay leaves.

2. Also add to the mixture the garlic powder, sugar, curry powder, paprika, salt, pepper, parsley, and Worcestershire sauce. Bring it to a boil, then cover and simmer for 90 minutes over medium-low heat. It'll be very thick with the soup. If desired, add more broth or less barley.

3. Before serving, remove the bay leaves.

Grilled Corn Salad

(Ready in 1 Hour and 10 Minutes, Serve 6, Difficulty: Hard)

Nutrition per Serving:

Calories 210, Protein 3.4 g, Carbohydrates 19.7 g, Fat 2.8 g, Cholesterol 0mg, Sodium 43.4mg.

Ingredients:

- 6 ears of freshly shucked corn
- 1 green pepper, diced
- 2 Roman(plum) tomatoes, diced
- ¼ cup of diced red onion
- ½ bunch of fresh cilantro, chopped, or to taste
- 2 teaspoons of olive oil, or to taste
- Salt and ground black pepper, to taste

Instructions:

1. Preheat the medium-hot outdoor grill and lightly oil the grill.

2. On the preheated grill, cook the corn, occasionally turning, until the corn is tender and black specks appear, set aside for about 10 minutes, until just cool enough to handle. Slice the kernels off the cob, then place them in a bowl.

3. Combine the green pepper, cilantro, diced tomato, onion, and olive oil with the warm corn kernels. Season with salt and pepper, and mix until mixed evenly. To allow flavors to blend before serving, set aside for at least 30 minutes.

Cream of Almond Soup

(Ready in 40 Minutes, Serve 2, Difficulty: Easy)

Nutrition per Serving:

Calories 287, Protein 13 g, Carbohydrate 3 g, Fat 26 g, Sodium 219mg.

Ingredients:

- 800ml of vegetable stock
- 200ml of skimmed milk
- 100 g of toasted, powdered almonds
- 50 g of butter
- 50 g of flour
- Salt and pepper, to taste
- 1 pinch of nutmeg, grated
- 2-3 drops of almond essence
- 10 g of toasted almond flakes

Instructions:

1. Melt the butter over low heat in a heavy-bottomed saucepan.

2. Put in the flour and milk until a smooth roux is obtained, stirring constantly.

3. Now add the powdered almonds and eventually and the vegetable stock, and simmer gently.

4. Add the seasoning and serve with almond flakes.

Flax Seed Raita (Indian Recipe)

(Ready in 25 Minutes, Serve 8, Difficulty: Easy)

Nutrition per Serving:

Calories 144, Protein 5.2 g, Carbohydrates 7.4 g, Fat 8.1 g, Cholesterol 16mg.

Ingredients:

- 3 tablespoons of flax ground seeds
- 1 cup of bottle grated gourd
- 1 cup of low-fat curd
- ½ cup of finely chopped, mint leaves
- 1 ½ teaspoon of coarsely ground, roasted cumin seeds
- Sal, to taste
- 1 cup of water

Instructions:

1. Combine water with the bottle guard. Cover and cook for 4 minutes on a medium flame.

2. Combine all the ingredients in a deep bowl, including the cooked gourd bottle, and blend well.

3. For at least 1 hour, refrigerate and serve chilled.

Basic Italian Bean Soup

(Ready in 25 Minutes, Serve 4, Difficulty: Normal)

Nutrition per Serving:

Calories 210, Protein 8.9 g, Carbohydrates 34.6 g, Fat 4.3 g, Cholesterol 0mg, Sodium 997.3mg.

Ingredients:

*   Olive oil
*   1 large onion, diced
*   2 cloves of garlic, or more to taste
*   2 cups of tomato sauce
*   24 ounces of prepared cannellini beans
*   1 tablespoon of dried basil
*   ½ teaspoon of oregano
*   Salt and ground black pepper, to taste

Instructions:

1. Heat the olive oil over medium to high heat in a pot. In hot oil, cook and stir onion until tender, about 5 minutes, add garlic and proceed to cook until fragrant, about 1-2 more minutes.

2. Add the tomato sauce to the pot and stir. Add the peppers, basil, oregano, salt, and pepper to the cannellini.

3. Bring the mixture to a boil, reduce the heat to medium-low, and cook 5-7 more minutes until the beans are hot.

Smooth Sweet Tea

(Ready in 3 Hours and 20 Minutes, Serve 8, and Difficulty: Hard)

Nutrition per Serving:

Calories 127, Protein 0 g, Carbohydrates 18.7 g, Fat 0 g, Cholesterol 0mg, Sodium 41.3mg.

Ingredients:

*   1 pinch of baking soda
*   2 cups of boiling water
*   6 tea bags
*   ¾ cup of white sugar
*   6 cups of cool water

Instructions:

1. In a 64-ounce heat-proof glass pitcher, sprinkle a pinch of baking soda. Pour in the boiling water, and then add the tea bags. Cover, and allow for 15 minutes to steep.

2. Remove the tea bags, discard them and whisk in the sugar until dissolved.

3. Use cool water to pour in and refrigerate until cold.

Skinny Taco Stuffed Peppers

(Ready in 30 Minutes, Serve 4, Difficulty: Normal)

Nutrition per Serving

Calories 191, Protein 19 g, Carbohydrates 4 g, Fat 3 g, Fiber 0 g, Sugars 1 g, Sodium 273mg.

Ingredients:

*   2 large green peppers, halved lengthwise, and seeded
*   453 g of lean ground turkey
*   1 tablespoon of less sodium taco seasoning
*   ¼ cup of tomato sauce
*   ¼ cup of reduced-fat sharp cheddar shredded cheese

Instructions:

1. Preheat the oven to 176 degree Celsius (350 degrees Fahrenheit).

2. Brown ground turkey in a big, medium-hot skillet.

3. Add 1 tablespoon of water and the turkey seasoning and stir.

 Add the sauce. Add a little extra of the meat if it is too dry. When the turkey is heated thoroughly, turn the heat to medium.

4. Add cheese and blend thoroughly.

5. Cut the green peppers, top to bottom in half. Cut a semi-circle around the stem, and in one cut, extract the stem and seeds.

6. Repeat until there are 4 halves.

7. Place the 2 halves in boiling water for 5 minutes at a time. After cooking, the "skin" will lose a little brightness.

8. Place peppers open side up in a baking dish and fill with your meat mixture.

9. Bake for 20-25 minutes in the oven.

10. Place and sprinkle with the toppings of your choice on plates.

Oats Khichdi

(Ready in 30 Minutes, Serve 6, Difficulty: Easy)

Nutrition per Serving:

Calories 157, Protein 6.6 g, Carbohydrate 20.6 g, Fat 5.4 g, Fiber 3.1 g.

Ingredients:

*   1/3 cup of quick-cooking oats
*   1/3 cup of split skinned moong dal
*   ½ teaspoon of cumin seeds
*   ¼ teaspoon of turmeric powder
*   ¼ tablespoon of red chili powder
*   1 small onion, finely chopped
*   1 medium tomato, finely chopped

- 1 small carrot, chopped
- 45 g of green peas
- ¾ teaspoon of finely chopped ginger
- ½ teaspoon of chopped green chilies
- 1 tablespoon of salt
- ½ tablespoon of extra virgin olive oil
- 2 cups of water

For Garnishing:

- ½ tablespoon of chopped fresh coriander leaves

Instructions:

1. In a pressure cooker, add oil, heat the oil, add cumin seeds and let them crackle.

2. Add the chopped onion and cook until translucent, add the ginger and green chilies, and cook for a few seconds.

3. Add the turmeric and red chili powder, then add the tomatoes. Let them cook until they're tender.

4. Add all vegetables and oats, along with rinsed moong dal. Cook for a couple of seconds.

5. Add water and adjust salt as per taste.

6. Cook for 8 minutes, through pressure.

7. Let the pressure calm down and open the lid.

8. Serve hot, served with yogurt, garnished with chopped coriander leaves or green chilies.

Slow Cooked Corned Beef for Sandwiches

(Ready in 4 Hours and 15 Minutes, Serve 1, and Difficulty: Normal)

Nutrition per Serving:

Calories 229, Protein 15 g, Carbohydrates 4.2 g, Fat 15.1 g, Cholesterol 77.9mg, Sodium 904.3mg.

Ingredients:

- 2(1360 g) of corned beef briskets with spice packets
- 2(12 fluid ounces) bottles of beer
- 2 bay leaves
- ¼ cup of peppercorns
- 1 bulb of clove garlic, separated and peeled

Instructions:

1. Place the briskets with the corned beef in a large pot. Sprinkle with 1 of the packets of spice and discard the other or save it for other uses. Pour in the beer and fill the saucepan with enough water to cover 1 inch of the briskets. Add the bay leaves, garlic, and peppercorns.

2. Reduce the heat to medium-low until the liquid comes to a boil, then simmer for 4-5 hours, checking hourly and adding more water if needed to keep the meat covered.

3. Remove the meat from the pot slowly, as it is going to be incredibly tender. Set it on a cutting board and allow it to rest for about 10 minutes before it firms up a little.

4. To serve, slice or shred, discard the cooking liquid, but it can be used for cooking cabbage and other vegetables if desired.

Spicy Papadum (Indian Recipe)

(Ready in 25 Minutes, Serve 6, Difficulty: Easy)

Nutrition per Serving:

Calories: 76, Protein 1.6 g, Carbohydrates 7 g, Fiber 2.8 g, Fat 0.3 g.

Ingredients:

- 1 cup tomato, chopped
- 1 cup onion, chopped
- 1 tablespoon of chopped coriander leaves
- 2 tbsp Lemon
- 1 teaspoon of salt
- 1 teaspoon of pepper
- Papadum

Instructions:

1. In a mug, mix the vegetables with the lemon juice, salt, and pepper. Take the papadums and cook them deep in a wok until they are crispy and crunchy. Put fried Papadum in a dish and uniformly place the spices and veggie mixture over it.

2. Serve with your favorite cold beer.

Slow Cooker Italian Beef Sandwiches

(Ready in 8 Hours and 10 Minutes, Serve 1, and Difficulty: Hard)

Nutrition per Serving:

Calories 318, Protein 39.4 g, Carbohydrates 1.6 g, Fat 15.8 g, Cholesterol 100.4mg, Sodium 819.1mg.

Ingredients:

- 1(3721 g) rump roast
- 3 cups of water
- 2 tablespoons of dried basil
- 1 tablespoon of dried oregano
- 1 tablespoon of salt
- 1 tablespoon of garlic powder
- 1 tablespoon of parsley flakes
- 3 bay leaves
- 1 ½ teaspoons of red pepper flakes
- ⅓ teaspoon of ground black pepper, or to taste

Instructions:

1. In a slow cooker, combine the roast, basil, water, oregano, cinnamon, garlic powder, red pepper flakes, parsley flakes, bay leaves, and black pepper.

2. In a slow cooker, cook for 8-10 hours, set to low. Use 2 forks to remove bay leaves and shred beef.

Sago Vada (Indian Recipe)

(Ready in 40 Minutes, Serve 6, Difficulty: Normal)

Nutrition per Serving:

Calories126, Protein 1.7 g, Carbohydrates 12.8 g, Fiber 0.7 g.

Ingredients:

- 1 cup of soaked sabudana
- ½ cup of grounded peanuts
- 1 teaspoon of green chilies
- 1 teaspoon of salt
- 1 teaspoon of red chili powder
- 1 cup of boiled potatoes
- 1 tablespoon of coriander leaves
- 1 tablespoon of lemon juice
- A long curd, to serve

Instructions:

1. Take a bowl of soaked sabudana.

2. Add ground peanuts to it, along with green chilies, salt, boiled potatoes, red chili powder, cilantro leaves, and lemon juice.

3. Combine the ingredients thoroughly to make a thick paste, mash.

4. Make small, round, tikki-like mixture balls.

5. For deep frying, put these balls in hot oil.

6. Fry them until the brown is golden.

7.Serve Sabudana Vada along with curd.

Baked Namak Para with Roasted Almond Dip

(Ready in 30 Minutes, Serve 4, Difficulty: Easy)

Nutrition per Serving:

Calories: 159, Protein 43.598 g, Carbohydrates 0 g, Fats 58.88 g, Cholesterol 0 g, Fiber 0 g, Saturated Fats: 5.975 g, Monounsaturated Fats: 37.609 g, Polyunsaturated Fats: 12.16 g.

Ingredients:

For Almond Dip:

- ½ cup of crushed, roasted almonds
- 1 cup of chopped tomato
- 2 cloves of garlic
- 1 basil sprig
- ½ lemon
- ½ teaspoon of salt
- ½ teaspoon of pepper

For Namak Para:

- 250 g of refined flour
- 10 g of sugar
- 1 teaspoon of salt
- 20 ml of olive oil
- 150 ml of water

Instructions:

Prepare the Dip:

1. Place the tomatoes in a bowl. Crush and chop the garlic and add to the tomatoes.

2. Finely chop up the sprig of basil and add the rest of the ingredients to the tomatoes.

3. Refrigerate it for a while.

Prepare Namak Para:

1. With the given ingredients, prepare the dough, and let it rest for 10 minutes.

2. Now, roll out a very thin sheet and bake it for 10-12 minutes in a preheated oven at 200 degrees Celsius (392 F).

3. Remove and break into bits.

4. Serve it with the almond sauce.

Spicy Grilled Cheese Sandwich

(Ready in 5 Minutes, Serve 6, Difficulty: Easy)

Nutrition per Serving:

Calories 213, Protein 10.7 g, Carbohydrates 28.2 g, Fat 22.1 g, Cholesterol 57.2mg, Sodium 846.4mg.

Ingredients:

- 2 tablespoons of butter or margarine
- 4 slices of white bread
- 2 slices of American cheese
- 1 roman (plum) tomato, thinly sliced
- ¼ small onion, chopped
- 1 jalapeno pepper, chopped

Instructions:

1. Over low heat, heat a large skillet. Spread butter or margarine over 2 slices of bread on 1 side.

2. Place the buttered side of both pieces in the skillet. Place each one with a slice of cheese and top with the tomato, onion, and jalapeno strips.

3. Butter the remaining slices of bread on one side and put them on top of the buttered side. If the sandwiches are toasted at the bottom, flip and fry until the other side is brown.

Easy Coconut Rice (South Indian Recipe)

(Ready in 35 Minutes, Serve 4, Difficulty: Easy)

Nutrition per Serving:

Calories 290, Protein: 5.4 g, Carbohydrate: 30 g, Fat 16.5 g, Fiber 4.2 g.

Ingredients:

- 2 tablespoons of oil
- ½ tablespoon of peanut
- 1 teaspoon of mustard seeds
- 1 teaspoon of cumin seeds
- ½ tablespoon of soaked chickpeas
- ½ tablespoon of soaked black gram
- 10 curry leaves
- 1 red whole chili
- ½ green chili
- 12 cashewnuts
- ½ teaspoon of salt
- 1 cup of grated coconut
- 2 cups of basmati rice (cooked)
- 2 tablespoons of grated coconut

Instructions:

1. Take a pan of oil and add the peanuts.

2. Add the mustard seeds to the peanut and cook them together, then add the cumin seeds and mix them, followed by the black gram and the soaked chana.

3. Cook all the ingredients together.

6. Now add the curry leaves, the whole red chili, and the chili green.

7. Cook them completely.

8. Add the cashew nuts to the pan, followed by salt, and combine well.

9. Now add to the pan the grated coconut.

10. To infuse the coconut flavor completely, combine the coconut thoroughly with the other ingredients.

11. Put the cooked rice in the pan now.

12. Mix them well.

13. To the rice, add grated coconut and mix again.

14. Serve it hot.

Chicago-Inspired Italian Beef Sandwich

(Ready in 1 Hour and 25 Minutes, Serve 4, Difficulty: Hard)

Nutrition per Serving:

Calories 406, Protein 29.3 g, Carbohydrates 35.7 g, Fat 15.7 g, Cholesterol 78.7mg, Sodium 1398.8mg.

Ingredients:

- 1 tablespoon of vegetable oil
- 6 cloves of garlic, sliced
- 2 tablespoons of white vinegar
- 1 tablespoon of dried oregano
- 1 ½ teaspoon of salt, or to taste
- 1 teaspoon of dried thyme
- 1 teaspoon of dried rosemary
- 1 teaspoon of freshly ground black pepper
- 1 bay leaf
- ¼ teaspoon of red pepper flakes, or to taste
- 3 cups of chicken broth, or as needed
- 4 ciabatta rolls, sliced in ½
- 1 cup of chopped giardiniera (pickled Italian vegetables)
- 2 teaspoons of chopped fresh flat-leaf parsley

Instructions:

1. With a pinch of black pepper and salt, season the beef. Heat the vegetable oil in a big pot over high heat. Cook and stir the beef for 5-8 minutes before it is browned in hot oil.

2. Garlic, vinegar, oregano, 1 1/2 teaspoons of garlic, thyme, rosemary, one teaspoon black pepper, bay leaf and red pepper are added to the beef. To cover 1 inch of the steak, add enough chicken broth into the beef mixture and bring it to a simmer.

3. Use a lid to cover the pot, reduce the heat to low, and simmer for 1-1 1/2 hours until the meat is tender.

4. Using a strainer or slotted spoon to transfer meat to another container and pour about ½ a cup of meat broth into the pot. And use a wooden spoon to gently divide the meat into smaller pieces. Cover the pot and keep it warm with a cap or aluminum foil.

5. To taste, season with salt and pepper. From the top of the broth left in the first bath, skim off the extra grease. To keep the broth warm, use a lid or aluminum foil to cover the pot.

6. Place the halves of a rollout on a work surface and spoon 2-3 teaspoons of meat broth over each half. On top of the roll's lower half is a generous amount of beef and a spoonful of pickled vegetables. Place on them with sandwich tops. Repeat with the remaining buns, soup, meat, and pickled vegetables to make three more sandwiches.

7. Spoon the hot meat broth into ramekins, and finish each ramekin with 1/2 teaspoon of parsley. Serve with hot broth sandwiches.

Summer Squash Salad

(Ready in 25 Minutes, Serve 6, Difficulty: Easy)

Nutrition per Serving:

Calories197, Protein 3.9 g, Carbohydrate 3.3 g, Fat 19.7 g, Sodium 323.9mg.

Ingredients:

- ¼ cup of white balsamic vinegar
- ¼ cup of lemon juice
- 2 teaspoon of lemon rind
- 2 red chilies
- 2 cloves of garlic, crushed
- 1 tablespoons of olive oil

- 150 g of summer squash(zucchini)
- Sea salt, to taste
- Black pepper, to taste
- Basil leaves

Instructions:

1. Crush 2 cloves of garlic cloves.

2. Now, placed the white balsamic vinegar, lemon rind, red chili, lemon juice, and olive oil in a bowl. Along with sea salt and freshly ground black pepper, add the crushed garlic cloves Blend and mix.

3. Add to the mixture the thinly sliced summer squash and toss to cover it.

4. Keep it aside and leave for 10 minutes to marinate.

5. Place the marinated summer squash and garnish with the baby basil leaves on a serving plate.

Strawberry Parfait Recipe

(Ready in 10 Minutes, Serve 4, Difficulty: Easy)

Nutrition per Serving:

Calories 128, Protein 17.1 g, Carbohydrates 37.2 g, Sugars 22 g, Fat 8.3 g.

Ingredients:

- 50 g of muesli
- 50 g of curd
- 30 g of strawberry puree
- 20 g of honey
- 10 g of maple syrup

Instructions:

1. In a glass first, arrange a sheet of muesli, then strawberry puree, followed by curd.

2. Use honey and maple syrup to garnish.

Sakkarai Pongal

(Ready in 55 Minutes, Serve 6, Difficulty: Normal)

Nutrition per Serving:

Calories: 227, Protein 3.8 g, Carbohydrates 48.7 g, Fiber 1.4 g, Fat 6.9 g.

Ingredients:

- 1 cup of rice
- ¼ cup of yellow moong dal
- 4 cup of milk
- 1 cup of jaggery
- 3 teaspoons of cashew nuts
- 3 teaspoons of raisin
- 5 cardamom nuts
- ¼ cup of ghee
- ½ cup of coconut

Instructions:

1. Soak the rice and cook it with yellow ghee moong dal and mash it properly on a slow flame. Add the jaggery and blend thoroughly.

2. Place ghee in another pan and add cashew nut, raisin, and cardamom. Get it golden, and then add it to the rice mixture.

3. Remove and serve until hot.

Popular in Italian Recipes

(Ready in 1 Hour and 25 Minutes, Serve 4, And Difficulty: Hard)

Nutrition per Serving:

Calories 306, Protein 25.3 g, Carbohydrates 15.7 g, Fat 15.7 g, Cholesterol 78.7mg, Sodium 1398.8mg.

Ingredients:

- 680 g of boneless beef chuck, cut into 2-inch pieces
- Salt and ground black pepper, to taste
- 1 tablespoon of vegetable oil
- 6 cloves of garlic, sliced
- 2 tablespoons of white vinegar
- 1 tablespoon of dried oregano
- 1 ½ teaspoon of salt, or to taste
- 1 teaspoon of dried thyme
- 1 teaspoon of dried rosemary
- 1 teaspoon of freshly ground black pepper
- 1 bay leaf
- ¼ teaspoon of red pepper flakes, or to taste
- 3 cups of chicken broth, or as needed
- 4 ciabatta rolls, sliced in ½
- 1 cup of chopped giardiniera (pickled Italian vegetables)
- 2 teaspoons of chopped fresh flat-leaf parsley

Instructions:

1. Season the beef with a pinch of black pepper and salt. Heat the vegetable oil over high heat in a heavy pot. Cook and stir the beef until browned in hot oil, for 5-8 minutes.

2. Poon the beef with black pepper, bay leaf, and red pepper flakes. Pour enough chicken broth into the beef mixture to cover 1 inch of the meat and bring it to a simmer.

3. Cover the pot with a lid, reduce the heat to low, and simmer for 1-1 1/2 hour until the meat is fork-tender.

4. Transfer meat to a separate pot with a strainer or slotted spoon and pour about 1/4 cup of meat broth into the pot. To gently break the meat into smaller chunks, use a wooden spoon. Use a lid or aluminum foil to cover the pot and keep it warm.

5. Season with salt and pepper to taste. Skim the excess grease from the top of the broth remaining

in the first pot. Use a lid or aluminum foil to cover the pot and keep the broth warm.

6. On a work surface, lay the halves of a rollout and spoon 2-3 tablespoons of meat broth over each 1/2. A generous portion of meat and a spoonful of pickled vegetables are on top of the roll's bottom ½. Place the top on the sandwich.

7. Repeat to create three more sandwiches with the remaining buns, broth, meat, and pickled vegetables.

8. Spoon the hot meat broth into ramekins and top 1/2 teaspoon of parsley with each ramekin. For dipping, serve sandwiches with hot broth.

Peach, Raspberry and Nuts Smoothie

(Ready in 20 Minutes, Serve 2, Difficulty: Easy)

Nutrition per Serving:

Calories 311, Protein 4 g, Carbohydrates 25 g, Fat 3 g, Fiber 4 g, Sodium 48mg.

Ingredients:
- 100 g of fresh raspberries
- 3 small, ripe banana
- 50 almonds, soaked
- 100 fresh peach slices
- 200 g of low-fat yogurt

For Topping:
- Fresh raspberry
- Peach fruit slices
- Almonds, soaked

Instructions:

1. In a mixer, combine all the ingredients.

2. Place it in the smoothie bowl.

3. Garnish with toppings and serve chilled.

Buckwheat Blinis Sandwich with Beetroot and Feta

(Ready in 55 Minutes, Serve 4, Difficulty: Normal)

Nutrition per Serving:

Calories 229, Protein 2.7 g, Carbohydrates 5.7 g, Fat 3.2 g, Cholesterol 21.7mg, Sodium 75.5mg.

Ingredients:
- 150 gram of buckwheat flour
- ½ teaspoon of baking powder
- 2 g of salt
- 1 teaspoon of yogurt
- 1 ½ teaspoon of vinegar
- 150ml of water
- 10 gram of jalapenos
- 10ml of clarified butter
- 160 g of beetroot, chopped
- 35 g of castor sugar
- 75ml of vinegar
- ½ teaspoon of cumin powder
- ½ teaspoon of coriander powder
- 20 g of walnut
- 80 g of feta

Instructions:

1. In a medium-sized bowl, sift the buckwheat flour.

2. Add baking powder, salt, vinegar, yogurt, and blend well. Add water slowly.

3. To the mixture, add sliced jalapenos, which should have a pancake batter's consistency for 15 minutes, set aside.

4. In a non-stick pan over moderate heat, melt a little butter.

5. In the hot skillet, spoon tablespoon-size mounds of batter and cook until bubbles form on the surface and the rim, the blinis are browned.

6. Blinis is turned and cooked for 15 seconds longer.

7. Peel the beetroot and finally chop it.

8. Over low heat, melt the sugar. In the pan, add chopped beetroot, vinegar, water, cumin powder, cilantro powder and cook for 10-15 minutes, stirring frequently.

9. Add chopped walnut to the mixture, remove from the heat, and allow to cool.

10. Place each blini with 1 tablespoon of beetroot mixture and top with feta cheese.

11. Garnish and serve with a rocket leaf.

Banana Coconut Idli

(Ready in 45 Minutes, Serve 6, Difficulty: Normal)

Nutrition per Serving:

Calories: 450, Protein 1 g, Carbohydrate 30 g, Fat 0 g, Sodium 0mg, Sugars 19 g.

Ingredients:

For Banana Idli:
- 1 cup of idli batter
- 4 tablespoons of. jaggery powder
- 1 pinch of salt
- 1 pinch of cardamom powder
- ½ ripe banana, chopped

For Coconut Jaggery Cream:
- 1 cup of coconut milk
- 2 tablespoons of jaggery powder

Instructions:

1. For banana idli, add all the ingredients together.

2. Grease with sugar, spoon some batter into the mold, and steam until done. When finished, remove it from the mold.

3. Heat the coconut milk in the jaggery sauce and add the jaggery powder. Stir until dissolved. With warm coconut sauce, serve warm idlis.

Slow Cooker Spicy Black-Eyed Peas

Nutrition per Serving:

Calories 199, Protein 14.1 g, Carbohydrates 30.2 g, Fat 2.9 g, Cholesterol 9.6mg, Sodium 341.4mg.

(Ready in 6 Hours and 30 Minutes, Serve 10, and Difficulty: Hard)

Ingredients:

- 6 cups of water
- 1 cube of chicken bouillon
- 453 g of sorted, rinsed and, dried black-eyed peas
- 1 onion, diced
- 2 cloves of garlic, diced
- 1 red bell pepper, stemmed, seeded, and diced
- 1 jalapeno chile, seeded and minced
- 8 ounces of diced ham
- 4 slices of bacon, chopped
- ½ teaspoon of cayenne pepper
- 1 ½ teaspoon of cumin
- Salt, to taste
- 1 teaspoon of ground black pepper

Instructions:

1. Pour the water into a slow cooker to dissolve, add the bouillon cube, and stir.

2. Mix in the black-eyed peas, the onion, the jalapeno pepper, the garlic, the bell pepper, the ham, the cayenne pepper, the bacon, the salt, and the pepper, and mix well. Cover the slow cooker and simmer for 6-8 hours, until the beans are tender.

Veg Summer Rolls

(Ready in 40 Minutes, Serve 6, Difficulty: Normal)

Nutrition per Serving:

Calories 81, Protein 3 g, Carbs 16 g, Fat 0 g, Fiber 1 g.

Ingredients:

- 2 rice paper sheets
- 25 g of iceberg lettuce
- 25 g of carrot
- 10 g of bean sprouts
- 15 g of cucumber
- 15 g of tofu
- 5 basil leaves
- 5 mint leaves
- 5 coriander leaves
- 15 g of rice noodles (soaked in warm water for 20-25 minutes)
- 5 cups of peanuts, roasted

For the Hoisin Peanut Sauce:

- 45 g of hoisin sauce
- 30 roasted peanuts
- 5 chopped garlic
- 15ml of oil
- 10 chopped red chilies
- 50ml of water

Instructions:

1. Make a paste from the peanuts roasted (Add 15ml of water and 15ml of cooking oil, grind in a mixer until a smooth paste. Add a little more water if required). Add the peanut paste, garlic, hoisin sauce, and chilies into a non-stick pan.

2. Add about 50ml of water and let it boil until the sauce thickens. Allow cooling.

3. Slice the carrot and cucumber thinly. Let the tofu sliced into batons.

4. Take a sheet of rice paper and put it for 10-15 seconds in water. Place it on a flat surface by wiping your hands with excess water.

5. Layer it with slices of cucumber and carrot, accompanied by sprouts of tofu, beans, roasted peanuts, basil leaves, iceberg lettuce, mint leaves, and coriander leaves.

6. Over it, put the rice noodles and chicken. Drizzle more sauce.

7. Roll the rice paper. Fold the sides after the first roll and roll further. To prevent the filling from dropping out, ensure that it is rolled tightly.

8. At a slant, cut the roll and serve with the hoisin peanut sauce.

9. For the second layer, repeat the procedure.

Gluten-Free Christmas Cake

(Ready in 2 Hours and 20 Minutes, Serve 20, and Difficulty: Hard)

Nutrition per Serving:

Calories 257, Protein 3 g, Carbohydrates 38 g, Fat 11 g, Saturated Fat 4 g, Sodium 145.29mg.

Ingredients:

- 300 g of Christmas dry fruits, pre-soaked
- ½ tablespoon orange zest
- ½ tablespoon lemon zest
- 200ml of jaggery syrup
- 150 g almond flour

- 100 g apples, grated
- 176 g butter, softened
- 4 medium eggs

Instructions:

1. Preheat the oven to 140 degrees.

2. In a large bowl, placed the remaining ingredients except for the almond flour.

3. When well mixed, beat with a hand-held electric mixer. Fold well with the almond flour.

4. Grease a deep 9 inches (approx.) round tin with butter or a 20 cm square cake tin with a double layer of baking paper, then grease the paper. Onto the packed tin, spoon the mixture.

5. And use a disc of baking paper to level the top and cover.

6. Bake until firm to the touch for around 2 hours, and a skewer pushed into the middle comes out clean. Keep the cake in the tin to cool.

7. Remove the baking paper disc when the cake has cooled, pierce the top with a skewer in many places, then pour over a touch of brandy. Remove the tin from the cake but store it in the baking paper.

8. Wrap it with more baking paper, then wrap it with foil. Then store it in a cool place.

9. Glace fruit, marzipan, or ready-to-use icing will decorate the cake.

Apple and Almond Curry (Indian Recipe)

(Ready in 1 Hour, Serve 6, Difficulty: Easy)

Nutrition per Serving:

Calories 316, Protein 6 g, Fat 14 g (80% monounsaturated, 15% polyunsaturated, and 5% saturated), carbohydrate 6 g, Fiber 3 g.

Ingredients:

- 150 g almonds, peeled
- 20 g ginger
- 5 g white pepper powder
- 10 g honey
- 2 tablespoon cumin

For topping Cream:

- 10 tbsp. refined oil
- 5 g Shahi cumin
- 5 no fennels
- 2 tbsp. cinnamon
- Salt, to taste
- 200 litres veg stock

Ingredients:

1. Create a puree, blanch the almonds, and hold them aside.

2. Heat a little oil in a pan, add ginger and green apple dices to boil with a little water.

3. To produce a puree, cool it off.

4. Add a little of the refined oil, Shahi cumin, fennel, and cinnamon to a separate saucepan and sauté well.

5. To cook, add almond puree for some time, then add apple puree.

6. After that, cook for 20 minutes, add a good vegetable reserve, and add sugar, pepper, and cumin powder.

7. Check the seasoning.

8. Finish with toasted cream and almond flakes that have skin

Almond and Cranberry Poha

(Ready in 35 Minutes, Serve 4, Difficulty: Easy)

Nutrition per Serving:

Calories: 362, Protein 78.1 g, Carbohydrates 0 g Fats 157.6 g, Cholesterol 0mg, Fiber 0 g.

Ingredients:

- 200 g of almond flakes
- 450 g of onion
- 200 g of poha
- 100 g of frozen dried cranberries
- 15 g of salt
- 20ml of oil
- 15 g of curry leaves
- 5 g of green chilies
- 100 g of fresh coconut

Ingredients:

1. Soak poha in cold water, strain, and keep it aside. Soak 3/4th of the almond flakes and toast the rest of them in water.

2. Add the chopped green chilies, mustard seeds, curry leaves, and sauté in the oil.

3. Now add the poha and almonds soaked in it, then add the seasoning.

4. Add the cranberries and add the sliced cilantro and the freshly grated coconut.

5. Add the poha to the toasted almonds.

6. Serve it spicy with a coriander sprig as a garnish.

Almond and Raw Banana Galawat

(Ready in 30 Minutes, Serve 1, Difficulty: Normal)

Nutrition per Serving:

Calories 124, Protein 29 g, Carbohydrates N/A, Fats 85 g, Saturated Fats 8.6 g, Monounsaturated Fats 36 g, Polyunsaturated Fats 22.6 g, Cholesterol N/A, Fiber N/A.

Ingredients:

- 80 g of peeled almond slivers
- 150 g of boiled banana
- 25 g of almond paste
- 20ml of cooking cream
- 15 ml refined oil
- 2 g of mace powder
- 2 g of cardamom powder
- 20 g of ginger garlic paste
- 5 g garam masala powder
- 3 g red chili powder
- Salt, to taste
- 50 g of tempura batter

Instructions:

1. Finely grate the boiled banana. In a pan, heat the oil and add the ginger garlic paste and cook well to a light brown color.

2. Then add red chili powder, garam masala, and cook with the mixture. Now combine the almonds paste and cook for 1 minute.

3. Add the grated banana, then cook until the mixture leaves the pan sides. Adjust the seasoning and finish with mace and cardamom powder.

4. Cool the mixture and divide it into small, similar size dumpling.

5. Give them a patty shape, a tempura batter coat, and an almond sliver crumb.

6. In a non-stick pan, grill the patties until golden.

7. Serve it warm.

River Sole for Your Soul

(Ready in 50 Minutes, Serve 6, Difficulty: Normal)

Nutrition per Serving:

Calories 186, Protein 17.1 g, Carbohydrate 0 g, Fat 1.9 g, Sodium 95mg, Potassium 230mg.

Ingredients:

- 1 kg of sole fillet
- 5-10 large shrimps (Optional)
- 1 kg of peeled, sliced potatoes
- 3 onions, sliced
- 5 cloves of garlic, chopped
- ½ red/ green capsicum
- Parsley or coriander
- Few dashes of hot sauce
- 1 teaspoon of paprika
- 1 cup of olive oil
- 50 ml of white wine
- Rock salt, to taste
- Toasted garlic bread

Instructions:

1. Place the sliced onions, garlic, tomatoes, coriander, peppers, or parsley, sliced potatoes, and fish in a saucepan, forming layers.

2. In the upper layer, put the sliced onions and peppers, paprika, and salt. Evenly spread the olive oil over the layers.

3. Add seasoning and white wine, and a little water until all layers are set.

4. Cover the pan to get it to a boil.

5. Do not ever stir this dish,

6. Cover the pan and let it cook on a low flame. Once the potato is cooked, check that it is ready for serving.

7. Serve this stew with toasted garlic bread, so the soup appears rich and soupy.

Peach, Raspberry, and Nuts Smoothie

(Ready in 20 Minutes, Serve 8, Difficulty: Easy)

Nutrition per Serving:

Calories 321, Protein 12 g, Carbohydrates 48 g, Fat 12 g, Saturated Fat 3 g, Cholesterol 9mg, Sodium 73mg, Fiber 10 g, Sugar 33 g.

Ingredients:

- 100 g of fresh raspberries
- 3 small, ripe bananas
- 50 almonds, soaked
- 100 fresh peach slices
- 200 g of low-fat yogurt

For Topping:

- Fresh raspberry
- Peach fruit slices
- Almonds, soaked

Instructions:

1. In a mixer, combine all the ingredients until smooth.

2. Put the smoothie in a bowl.

3. Serve chilled after garnished with the toppings.

Green Pea Upma (Indian recipe)

(Ready in 25 Minutes, Serve 4, Difficulty: Easy)

Nutrition per Serving:

Calories 224, Protein 7 g, Carbohydrates 36 g, Fat 5 g.

Ingredients:

- 1 cup of roasted semolina
- ¼ cup of green peas
- 1 onion, finely chopped
- 2 green chilies, finely chopped
- 2 cups of hot water

For Tempering:

* 1 tablespoon of extra virgin olive oil
* ¾ teaspoon of mustard seeds
* 1 sprig of curry leaves
* 1 sprig ginger, grated
* Salt, to taste

For Garnishing:

* 2 sprigs of fresh coriander leaves (Optional)
* ½ tablespoon of boiled peas
* 1 sprig of curry leaves (cooked)

Instructions:

1. In a thick bottomed pan, heat oil and add mustard seeds. Let them crackle.

2. Add the curry leaves and grated ginger, and cook before the ginger's raw aroma disappears.

3. Now add the finely chopped onion, cook until smooth, add the green chilies, and cook for 2 minutes.

4. Now add the gently roasted semolina, add the green peas, cook, and add the hot water for 2 minutes.

5. To taste, add the salt. Stir to avoid lumps forming.

6. Cover it now and cook on a very slow heat until all the water is absorbed and the green peas and semolina are cooked.

7. Serve hot with sliced leaves of coriander or grated fresh coconut.

Saturday Chicken Stock

(Ready in 6 Hours and 20 Minutes, Serve 16, and Difficulty: Hard)

Nutrition per Serving:

Calories 213, Protein 0.5 g, Carbohydrates 4 g, Fat 0.9 g, Cholesterol 0mg, Sodium 27.5mg.

Ingredients:

* 1 tablespoon of olive oil
* 2 rotisserie chicken carcasses, broken into pieces
* 4 carrots, cut into chunks
* 2 large onions, cut into chunks
* 3 stalks of celery, with leaves
* ½ cup of dry white wine
* 1 tablespoon of whole peppercorns
* 5 whole cloves of garlic
* 2 bay leaves
* 1 sprig fresh thyme
* 5 quarts of water

Instructions:

1. Preheat the oven to 400 degrees Fahrenheit (200 degrees Celsius).

2. Top with chicken carcass pieces, cabbage, onions, and celery. Add olive oil into the bottom of a large roasting pan.

3. Roast in a preheated oven until bones and vegetables are browned, stirring regularly for around 1 hour.

4. Move to an 8-quart stockpot of roasted chicken bones and vegetables. Pour the wine into the roasting pan, scrub the sides, pour into the stockpot to release any browned bits of bread.

5. Fill the stockpot with peppercorns, garlic, bay leaves, and thyme. Cover the mixture with water and let it boil slowly. Set the heat to low and simmer for at least 5 hours, straining off the fat as needed.

6. Strain stock, refrigerate or freeze stock using a cheesecloth.

Baked Ragi Murukku

(Ready in 35 Minutes, Serve 6, Difficulty: Easy)

Nutrition per Servings:

Calories 239, Carbohydrates 5 g, Fat 1 g, Cholesterol 3mg, Sodium 3mg, Potassium 12mg.

Ingredients:

* 250 g of ragi flour
* 150 g of besan flour
* 5 g of ginger
* 5 g of chili
* 2 g of garlic paste
* 5 g of salt
* 20ml of oil

Ingredients:

1. Collect and knead the dry ingredients together. Add the oil and the amount of needed water.

2. Let it become a semi-soft dough. Make the two sides equal.

3. Taking ½ of the dough into a Chakli machine.

4. Press the dough out of the roundels. Place the chaklis in a preheated oven. Bake them for 15-20 minutes at 180 C (360 degrees Fahrenheit).

5. Take the other ½ and repeat the same process. Let it cool off. The Chakli whirls are ready to use.

Coconut Lime Quinoa Salad

(Ready in 35 Minutes, Serve 3, Difficulty: Easy)

Nutrition per Serving:

Calories 310, Total Carbohydrate 56 g, Total Fat 7 g, Saturated Fat 3 g, Trans Fat 0 g, Cholesterol 0mg, Sodium 218mg.

Ingredients:

* 1 cup of uncooked quinoa
* 2 cups of water

- ½ cup of sliced red onion
- 3 cups of diced cucumber
- 1 ½ cup of purple cabbage
- ½ cup of ripened, diced avocado
- 4 segments of orange for garnishing
- 2 cups of defrosted, shelled edamame
- ½ cup of unsweetened toasted coconut flakes
- ¼ cup of chopped almonds
- Few shakes of black pepper

For the Dressing:

- 2 tablespoons of orange juice
- 1 lime, juiced
- 2 tablespoons of apple cider vinegar
- 2 tablespoons of olive oil

Instructions:

1. According to box instructions, boil quinoa in water. This should take between 12-15 minutes because it is necessary to absorb all the water. Remove it from the heat, use a fork to fluff it and allow it to cool.

2. Whisk the dressing together in a small bowl and set it aside.

3. As seen above, prepare all the remaining ingredients and toss them together in a very large bowl. Add it to the mixture after the quinoa has cooled, along with the dressing. Stir to coat well.

4. While this salad can be enjoyed instantly if you wish, let it rest for at least 30 minutes for the best results, or overnight if you can.

Hassel Back Sweet Potatoes

(Ready in 1 Hour. and 10 Minutes, Serve 4, Difficulty: Normal)

Nutrition per Serving:

Calories 226, Protein 3 g, Carbs 40 g, Fat 6 g.

Ingredients:

- 4 medium sweet potatoes
- 6 tablespoons of butter, unsalted
- 1/3 cup of brown sugar
- 1 teaspoon of pure vanilla extract
- ½ teaspoons of ground cinnamon
- ½ teaspoons of Himalayan pink salt/rock salt

Instructions:

1. In the oven center, place an oven rack and preheat the oven to 218 degree Celsius (425 degrees Fahrenheit).

2. To give it a flat surface to stand on as you slice it, shave a thin sliver from one side of each potato. Make thin slices about 1/16-inch thick into the potato, stopping before cutting all the way through.

3. On a separate sheet of foil, place each potato. To seal them, shape the foil around the potatoes but leave the tops open and exposed.

4. On a rimmed baking sheet, place the potatoes.

5. Melt the butter over medium-high heat in a small skillet, stirring periodically, until browned and nutty, for 2- 3 minutes.

6. Stir in the brown sugar, vanilla, salt, and cinnamon. Over the potatoes, drizzle the butter mixture and pinch the foil together on top to seal the potato inside.

7. Bake for 45 minutes, then leave for a few moments to cool down. Remove the potatoes from the foil, place them on a serving dish, and drizzle each foil packet with the leftover sauce.

8. Sprinkle with some nuts as you serve.

Creamy Cauliflower Mash

(Ready in 35 Minutes, Serve 8, Difficulty: Normal)

Nutrition per Serving:

Calories 246, Protein 7 g, Carbohydrates 34 g, Fat 8 g.

Ingredients:

- 3 cups of steamed, chopped cauliflower florets
- 1/2 cup of soaked, drained cashews
- 1/4 cup of water
- 1 lemon, juiced
- 1/4 teaspoon of salt
- 1 1/2 cups of cooked millet

Instructions:

1. Add the lemon juice, cashews, water, and salt to a food processor or blender and then process until smooth. Add the cauliflower and until well combined, continue to process.

2. Slowly add and process the millet until the desired consistency is achieved.

Quinoa & Smoked Tofu Salad

(Ready in 45 Minutes, Serve 2, Difficulty: Normal)

Nutrition per Servings:

Calories 206, Protein 10 g, Carbohydrates 23 g, Fat 8 g.

Ingredients:

- 1 cup of rinsed quinoa
- 2 cups of water
- 3/4 teaspoon of salt, divided
- 1/4 cup of lemon juice
- 2 tablespoons of extra-virgin olive oil
- 2 cloves of garlic, minced

- 1/4 teaspoon of ground black pepper
- 1(6 ounces) package of baked smoked tofu, diced
- 1 yellow bell pepper, diced
- 1 cup of halved grape tomatoes
- 1 cup of diced cucumber
- 1/2 cup of chopped fresh parsley
- 1/2 cup of chopped fresh mint

Instructions:

1. In a medium saucepan, add the water and 1/2 teaspoon salt and place over medium-high heat. Bring it to a boil, add the quinoa and bring it back to the boil. Reduce to low, cover, and cook, about 15-20 minutes, until water has been fully absorbed.

2. Meanwhile, add the lemon juice, garlic, olive oil, pepper, and the remaining 1/4 of a teaspoon of salt to a large mixing bowl. Until well combined, whisk together.

3. On a baking sheet, spread the quinoa out to cool for at least 10 minutes. To make the dressing, add the cooled quinoa, tomatoes, tofu, bell pepper, cucumber, parsley, and mint. Toss until it is coated well.

Matcha Tea Macaroons

(Ready in 1 Hour and 15 Minutes, Serve 12, Difficulty: Normal)

Nutrition per Serving:

Calories 127, Protein 2 g, Carbohydrates 18 g, Fat 5 g, Fiber 0 g, Sugar 17 g.

Ingredients:

For Macaroons:
- 5 egg whites
- 20 g of breakfast sugar
- 368 g of icing sugar
- 425 g of almond powder
- 1 tablespoon of matcha powder

For White Chocolate Ganache:
- 60ml of heavy cream
- 170 g of chopped white chocolate

Instructions:

Prepare Macaroon Shells:

1. Place and set aside 2 silicone mats on 2 wide baking trays.

2. Mix the almond flour, icing sugar, and matcha powder well. Set aside.

3. Whip the egg whites at a medium-low speed using an electric mixer until they are frothy. Sprinkle the granulated sugar slowly and continue to whip until it forms stiff peaks.

4. To fit the remaining materials, move the egg whites to a wide bowl.

5. Fold ¼ of the blend of almond flour gently into the whites. Fold in the remaining almond mixture gradually until a moist, gloppy batter forms. It needs to have hot lava consistency.

6. Rapidly fill the batter with a pastry bag, or the meringue may loosen. Pipe into 2-inch rounds, spaced about 1-inch apart, onto the prepared baking sheets.

7. Let the macarons rest at room temperature for 25-40 minutes, until the tops are dry and smooth skin has formed.

8. Adjust the oven rack to the middle position for 10 minutes before baking and heat the oven to 160 degrees Celsius (320 F).

9. Bake on the one hand for 6 minutes, turn the tray around and bake for another 6 minutes. At a time, bake one pan.

10. Slide the silicone mat carefully onto a wire rack or the marble tabletop immediately after baking, and cool completely.

Prepare White Chocolate Ganache:

1. Put it to a boil with the milk. Pour over the white diced chocolate and mix to an even consistency. Using a spatula made of wood and not a machine. Leave to cool at room temperature to thicken more.

2. Pour into a piping bag once thick enough to pipe, pipe gently onto one macaroon shell, and put the other macaron shell on top. Push a little until the ganache spreads to the sides.

3. Serve.

Spicy Curd Fry (Indian Recipe)

(Ready in 15 Minutes, Serve 2, Difficulty: Easy)

Nutrition per Serving:

Carbs 11 g, Protein 6 g, Fat 9 g, Fiber 2 g, Sugar 7 g, Sodium 25.4 g.

Ingredients:
- 1 onion, chopped
- 1 tomato, chopped
- 10-12 pieces of curry leaves
- ½ teaspoon of turmeric
- ½ teaspoon of salt
- ½ teaspoon of red chili powder
- 1 teaspoon of butter
- 1 bowl of chilled curd

Instructions:

1. Place some butter in a frying pan.

2. Add the onion and tomatoes and fry them together.

3. Stir in the turmeric, salt, and red chili pepper. Mix thoroughly.

4. Put the curry leaves together, mix well, and cook for a while.

5. The cooked tadka is added to the chilled curd.

6. Serve cold.

Baked Vegetables Casserole

(Ready in 30 Minutes, Serve 6, Difficulty: Easy)

Nutrition per Serving:

Calories 158.5, Protein 9.7 g, Fat 5.7 g, Cholesterol 5.9mg, Sodium 479.9mg,

Sugars 3.4 g.

Ingredients:

- 4 cups of vegetables (Your choice)
- 2 cups of cubed bread
- 1 cup of milk
- ¼ cup of butter milk
- 1 tablespoon of butter
- 1 teaspoon of olive oil
- 2 egg whites
- 1 bunch of rosemary
- 2-3 saga leaves
- Salt, to taste
- 1 teaspoon of chili peppers, roasted

Instructions:

1. Preheat the oven for 5 minutes at 140 degrees Celsius (284 F).

2. Grease an oven-proof dish with olive oil and toss butter with vegetables, bread, salt, and herbs to make them well coated.

3. Roast the vegetables at 180 degrees Celsius (356 F) for 15 minutes in the oven.

4. Combine the milk, butter, cheese, and eggs until the vegetables are roasted.

5. Take it out and pour in the milk and egg mixture after the vegetables are roasted and put it back in the oven.

6. Tear it into pieces if you are using cheese slices, then put it on top of the vegetables.

7. Cook for 15 minutes, until the mixture of milk and eggs is well cooked.

8. Serve it warm.

Barley Paratha (Indian Recipe)

(Ready in 40 Minutes, Serve 6, Difficulty: Easy)

Nutrition per Serving:

Calories 377, Protein 10 g, Carbohydrates 55 g, Fat 11 g.

Ingredients:

For Dough:

- 2 cups barley flour
- ½ teaspoon of salt
- ½ teaspoon of bishop's weed
- 1 teaspoon of fennel
- 1 tablespoon of ghee
- ½ cup of water

For Filling:

- 1 cup of sattu
- ½ teaspoon of bishop's weed
- ½ teaspoon of salt
- 1 tbsp.of garlic paste
- 1 tbsp. of ginger paste
- 1 tbsp. of green chili
- ½ teaspoon of red chili powder
- 1 medium sized onion
- ½ teaspoon of lemon juice
- 1 teaspoon of pickle spicy
- 1 teaspoon of mustard oil
- ½ cup of coriander leaves

Instructions:

Prepare the Dough:

1. In a bowl, take flour and add salt, weed from the bishop, fennel, and ghee. Add the amount of water needed and prepare the soft dough.

Prepare the Stuffing:

1. Put sattu in a bowl. Add the weed, salt, green chili, ginger-garlic paste, and red chili powder from the bishop.

2. Add the onion, lemon juice, mustard oil, pickle spicy, and cilantro leaves. Mix thoroughly.

3. The addition of the necessary amount of water makes the stuffing moist to easily be filled.

Prepare Sattu Paratha:

1. For making parathas make balls out of the dough.

2. To prevent the dough from sticking, sprinkle flour over the rolling surface.

3. Roll out to make parathas and fill in the center with a portion of sattu.

4. Enfold the filling properly to roll it again to make flat balls.

5. Heat the Paratha pan and cook on both sides.

6. On both sides, add a generous amount of ghee and cook until golden brown.

7. Keep the flame low for better cooking.

8. Sattu Parathas are ready to be served hot with your choice of gravy, curd, or pickle.

Easy White Bean Salad

(Ready in 15 Minutes. Serve 6, Difficulty: Easy)

Nutrition per Serving:

Calories 142, Protein 6 g, Carbohydrates 25 g, Fat 11 g.

Ingredients:

- 2(15 ounces) cans of Great Northern beans, drained and rinsed
- 226 g of chopped plum tomatoes
- ½ cup of chopped fresh basil leaves
- 1 teaspoon of salt
- ½ teaspoon of ground black pepper
- 3 cloves of garlic, minced
- 4 tablespoons of extra-virgin olive oil

Instructions:

1. Coat the cooking spray with a large non-stick skillet and place over medium heat. Add the garlic and sauté for 1-2 minutes until just lightly browned.

2. Meanwhile, add the beans, tomatoes, basil, salt, and pepper into a large salad bowl. Over the salad, pour the garlic and oil and toss to combine.

3. Let the salad sit for at least 30 minutes to make it possible to combine the flavors.

Quinoa and Sesame Crackers with Orange Hummus

(Ready in 50 Minutes, Serve 8, Difficulty: Normal)

Nutrition per Serving:

Calories 331, Protein 1 g, Carbohydrates 2 g, Fat 1 g, Saturated Fat 1 g, Cholesterol 8mg, Sodium 39mg.

Ingredients:

- 200 gram of white quinoa
- 500ml of water to cook quinoa
- ½ teaspoon of baking powder
- 50 gram of rice flour
- 5 gram of salt
- 15 gram of sesame seeds
- 2 fresh oranges
- 150 g of boiled chickpeas
- 20 g of tahini paste
- 2 pinches of smoked paprika
- Salt, to taste

Instructions:

1. Preheat the oven to 176 degree Celsius (350°F)

2. Bring quinoa to a boil over moderate heat, then simmer until fully cooked and consistency is achieved like porridge.

3. Remove it from the heat and let it cool down.

4. To blend, add rice flour, baking powder, season with salt and mix well.

5. Using a spatula, spread the quinoa batter on to the silpat®.

6. Sprinkle with the sesame seeds and cook for 10-12 minutes.

7. Take it out of the oven and allow it to cool.

8. Using the fine side of your grater, prepare the orange zest. When the zest has been extracted, split the orange in ½ and squeeze out the orange juice.

9. Add the boiled chickpeas, smoked paprika, orange juice, tahini paste, salt, and process until well mixed in a food processor.

10. Move the hummus and search for seasoning in a serving bowl. Serve with crackers made from quinoa. Enjoy!

Sautéed Cauliflower

(Ready in 15 Minutes. Serve 8, Difficulty: Easy)

Nutrition per Serving:

Calories: 38, Protein 3 g, Carbohydrates 8 g, Fat 0 g.

Ingredients:

- 4 cups of chopped cauliflower florets
- 2 tablespoons of water
- 2 teaspoons of red wine vinegar
- 1 cup of halved grape tomatoes
- 2 tablespoons of chopped fresh parsley
- 1 tablespoon of minced garlic
- 1/4 teaspoon of salt
- 1/4 teaspoon of ground black pepper

Instructions:

1. Coat the cooking spray with a large non-stick skillet and put it over medium heat. Add the cauliflower and cook for 4 minutes, then cover and cook.

2. Pour in the vinegar and water, stir to mix, and cover. Cook for about 4 more minutes until the cauliflower is golden and soft, and the liquid has evaporated.

3. Tomatoes, parsley, garlic, salt, and pepper should be added. Cook for about 2 more minutes, stirring regularly until the tomatoes have softened and the flavors have blended.

Kappa (Tapioca)

(Ready in 40 Minutes, Serve 6, Difficulty: Normal)

Nutrition per Serving:

Calories 100, Protein 0 g, Carbohydrates 26 g, Fat 0 g, Fiber 0 g, Sugar 0 g.

Ingredients:

* 2 Tapioca, cubed
* Tapioca water to cook
* Salt, to taste

To Grind:

* 1 Coconut
* 1 cumin seed
* 2 clove of garlic
* 1-2 green chili
* ¼-1/2 teaspoon of turmeric powder
* Salt, to taste
* Enough water to grind into a coarse paste

For Tempering:

* 2 tablespoons of coconut oil/vegetable oil
* 1 teaspoon of mustard seeds
* 3 small onions, finely chopped
* 3 red dry whole chili
* 1 sprig of curry leaves

Instructions:

1. Peel off the tapioca, cut it into cubes, and wash it under running water.

2. Boil the tapiocas until tender and well cooked, along with water and a little salt.

3. Drain and keep the water aside.

4. Grind ingredients in a blender to a coarse paste.

5. Add the cooked tapiocas as well as the ground paste into a large saucepan.

6. Cook until the gravy begins to thicken and is well mixed for around 5-10 minutes. You could use a wooden spoon to mash the tapiocas gently if you want.

7. Remove from the heat and cover aside.

8. Over medium heat, heat a small pan and add oil.

9. Add the mustard seeds as the oil gets hot and let it splutter.

10. Add the small sliced onions and cook them for a few minutes.

11. Add the dried red chilies and the curry leaves and cook before the onions turn brown.

12. Pour this mixture on the cooked tapioca.

13. For some time, leave the tapioca covered so that the tempering flavors will get into the bowl.

14. Along with your favorite fish curry, serve warm.

Three Bean Salad

(Ready in 10 Minutes, Serve 8, Difficulty: Easy)

Nutrition per Serving:

Calories 194, Protein 6 g, Carbohydrates 22 g, Fat 9 g.

Ingredients:

* 1(16 ounces) can of green beans, drained and rinsed
* 1(16 ounces) can of yellow wax beans, drained and rinsed
* 1(16 ounces) can of red kidney beans, drained and rinsed

4 tablespoons of Stevia® or another natural sweetener

* 2/3 cup of vinegar
* 1/4 cup of vegetable oil
* 1/2 teaspoon of salt
* 1/2 teaspoon of ground black pepper
* 1 onion, sliced thinly

Instructions:

1. Add the stevia, vinegar, oil, salt, and pepper into a large mixing bowl and whisk together to make the dressing. Pour in the onions and beans and toss to coat them.

2. Cover and place in the refrigerator to chill for at least 4 hours or overnight, best if occasionally stirred. Before serving, you can drain the excess liquid if desired.

Asian Chicken Lettuce Wraps (Whole30, Paleo, Low Carb)

(Ready in 35 Minutes, Serve 8, Difficulty: Normal)

Nutrition Per Serving:

Calories 180, Protein 13 g, Carbohydrates 7 g, Fat 11 g, Sodium 421mg, Potassium 376mg.

Ingredients:

* 2 tablespoons of chopped garlic
* 1 large shallot, chopped
* 3 thin slices of ginger about 3 thin slices, chopped
* ⅔ cup of chopped carrots (about 1 medium-size carrot)
* ⅔ cup of chopped celery
* 5-6 whole water chestnuts chopped (Optional)
* 226 grams of raw shrimp peeled, deveined, and diced.
* 2 tablespoons of avocado oil
* 226 grams of ground chicken breast
* ¼ teaspoon of coarse salt, to taste
* ⅛ teaspoon of white pepper

For sauce:

* 3 tablespoons of almond butter
* 2 tablespoons of coconut aminos
* 2 teaspoons of hot pepper sauce (Optional)
* 3-4 tablespoons of apple juice or water

For Serve and Garnish:

- 1-2 heads of butter lettuce
- 3 tablespoons of chopped, toasted almond or cashew nuts
- 1 bulb of scallion, chopped

Instructions

1. Prepare the garlic ingredients for the chestnuts. Dice it to a bite-size if you are using shrimp. In a single bowl, cook the sauce. Ready to use, set them aside.

2. Add 2 tablespoons of oil to a well-heated wide skillet or wok. Over medium-high heat, cook the garlic, shallot, and ginger with 1 pinch of salt for around 10 seconds or until it smells fragrant.

3. Add chicken ground. With salt and pepper, season. Cook until the meat is thoroughly cooked, around 2-3 minutes or so. Lower the heat to low, then cook for an extra 2 minutes. It should not be wet and watery for your skillet; otherwise, the dish would be less delicious.

4. Add the carrots and celery and turn the heat to medium-high, with a salt and season pinch. cook for 1 minute, adding chestnuts and shrimp.

5. Add 2 tablespoons of sauce and stir-fry for about 10 seconds to coat all over. Keep the sauce to a minimum so that the texture is not soggy nor crunchy. Taste as per choice and remove from heat.

6. Place the lettuce wraps over a wide serving tray/plate to eat. In the middle, fill each lettuce cup with several mixture tablespoons. Garnish with almonds and scallions. To the side, serve the extra sauce. At room temperature, serve.

Barnyard Millet Dosa (Indian Recipe)

(Ready in 25 Minutes, Serve 8, Difficulty: Easy)

Nutrition per Serving:

Calories: 109, Protein 2.55 g, Carbs 19.2 g, Fat 2.52 g, Fiber 2.46 g.

Ingredients:

For Dosa:

- 1 cup of Barnyard millet
- 3 tablespoon of chestnut flour
- Rock salt, to taste

For Frying Ghee

Stuffing:

- 2 boiled, mashed potatoes
- 2 tablespoons of desi ghee
- Sendha Namak, to taste
- 2 whole red chilies
- ½ teaspoon of turmeric powder
- 1 teaspoon of cumin seeds
- 1 tablespoon of chopped ginger
- 1 teaspoon of chopped chilies
- 1 tablespoon of chopped coriander

Instructions:

1. Soak the barnyard millet for 15-20 minutes. Drain the rough batter and roll it out (not too thin). Mix the chestnut flour with the prepared batter and keep it at room temperature for 30 minutes.

2. Soak and mash the chilies to make a perfect paste with a little water.

3. Heat ghee in a saucepan, add cumin seed, bring in the chopped ginger and green chilies when it crackles.

4. Add the boiled crushed potatoes and fry nicely. Add the turmeric powder, rock salt, and red chili paste.

5. Add chopped cilantro. Remove and place aside.

6. Heat a non-stick pan now. Grease it.

7. In the middle of the pan, pour a ladle full of dosa batter and spread it evenly with the aid of the spoon, like a round disk.

8. Sprinkle with oil and let it cook.

9. In the dosa center, place the prepared potato Spicy and flip 1/2 and fold the dosa in the form of a half-moon and serve hot with coconut and peanut chutney.

Curd Rice

(Ready in 25 Minutes, Serve 8, Difficulty: Easy)

Nutrition per Serving:

Calories 376, Protein 8.5 g, Carbohydrate 36.9 g, Fat 18.7 g, Fiber 1.8 g.

Ingredients:

- 1 cup of rice
- 3 cups of water
- 1 ½ cup of curd
- ½ cup of milk
- 1 carrot
- 1 green chili
- 1 teaspoon of ginger
- 1 teaspoon of salt
- 1 bunch of coriander leaves
- 2 teaspoon of oil
- 2 teaspoon of mustard seeds
- 1 teaspoon of chickpeas
- 2 teaspoon of black gram
- 2 bunch of curry leaves
- 2 red chili
- ½ teaspoon of hing

Instructions:

1. Add rice and water and cook it under pressure.

2. To make it soggy, mix the pressure-cooked rice a little bit.

3. Fill it with curd and milk and mix well.

4. Put the carrot, the green chili, the ginger, the salt, and the coriander's leaves. Thoroughly stir the ingredients.

5. Take a pan now, heat it, and pour in some oil.

6. To make a tadka, add mustard seeds, curry leaves, chickpeas, black gram, red chili, and hinges together.

7. Cook them thoroughly.

8. Place the curd rice in a bowl to serve and pour the tadka over it.

Garlic Rosemary Mushrooms

(Ready in 15 Minutes. Serve 4, Difficulty: Easy)
Nutrition per Serving:

Calories 154, Protein 6 g, Carbohydrates 7 g, Fat 1 g.

Ingredients:

*   453 g of mixed mushrooms, cut into 1/4-inch slices
*   2 cloves of garlic, finely chopped
*   1/2 tablespoon of chopped fresh rosemary
*   1/4 teaspoon of salt
*   1/8 teaspoon of ground black pepper
*   1/4 cup of dry white wine

Instructions:

1. Coat in the cooking spray with a large skillet and put over medium heat. Add the mushrooms, rosemary, garlic, salt, and pepper.

2. Cook until mushrooms are tender, about 8 minutes, stirring occasionally. Pour in the wine and stir, cook for 2 minutes until it is mostly evaporated.

Asparagus Stir-Fry

(Ready in 20 Minutes, Serve 9, Difficulty: Easy)
Nutrition per Serving:

Calories 306, Protein 3 g, Carbohydrates 6 g, Fat 0 g.

Ingredients:

*   1/4 medium onion, chopped
*   453 g of trimmed fresh asparagus
*   1 clove of garlic, thinly sliced
*   2 teaspoons of teriyaki sauce

Instructions:

1. Coat in the cooking spray with a large skillet and put over medium heat. Add the onions and cook for 1-2 minutes, until tender.

2. Add the asparagus and garlic and cook until the asparagus is slightly tender, for 3-5 minutes. To let the flavors, mix, pour in the teriyaki sauce, and stir for an extra minute.

Eggplant "Bacon"

(Ready in 20 Minutes, Serve 12, Difficulty: Easy)
Nutrition per Serving:

Calories: 127, Protein 2 g, Carbohydrates 16 g, Fat 7 g.

Ingredients:

*   1 large eggplant, sliced lengthwise into 1/4-inch thick (or less) slices
*   2 tablespoons of tamari
*   2 tablespoons of maple syrup
*   2 tablespoons of apple cider vinegar
*   2 tablespoons of extra-virgin olive oil
*   1 teaspoon of chili powder
*   1/4 teaspoon of smoked paprika
*   1/8 teaspoon of ground black pepper

Instructions:

1. In a wide zip lock bag, put all of the ingredients, seal, and shake to coat. Refrigerate and marinate for at least an hour.

2. Preheat the oven to 176 degrees Celsius (350 Fahrenheit).

3. On a baking sheet, spread out slices and bake, sometimes basting with the marinade, for about 45 minutes or until crispness is desired.

Salty Edamame

(Ready in 15 Minutes, Serve 4, Difficulty: Easy)
Nutrition per Serving:

Calories: 50, Protein 4 g, Carbohydrates 5 g, Fat 1 g.

Ingredients:

*   1 cup of edamame, in the shell
*   Salt, to taste

Instructions:

1. Over medium-low heat, place a large saucepan. Add 2 quarts of edamame and water. Cover and simmer for about 5-8 minutes, until tender.

2. Drain and add salt to sprinkle.

Sherry-Asiago Cream Brussels Sprouts

(Ready in 25 Minutes, Serve 4, Difficulty: Easy)
Nutrition per Serving:

Calories 114, Protein 8 g, Carbohydrates 15 g, Fat 4 g.

Ingredients:

*   453 g of trimmed, halved Brussels sprouts
*   2 tablespoons of minced shallots

- 1 tablespoon of all-purpose flour
- 2/3 cup of skim milk
- 2 tablespoons of dry sherry
- 1/3 cup of shredded Asiago cheese
- 1/4 teaspoon of salt
- 1/8 teaspoon of ground black pepper

Instructions:

1. Place a large saucepan over medium-high heat with around 1 inch of water and bring to a boil. Put the Brussels sprouts and steam in a steamer basket until tender, around 7-9 minutes.

2. Meanwhile, cover in a cooking spray with a small saucepan and put over medium heat. Add the shallots and sauté for 1-2 minutes, until tender. To mix, add the flour and combine.

3. Pour in the milk and the sherry, bring to a boil, and whisk continuously. Reduce heat to medium-low and simmer until thickened, often whisking, for about 3 minutes.

4. Stir in the cheese, salt, and pepper and remove from the heat. In a large bowl, put the Brussels sprouts and pour in the sauce. Toss to coat.

Semiya Upma (Indian Recipe)

(Ready in 30 Minutes, Serve 12, Difficulty: Easy)

Nutrition per Serving:

Calories 180, Protein 2.6 g, Carbohydrates 17.4 g, Fat 11.1 g, Fiber 1.5 g.

Ingredients:

- 2 tablespoons of oil
- 1 teaspoon of mustard seeds
- 1 teaspoons of cumin seeds
- 1 teaspoon of peanuts
- ½ teaspoons of sesame seeds
- 1 teaspoon of black gram
- 7-8 curry leaves
- 11-12 cashew nuts
- 1 onion, chopped
- ¼ cup of chopped carrot
- ¼ cup of chopped beans
- ¼ cup of peas
- 1 teaspoon of ginger
- 1 green chili
- 1 teaspoon of salt
- ½ teaspoon of turmeric powder
- 1 cup of vermicelli
- 1 cup of water

Instructions:

1. In a pan, heat oil.

2. Add the mustard seeds, peanuts, sesame, black gram, curry leaves, and cashew nuts.

3. For a while, cook them and add the onion and combine thoroughly.

4. Along with ginger, peas, and green chili, add chopped carrot and beans. Stir occasionally.

5. Add the salt and turmeric powder and blend until the color is yellowish.

6. Pour the vermicelli slowly into the pan.

7. Stir slowly by adding water as needed.

8. To let it cook on a medium flame, cover the pan for a while.

9. If the water has evaporated, remove the lid and check.

10. Semiya Upma is ready for a hot serving.

Sautéed Spinach

(Ready in 15 Minutes, Serve 6, Difficulty: Easy)

Nutrition per Serving:

Calories 269, Protein 4 g, Carbohydrates 14 g, Fat 1 g.

Ingredients:

- 6 cups (10-ounce bag) of rinsed fresh spinach
- 2 tablespoons of golden raisins
- 1 tablespoon of pine nuts
- 2 cloves of garlic, minced
- 2 teaspoons of balsamic vinegar
- 1/8 teaspoon of salt
- Ground black pepper, to taste
- 1 tablespoon of shredded, low-fat parmesan cheese

Instructions:

1. Coat a large non-stick skillet or saucepan with a cooking spray and place over medium-high heat. Add the raisins, pine nuts, and garlic once it is hot. Cook until fragrant, for approximately 30 seconds.

2. Stir in the spinach and cook for about 2 minutes, until wilted. Put the vinegar, salt, and pepper away from the heat. Sprinkle with parmesan and toss.

Corn & Edamame Succotash

(Ready in 15 Minutes, Serve 4, Difficulty: Easy)

Nutrition per Serving:

Calories 126, Protein 6 g, Carbohydrates 15 g, Fat 5 g.

Ingredients:

- 1 tablespoon of canola oil
- 1/2 cup of chopped red bell pepper
- 1/4 cup of chopped onion
- 2 cloves of garlic, minced

* 2 cups of fresh corn kernels
* 3 tablespoons of dry white wine
* 1 1/2 cups of cooked edamame beans according to package
* 2 tablespoons of rice vinegar
* 2 tablespoons of chopped fresh parsley
* 2 tablespoons of chopped fresh basil
* 1/2 teaspoon of salt
* 1/4 teaspoon of ground black pepper

Instructions:

1. Over medium heat, position a large non-stick skillet, add the oil and heat. Add the bell pepper, onion, and garlic once it is warmed. Cook for about 2 minutes, until the vegetables are tender.

2. Add the corn, white wine, and edamame and sauté for approximately 4 minutes until the flavors are well mixed.

3. Stir in the parsley, basil, vinegar, salt, and pepper and remove from the heat.

Speedy Pita Pizza

(Ready in 10 Minutes, Serve 2, Difficulty: Easy)

Nutrition per Serving:

Calories 229, Protein 32 g, Carbohydrates 28 g, Fat 9 g.

Ingredients:

* 1 whole-grain pita
* 1 cup of baby spinach
* 1/2(14 ounces) package of cubed, low-fat extra-firm tofu
* 1/4 cup of shredded, low-fat mozzarella cheese
* 1/2 lemon, juiced
* Salt and ground black pepper, to taste

Instructions:

1. Place the tofu, spinach, and mozzarella on top of the pita. Season with pepper and salt and sprinkle with lime juice.

2. Set in a toaster oven (4-5 minutes) or microwave oven (2-3 minutes) until the cheese has melted to the desired consistency.

Mediterranean Broccoli

(Ready in 20 Minutes. Serve 6, Difficulty: Easy)

Nutrition per Serving:

Calories 284, Protein 2 g, Carbohydrates 8 g, Fat 4 g.

Ingredients:

* 1 cup of cherry tomatoes
* 1 tablespoon of extra-virgin olive oil
* 2 cloves of garlic, minced

* 1/4 teaspoon of salt
* 1/2 teaspoon of lemon zest
* 1 tablespoon of lemon juice
* 1/4 cup of pitted and sliced black olives
* 1 teaspoon of dried oregano
* 2 teaspoons of capers, rinsed

Instructions:

1. Preheat the oven to 232 degree Celsius (450 Fahrenheit). Coat the cooking spray with a baking sheet.

2. Add the broccoli, olive oil, tomatoes, garlic, salt to a large mixing bowl, and toss to cover. Spread out on the baking sheet and bake for 10 to 12 minutes until the broccoli starts to brown.

3. Meanwhile, combine lemon zest, olives, lemon juice, oregano, and capers to the large mixing bowl. Add the vegetables that have been cooked and stir to combine.

Cranberry Apricot Squash

(Ready in 15 Minutes, Serve 4, Difficulty: Easy)

Nutrition per Serving:

Calories 172, Protein 2 g, Carbohydrates 32 g, Fat 6 g.

Ingredients:

* 453 g of delicate squash, seeded and chopped into bite-sized pieces
* 1 tablespoon of extra-virgin olive oil
* 1 tablespoon of apple cider
* 1/4 of teaspoon salt
* 1/4 teaspoon of ground black pepper
* 1/4 cup of chopped dried apricots
* 1/4 cup of dried cranberries
* 2 tablespoons of finely chopped chives
* 2 tablespoons of toasted sliced almonds

Instructions:

1. Place a large saucepan over medium heat with about 1 inch of water and bring to a boil. Place the squash in a steamer basket and steam for about 5-7 minutes, until tender.

2. Add the olive oil, apple cider, salt, and pepper to a large mixing bowl and whisk until well combined. Add and toss to coat the squash, apricots, cranberries, and chives. Use almonds to sprinkle.

Spiced Red Cabbage

(Ready in 1 hr. 5 Minutes, Serve 6, Difficulty: Hard)

Nutrition per Serving:

Calories 364, Protein 2 g, Carbohydrates 11 g, Fat 3 g.

Ingredients:

* 1/2 medium head red cabbage, diced
* 1 tablespoon of canola oil
* 1/2 cup of chopped onion
* 1 medium apple, quartered
* 3 tablespoons of tarragon vinegar
* 1 teaspoon of Stevia® or another natural sweetener
* 1 bay leaf
* 1 teaspoon of salt
* 1/4 teaspoon of ground black pepper
* 1/8 teaspoon of ground cloves

Instructions:

1. In a large saucepan, add 1 inch of water and place over medium-high heat. Stir in the cabbage and bring it to a boil. For 4-5 minutes, reduce heat, cover, and simmer until crisp and drain.

2. Return the remaining ingredients to the pan, add them, and mix well. Cover and cook for 1 hour or until the cabbage is soft. Before serving, remove the bay leaves.

Italian Style Snap Peas

(Ready in 30 Minutes. Serve 4, Difficulty: Easy)

Nutrition per Serving:

Calories 249, Protein 4 g, Carbohydrates 14 g, Fat 3 g.

Ingredients:

* 1 large leek (white part only), washed, halved lengthwise, and cut into 2-inch strips
* 453 g of trimmed sugar snap peas
* 2 teaspoons of extra-virgin olive oil
* 1/2 teaspoon of salt
* 1 cup of halved cherry tomatoes
* 1 teaspoon of dried oregano

Instructions:

1. Preheat the oven to 218 degrees C (425 Fahrenheit). Coat the cooking spray with a baking sheet.

2. Add the peas, olive oil, leeks, and salt into a large mixing bowl. To combine, toss.

3. Spread the mixture out for 15 minutes on the baking sheet and roast. Add the tomatoes and roast for another 10 minutes or until the vegetables begin to brown. Use oregano to sprinkle.

Low-Calorie Microwave Dhokla (Indian Recipe)

(Ready in 30 Minutes, Serve 6, Difficulty: Easy)

Nutrition per Serving:

Calories 267, Protein 10.2 g, Carbohydrates 34.4 g, Fat 9.8 g, Sugars 2.6 g.

Ingredients:

* 1 cup of besan 1 tsp suji
* 1 teaspoon of ginger, green chili paste
* 1 teaspoon of salt
* 1/2 lemon, juiced
* 1 teaspoon of turmeric powder
* 2 tablespoons of. curd
* 1 cup of water
* 1 teaspoon of fruit salt

For Tadka:

* 2 teaspoon of oil
* 1 teaspoon of mustard seeds
* 15-20 curry leaves
* 2 green chilies
* 1 teaspoon of sesame seeds
* 1 cup of water

For Garnish:

* Coriander leaves
* Grated coconut

Instructions:

1. In a big deep bowl, take besan. Use green chili paste to add suji and ginger to it.

2. Thoroughly mix them, add salt and lemon juice, and mix again. Add the turmeric powder and curd and thoroughly whisk.

3. Pour some water in the bowl and whisk thoroughly to make a thick batter of the put fruit salt in the batter and mix.

4. Transfer the batter for 6-8 minutes to a microwave-friendly utensil and heat it on high power.

5. Put the mustard seeds in a hot oil pan and prepare the tadka. Cook the curry leaves and green chilies a little, then add them to the tadka and cook thoroughly. Add the sesame seeds and some water to balance them well.

4.Pour the tadka over cooked dhokla. Garnish with grated coconut and coriander leaves.

5. Slice the dish into the appropriate sizes and serve it fresh.

Taco Salad for a Large Crowd

(Ready in 35 Minutes, Serve 26, Difficulty: Normal)

Nutrition per Serving:

Calories 26, Protein 10 g, Fat 15 g, Saturated Fat 4 g, Cholesterol 24mg, Sodium 696mg, 23 g, Sugars 7 g, Fiber 3 g.

Ingredients:

* 907 g of ground beef

* 2 envelopes of taco seasoning, divided
* 1 medium head iceberg lettuce
* 1 package (10 ounces) of nacho-flavored tortilla chips, coarsely crushed
* 2 pints of grape tomatoes, halved
* 2 cans (16 ounces) of kidney beans, rinsed and drained
* 3 cans (2-1/4 ounces) of sliced ripe olives, drained
* 1-1/2 cups of shredded cheddar cheese
* 1 large sweet onion, chopped
* 2 cans (4 ounces) of chopped green chilies
* 1-1/2 cups of Thousand Island salad dressing
* 1-1/3 cup of sauce
* 1/3 cup of sugar

Instructions:

1. Cook beef in a Dutch oven over medium heat with 1 envelope plus 2 tablespoons of taco seasoning until no longer pink, then rinse.

2. Combine the lettuce, chips, cheese, tomatoes, beans, olives, onion, chili, and beef mixture in a very large serving dish.

3. Combine the salad dressing, sugar, sauce, and remaining taco seasoning in a small bowl, pour over the salad, and coat.

Mustard-Parmesan Whole Roasted Cauliflower

(Ready in 1 Hour and 5 Minutes, Serve 2, Difficulty: Normal)

Nutrition per Serving:

Calories 107, Protein 2.5 g, Carbohydrates 6.2 g, Fat 8.9 g, Sodium 745mg, Potassium 189mg.

Ingredients:

* 2 large cauliflowers
* 1 clove of garlic, halved
* ¼ cup of olive oil
* 4 tablespoons of Dijon mustard
* Kosher salt
* Freshly ground of black pepper
* ½ cup of fresh parsley leaves, chopped
* ¼ cup of parmesan, grated
* Lemon wedges

Instructions:

1. In the bottom of the oven, place an oven rack and preheat to 232 Celsius (450 degrees Fahrenheit). Line a sheet with foil for baking.

2. Remove the leaves from the cauliflower, then trim the stem flush with the head's bottom, so the cauliflower sits flat on the prepared baking sheet.

3. With the sliced garlic, rub the outside of each head.

4. In a small bowl, whisk together the oil, 3 tablespoons of mustard, 1/2 teaspoon of salt, and a few tiny pieces of black pepper.

5. On the prepared baking sheet, place the cauliflower and brush the whole outside and inside with the mustard-oil mixture.

6. Roast the cauliflower until it is nicely charred and tender, 50 minutes to 1 hour (a long skewer inserted in the center of the cauliflower can pass through easily). Let them rest for a couple of minutes.

7. Meanwhile, in a small bowl, combine the parsley and the parmesan. Brush with the remaining one tablespoon mustard the outside of the roasted cauliflower heads all over and generously sprinkle the Parmesan mixture.

Katie's Yogurt Veggie Salad

(Ready in 1 Hour and 50 Minutes, Serve 4, Difficulty: Hard)

Nutrition per Serving:

Calories 311, Protein 8.9 g, Carbohydrates 22 g, Fat 0.4 g, Cholesterol 3.9mg, Sodium 128.9mg.

Ingredients:

* 25 ounces of non-fat plain yogurt
* ½ large English cucumber, halved, seeded, and grated
* 1 carrot, grated
* Salt, to taste
* ½ onion, diced
* ½ red bell pepper, diced
* 1 stalk of celery, diced
* ¼ cup of chopped fresh parsley
* ¼ lemon, juiced
* 1 tablespoon of chopped fresh mint, or to taste
* 2 teaspoons of ground cumin
* Salt and ground black pepper, to taste

Instructions:

1. Spoon the yogurt into a colander lined with cheesecloth and put it aside for at least 30 minutes until most of the water has drained.

2. Sprinkle with salt and put the grated cucumber and grated carrot in a cheesecloth-lined colander. To drain excess water, place a heavy object, such as a bowl, on top of the cucumber and carrot, for 15-20 minutes.

3. In a bowl, mix the milk, cucumber, carrot, cabbage, red bell pepper, celery, parsley, lemon juice, mint, and season with black salt pepper.

4. Refrigerate for at least 1 hour for the flavors to blend.

Asian Ginger Broccoli

(Ready in 15 Minutes. Serve 12, Difficulty: Easy)

Nutrition per Serving:

Calories: 176, Protein 4 g, Carbohydrates 8 g, Fat: 4 g.

Ingredients:

- 1 tablespoon of canola oil
- 2 tablespoons of minced garlic
- 4 teaspoons of minced fresh ginger
- 5 cups of halved broccoli crowns
- 3 tablespoons of water
- 1 tablespoon of rice vinegar

Instructions:

1. Heat oil over medium-high heat in a large skillet. Add the garlic and ginger and cook for about 45 seconds until it is fragrant. Add the broccoli and sauté for about 2 minutes, until the broccoli is bright green.

2. Pour the water in, stir and cover with it. Reduce the heat to medium and cook for around 3 minutes until the broccoli is tender. Toss the vinegar with it.

Carrot Fries

(Ready in 50 Minutes, Serve 8, Difficulty: Normal)

Nutrition per Serving:

Calories 104, Protein 1 g, Carbohydrates 7 g, Fat 5 g.

Ingredients:

- 2 large carrots, cut into fry shape wedges
- 1 teaspoon of coconut oil
- 1/4 teaspoon of salt
- 1/8 teaspoon of ground black pepper

Instructions:

1. Preheat the oven to 450 degrees Fahrenheit (232 Celsius). Coat the baking sheet with a cooking spray.

2. Add all of the ingredients to a large mixing bowl. Toss until combined well. On the baking sheet, spread the carrots and bake for 40-45 minutes, or until lightly browned.

Chapter 4: Vegan Recipes

In this chapter we are going to give you some delicious and mouthwatering recipes on Octavia Vegan recipes.

Penne Pasta with Cannellini Beans and Escarole

(Ready in 30 Minutes, Serve 8, Difficulty: Easy)

Nutrition per Serving:

Calories 310, Protein 13.7 g, Carbohydrates 60.1 g, Fat 2 g, Cholesterol 0mg, Sodium 267.5mg.

Ingredients:

- 1(16 ounces) package of dry penne pasta
- 1 head of escarole, chopped
- 1(15.5 ounces) can of cannellini beans, with liquid
- 1(14.5 ounces) can of diced tomatoes with garlic and onion, drained
- Salt and ground black pepper, to taste

Instructions:

1. Put to a boil a big pot of lightly salted water and cook the penne pasta for 8-10 minutes or until the pasta is drained al dente.

2. Cook and mix the escarole, cannellini beans, and liquid in a skillet over medium heat, and dice the tomatoes with garlic and onion until cooked through. With salt and pepper, season. To eat, toss in the boiled pasta.

Spinach, Red Lentil, and Bean Curry

(Ready in 35 Minutes, Serve 4, Difficulty: Easy)

Nutrition per Serving:

Calories 328, Protein 18 g, Carbohydrates 51.9 g, Fat 8.3 g, Cholesterol 1.7mg, Sodium 633mg.

Ingredients:

- 1 cup of red lentils
- ¼ cup of tomato puree
- ½ (8 ounces) container of plain yogurt
- 1 teaspoon of garam masala
- ½ teaspoon of ground dried turmeric
- ½ teaspoon of ground cumin
- ½ teaspoon of Ancho chile powder
- 2 tablespoons of vegetable oil
- 1 onion, chopped
- 2 cloves of garlic, chopped
- 1(1 inch) piece fresh ginger root, grated
- 4 cups of loosely packed fresh spinach, coarsely chopped
- 2 tomatoes, chopped
- 4 sprigs of fresh cilantro, chopped
- 1(15.5 ounces) can of mixed beans, rinsed and drained.

Instructions:

1. Rinse the lentils and put enough water in a saucepan to cover them. Bring it to a boil. Lower the heat, cover the kettle and boil for 20 minutes over low heat, drain.

2. Stir the tomato puree and yogurt together in a dish. Season with garam masala, turmeric, chili powder, and cumin. Remove before creamy.

3. Heat oil over low heat in a pan. Add the onion, garlic, and ginger, then simmer until the onion starts to brown. Stir in the spinach, then simmer until wilted and dark green. Stir in the yogurt mixture gradually. Then the tomatoes and cilantro are combined.

4. Stir in the mixture of lentils and mixed beans once well balanced. Heat through, 5 minutes, approximately.

Slow Cooker Eggplant Curry

(Ready in 9 Hours and 15 Minutes, Serve 6, and Difficulty: Hard)

Nutrition per Serving:

Calories 197, Protein 7.8 g, Carbohydrates 47.6 g, Fat 1.4 g, Cholesterol 0mg, Sodium 631.4mg.

Ingredients:

- Cooking spray
- 2 large egg plants, peeled and chopped
- 1(28 ounces) can of diced tomatoes
- 1 large onion, diced
- 4 cloves of garlic, chopped
- 1 tablespoon of curry powder
- 1 teaspoon of garam masala
- 1 teaspoon of cayenne pepper
- ½ teaspoon of salt
- ½ teaspoon of ground black pepper
- 6 whole-wheat tortillas

Instructions:

1. Spray a slow cooker with cooking spray. Add eggplants, tomatoes, onion, garlic, curry powder, garam masala, cayenne, and salt, and pepper, mix well.

2. Cook on Low until soft and fragrant, about 9 hours.

3. Serve eggplant curry on tortillas.

Quick Vegetarian Spaghetti

(Ready in 35 Minutes, Serve 8, Difficulty: Easy)

Nutrition per Serving:

Calories 279, Protein 10.3 g, Carbohydrates 57.8 g, Fat 1.6 g, Cholesterol 0mg, Sodium 468mg.

Ingredients:

- 453 g of uncooked spaghetti
- 1 cup of broccoli florets
- 1(15 ounces) can of whole kernel corn, drained
- 1 cup of fresh sliced mushrooms
- 1 cup of sliced carrots
- 2(8 ounces) cans of tomato sauce

Instructions:

1. Boil a big pot of salted water, add the spaghetti, and put the water back to a boil. Cook until al dente is spaghetti, then drain well.

2. In a big sauce pot, add the broccoli, peas, mushrooms, carrots, and tomato sauce. Cook for 15-20 minutes or until the vegetables are tender, over medium heat. To keep the sauce from sticking, whisking regularly.

3. Serve over pasta with sauce.

Spicy Couscous with Dates

(Ready in 30 Minutes, Serve 2, Difficulty: Easy)

Nutrition per Serving:

Calories 129, Protein 18 g, Carbohydrates 111.9 g, Fat 10.6 g, Cholesterol 0mg, Sodium 314.5mg.

Ingredients:

- 2 whole star anise pods
- Salt, to taste
- 3 cloves of garlic, peeled and chopped
- ½ red bell pepper, chopped
- 2 dried hot red peppers, diced
- ½ teaspoon of ground black pepper
- 4 large fresh mushrooms, chopped
- 1 tablespoon of lemon juice
- ¼ cup of chopped dates
- 1 teaspoon of ground cinnamon
- 1 cup of uncooked couscous
- 1 ½ cups of vegetable stock

Instructions:

1. Heat the oil over low heat in a medium saucepan, and sauté the onion until it is tender. Using the anise pods and salt to season. Blend the garlic, red bell pepper, spicy dried red peppers, and black pepper. Continue to cook and stir until you have tender vegetables.

2. Stir in the vegetable mixture with the mushrooms and lemon juice. Add in the dates and cinnamon, and cook for around 10 minutes over low heat.

3. In a medium saucepan, position the couscous and cover with vegetable supply. Bring it to a boil. Reduce heat to low levels. Cover and boil until the moisture has been drained, 3-5 minutes.

4. With a fork, mix in the vegetables and eat. Fluff couscous.

Slow Cooker Vegetarian Curry

(Ready in 5 Hours and 15 Minutes, Serve 6, and Difficulty: Hard)

Nutrition per Serving:

Calories 124, Protein 6.7 g, Carbohydrates 32.1 g, Fat 0.7 g, Cholesterol 0mg, Sodium 44.6mg.

Ingredients:

- 1 head of cauliflower, chopped
- 1 ½ cups of green peas
- 3 potatoes, chopped
- 3 tomatoes, chopped
- 1 cup of water
- 1 ½ teaspoon of ground cumin
- 1 teaspoon of curry powder
- ¾ teaspoon of ground turmeric
- ½ teaspoon of chili powder

Instructions:

1. In a slow cooker, blend the cauliflower, peas, potatoes, onions, water, curry powder, turmeric, and chili powder.

2. Cook until vegetables are tender, 5-6 hours. Cook on medium heat.

Vegetarian Oven-Baked Brown and Wild Rice with Eggplant

(Ready in 1 Hour and 45 Minutes, Serve 8, Difficulty: Hard)

Nutrition per Serving:

Calories 344, Protein 13.7 g, Carbohydrates 63.8 g, Fat 4.7 g, Cholesterol 1.8mg, Sodium 739.6mg.

Ingredients:

- 2 cups of brown rice
- 1 cup of diced onion
- ¼ teaspoon of black pepper
- ¼ teaspoon of turmeric
- 4 cups of vegetable broth
- 1 small eggplant
- 1 cup of plain yogurt
- 1 large tomato, chopped
- 1(15 ounces) can of navy beans

- 1(15 ounces) can of garbanzo beans
- 1 tablespoon of olive oil
- 2 teaspoons of minced garlic
- ½ teaspoon of salt

Instructions:

1. Sauté the onion in the oil in a saucepan until it is finely browned. Garlic, cinnamon, pepper, and turmeric are added. Add the rice and broth to the mixture, bring to a boil, simmer, cover, and cook for 30 minutes.

2. Peel and trim the eggplant into ¼-inch slices while the rice is frying. Sprinkle with salt and leave for about 10 minutes to put aside. Clean, clean, and pat.

3. Salt the eggplant gently and brush it with oil. Set aside, brown both sides in a hot skillet.

4. Mix the yogurt and pass the mixture to a large shallow casserole dish until the rice is cooked. Spread the navy and garbanzo beans over the rice and finish with a plate of sliced tomatoes and eggplant. Bake in a preheated 350 degrees Fahrenheit (176 Celsius). oven, uncovered, for around 20 minutes.

Black-Eyed Peas and Tortillas

(Ready in 25 Minutes, Serve 4, Difficulty: Normal)

Nutrition per Serving:

Calories 287, Protein 15.1 g, Carbohydrates 76.8 g, Fat 13.2 g, Cholesterol 0mg, Sodium 1248.8mg.

Ingredients:

- 1 tablespoon olive oil
- ¼ cup finely chopped onion
- 1(15.5 ounces) can black-eyed peas, drained
- ½ cup vegetable stock
- 1 fresh jalapeno pepper, chopped
- 1 clove of garlic, minced
- 1 tablespoon of fresh lime juice
- Salt and pepper, to taste
- 4(12 inches) flour tortillas

Instructions:

1. Heat the olive oil over medium heat in a medium skillet and cook the onion until it is tender.

2. Combine the black-eyed peas, vegetable reserve, jalapeno, lime juice, and garlic cloves Season to taste with salt and pepper, and continue cooking until hot.

3. Wrap the mixture in the tortillas to serve.

Black Bean Veggie Burgers

(Ready in 45 Minutes, Serve 4, Difficulty: Normal)

Nutrition per Serving:

Calories 198, Protein 11.2 g, Carbohydrates 33.1 g, Fat 3 g, Cholesterol 46.5mg, Sodium 607.3mg.

Ingredients:

- 1(16 ounces) can of black beans, drained and rinsed
- ½ green bell pepper, cut into 2-inch pieces
- ½ onion, cut into wedges
- 3 cloves of garlic, peeled
- 1 egg
- 1 tablespoon of chili powder
- 1 tablespoon of cumin
- 1 teaspoon of Thai chili sauce or hot sauce
- ½ cup bread crumbs

Instructions:

1. When grilling, preheat a high-heat grill and gently grease a sheet of aluminum foil. Preheat the oven to 375 degrees Fahrenheit (190 degrees Celsius) before baking, and gently grease your baking sheet.

2. Mash the black beans with a fork in a medium bowl until they are dense and pasty.

3. Cut the bell pepper, onion, and garlic thinly in a food processor. Stir in the mashed beans, then.

4. Stir the egg, chili powder, and chili sauce together in a small cup.

5. Stir in the mashed beans with the egg mixture. Until the paste is moist and stays together, add in bread crumbs. Break the mixture into 4-patties.

6. When grilling, put the patties on the foil and grill on either side for about 8 minutes. When baking, put the patties on the baking sheet and bake on each side for about 10 minutes.

Cinnamon Apple Toast

(Ready in 30 Minutes, Serve 2, Difficulty: Easy)

Nutrition per Serving:

Calories 239, Protein 4 g, Carbohydrates 53.9 g, Fat 1.5 g, Cholesterol 0mg, Sodium 141.7mg.

Ingredients:

- 1 tablespoon of corn-starch
- 1 dash of cinnamon
- ¼ teaspoon of nutmeg
- 1 ¼ cups of unsweetened apple juice
- 1 apple, peeled, cored and thinly sliced
- 2 slices of whole wheat bread
- 1 tablespoon of apple syrup
- ¼ teaspoon of cinnamon
- 2 teaspoons of light brown sugar

Instructions:

1. Combine the corn-starch, cinnamon, nutmeg, and apple juice in a shallow saucepan and whisk until well mixed. Bring it to a boil, then drop it to a

simmer. Cook and whisk for 5 minutes or until the mixture thicken slightly. Store in the refrigerator in a tight air jar before ready to use.

2. Preheat the oven to 500 Fahrenheit degrees (260 degrees Celsius).

3. In a microwave-safe oven, put the apples and drizzle them with apple syrup. Microwave on high for 1 minute, or set aside before tender. Toast the bread and line it with apple slices. Drizzle sugar with it.

4. Bake for 5 minutes in the preheated oven, closely watching to avoid fire. If needed, sprinkle with cinnamon. Immediately serve.

Cabbage and Rice
(Ready in 35 Minutes, Serve 8, Difficulty: Easy)
Nutrition per Serving:

Calories 150, Protein 4.2 g, Carbohydrates 30.4 g, Fat 1.6 g, Cholesterol 0mg, Sodium 249.9mg.

Ingredients:
- 1 cup of long-grain white rice
- 2 cups of water
- 2 teaspoons of olive oil
- 1 medium onion, chopped
- 1 clove of garlic, crushed
- 1 head of cabbage, cored and shredded
- 1(14.5 ounces) can of diced tomatoes
- ½ cup of jalapeno pepper rings

Instructions:

1. Combine the rice and water in a saucepan. Bring it to a boil. Cover and minimize to the low heat. Simmer for 15-20 minutes until the rice is tender and water is absorbed.

2. Meanwhile, in a big kettle, heat the olive oil. Add the onion and garlic, cook and stir for about 3 minutes, until fragrant. Add the cabbage and boil, stirring regularly, for about 10 minutes, until the cabbage is finished.

3. Placed the onions, pepper rings, and cooked rice in the mixture. To mix the flavors, boil for 10-15 minutes.

Vegan Black Bean Burgers
(Ready in 35 Minutes, Serve 4, Difficulty: Easy)
Nutrition per Serving:

Calories 126, Protein 11.6 g, Carbohydrates 51.7 g, Fat 1.4 g, Cholesterol 0mg, Sodium 1263.5mg.

Ingredients:
- 1(15 ounces) can of black beans, drained and rinsed
- ⅓ cup of chopped sweet onion
- 1 tablespoon of minced garlic
- 3 baby carrots, grated (Optional)
- ¼ cup of minced green bell pepper (Optional)
- 1 tablespoon of corn-starch
- 1 tablespoon of warm water
- 3 tablespoons of Chile-garlic sauce
- 1 teaspoon of chili powder
- 1 teaspoon of ground cumin
- 1 teaspoon of seafood seasoning
- ¼ teaspoon of salt
- ¼ teaspoon of ground black pepper
- 2 slices of whole-wheat bread, torn into small crumbs
- ¾ cup of unbleached flour, or as needed

Instructions:

1. Preheat the oven to 350 degrees Fahrenheit (176 degrees Celsius). Grease the baking tray.

2. Add the cabbage, garlic, carrots, and green bell pepper and mash the black beans in a dish. Combine.

3. In a separate dish, whisk together the corn-starch, water, Chile-garlic sauce, chili powder, seafood seasoning, salt, and black pepper. Stir the combination of corn-starch into the black bean mixture.

4. Mix the whole-wheat bread with a mixture of beans. Stir the flour into the bean mixture, 1/4 cup at a time, until a moist batter emerges.

5. Spoon 'burger-sized' mounds of batter, around 3/4-inch thick per mound, onto the prepared baking dish. Shape yourself into burgers.

6. Cook in the preheated oven until the center is baked and the outside is crispy, about 10 minutes on either side.

Red Lentil Curry
(Ready in 40 Minutes, Serve 8, Difficulty: Normal)
Nutrition per Serving:

Calories 219, Protein 12.1 g, Carbohydrates 32.5 g, Fat 2.6 g, Cholesterol 0mg, Sodium 571.9mg.

Ingredients:
- 2 cups of red lentils
- 1 large onion, diced
- 1 tablespoon of vegetable oil
- 2 tablespoons of curry paste
- 1 tablespoon of curry powder
- 1 teaspoon of ground turmeric
- 1 teaspoon of ground cumin
- 1 teaspoon of chili powder
- 1 teaspoon of salt
- 1 teaspoon white sugar
- 1 teaspoon of minced garlic

- 1 teaspoon of minced fresh ginger
- 1(14.25 ounces) can of tomato puree.

Instructions:

1. Wash the lentils until the water runs clean in cold water. Place the lentils in a pot with enough water to cover, bring to a boil, place a cover on the pot, reduce heat to medium-low, and simmer, adding water for 15-20 minutes during cooking, as required, until tender. Drain.

2. Heat the vegetable oil over medium heat in a large skillet, cook and stir the onions in the hot oil until they are caramelized about 20 minutes.

3. In a big bowl, combine the curry paste, curry powder, turmeric, chili powder, cinnamon, sugar, garlic, and ginger. Stir in the onions. Boost the fire to high and simmer for 1-2 minutes, stirring continuously, until fragrant.

4. Remove from the heat, stir in the tomato puree and stir in the lentils.

Vegan Holiday Roast with Mashed Vegetables

(Ready in 10 Minutes, Serve 4-6, Difficulty: Easy)

Nutrition per Serving:

Calories 246, Protein 19 g, Carbohydrates 22 g, Fat 9 g, Fiber 3g.

Ingredients:

- 1, 1 lb. (thawed) vegan stuffed roast
- 2 cups diced potato
- 2 cups diced carrots
- 1 cup diced yellow onion
- ¾-1 cup of veggie broth
- 4 minced garlic cloves
- 1 tablespoon almond milk
- 1 teaspoon olive oil
- Salt and pepper to taste

Instructions:

1. In your pressure cooker, heat the oil.

2. Cook the garlic and onion for 1 minute when it is hot.

3. Add the vegetables, salt, and potatoes and combine.

4. On top of the vegetables, put the roast on top and spill over the broth.

5. Cover the lid and seal it

6. Select 'manual' and cook for 8 minutes at low pressure or around 6 minutes at high pressure.

7. Hit 'cancel' and quick-release when the time is up.

8. Let the roast out.

9. For the vegetables, add almond milk and pepper and mash to your perfect consistency.

10. Serve.

Vegan "Shrimp" Ceviche

(Ready in 45 Minutes, Serve 6, Difficulty: Normal)

Nutrition per Serving:

Calories 116, Protein 1.5 g, Carbohydrates 15.4 g, Fat 0.3 g, Cholesterol 0mg, Sodium 166.9mg.

Ingredients:

- 453 g of carrots, peeled and grated
- 1 cup of chopped onion
- 1 cup of chopped fresh cilantro
- 1 serrano pepper, seeded and chopped
- 3 limes, juiced
- 3 tablespoons of ketchup
- Salt, to taste

Instructions:

1. In a glass bowl, combine the carrots, onion, cilantro, and serrano pepper.

2. Stir in the ketchup and lime juice. Put aside for 30 minutes and season with salt.

Easy Tofu Shirataki Stir-Fry Style

(Ready in 30 Minutes, Serve 6, Difficulty: Easy)

Nutrition per Serving:

Calories 139, Protein 5.7 g, Carbohydrates 29.8 g, Fat 0 g, Cholesterol 0mg, Sodium 628.4mg.

Ingredients:

- 1(16 ounces) package of frozen vegetable medley
- 1(8 ounces) package of angel hair-style tofu Shirataki noodles, or to taste
- ½ teaspoon of minced garlic
- 2 teaspoons of soy sauce, or to taste
- ½ teaspoon of ground ginger, or to taste

Instructions:

1. In the pot, microwave the vegetables until they are thawed and cooked, about 5 minutes. Let it cool off for about 1 minute.

2. Drain and thoroughly rinse the Shirataki noodles and put them in a microwave-safe dish.

3. In the microwave, cook the noodles until mostly heated, around 1 minute.

4. Heat a saucepan and add garlic over medium heat. Cook for around 1 minute before fragrant. Add the fried pasta, soy sauce, mixed vegetables, and ginger. Cook and stir until heated and blended with flavors, 2-3 minutes. Stir in spicy sauce.

Tunisian Pasta with Lentils

(Ready in 1 Hour and 15 Minutes, Serve 8, and Difficulty: Hard)

Nutrition per Serving:

Calories 124, Protein 13.5 g, Carbohydrates 61.1 g, Fat 3 g, Cholesterol 0mg, Sodium 512.4mg.

Ingredients:

- 1 tablespoon of olive oil, or as needed
- 1 large onion, chopped
- 1 large carrot, grated
- 3 cloves of garlic, crushed
- 1(28 ounces) can of crushed tomatoes
- 4 cups of cold water
- 1(19 ounces) can of lentils, drained and rinsed
- 1 teaspoon of paprika
- 1 teaspoon of ground cumin
- 1 teaspoon of salt
- ¼ teaspoon of ground black pepper
- 1(16 ounces) package of spaghetti, broken into 1 ½-inch piece

Instructions:

1. Heat oil over low heat in a big pot. In hot oil, cook the onion, carrot, and garlic for around 5 minutes, until tender. Add the tomatoes, reduce the heat to medium, and cook for 10 minutes until the carrots and onions are mushy. Stir in the sugar, lentils, paprika, salt, and pepper and bring to a boil for around 5 minutes over high heat.

2. Stir in the pasta and put it to a boil again for about 5 minutes. Turn off the fire, cover the pot, and leave it on the burner. Let them settle down for 15 minutes. Stir, cover again, and let sit for about 15 more minutes until the pasta is tender but firm to the bite. Mix and serve.

Vegan Stuffed Peppers with Rice

(Ready in 55 Minutes, Serve 6, Difficulty: Normal)

Nutrition per Serving:

Calories 229, Protein 19.2 g, Carbohydrates 51.8 g, Fat 2.6 g, Cholesterol 0mg, Sodium 1116.1mg.

Ingredients:

- 4 red bell peppers, tops, and seeds removed
- Salt, to taste
- 1 cup of vegan "ground beef," frozen (such as Beyond Meat®)
- 1 cup of diced onion
- 1 cup of diced tomatoes
- 1(14 ounces) can of vegetable broth, divided
- 1 teaspoon of garlic powder
- 1 teaspoon of chili powder
- ½ teaspoon of ground black pepper
- 1 cup of water
- 1(8 ounces) package of Spanish rice mix
- 1 cup of black beans, rinsed and drained
- 1 cup of corn, drained
- 1 tablespoon of nutritional yeast (optional)
- 4 ounces of tomato sauce

Instructions:

1. To a simmer, put a big pot of water. Add the bell peppers and cook for 8-10 minutes, until tender. Drain and sprinkle salt on the inside. Place 10 minutes free.

2. The oven should be preheated to 350 degrees Fahrenheit (176 degrees Celsius). Line an aluminum foil baking tray with it.

3. In a large skillet over medium-high heat, mix vegan ground beef, onion, diced tomatoes, 2/3 cup broth, garlic powder, chili powder, black pepper, and salt bring to a high boil. Cook until all but 1/3 cup of liquid has steamed off or been consumed, 5-10 minutes, stirring periodically. Remove from the heat.

4. In a saucepan, mix water, 1 cup broth, and Spanish rice packet over medium heat. Bring to a boil, simmer, and cook for 8 minutes. Minimize pressure. Add the corn and black beans and mix to blend. Add the mixture of ground beef with adequate liquid to keep the rice stuffing moist. Add and stir in the nutritional yeast until well mixed.

5. Drain the peppers with any extra water. Using a spoon to stuff with rice mixture, packing securely to fill off. In the prepared baking pan, put the stuffed peppers and spoon the extra rice mixture around them. Pour the tomato sauce over the rice and peppers with aluminum foil shell.

6. Bake for 20 minutes in the preheated oven. Remove the foil and bake for an extra 10 minutes, uncovered. Until eating, let the peppers rest for 5 minutes.

Wild Rice Stuffed Acorn Squash

(Ready in 1 Hour and 30 Minutes, Serve 8, Difficulty: Normal)

Nutrition per Serving:

Calories 187, Protein 5.1 g, Carbohydrates 39.2 g, Fat 2.1 g, Cholesterol 2.8mg, Sodium 637.2mg.

Ingredients:

- 2 acorn squash, halved and seeded
- 1(6 ounces) package of dry cornbread stuffing mix
- 2 teaspoons of butter
- 1 onion, diced
- 1 clove of garlic, minced
- 1 cup of chopped fresh mushrooms

- 1 cup of long grain and wild rice mix
- 2 sprigs of fresh sage, chopped
- 2 cups of vegetable stock

Instructions:

1. Preheat the oven to 350 degrees Fahrenheit (176 degrees Celsius). Grease 2 baking pans gently, put the cleaned-out squash in the pans, and cut side down. Bake in the preheated oven for around 25 minutes until barely moist to the touch.

2. As instructed on the box, make the stuffing blend, and set aside.

3. In a saucepan, melt the butter over medium heat and cook and stir the onion and garlic for about 10 minutes until the onion is translucent. Stir in the mushrooms and simmer for another 5 minutes before they give up their juice. Combine the rice and sage mixture and cook and stir the rice and vegetables for about 5 minutes before the vegetables begin to tan. Pour in the stock of vegetables, stir to blend, cover, and reduce the heat. Simmer the rice mixture for 30-40 minutes, until tender.

4. Mix the cooked rice mixture gently with the stuffing in a tub, then pile the mixture without packing it into the squash centers. Put the stuffed squash back in the oven and cook for 15 more minutes, until the squash is tender and the stuffing is sweet.

Meyer Lemon Avocado Toast

(Ready in 13 Minutes, Serve 4, Difficulty: Easy)

Nutrition per Serving:

Calories 272, Protein 3.6 g, Carbohydrates 11.8 g, Fat 1.2 g, Cholesterol 0mg, Sodium 270.7mg.

Ingredients:

- 2 slices of whole-grain bread
- ½ avocado
- 2 tablespoons of chopped fresh cilantro, or more to taste
- 1 teaspoon of Meyer lemon juice, or to taste
- ¼ teaspoon of Meyer lemon zest
- 1 pinch of cayenne pepper
- 1 pinch of fine sea salt
- ¼ teaspoon of chia seeds

Instructions:

1. Toast slices of bread to the perfect thickness, for 3-5 minutes.

2. Stir in the cilantro, Meyer lemon juice, Meyer lemon zest, cayenne pepper, and sea salt, and mix the avocado in a dish.

Spread the combination of avocado onto the toast and finish with chia seeds.

Slow Cooker Root Vegetable Tagine

(Ready in 9 Hours and 50 Minutes, Serve 8, and Difficulty: Hard)

Nutrition per Serving:

Calories 124, Protein 2.8 g, Carbohydrates 31 g, Fat 0.7 g, Cholesterol 0mg, Sodium 187.4mg.

Ingredients:

- 453 g of parsnips, peeled and diced
- 453 g of turnips, peeled and diced
- 2 medium onions, chopped
- 453 g of carrots, peeled and diced
- 6 dried apricots, chopped
- 4 pitted prunes, chopped
- 1 teaspoon of ground turmeric
- 1 teaspoon of ground cumin
- ½ teaspoon of ground ginger
- ½ teaspoon of ground cinnamon
- ¼ teaspoon of ground cayenne pepper
- 1 tablespoon of dried parsley
- 1 tablespoon of dried cilantro
- 1(14 ounces) can of vegetable broth.

Instructions:

1. Toss the parsnips, turnips, onions, carrots, apricots, and prunes together in a slow cooker. Add turmeric, ginger, cinnamon, cayenne pepper, parsley. Pour the vegetable broth into it.

2. Cover, then cook on low for 9 hours.

Black Beans and Rice

(Ready in 30 Minutes, Serve 10, Difficulty: Easy)

Nutrition per Serving:

Calories 140, Protein 6.3 g, Carbohydrates 27.1 g, Fat 0.9 g, Cholesterol 0mg, Sodium 354.4mg.

Ingredients:

- 1 teaspoon of olive oil
- 1 onion, chopped
- 2 cloves of garlic, minced
- ¾ cup of uncooked white rice
- 1 ½ cups of low Sodium, low-fat vegetable broth
- 1 teaspoon of ground cumin
- ¼ teaspoon of cayenne pepper
- 3 ½ cups of canned black beans, drained

Instructions:

1. Heat the oil in a stockpot over medium-high heat. Add the garlic and onion and cook for 4 minutes. For 2 minutes, add the rice and sauté.

2. Cook for 20 minutes, add the vegetable broth, bring to a boil, cover, and lower the pressure. Add the black beans and seasoning.

Sweet Potato Black Bean Burgers

(Ready in 1 Hour and 16 Minutes, Serve 6, Difficulty: Hard)

Nutrition per Serving:

Calories 227, Protein 10.8 g, Carbohydrates 44.7 g, Fat 1 g, Cholesterol 0mg, Sodium 746.3mg.

Ingredients:

- 1 large sweet potato
- 1 cooking spray
- 2(15 ounces) cans of black beans, rinsed and drained
- ½ cup of quick cooking oats
- ¼ cup of chopped onion
- 1 tablespoon of Dijon mustard
- 1 teaspoon of ground cumin
- ¼ teaspoon of freshly grated ginger
- ¼ teaspoon of salt
- 1 pinch of ground cinnamon

Instructions:

1. Preheat the oven to 400 degrees Fahrenheit (204 degrees Celsius). Place a few holes with a fork in the sweet potato on a greased baking sheet.

2. Bake in the preheated oven for 35-45 minutes, until the sweet potato can comfortably be pierced with a fork. Remove from the oven and cool until handling is comfortable. Reduce the sum of heat to 350 degrees Fahrenheit (176 degrees Celsius). Use cooking spray to spray a baking sheet.

3. Peel the sweet potato, then put it in a wide dish. Add the black beans, then use a whisk or fork to mash them. Combine the oats, carrots, Dijon mustard, ginger, salt, and cinnamon and blend until well mixed. Shape the mixture with wet hands into 6-patties and put on a prepared baking sheet.

4. Bake until baked in the middle and crisp on the bottom, about 8 minutes on either side, in the preheated oven.

Vegan Bean Taco Filling

(Ready in 30 Minutes, Serve 8, Difficulty: Easy)

Nutrition per Serving:

Calories 142, Protein 7.5 g, Carbohydrates 14 g, Fat 2.5 g, Cholesterol 0mg, Sodium 596.3mg.

Ingredients:

- 1 tablespoon of olive oil
- 1 onion, diced
- 2 cloves of garlic, minced
- 1 bell pepper, chopped
- 2(14.5 ounces) cans of black beans, rinsed, drained, and mashed
- 2 tablespoons of yellow cornmeal
- 1 ½ tablespoon of cumin
- 1 teaspoon of paprika
- 1 teaspoon of cayenne pepper
- 1 teaspoon of chili powder
- 1 cup of salsa

Instructions:

1. Heat olive oil over low heat in a medium skillet. Stir in the cabbage, bell pepper, and garlic, and fry until tender. Stir in the beans and mash.

2. Put some cornmeal. Mix the paprika, cayenne, salsa, and chili powder. Cover it, then simmer for 5 minutes.

Vegetarian Shepherd's Pie

(Ready in 1 Hour and 35 Minutes, Serve 1, Difficulty: Hard)

Nutrition per Serving:

Calories 218, Protein 6.2 g, Carbohydrates 29.8 g, Fat 5.2 g, Cholesterol 0mg, Sodium 147.1mg.

Ingredients:

- 2 cups of vegetable broth, divided
- 1 teaspoon of yeast extract spread, (such as Marmite®/Vegemite®)
- ½ cup dry lentils
- ¼ cup of pearl barley
- 1 large carrot, diced
- ½ onion, finely chopped
- ½ cup of walnuts, coarsely chopped
- 3 potatoes, chopped
- 1 teaspoon of all-purpose flour
- ½ teaspoon of water
- Salt and pepper, to taste

Instructions:

1. Preheat the oven to 350 degrees Fahrenheit (176 degrees Celsius).

2. Combine, ¼ cups of broth, yeast extract, lentils, and barley in a large saucepan over medium-low heat. For 30 minutes, boil.

3. Meanwhile, mix the remaining 3/4 cup broth, carrot, onion, and walnuts in a medium saucepan and cook until tender, about 15 minutes.

4. Meanwhile, put it to a boil with a big pot of salted water. Add the potatoes and cook for about 15 minutes, until tender but still solid. Mash and rinse.

5. Mix the flour and water, stir in the carrot mixture and boil until thickened. Combine a mixture of carrots with a mixture of lentils and season with salt and pepper. Pour the mixture into a bowl of 2 quarts of casserole. Spoon fried potatoes over a blend of lentils.

6. Bake in a preheated oven for about 30 minutes, until finely browned on top.

Oven Roasted Red Potatoes and Asparagus

(Ready in 1 Hour, Serve 6, Difficulty: Normal)

Nutrition per Serving:

Calories 149, Protein 4.2 g, Carbohydrates 23.5 g, Fat 4.9 g, Cholesterol 0mg, Sodium 650.5mg.

Ingredients:

- 680 g of red potatoes, cut into chunks
- 2 tablespoons of extra virgin olive oil
- 8 cloves of garlic, thinly sliced
- 4 teaspoons of dried rosemary
- 4 teaspoons of dried thyme
- 2 teaspoons of kosher salt
- 1 bunch of fresh asparagus, trimmed and cut into 1-inch pieces
- Ground black pepper to taste

Instructions:

1. Preheat oven to 425 degrees Fahrenheit (218 degrees Celsius).

2. In a large baking dish, toss the red potatoes with ½ the olive oil, garlic, rosemary, thyme, and ½ the kosher salt. Cover with aluminum foil.

3. Bake 20 minutes in the preheated oven. Mix in the asparagus, remaining olive oil, and remaining salt. Cover, and continue cooking 15 minutes, or until the potatoes are tender. Increase oven temperature to 450 degrees Fahrenheit (232 degrees Celsius).

4. Remove foil, and continue cooking 5-10 minutes, until potatoes are lightly browned. Season with pepper to serve.

Veggie Bagel Sandwich

(Ready in 15 Minutes, Serve 4, Difficulty: Easy)

Nutrition per Serving:

Calories 234, Protein 14.3 g, Carbohydrates 63.7 g, Fat 2.9 g, Cholesterol 0mg, Sodium 680.9mg.

Ingredients:

- 1 bagel, sliced in half
- 1 tablespoon of coarse-grain brown mustard
- 1 leaf of romaine lettuce
- 2(1/4 inch-thick) rings green bell pepper
- 4 slices of cucumber
- 2 slices of tomato
- Salt and freshly ground black pepper, to taste
- 2 slices of red onion
- ½ cup of alfalfa sprouts

Instructions:

1. Spread mustard over the bagel's sliced edges. Layer 1 ½ with the cabbage, green pepper, cucumber, and tomato.

2. Season the tomatoes with pepper and salt. Top with sprouts of onion and alfalfa, then fill with the remaining ½ bagel.

Spiced Pumpkin Seeds

(Ready in 1 Hour and 10 Minutes, Serve 4, Difficulty: Hard)

Nutrition per Serving:

Calories 90, Protein 3 g, Carbohydrates 8.9 g, Fat 5.1 g, Cholesterol 0mg, Sodium 213.7mg.

Ingredients:

- 1 ½ tablespoon of margarine, melted
- ½ teaspoon of salt
- ⅛ teaspoon of garlic salt
- 2 teaspoons of Worcestershire sauce
- 2 cups of raw whole pumpkin seeds

Instructions:

1. Preheat the oven to 275 degrees Fahrenheit (135 degrees Celsius).

2. Combine the Worcestershire sauce, margarine, and cinnamon, garlic salt, and pumpkin seeds. Mix and put thoroughly in a shallow baking dish.

3. Bake for 1 hour, periodically stirring.

Oven Baked Tempeh

(Ready in 1 Hour and 10 Minutes, Serve 6, Difficulty: Normal)

Nutrition per Serving:

Calories 118, Protein 7.7 g, Carbohydrates 13.8 g, Fat 2.8 g, Cholesterol 0mg, Sodium 253.3mg.

Ingredients:

- 1 ½ teaspoons of olive oil
- ⅛ teaspoon of crushed red pepper flakes
- 1 leek, sliced
- ⅓ cup of chopped shallots
- ½ cup of chopped red bell pepper
- 4 cloves of garlic, minced
- 2 cups of halved baby carrots
- 1 cup of diced zucchini
- 1(8 ounces) package of seasoned tempeh
- ½ cup of dry sherry
- 1 tomato, chopped
- 1 tablespoon of tamari

Instructions:

1. Preheat the oven to 350 degrees Fahrenheit (176 degrees Celsius).

2. Layer with oil and crushed red pepper in a stovetop-safe and ovenproof 2-quart casserole bowl. Sauté over medium heat for 1 minute. Tie the leek, the red bell pepper, the shallot, and the garlic together. cook for 3 minutes. Add the carrots and zucchini, stirring at least 5 more minutes.

3. Stir in tempeh and cook for an additional 5 minutes. Add the tamari, sherry, and tomato. cook for just an extra 5 minutes.

Cover the casserole tray and bake at 350 degrees Fahrenheit (176 degrees Celsius) for 30 minutes.

Easy Creamy Vegan Mushroom Risotto

(Ready in 45 Minutes, Serve 6, Difficulty: Normal)

Nutrition per Serving:

Calories 327, Protein 12.4 g, Carbohydrates 65.7 g, Fat 1.9 g, Cholesterol 0mg, Sodium 921.2mg.

Ingredients:

* 1 onion, chopped
* 2 cloves of garlic, minced
* 2 teaspoons of Provence herb
* 2 ¼ cups of vegetable broth, or as needed, divided
* 2 cups of white mushrooms, sliced
* ½ cup of chopped leek
* 1 cup of Arborio rice
* 1 cup of soy milk
* 1 tablespoon of white wine vinegar
* 1 cup of frozen peas
* 2 tablespoons of lemon juice
* 2 tablespoons of nutritional yeast
* 1 teaspoon of salt
* ½ teaspoon of ground black pepper

Instructions:

1. Over a medium-high flame, heat a large saucepan. Cook the tomato, ginger, and Provence herbs. Should the mixture be too dry, add some vegetable broth to the mixture. Add the mushrooms and leeks and cook for 3-4 minutes, until heated.

2. Pour the leftover rice and vegetable broth into the mushroom mixture. Add vinegar and soy milk. Let it boil for 15-20 minutes before the liquid is absorbed, stirring periodically.

3. Stir in the rice mixture with the peas, lemon juice, and nutritional yeast. Cook until the peas, about 3 minutes, are cooked through. Turn off the heat, add salt and pepper, to season.

Easy, Healthy Falafel

(Ready in 30 Minutes, Serve 1, Difficulty: Normal)

Nutrition per Serving:

Calories 246, Protein 1.6 g, Carbohydrates 7.8 g, Fat 1 g, Cholesterol 0mg, Sodium 106.9mg.

Ingredients:

* 1(14 ounces) can of chickpeas
* 1 onion, chopped
* 3 tablespoons of chopped flat, leaf parsley, or to taste
* 2 teaspoons of olive oil
* 2 cloves of garlic, chopped, or to taste
* 1 teaspoon of coriander
* 1 teaspoon of cumin
* Salt and pepper, to taste
* 2 tablespoons of all-purpose flour
* ½ teaspoon of baking powder

Instructions:

1. The oven should be preheated to 400 degrees Fahrenheit (204 degrees Celsius).

2. In the bowl of a food processor, combine the chickpeas, cabbage, parsley, oil, garlic, cilantro, and salt, and pepper, pulse until everything is combined. Add flour and baking powder and pulse until the mixture begins to bind together and forms a ball and if necessary, scrape the sides of the bowl.

3. To extract even volumes of the mixture, use two dessert spoons and form them into 15 small patties. On a baking sheet, put the patties.

4. Bake for 25-30 minutes in the preheated oven until golden brown, turning the falafel over carefully after 10 minutes.

Red Beans and Spaghetti

(Ready in 1 Hour and 30 Minutes, Serve 8, and Difficulty: Hard)

Nutrition per Serving:

Calories 230, Protein 13.7 g, Carbohydrates 59.2 g, Fat 1.1 g, Cholesterol 0mg, Sodium 6.8mg.

Ingredients:

* 226 g dry kidney beans, soaked overnight
* 1(16 ounces) package of uncooked spaghetti
* Salt, to taste

Instructions:

1. Rinse the beans, then put them in a big jar. Cover with water and over medium-high heat, bring to a boil. Reduce heat to medium-low and simmer, partly covered, until the beans are tender, add more water to stop drying and scorching, around 1 hour, if necessary.

2. Add spaghetti when the beans are tender, and simmer until al dente. Season to taste with salt.

Smoky Black Bean Burgers

(Ready in 55 Minutes, Serve 4, Difficulty: Normal)

Nutrition per Serving:

Calories 128, Protein 7.5 g, Carbohydrates 23.4 g, Fat 1.5 g, Cholesterol 0mg, Sodium 753.5mg.

Ingredients:

- 1 tablespoon of ground flax seed
- 3 tablespoons of water
- 1(15 ounces) can of black beans, drained, rinsed, and mashed
- ¼ cup of panko bread crumbs
- 1 clove of garlic, minced
- ½ teaspoon of salt
- ½ tablespoon of Worcestershire sauce
- ⅛ teaspoon of liquid smoke flavoring
- Cooking spray

Instructions:

1. In a small bowl, mix the ground flaxseed and water. Let it sit for about 5 minutes to thicken.

2. In a bowl, blend the flax mix, black beans, panko bread crumbs, garlic, cinnamon, Worcestershire sauce, and liquid smoke until mixed. Shape the batter into 4 patties and place it on a tray. Chill in the refrigerator for about 30 minutes before set.

3. Spray the cooking spray on a skillet and place the patties in the skillet over medium heat. Cook until browned, about 5 minutes on each hand.

Buddhist Monk Dumplings

(Ready in 2 Hours and 30Minutes, Serve 10, Difficulty: Hard)

Nutrition per Serving:

Calories 188, Protein 5.8 g, Carbohydrates 36.2 g, Fat 2 g, Cholesterol 0mg, Sodium 45.9mg.

Ingredients:

- 1 potato
- 2 teaspoons of vegetable oil
- 1 tablespoon of mustard seed
- ¼ teaspoon of cumin seeds
- 2 carrots, finely diced
- 1 onion, finely chopped
- 1 green of Chile, finely chopped
- 1 clove of garlic, finely chopped
- 1 teaspoon of ground turmeric
- 1 teaspoon of grated ginger
- ½ cup of finely shredded cabbage

- ¼ (14 ounces) package of firm tofu, crumbled
- ½ cup of water
- ¼ cup of chopped fresh cilantro
- 1 teaspoon of garam masala
- Salt, to taste

For Pastry:

- 3 cups of all-purpose flour
- 1 cup of water
- 1 pinch of salt

Instructions:

1. Place the potato in a large saucepan, cover it with salted water and bring it to a boil. Reduce the heat to medium-low and simmer for about 20 minutes, until soft. Mash and rinse. Set to cool aside.

2. Heat oil over low heat in a pan. Add the cumin seeds and mustard seeds and stir. Add the cabbage, cabbage, garlic, turmeric, green chili, and ginger. For 1 minute, cook and stir. Add the mashed potato, tofu, and cabbage and stir again. Add the water and cilantro, cook and stir for 7-8 minutes until the vegetables are soft and the water is dry. Stir well and Combine garam masala and salt. Remove from the heat and place to cool aside.

3. In a dish, mix the rice, water, and salt. Knead it into a ball and begin kneading for 10-12 minutes until the dough is very smooth. Wrap and relax for a minimum of 1 hour.

4. Take a dough knob and roll it out into a small circle with a diameter of around 4 inches. Spoon in the middle with a heaped teaspoon of filling and moisten the side with a little water. To form a crease, force the edges together, slightly overlap the top, and proceed to create a half-moon shape with small creases all over the edge. Repeat for the remaining filling and dough.

5. Using a steamer basket, fit a wide pan, and add about 2 inches of water. Bring it to a boil. Add the dumplings and steam for about 15 minutes before they are swollen and cooked through.

Calico Veggie Beans

(Ready in 1 Hour and 10 Minutes, Serve 8, Difficulty: Normal)

Nutrition per Serving:

Calories 229, Protein 11.7 g, Carbohydrates 61.3 g 2, Fat 0.6 g, Cholesterol 0mg, Sodium 774.8mg.

Ingredients:

- 1(15 ounces) can of black beans
- 1(15 ounces) can of kidney beans, drained
- 1(15 ounces) can of butter beans
- 1(15 ounces) can of lima beans, drained
- 1 cup of packed brown sugar
- 1 cup of chopped onion

- ½ cup of fresh tomato sauce
- ½ cup of chopped celery
- 3 tablespoons of white wine vinegar
- 1 teaspoon of mustard powder

Instructions:

1. Preheat the oven to 350 degrees Fahrenheit (176 degrees Celsius).

2. In a four-quarter casserole dish, mix the black beans, kidney beans, butter beans, lima beans, brown sugar, onion, tomato sauce, celery, vinegar, and mustard powder cover with aluminum foil.

3. Bake for 1 hour in the preheated oven.

Porcini Mushroom Pasta

(Ready in 55 Minutes, Serve 6, Difficulty: Normal)

Nutrition per Serving:

Calories 335, Protein 13.8 g, Carbohydrates 560.1 g, Fat 4.3 g, Cholesterol 0mg, Sodium 18.6mg.

Ingredients:

- 1 tablespoon of olive oil
- 2 cloves of garlic, minced
- ½ red onion, minced
- ½ cup of red bell pepper, julienned
- ½ cup of julienned carrots
- ½ cup of dry red wine
- 1 cup of rehydrated porcini mushrooms
- 1 ½ cup of crushed tomatoes
- 2 teaspoons of chopped fresh basil
- 1 teaspoon of dried rosemary, crushed
- Salt and pepper, to taste
- 6 cups of tagliatelle

Instructions:

1. Over medium heat, heat the oil in a large skillet. Add the onions and garlic and cook for 4 minutes, then add the red bell pepper and carrots and cook for another 4 minutes. Add the red wine, increase the heat, cook for 1 minute, reduce the heat to medium-low, add the mushrooms, and cook for 3 minutes.

2. Add the tomatoes, basil, and rosemary, season to taste with salt and pepper.

3. Simmer for 10 minutes, then serve over fried noodles with sauce.

Hot Tomato Sauce

(Ready in 30 Minutes, Serve 6, Difficulty: Normal)

Nutrition per Serving:

Calories 228, Protein 10.8 g, Carbohydrates 52.4 g, Fat 2.9 g, Cholesterol 67.2mg, Sodium 369.6mg.

Ingredients:

- 8 ounces of dry pasta
- 1 fresh red Chile pepper, chopped
- 1 red bell pepper, chopped
- 1 onion, chopped
- 1(28 ounces) can of diced tomatoes with juice
- 2 tablespoons of tomato puree
- 2 teaspoons of chili powder

Instructions:

1. Preheat the oven to 300 degrees Fahrenheit (150 degrees Celsius). To a simmer, put a big pot of lightly salted water. Cook for 8-10 minutes or until al dente, drain and add spaghetti.

2. Meanwhile, sauté the chili pepper, bell pepper, and onion in a broad skillet until tender. Add the onions, chili powder, and puree, and simmer for another 2 minutes. For a creamy sauce, puree with a hand blender, or puree in lots in a food processor.

3. In a 9 x13-inch baking dish, mix the pasta and sauce and bake for 15 minutes. Serve warm.

Vegetarian Black Bean Burgers

(Ready in 20 Minutes, Serve 6, Difficulty: Normal)

Nutrition per Serving:

Calories 128, Protein 12.2 g, Carbohydrates 56 g, Fat 1.5 g, Cholesterol 0mg, Sodium 615.8mg.

Ingredients:

- 2(15 ounces) cans of black beans
- 1 onion, diced
- 1 teaspoon of water, or as needed
- 2 cups of cooked brown rice
- ½ cup of corn
- ½ cup of cornmeal
- ¼ cup of salsa
- 2 teaspoons of garlic powder
- 2 teaspoons of ground cumin
- ½ teaspoon of chili powder

Instructions:

1. In a bowl, put the black beans and mash them to a smooth consistency.

2. The oven should be preheated to 350 degrees Fahrenheit (176 degrees Celsius). Line the parchment paper with a baking sheet.

3. Cook the onion in a skillet over medium heat for around 5 minutes, until translucent. To avoid sticking, add water if needed. Transfer the black beans to a bowl.

4. Stir in the bean mixture with the cooked rice, maize, cornmeal, salsa, garlic powder, and chili powder. Mix until uniformly mixed, using clean

hands. Roll the mixture into eight balls of the same size and shape the balls into patties. Move the patties to the baking sheet and cool until they are ready to bake.

5. Bake the burgers for 15 minutes on a paper-lined parchment baking sheet. Flip and bake until heated and browned, around an extra 15 minutes.

Nutritious and Delicious Pasta

(Ready in 40 Minutes, Serve 6, Difficulty: Normal)

Nutrition per Serving:

Calories 216, Protein 5.9 g, Carbohydrates 29.1 g, Fat 1 g, Cholesterol 27.3mg, Sodium 29.2mg.

Ingredients:

- 8 ounces of pasta
- 3 onions, minced
- 8 fresh mushrooms, sliced
- 1 teaspoon of onion powder
- 1 teaspoon of garlic powder
- 1(5.5 ounces) can of low-sodium, tomato-vegetable juice cocktail
- ½ cup of port wine
- 1 teaspoon of dried oregano
- 1 bay leaf
- 1 teaspoon of arrowroot powder
- 1 cup of water

Instructions:

1. In a large pot of hot, salted water, cook the pasta until al dente. Drain thoroughly.

2. Meanwhile, sauté the mushrooms and onions in ½ cup of water in a large saucepan. Garlic, onion powder, port wine, tomato juice, oregano, and basil are added. Add slowly to the saucepan after first dissolving the arrowroot in a bowl of 1/2 cup of water, stirring constantly. Within a minute, thickening can occur.

3. To the large saucepan, add the cooked and drained pasta and stir. Put the lid on, then serve warm for 3 minutes,

Pineapple, Black Beans, and Couscous

(Ready in 25 Minutes, Serve 2, Difficulty: Easy)

Nutrition per Serving:

Calories 227, Protein 24.7 g 5, Carbohydrates 141.2 g, Fat 1.3 g, Cholesterol 0mg, Sodium 1485.6mg.

Ingredients:

- ½ cup of water
- 1(15 ounces) can of pineapple chunks, drained (juice reserved)
- 1 cup of couscous
- 1(15 ounces) can of black beans, rinsed and drained
- ⅓ cup of warm water
- 2 tablespoons of taco seasoning mix

Instructions:

1. In a saucepan, mix 1/2 cup water and reserved pineapple juice over medium-low heat, bring to a boil and extract immediately from the heat. Stir couscous into the coating solvent. Put aside until the liquid is consumed and the couscous is soft, and fluff with a fork for about 5 minutes. Divide it into 2 dishes.

2. In a pan, whisk together the pineapple chunks and black beans over medium heat. In a shallow bowl, mix 1/3 cup of warm water and taco seasoning mix and pour over the black beans mixture. Cook and stir the mixture for 5-7 minutes, until hot. Couscous spoon to serve.

Veggie Sweet Potato Burgers

(Ready in 35 Minutes, Serve 8, Difficulty: Normal)

Nutrition per Serving:

Calories 140, Protein 6.1 g, Carbohydrates 27.3 g, Fat 1.3 g, Cholesterol 0mg, Sodium 89mg.

Ingredients:

- 1 cup of cooked brown rice
- 1 cup of cooked black beans; no salt added
- 1 cup of cooked, mashed sweet potatoes
- ¼ cup of chopped roasted red bell peppers
- ¼ cup of diced tomatoes
- 3 green onions, finely chopped
- ¼ cup of shredded carrots
- ¼ cup of chopped cilantro
- 1 tablespoon of no-salt-added chili powder
- 2 cloves of garlic, minced
- 1 teaspoon of hot pepper sauce (such as Tabasco®)
- 1 teaspoon of ground cumin

Instructions:

1. The oven should be preheated to 400 degrees Fahrenheit (204 degrees Celsius). Line the parchment paper with a baking sheet.

2. In a large bowl, add the rice, beans, sweet potatoes, red bell peppers, tomatoes, green onions, cilantro, chili powder, carrots, garlic, spicy pepper sauce, and cumin. Place the mixture into 4 equal patties on the prepared baking sheet.

3. Bake for 15 minutes in the preheated oven. Flip the patties and bake until mildly crisp and browned about 15 more minutes.

The Best Ever Vegan Sushi

(Ready in 1 Hour and 23 Minutes, Serve 6, Difficulty: Hard)

Nutrition per Serving:

Calories 299, Protein 8.9 g, Carbohydrates 36.8 g, Fat 13.6 g, Cholesterol 0mg, Sodium 337.8mg.

Ingredients:

- 1 cup of short-grain sushi rice
- 2 cups of water
- 1 pinch of salt
- 1 ½ teaspoon of vegetable oil
- ¼ cup of rice vinegar
- 2 tablespoons of white sugar
- ⅛ teaspoon of salt
- 1(16 ounces) package of extra-firm tofu
- 1 tablespoon of olive oil, or more as needed
- ¼ small onion, minced (Optional)
- 1 teaspoon of garlic, minced (Optional)
- ¼ cup of vegan mayonnaise (such as Follow Your Heart®)
- 2 tablespoons of Sriracha sauce, or to taste
- 2 sheets of nori, or as needed
- ½ avocado, peeled, pitted, and sliced
- ½ cup of matchstick-sliced Savoy cabbage
- ¼ cup of matchstick-cut carrots
- ¼ cup of matchstick-cut seeded cucumber

Instructions:

1. In a saucepan, combine the rice, water, and a pinch of salt and bring it to a boil. With a bamboo rice spatula or a thin wooden spoon, stir once. Lower the heat to low and cover-up. Cook for about 20 minutes until all the water is absorbed and the rice is tender. Let it cool.

2. Heat vegetable oil over medium heat in a small saucepan and add rice vinegar, sugar, and 1/8 teaspoon salt. Heat the mixture until it has dissolved all the sugar and the liquid starts to simmer. Remove from the heat and let cool for at least 10 minutes, until safe to handle. Slowly fold small portions of the cooled liquid into the cooled rice until the mixture is slightly sticky and wet, but you may not need all the liquid.

3. Use a paper towel to press the excess liquid out of the tofu. Have tofu cut into strips.

4. Over medium heat, heat the olive oil in a small skillet. Add the tofu, onion, and garlic strips, cook and stir until the tofu is brown, about 4 minutes on each side.

5. In a small bowl, blend the vegan mayonnaise and Sriracha.

6. Lay a sheet of nori on a sushi mat, rough side up. Firmly pat a thick, even layer of prepared rice over the nori with wet fingers, covering it fully. Arrange strips of tofu, avocado, cabbage, carrots, and cucumber in a line along the sheet's bottom edge.

7. Roll the nori over the filling and the sushi mat. Remove the mat and wrap the roll with plastic wrap, twisting to compress the roll ends tightly. Refrigerate for 5-10 minutes until set. Repeat with the filling and remaining nori.

8. Remove the sushi roll from the plastic wrap, slice it into pieces, and top it with the mayonnaise Sriracha.

9. Like shrimp tempura, fried tofu offers a satisfying crunch, whereas pan-seared is a bit creamier. You'll want the driest type you can find for fried tofu, such as the pre-marinated type sold in a vacuum-sealed package (instead of in liquid). With a paper towel, pat the tofu dry, slice it into 1/4-inch strips, dust them with corn-starch, and heat a few tablespoons of vegetable oil in a saucepan. Fry until golden brown on each side for 1-2 minutes.

Quick Vegan Sushi

(Ready in 50 Minutes, Serve 4, Difficulty: Normal)

Nutrition per Serving:

Calories 129, Protein 7.1 g, Carbohydrates 62.8 g 2, Fat 2.1 g, Cholesterol 0mg, Sodium 50.9mg.

Ingredients:

- Make-at-home sushi that is quick, easy, and vegan. Serve with wasabi and soy sauce.
- 1(7.4 ounces) package of precooked brown rice
- 2 sheets nori (dry seaweed)
- 1 bamboo mat
- 1 cucumber, sliced into thin strips
- 1 carrot, sliced into thin strips

Instructions:

1. In a microwave-safe bowl, put the cooked rice and partially cover it. Microwave on high, around 1 minute, before hot.

2. Place 1 nori sheet on a bamboo mat. Using a little water on your hands or a spoon to prevent the rice from sticking. Spread ½ of the rice equally on the nori mat. On the top ½ of the rice, put 1/2 of the cucumber and carrot slices, and roll nori sheet around rice and veggies using the bamboo mat to help. With the remaining nori sheets and vegetables, repeat.

3. Break each roll into six small pieces and place them in the refrigerator for about 20 minutes to cool.

Vegan Mushroom-Stuffed Cabbage Rolls

(Ready in 1 Hour and 50 Minutes, Serve 12, Difficulty: Normal)

Nutrition per Serving:

Calories 167, Protein 4.9 g, Carbohydrates 23.7 g, Fat 7.6 g, Cholesterol 0mg, Sodium 218mg.

Ingredients:

- 1 large head cabbage, cored
- 2 tablespoons of olive oil, divided
- 1 medium onion, minced
- ¼ cup of fresh thyme leaves, divided
- 3 cloves of garlic, chopped
- 340 g of mushrooms, finely chopped
- ½ cup of raisins
- 1 teaspoon of ground cinnamon
- ¾ cup of walnuts, roughly chopped
- 1 teaspoon of sea salt, or to taste, divided
- ½ cup of uncooked brown rice
- 1(16 ounces) can of crushed tomatoes, divided
- Ground black pepper, to taste

Instructions:

1. To a boil, bring a large pot of lightly salted water. Drop the cabbage into the pot and soak it fully in the water. For 10 minutes, cook. Remove from the water and allow for about 10 minutes to cool enough to handle. Carefully pull the leaves off.

2. The oven should be preheated to 350 degrees Fahrenheit (176 degrees Celsius).

3. Heat 1 tablespoon of oil over medium to high heat in a large skillet. Add the onion, 1/3 of the garlic, and the thyme. Cook for about 5 minutes, until the onions are translucent. Add the mushrooms, cinnamon, and raisins and cook for about 3 minutes. Stir in the walnuts and add 1/3 of the sea salt to season. Transfer the mixture to a large bowl and add the rice into a uniform mixture, mixing the stuffing.

4. Grease a baking dish with the remaining olive oil and use a thin layer of tomatoes to line the bottom. Sprinkle 1/3 of the thyme, 1/3 of the sea salt, and pepper lightly to taste.

5. Scoop into a cabbage leaf around a heaping tablespoon of stuffing and first fold into the sides, then roll and place in the prepared pan. Repeat with the leaves and the stuffing remaining. To close up any broken rolls, use any torn leaves. Top the remaining tomatoes with the rest of the thyme. Season with the remaining pepper and salt.

6. Use aluminum foil or a cover to cover the baking dish.

7. Bake until tender in the preheated oven, about 45 minutes.

Zucchini with Chickpea and Mushroom Stuffing

(Ready in 1 Hour, Serve 8, Difficulty: Normal)

Nutrition per Serving:

Calories 107, Protein 4.5 g, Carbohydrates 18.4 g, Fat 2.7 g, Cholesterol 0mg, Sodium 170mg.

Ingredients:

- 4 zucchinis, halved
- 1 tablespoon of olive oil
- 1 onion, chopped
- 2 cloves of garlic, crushed
- ½ (8 ounces) package of button mushrooms, sliced
- 1 teaspoon of ground coriander
- 1 ½ teaspoons of ground or to taste
- 1(15.5 ounces) can of chickpeas, rinsed and drained
- ½ lemon, juiced
- 2 tablespoons of chopped fresh parsley
- Sea salt, to taste
- Ground black pepper, to taste

Instructions:

1. Preheat the oven to 350 degrees Fahrenheit (176 degrees Celsius). Grease a shallow baking dish.

2. Scoop the zucchini meat out of it, chop the flesh, and set it aside. In the prepared dish, put the shells.

3. Heat oil over medium heat in a large skillet. Sauté the onions for 5 minutes, add the garlic and cook for another 2 minutes. Stir in the chopped mushrooms and zucchini and cook for 5 minutes. Stir in cilantro, lemon juice, chickpeas, parsley, salt, and pepper. A combination of spoons into zucchini shells.

4. Bake for 30-40 minutes in a preheated oven, or until the zucchini is tender.

Homemade Vegetable Sushi

(Ready in1 Hour and 10 Minutes, Serve 18, Difficulty: Hard)

Nutrition per Serving:

Calories 216, Protein 1.1 g, Carbohydrates 10.5 g, Fat 1.7 g, Cholesterol 0mg, Sodium 4.1mg

Ingredients:

- 1 cup of sushi rice
- 1 cup of water
- 3 sheets sushi nori (dry seaweed)
- ⅓ cup of rice vinegar
- 1 small cucumber, cut into matchstick-size pieces
- 1 carrot, cut into matchstick-size pieces
- 1 avocado, sliced

Instructions:

1. In cool water, clean the sushi rice and drain. Put the rice and 1 cup of water in a rice cooker. Seal and pick the setting as instructed by the manufacturer, cook until tender, around 15 minutes. With a fork, fluff, and let sit for 10 minutes.

2. On the sugar, add the rice vinegar and toss to coat. Let it cool absolutely for about thirty minutes.

3. Cover the plastic wrap with a bamboo sushi mat and put it on a cutting board. On the covered sushi mat, put a sheet of nori and cover it with cooled rice.

4. Spread out on top of 1/3 of the cucumber, carrot, and avocado, placing them around the boards bottom third. To help roll the nori up, use the sushi mat. Repeat with the nori, corn, and vegetables left. To cut each roll into six similar pieces, use a sharp knife.

Pressure Cooker Sambar (Indian Lentil Curry)

(Ready in 30 Minutes, Serve 4, Difficulty: Easy)
Nutrition per Serving:

Calories 238, Protein 14.8 g, Carbohydrates 41 g, Fat 2.4 g, Cholesterol 0mg, Sodium 47.2mg.

Ingredients:

- 6 ½ cups of water, divided
- 1 cup of yellow lentils
- 1 cup of chopped eggplant
- 1 teaspoon of turmeric powder
- Salt, to taste
- 1 tablespoon of tamarind paste
- 2 teaspoons of ground red Chile powder
- 1 teaspoon of vegetable oil, or as needed
- 1 whole dried-red Chile
- 4 curry leaves, or more to taste
- 1 teaspoon of whole cumin seeds
- 1 teaspoon of mustard seeds
- 1 pinch of asafoetida powder

Instructions:

1. In a pressure cooker, mix 4 cups of water, lentils, eggplant, turmeric, and salt. Cover the cooker safely and position the pressure regulator over the vent as instructed by the manufacturer. Heat until steam, about 10 minutes, exits in a constant flow and makes a whistling sound. Switch the temperature until the controller is rocking softly. Cook and exit from the heat for 3 minutes. As per the manufacturer's instructions, let the pressure release naturally for 5-10 minutes. Unlock the lid and remove it.

2. Add to the pressure cooker the remaining 2 1/2 cups of water, tamarind paste, and chili powder. Cover the cooker safely and position the pressure regulator over the vent as instructed by the manufacturer. Heat until steam, about 10 minutes, exits in a constant flow and makes a whistling sound. Remove from heat. As per the manufacturer's instructions, let the pressure release naturally for 5-10 minutes. Unlock the lid and remove it.

3. In a shallow saucepan, mix the oil, dried chili, curry leaves, cumin seeds, mustard seeds, and asafoetida powder over low heat. Cook for about 1 minute before the spices begin to sputter a little. Move the spice mixture and the lentils to the pressure cooker. Season with salt.

Veggeroni

(Ready in 1 Hour and 20 Minutes, Serve 12, Difficulty: Hard)
Nutrition per Serving:

Calories 144, Protein 17.1 g, Carbohydrates 13.1 g, Fat 2.1 g, Cholesterol 0.1mg, Sodium 375.6mg.

Ingredients:

- 2 cups of wheat gluten
- ½ cup of isolated protein powder
- 1 tablespoon of agar-agar powder
- 1 ½ tablespoons of paprika
- 1 teaspoon of ground black pepper
- ½ teaspoon of red pepper flakes
- ½ teaspoon of cayenne pepper
- 1 tablespoon of fennel seed
- 2 teaspoons of garlic powder
- 1 envelope of dry onion soup mix
- 1 envelope of dry tomato soup mix
- 1 ½ cups of water
- 1 tablespoon of vegetable oil
- 1 teaspoon of liquid smoke flavoring

Instructions:

1. Preheat the oven to 325-degree Fahrenheit (165 degrees Celsius).

2. In a mixer, add gluten, protein powder, agar-agar, paprika, black pepper, red pepper, cayenne pepper, fennel seed, garlic powder, onion soup paste, and tomato soup. Grind the powder for 2-3 minutes, then pour it into a large mixing cup.

3. In the powdered mixture, stir the water, oil, and liquid smoke flavoring until moistened, knead the dough for 3-5 minutes. Shape the dough into a log of 2-3 inches, tightly wrap it in aluminum foil, and put it on a baking sheet.

4. Bake the Veggeroni for 1 hour in a preheated oven. Until slicing, cool absolutely.

Spicy Vegan Chili

(Ready in 1 Hour, Serve 8, Difficulty: Normal)

Nutrition per Serving:

Calories 354, Protein 11.8 g, Carbohydrates 52.8 g, Fat 11.1 g, Cholesterol 0mg, Sodium 1405.2mg.

Ingredients:

- 1 tablespoon of canola oil
- 1 large green bell pepper, diced
- 1 large onion, diced
- 2 jalapeno peppers, chopped (Optional)
- ¼ cup of chili powder
- 1 ½ teaspoon of salt
- ½ teaspoon of ground cumin
- 2 cloves of garlic, minced
- 1(28 ounces) can of crushed tomatoes
- 1(15 ounces) can of black beans
- 1 ½ cups of water
- 1 cup of rinsed, uncooked white rice
- 1(15 ounces) can of corn
- ½ teaspoon of ground black pepper
- 1(8 ounces) package of shredded mozzarella-style vegan cheese

Instructions:

1. Heat oil over medium-high heat in a pan. Cook the bell pepper, onion, and jalapeno peppers for about 3 minutes until tender. Add chili powder, cinnamon, garlic, and cumin. Cook for about 10 minutes, stirring regularly, making sure that the chili powder doesn't burn.

2. Stir in a pot of tomatoes, beans, water, and rice. Bring it to a boil. Reduce the heat to medium, cover, and simmer for about 20 minutes until the rice is thoroughly cooked. If extra water is needed, check every 10-15 minutes. Add ¼ cup at a time.

3. Stir in the chili and cook the corn and pepper until heated, about 5 minutes.

Quick Stuffed Tomatoes

(Ready in 55 Minutes, Serve 4, Difficulty: Normal)

Nutrition per Serving:

Calories 224, Protein 11.4 g, Carbohydrates 47.7 g, Fat 1.1 g, Cholesterol 1.3mg, Sodium 283.9mg.

Ingredients:

- 4 large tomatoes
- 1 ½ cups of vegetable broth
- ½ cup of heat-dried tomatoes, chopped
- 1 cup of couscous
- ¼ cup of shredded non-Fat mozzarella cheese
- ¼ cup of chopped fresh basil
- 2 tablespoons of minced fresh mint leaves
- ¼ teaspoon of ground black pepper

Instructions:

1. Preheat the oven to 375 degrees Fahrenheit (190 degrees Celsius).

2. Cut the fresh tomatoes in ½ crosswise and set aside to scoop out the pulp. To drain, invert the tomato shells onto paper towels.

3. Bring the broth and heat-dried tomatoes to boil in a small saucepan. Remove the heat from the saucepan and stir the couscous in. Cover to prepare for 5 minutes to stand.

4. Stir in the cheese, basil, pepper, and mint. Then stir in the tomato pulp gently.

5. In an 11x7 inch baking dish, put the tomato shells. Spoon the mixture of couscous into the shells, pressing the mixture into the shells tightly. Bake at 190 degrees Celsius (375 degrees F) for 25-30 minutes or until totally cooked.

Guacamole

(Ready in 10 Minutes, Serve 4, Difficulty: Easy)

Nutrition Per Serving:

Calories 262, Protein 3.7 g, Carbohydrates 18 g, Fat 22.2 g, Cholesterol 0mg; Sodium 595.7mg.

Ingredients:

- 3 avocados, peeled, pitted, and mashed
- 1 lime, juiced
- 1 teaspoon of salt
- ½ cup of diced onion
- 3 tablespoons of chopped fresh cilantro
- 2 Roman (plum) tomatoes, diced
- 1 teaspoon of minced garlic
- 1 pinch of ground cayenne pepper (Optional)

Instructions:

1. Mash the avocados, lime juice, and salt together in a medium bowl.

2. Combine the cabbage, coriander, tomato, and garlic. Stir in the pepper with cayenne.

3. For the best flavor, refrigerate for 1 hour or serve immediately.

Vegan Stuffed Peppers

(Ready in 55 Minutes, Serve 6, Difficulty: Normal)

Nutrition per Serving:

Calories 289, Protein 13.5 g, Carbohydrates 59.2 g, Fat 2 g, Cholesterol 0mg, Sodium 1982.3mg.

Ingredients:

- 4 red bell peppers, halved lengthwise and seeded

- 1 cup of water
- ½ cup of bulgur
- 1(24 ounces) of jar tomato sauce, or more to taste
- 2 cups of arugula
- 1 cup of corn kernels
- ½ cup of garbanzo beans, drained
- ½ cup of lima beans, drained
- ½ cup of black beans, rinsed and drained
- ½ cup of kidney beans, rinsed and drained
- 1 teaspoon of salt
- ½ teaspoon of paprika
- ½ teaspoon of dried basil
- ½ teaspoon of dried oregano

Instructions:

1. Preheat the oven to 350 degrees Fahrenheit (176 degrees Celsius). Line the aluminum foil with a 9x11-inch baking pan. In a baking pan, arrange the bell pepper halves.

2. In a shallow saucepan, put the water and the bulgur to a boil. Cover and cook for 12-15 minutes, until the bulgur is tender. Drain all extra water.

3. In a large dish, mix the bulgur, tomato sauce, arugula, corn, garbanzo beans, lima beans, black beans, kidney beans, cinnamon, paprika, basil, and oregano. With a bulgur mixture, fill each bell pepper half generously.

4. Bake for 25-30 minutes in the preheated oven until bubbly and hot.

Flavorful Rice

(Ready in 25 Minutes, Serve 8, Difficulty: Easy)

Nutrition per Serving:

Calories 231, Protein 6.1 g, Carbohydrates 60.5 g 2, Fat 4 g, Cholesterol 0mg, Sodium 81.9mg

Ingredients:

- 4 ½ cups of water
- 3 cups of uncooked white rice
- 2 tablespoons of olive oil
- 2 tablespoons of distilled white vinegar
- ½ teaspoon of dried basil
- ½ teaspoon of dried oregano
- 1 pinch of salt
- 1 pinch of ground black pepper
- 1(14.5 ounces) can of diced tomatoes, drained

Instructions:

1. Mix the sugar, flour, olive oil, vinegar, salt, pepper, basil, oregano, and tomatoes in your rice steamer. Cook in according to steamer settings.

Lentil Soup

(Ready in 25 Minutes, Serve 6, Difficulty: Normal)

Nutrition per Serving:

Calories 249, Protein 18.3 g, Carbohydrates 48.2 g, Fat 10 g, Cholesterol 0mg, Sodium 130.5mg

Ingredients:

- 1 onion, chopped
- ¼ cup of olive oil
- 2 carrots, diced
- 2 stalks of celery, chopped
- 2 cloves of garlic, minced
- 1 teaspoon of dried oregano
- 1 bay leaf
- 1 teaspoon of dried basil
- 1(14.5 ounces) can of crushed tomatoes
- 2 cups of dry lentils
- 8 cups of water
- ½ cup of spinach, rinsed and thinly sliced
- 2 tablespoons of vinegar
- Salt, to taste
- Ground black pepper, to taste

Instructions:

1. Heat oil over medium heat in a large soup pot. Cook and stir until the onion is tender. Add the tomatoes, carrots, and celery. Stir in the garlic, bay leaves, basil, and oregano and cook for 2 minutes.

2. Stir in the lentils and stir in the tomatoes and water. Bring it to a boil. Reduce the heat and boil for 1 hour at least. Stir in the spinach when ready to eat, and simmer until it wilts. Stir in the vinegar, and if necessary, season with salt and pepper and more vinegar to taste.

Vegan Lentil Loaf with Greek Flavors

(Ready in 2 Hours and 30 Minutes, Serve 8, and Difficulty: Normal)

Nutrition per Serving:

Calories 243, Protein 14.6 g, Carbohydrates 42 g, Fat 2.5 g, Cholesterol 0mg, Sodium 236.9mg

Ingredients:

- 2 cups of French green lentils
- Water, to cover
- ½ teaspoon of onion powder
- ½ teaspoon of celery salt
- ½ teaspoon of garlic salt
- 1 green bell pepper, minced
- 2 stalks of celery, minced
- 2 carrots, minced
- 2 cloves of garlic, minced

- 1 bunch of fresh parsley, chopped
- 1 cup of cooked brown rice
- ⅓ cup of chia seeds
- 1 lemon, zested and juiced
- 1 teaspoon of dried oregano
- 1 teaspoon of dried mint
- Salt and ground black pepper, to taste

Instructions:

1. Pour enough water to cover 2 inches, combine onion powder, celery salt, and garlic salt, and put the lentils in a jar. Cook the lentils, occasionally stirring, until tender, about 40 minutes, over medium heat. Slightly cool the lentils and add them to a food processor and blend until smooth.

2. Preheat the oven to 350 degrees Fahrenheit (176 degrees Celsius). Grease a pan with a 9x5-inch loaf.

3. In a big cup, combine the lentils, green bell pepper, celery, carrots, and garlic cloves Combine the lentil mixture to the parsley, brown rice, chia seeds, lemon zest, lemon juice, oregano, mint, salt, and pepper, and blend well. Pour the mixture of lentils into a prepared loaf tray.

4. Bake until baked through around 1 1/2 hours in the preheated oven. Before slicing, cool a little bit, about 15 minutes.

Pasta

(Ready in 25 Minutes, Serve 3, Difficulty: Normal)

Nutrition per Serving:

Calories 218, Protein 8.5 g, Carbohydrates 34.7 g, Fat 2.3 g, Cholesterol 0mg, Sodium 438.9mg.

Ingredients:

- ⅓ cup of soy flour
- 1 cup of whole wheat flour
- ½ cup of spelt flour
- ¾ teaspoon of salt
- ½ cup of water, or as needed

Instructions:

1. Stir together the whole wheat flour, soy flour, spelled meal, and salt in a medium dish. Add water, and combine with the dough hook. To form a stiff yet pliable dough, use more water as needed. For about 10 minutes, mix or knead by hand. Cover, let the dough sit for 30 minutes, or rest for at least an hour if you don't have a pasta machine.

2. Divide the dough into four parts, making things easier to roll. If you have one, pass the dough through a pasta machine or use a rolling pin to roll on a floured surface quite thinly, but not transparently.

3. Allow the pasta sheet to dry for a couple of minutes while you are making noodles. Flour dust, and roll into a loose channel. For linguine, or to the required size, slice the tube into 1/4-inch slices.

4. To cook: Put to a boil a big pot of lightly salted water. Add the pasta, then cook until al dente, depending on the thickness, for 1-5 minutes. Cooked pasta can float to the water's top.

Ginger Veggie Stir-Fry

(Ready in 40 Minutes, Serve 6, Difficulty: Normal)

Nutrition per Serving:

Calories 119, Protein 2.2 g, Carbohydrates 8 g, Fat 9.3 g, Cholesterol 0mg, Sodium 903.3mg.

Ingredients:

- 1 tablespoon of corn-starch
- 1 ½ cloves of garlic, crushed
- 2 teaspoons of chopped fresh ginger root, divided
- ¼ cup of vegetable oil, divided
- 1 small head broccoli, cut into florets
- ½ cup of snow peas
- ¾ cup of julienned carrots
- ½ cup of halved green beans
- 2 tablespoons of soy sauce
- 2 ½ tablespoons of water
- ¼ cup of chopped onion
- ½ tablespoon of salt

Instructions:

1. Mix the corn-starch, garlic, 1 teaspoon of ginger, and 2 teaspoons of vegetable oil in a wide bowl until the corn-starch dissolves. Combine the broccoli, carrots, snow peas, and green beans in a finely seasoned toss.

2. In a broad skillet or wok over medium heat, heat the remaining 2 tablespoons of oil. For 2 minutes, cook vegetables in oil, stirring continuously to avoid burning. Stir in the water and soy sauce. Mix the onion, salt, and 1 teaspoon of the remaining ginger. Cook until it is soft but still crisp with vegetables.

Vegan Fajitas

(Ready in 1 Hour and 10 Minutes, Serve 6, Difficulty: Hard)

Nutrition per Serving:

Calories 198, Protein 3 g, Carbohydrates 17.9 g, Fat 14.4 g, Cholesterol 0mg, Sodium 130.2mg.

Ingredients:

- ¼ cup of olive oil
- ¼ cup of red wine vinegar
- 1 teaspoon of dried oregano
- 1 teaspoon of chili powder

- Garlic salt, to taste
- Salt and pepper, to taste
- 1 teaspoon of white sugar
- 2 small zucchinis, julienned
- 2 medium yellow squash, julienned
- 1 large onion, sliced
- 1 green bell pepper, cut into thin strips
- 1 red bell pepper, cut into thin strips
- 2 tablespoons of olive oil
- 1(8.75 ounces) can of whole kernel corn, drained
- 1(15 ounces) can of black beans, drained

Instructions:

1. Mix the olive oil, mustard, oregano, chili powder, garlic salt, salt, pepper, and sugar in a big dish. Add some zucchini, yellow squash, cabbage, green pepper, and red pepper to the marinade. Marinate the vegetables for at least 30 minutes, but not more than 24 hours in the refrigerator.

2. Heat oil over medium-high heat in a large skillet. Drain the vegetables and cook for about 10 to 15 minutes, until tender. Stir in the beans and corn, raise the heat to high for 5 minutes, and brown the vegetables.

Vegan Sweet Potato and Bean Burritos

(Ready in 40 Minutes, Serve 4, Difficulty: Normal)

Nutrition per Serving:

Calories 357, Protein 13.7 g, Carbohydrates 87.3 g, Fat 16.7 g, Cholesterol 2.5mg, Sodium 1121.1mg.

Ingredients:

- 1 cup of sweet potato, peeled and cut into ¼-inch cubes
- ½ cup of yellow onion, sliced
- 2 tablespoons of olive oil
- 1 tablespoon of taco seasoning mix
- ½ cup of vegan refried beans
- 4 large vegan tortillas
- 1 cup of cooked brown rice
- ¼ cup of salsa

Instructions:

1. Preheat the oven to 450 degrees Fahrenheit (232 degrees Celsius).

2. In a bowl, combine the onion, olive oil, sweet potatoes, and taco seasoning. Spread out on the baking sheet.

3. Roast in a preheated oven for approximately 30 minutes, or until desired.

4. In the middle of each tortilla, spread 1/4 of the beans. Use ¼ cup of rice, ¼ of the vegetable mixture, and one tablespoon of salsa to top each tortilla.

Grilled Tofu Skewers with Sriracha Sauce

(Ready in 1 Hour and 25 Minutes, Serve 2, Difficulty: Normal)

Nutrition per Serving:

Calories 30, Protein 16.8 g, Carbohydrates 19.4 g, Fat 19.8 g, Cholesterol 0mg, Sodium 2465.7mg.

Ingredients:

- 1(8 ounces) container of extra firm tofu, drained and sliced into large chunks
- 1 zucchini, cut into large chunks
- 1 red bell pepper, cut into large chunks
- 10 large mushrooms
- 2 tablespoons of Sriracha chili garlic sauce
- ¼ cup of soy sauce
- 2 tablespoons of sesame oil
- ¼ cup of diced onion
- 1 jalapeno pepper, diced
- Ground black pepper, to taste

Instructions:

1. Bring the tofu, zucchini, red bell pepper, and mushrooms together in a bowl. In a shallow cup, mix the Sriracha sauce, sesame oil, soy sauce, onion, jalapeno, and pepper, and pour the tofu and vegetables together. To coat, toss lightly. Cover and leave to marinate in the refrigerator for at least 1 hour.

2. Preheat the medium-high-heat outdoor grill and gently grease the grill.

3. On to skewers, thread tofu, and vegetables. Grill each skewer for 10 minutes, or until needed. As a dipping sauce, use the remaining marinade.

South-Western Pasta Salad

(Ready in 30 Minutes, Serve 8, Difficulty: Easy)

Nutrition per Serving:

Calories 217, Protein 6.5 g, Carbohydrates 27.2 g, Fat 10.3 g, Cholesterol 0mg, Sodium 468.3mg.

Ingredients:

- ½ (16 ounces) package of rotini pasta
- ⅓ cup of vegetable oil
- ¼ cup of fresh lime juice
- 2 tablespoons of chili powder, or to taste
- 2 teaspoons of ground cumin
- ½ teaspoon of salt
- 2 cloves of garlic, crushed
- 1 ½ cups of whole kernel corn

- 1(15 ounces) can of black beans, drained and rinsed
- ½ cup of diced green bell pepper
- ½ cup of diced red bell pepper
- ½ cup of fresh cilantro leaves
- 1 cup of chopped Roman(plum) tomatoes

Instructions:

1. To a boil, bring a large pot of lightly salted water. Cook for 8-10 minutes or until al dente, drain and add pasta.

2. Mix the oil, lime juice, salt, chili powder, and garlic in a large bowl. Stir in the pasta and set aside, occasionally stirring, to cool to room temperature.

3. Add the corn, beans, green pepper, red pepper, and ½ of the cilantro leaves. Spoon and garnish with the tomatoes and remaining cilantro on a plate. Chilled or at room temperature, serve.

Tempeh Gyros

(Ready in 9 Hours and 8 Minutes, Serve 4, and Difficulty: Hard)

Nutrition per Serving:

Calories 238, Protein 25.1 g, Carbohydrates 53.9 g, Fat 10.6 g, Cholesterol 0mg, Sodium 1085.9mg.

Ingredients:

- 1 cup of vegetable broth
- 2 tablespoons of soy sauce
- 2 tablespoons of lemon juice
- 2 teaspoons of dried oregano
- 2 teaspoons of ground thyme
- 1 ½ teaspoon of minced garlic
- 1(8 ounces) package of tempeh
- 4(6 inches) whole-wheat pitas
- 1 dash of pink Himalayan salt
- 1 dash of ground black pepper

For Tzatziki:

- 2 small cucumbers, peeled and grated
- 1(12.3 ounces) package of silken tofu
- 1 tablespoon(packed) of fresh dill
- 1 teaspoon of minced fresh garlic
- Salt and ground black pepper, to taste
- 2 tomatoes, sliced
- ½ red onion, thinly sliced

Instructions:

1. In a large bowl, combine the vegetable broth, soy sauce, lemon juice, oregano, thyme, 1 1/2 teaspoons of garlic, Himalayan salt, and a dash of pepper.

2. Bring it to a boil with a saucepan of water. Cut ½ of the tempeh and add to the boiling water. Boil to remove any bitter taste for 10 minutes. Transfer the tempeh to a cutting board and allow a slight cooling process.

3. In the vegetable broth marinade, cut tempeh into ¼ -inch slices and place them. Cover with plastic wrap and marinate 8 hours to overnight in the refrigerator, occasionally stirring to make sure the marinade is covered with tempeh.

4. Preheat the oven to 400 degrees Fahrenheit (204 degrees Celsius). Line the parchment paper with a baking sheet.

5. Transfer the marinated slices of tempeh to the cooked baking sheet.

6. Bake for 30-35 minutes in the preheated oven, turning halfway through until golden brown and starting to crisp at the edges.

7. Place pitas for 3-5 minutes in the hot oven until warmed through.

8. Use a paper towel to squeeze excess water from the cucumbers. In a food processor, put the tofu, cucumbers, dill, and 1 teaspoon of garlic, salt, and pepper. Mix until the Tzatziki is well blended. If desired, modify the seasonings.

9. Put ¼ of the slices of tempeh, tomatoes, and red onions on top of a pita to assemble a gyro with Tzatziki cover. Repeat with the remaining tempeh pita, onion, and tomatoes.

Perfect Sushi Rice

(Ready in 25 Minutes, Serve 15, Difficulty: Easy)

Nutrition per Serving:

Calories 112, Protein 1.7 g, Carbohydrates 23.5 g, Fat 1 g, Cholesterol 0mg, Sodium 158.2mg.

Ingredients:

- 2 cups of uncooked glutinous white rice (sushi rice)
- 3 cups of water
- ½ cup of rice vinegar
- 1 tablespoon of vegetable oil
- ¼ cup of white sugar
- 1 teaspoon of salt

Instructions:

1. Heat oil over medium heat in a large soup pot. Cook and stir until the onion is tender. Add the tomatoes, carrots, and celery. Stir in the garlic, bay leaves, basil, and oregano and cook for 2 minutes.

2. Stir in the lentils and stir in the tomatoes and water. Bring it to a boil. Reduce the heat and boil for 1 hour at least. Stir in the spinach when ready to eat, and simmer until it wilts.

3. Stir in the vinegar, and if necessary, season with salt and pepper and more vinegar to taste.

Jackfruit Vegan Tacos

(Ready in 13 Minutes, Serve 4, Difficulty: Easy)

Nutrition per Serving:

Calories, 258 Protein 1.6 g, Carbohydrates 27.8 g, Fat 13.3 g 2, Cholesterol 0mg, Sodium 1147.7mg.

Ingredients:

* 2(20 ounce) cans jackfruit in brine, drained, rinsed, and cut into bite-sized pieces
* 1 tablespoon of vegetable oil
* 1 tablespoon of water, or more as needed
* 2 tablespoons of taco seasoning mix, or to taste
* 4 taco shells
* ½ cup of salsa, or to taste

Instructions:

1. Heat oil over medium heat in a small saucepan. Add the jackfruit, cook for 2-3 minutes and stir. Add 1 tablespoon of taco seasoning and water and stir until well combined, about 1 minute. Add 1 tablespoon of additional water at a time, as required.

2. Place each taco shell with a small amount of jackfruit and add 2 tablespoons of salsa.

Spiralized Cucumber and Jicama Tostada Salad with Avocado

(Ready in 50 Minutes, Serve 4, Difficulty: Normal)

Nutrition per Serving:

Calories 217, Protein 3.1 g, Carbohydrates 28.2 g, Fat 6.2 g, Cholesterol 0mg, Sodium 141.1mg.

Ingredients:

* 1 jicama, cut into spirals
* 1 English cucumber, cut into spirals
* ½ red onion, cut into spirals
* 2 mini sweet bell peppers, cut into matchstick pieces
* 1 large jalapeno, cut into spirals
* 1 lime, juiced
* 1 tablespoon of avocado oil
* 2 avocados, mashed
* 1 pinch of garlic salt, or to taste
* 4 prepared tostada shells
* 10 grape of tomatoes, halved
* ¼ cup of chopped cilantro (optional)
* 1 lime, cut into wedges

Instructions:

1. In a mixing bowl, place the jicama, cucumber, red onion, and bell peppers together. Combine with lime juice and avocado oil and refrigerate until cooled, about 20 minutes.

2. With garlic salt, season the mashed avocado. Spread the avocado mixture evenly over the shells of the tostada.

3. Top evenly with the mixture of jicama and grape tomatoes.

4. Garnish with coriander and serve with wedges of lime.

Spicy Black Bean Vegetable Soup

(Ready in 50 Minutes, Serve 8, Difficulty: Normal)

Nutrition per Serving:

Calories 216, Protein 7.6 g, Carbohydrates 26.9 g, Fat 3.4 g, Cholesterol 0mg, Sodium 683.4mg.

Ingredients:

* 1 tablespoon of vegetable oil
* 1 onion, chopped
* 1 clove of garlic, minced
* 2 carrots, chopped
* 2 teaspoons of chili powder
* 1 teaspoon of ground cumin
* 4 cups of vegetable stock
* 2(15 ounces) cans of black beans, rinsed and drained
* 1(8.75 ounces) can of whole kernel corn
* ¼ teaspoon of ground black pepper
* 1(14.5 ounces) can of stewed tomatoes

Instructions:

1. Heat the oil over medium heat in a large saucepan and cook the onion, garlic, and carrots, occasionally stirring, for 5 minutes or until the onion is tender.

2. Add the chili powder and cumin and cook for 1 minute, stirring. Add stock, bring to a boil, one can of beans, corn, and pepper.

3. Meanwhile, mash the tomatoes together in a food processor or blender and add the remaining can of beans to the pot. Reduce heat for 10-15 minutes or until the carrots are tender, cover, and simmer.

Vegan Lasagna

(Ready in 1 Hour and 5 Minutes, Serve 9, Difficulty: Hard)

Nutrition per Serving:

Calories 312, Protein 32.5 g 6, Carbohydrates 69.9 g, Fat 15.8 g, Cholesterol 0mg, Sodium 1074.1mg.

Ingredients:

* 2 tablespoons of olive oil
* 1 ½ cups of chopped onion
* 3 tablespoons of minced garlic
* 4(14.5 ounces) cans of stewed tomatoes
* ⅓ cup of tomato paste

- ½ cup of chopped fresh basil
- ½ cup of chopped parsley
- 1 teaspoon of salt
- 1 teaspoon of ground black pepper
- 1(16 ounces) package of lasagna noodles
- 907 g of firm tofu
- 2 tablespoons of minced garlic
- ¼ cup of chopped fresh basil
- ¼ cup of chopped parsley
- ½ teaspoon of salt
- Ground black pepper, to taste
- 3(10 ounces) packages of frozen chopped spinach, thawed and drained

Instructions:

1. Make the sauce: Heat the olive oil in a large, heavy saucepan over medium heat. Place the onions in the saucepan and cook for about 5 minutes until they are soft. Add the garlic and cook for an extra 5 minutes.

2. In the saucepan, put the tomatoes, tomato paste, basil, and parsley. Stir well, turn the heat to medium, and cover the sauce for 1 hour to simmer. Add the pepper and salt.

3. Bring a large kettle of salted water to a boil while the sauce is boiling. Boil the Lasagna noodles for 9 minutes, then drain and rinse well.

4. The oven should be preheated to 400 degrees Fahrenheit (204 degrees Celsius).

5. In a large bowl, place the tofu blocks. Garlic, basil, and parsley are added. Add the salt and pepper and by squeezing pieces of tofu through your fingers, mash all the ingredients together. Stir occasionally.

6. Put the Lasagna together: Spread 1 cup of the tomato sauce over the bottom of a 9x13 inch casserole pan. Arrange a single sheet of Lasagna noodles and sprinkle the noodles with one-third of the tofu mixture.

7. Distribute the spinach over the tofu evenly. Next, top the tofu with 1 ½ cups of tomato sauce and top it with another sheet of noodles. 7. Then sprinkle the noodles with another 1/3 of the tofu mixture, top the tofu with 1 1/2 cups of tomato sauce, and place the tomato sauce over a final layer of noodles.

8. Finally, add the final 1/3 of the tofu to the noodles, and spread the remaining tomato sauce over everything.

9. Use foil to cover the pan and bake the Lasagna for 30 minutes. Serve it warm and enjoy it.

Spicy Vegan Potato Curry

(Ready in 1 Hour, Serve 6, Difficulty: Normal)

Nutrition per Serving:

Calories 207, Protein 10.1 g, Carbohydrates 50.6 g, Fat 20.1 g, Cholesterol 0mg, Sodium 1176.9mg.

Ingredients:

- 4 potatoes, peeled and cubed
- 2 tablespoons of vegetable oil
- 1 yellow onion, diced
- 3 cloves of garlic, minced
- 2 teaspoons of ground cumin
- 1 ½ teaspoon of cayenne pepper
- 4 teaspoons of curry powder
- 4 teaspoons of garam masala
- 1(1 inch) piece of fresh ginger root, peeled and minced
- 2 teaspoons of salt
- 1(14.5 ounces) can of diced tomatoes
- 1(15 ounces) can of garbanzo beans(chickpeas), rinsed and drained
- 1(15 ounces) can of peas, drained
- 1(14 ounces) can of coconut milk

Instructions:

1. In a large pot, place the potatoes and cover them with salted water. Bring to a boil over high heat, reduce heat to medium-low, cover and simmer for about 15 minutes until just tender. Drain and allow to dry for 1 minute or 2 while steaming.

2. Meanwhile, over medium heat, heat the vegetable oil in a large skillet. Stir in the garlic and onion, cook and stir until the onion is tender and translucent, about 5 minutes.

3. Season with cayenne pepper, garam masala, curry powder, ginger, salt, and cook for a further 2 minutes. Tomatoes, garbanzo beans, peas, and potatoes are all added.

4. Pour in the milk from the coconut and bring it to a simmer. Before serving, simmer for 5 to 10 minutes.

Easy Vegan Sheet Pan Roasted Cauliflower, Tomatoes, and Garbanzo Beans

(Ready in 35 Minutes, Serve 2, Difficulty: Easy)

Nutrition per Serving:

Calories 232, Protein 12.6 g, Carbohydrates 53.9 g, Fat 9.3 g, Cholesterol 0mg, Sodium 1075.5mg.

Ingredients:

- Cooking spray
- 1 tablespoon of olive oil
- 2 cloves of garlic, minced

- ½ teaspoon of salt
- ¼ teaspoon of ground black pepper
- 4 cups of sliced cauliflower
- 2 cups of cherry tomatoes
- 1(15 ounces) can of garbanzo beans, drained
- 1 lime, cut into wedges
- 1 tablespoon of chopped fresh cilantro

Instructions:

1. Preheat the oven to 450 degrees Fahrenheit (232 degrees Celsius). Cover a baking sheet with cooking spray and grease with aluminum foil.

2. In a bowl, blend the olive oil, garlic, salt, and pepper. Add the onions, cauliflower, and garbanzo beans and toss until well-seasoned. Spread out on the prepared baking sheet in a single layer. Add wedges of lime.

3. Roast in the preheated oven for about 25 minutes before the vegetables are caramelized. Remove the lime wedges and combine fresh cilantro to the top.

American-Style Red Beans and Rice

(Ready in 35 Minutes, Serve 4, Difficulty: Normal)

Nutrition per Serving:

Calories 121, Protein 14.7 g, Carbohydrates 101.1 g, Fat 5.1 g, Cholesterol 0mg, Sodium 711.9mg.

Ingredients:
- 1 tablespoon of olive oil
- 1(15 ounces) can of kidney beans
- 1 ½ cups of tomato sauce
- 4 ½ cups of water, divided
- ½ teaspoon of dried oregano
- ½ teaspoon of dried basil
- 1 pinch of dried thyme
- Salt and pepper, to taste
- 5 teaspoons of adobo seasoning, divided
- 2 cups of uncooked white rice

Instructions:

1. Combine the olive oil, kidney beans, tomato sauce, ½ cup water, basil, thyme, salt, oregano, pepper, and two teaspoons adobo in a large saucepan. Simmer at low temperatures.

2. Meanwhile, boil 4 cups of water. Combine rice and stir. Reduce the heat, cover, and simmer for 20 minutes or until all the liquid is absorbed and the rice is cooked.

3. Add the remaining 3 teaspoons of adobo. Over the rice, serve the beans.

Broccoli and Peanut Soba Noodles

(Ready in 25 Minutes, Serve 4, Difficulty: Easy)

Nutrition per Serving:

Calories 238, Protein 18 g, Carbohydrates 41.6 g, Fat 14.1 g, Saturates Fat 2.8 g, Sugars 5.9 g, Fiber 8.8 g, Salt 1.6 g.

Ingredients:
- 150 g of soba noodles
- ½ teaspoon of sesame oil
- Tenderstem® or purple sprouting
- 300 g of broccoli
- 100 g of edamame beans
- 2 tablespoons of smooth peanut butter
- 1 tablespoon of soy sauce
- 1 tablespoon of rice vinegar
- 1 tablespoon of ginger grated to make
- 1/2 clove of garlic, crushed
- Lime, juiced, plus wedges to serve
- Spring onions, sliced
- Coriander small bunch, chopped
- 2 tablespoons of roasted salted peanuts, chopped

Instructions:

1. Cook the noodles in salted boiling water, until tender, for 4 minutes. Drain and rinse thoroughly in cold water, then drain again, toss in the sieve with the sesame oil, and leave.

2. For 2-3 minutes, blanch the Tenderstem® until it is vibrant green and still has a bite, adding the edamame for the last 30 seconds. In cold water, refresh, and then drain well.

3. To make a dressing, whisk together the peanut butter, vinegar, ginger, soy sauce, garlic, and lime juice with a splash of boiling water.

4. Cut the Tenderstem® into bite-sized bits and add the noodles, edamame, spring onions, cilantro, and the dressing to a bowl. Well, toss well. Serve with the chopped peanuts scattered, with lime wedges to squeeze over.

Chapter 5: Soups Recipes

In this chapter, we are going to give you some delicious and mouthwatering recipes on Octavia Soups recipes.

Butternut Vegetable Soup

(Ready in 1 Hour and 45 Minutes, Serve 10, Difficulty: Hard)

Nutrition per Serving:

Calories 187, Protein 6.4 g, Carbohydrates 27.3 g, Fat 6.6 g, Cholesterol mg, Sodium 820.2mg.

Ingredients:

* ¼ cup of vegetable oil
* 1 cup of finely diced onion
* 2 teaspoons of minced garlic
* 4 large carrots, thinly sliced
* 2 cups of peeled and cubed butternut squash
* 12 cups of vegetable broth
* 2 red potatoes, cubed
* ½ teaspoon of dried thyme
* 1 teaspoon of salt
* ½ teaspoon of ground black pepper
* 4 cups of finely chopped kale leaves
* 1(16 ounces) can of great northern beans, rinsed and drained

Instructions:

1. Heat the vegetable oil over medium heat in a big Dutch oven. Stir in the garlic and onion, cook and stir until the onion is tender and translucent, around 5 minutes. Stir in the butternut squash and carrots, cook and stir for about 15 minutes before the squash starts to brown.

2. Pour the broth. Bring to a boil, stir in the red potatoes, thyme, salt, and pepper. Reduce the heat and boil for about 45 minutes until the vegetables are tender. Stir in the kale and the large northern beans and boil for about 10 minutes until the kale is tender.

3. In a mixer, pour about 3 cups of the broth, filling the pitcher no more than halfway full (you may have to do this in two batches). With a folded kitchen towel, keep the blender's lid down and start the blender carefully, using a few short pulses to transfer the soup before leaving it to puree.

4. To the soup pot, return the pureed part of the soup, leaving the remaining soup chunky. Alternately, right in the boiling pot, you should use a stick blender to partly puree the soup.

Squash and Apple Soup

(Ready in 35 Minutes, Serve 6, Difficulty: Easy)

Nutrition per Serving:

Calories 140, Protein 3.1 g, Carbohydrates 28.6 g, Fat 2.8 g, Cholesterol 4.8mg, Sodium 31.8mg.

Ingredients:

* 2 teaspoons of butter
* 1 onion, chopped
* 453 g of butternut squash, peeled and chopped
* 2 apples, peeled and chopped
* 1 small potato, peeled and chopped
* 1 teaspoon of grated fresh ginger root
* 1 pinch of white pepper
* 4 cups of water
* ¼ cup of apple cider
* 1 teaspoon of packed brown sugar
* ½ cup of plain yogurt
* 1 tablespoon of finely chopped toasted pecans

Instructions:

1. Cook the stew beef, onion, and celery in a large saucepan over medium-high heat for 5 minutes or until the meat is browned on all sides.

2. Add the bouillon, parsley, carrots, ground black pepper, and pasta with water and eggs.

3. Bring it to a boil, bring it to low heat, and cook for 30 minutes.

Cauliflower-Cheese Soup

(Ready in 45 Minutes, Serve 4, Difficulty: Normal)

Nutrition per Serving:

Calories 138, Protein 15.7 g, Carbohydrates 25.9 g, Fat 24.7 g, Cholesterol 74.9mg, Sodium 367.6mg.

Ingredients:

* ¾ cup of water
* 1 cup of chopped cauliflower
* 1 cup of cubed potatoes
* ½ cup of finely chopped celery
* ½ cup of diced carrots
* ¼ cup of chopped onion
* ¼ cup of butter
* ¼ cup of all-purpose flour
* 3 cups of milk
* Salt and pepper, to taste

- 4 ounces of shredded cheddar cheese

Instructions:

1. Combine the water, cauliflower, carrots, potatoes, celery, and onion in a large saucepan. It should be boiled for 5-10 minutes, or until tender. Only put aside.

2. Over medium pressure, melt the butter in a separate saucepan. Add the flour, then simmer for 2 minutes.

3. Remove from the heat, and stir in the milk gradually. Return to the heat and simmer until the mixture thickens. With the cooking liquid, stir in the vegetables and season with salt and pepper. Remove from the heat and whisk in the cheese until melted.

Slow Cooker Lentil and Ham Soup

(Ready in 11 Hours and 20 Minutes, Serve 6, and Difficulty: Hard)

Nutrition per Serving:

Calories 322, Protein 15.1 g, Carbohydrates 26.3 g, Fat 6.1 g, Cholesterol 19.7mg, Sodium 1169.6mg.

Ingredients:

- 1 cup of dried lentils
- 1 cup of chopped celery
- 1 cup of chopped carrots
- 1 cup of chopped onion
- 2 cloves of garlic, minced
- 1 ½ cups of diced cooked ham
- ½ teaspoon of dried basil
- ¼ teaspoon of dried thyme
- ½ teaspoon of dried oregano
- 1 bay leaf
- ¼ teaspoon of black pepper
- 32 ounces of chicken broth
- 1 cup of water
- 8 teaspoons of tomato sauce

Instructions:

1. Mix the lentils, carrots, celery, cabbage, garlic, and ham in a three ½-quart or larger slow cooker. Using basil, thyme, oregano, bay leaf, and pepper to season. Stir in the chicken broth, tomato sauce, and water.

2. Cover and simmer for 11 hours on low pressure. Before serving, discard the bay leaf.

Sweet Potato, Carrot, Apple, and Red Lentil Soup

(Ready in 1 Hour and 10 Minutes, Serve 6, Difficulty: Normal)

Nutrition per Serving:

Calories 232, Protein 9 g, Carbohydrates 52.9 g, Fat 9 g, Cholesterol 21.6mg, Sodium 876.3mg.

Ingredients:

- ¼ cup of butter
- 2 large sweet potatoes, peeled and chopped
- 3 large carrots, peeled and chopped
- 1 apple, peeled, cored, and chopped
- 1 onion, chopped
- ½ cup of red lentils
- ½ teaspoon of minced fresh ginger
- ½ teaspoon of ground black pepper
- 1 teaspoon of salt
- ½ teaspoon of ground cumin
- ½ teaspoon of chili powder
- ½ teaspoon of paprika
- 4 cups of vegetable broth
- Plain yogurt

Instructions:

1. Melt the butter over medium-high heat in a big heavy-bottomed pot. In the pot, combine the chopped sweet potatoes, carrots, apple, and onion. Stir and cook the apples and vegetables for about 10 minutes before the onions are translucent.

2. In a pot with the apple and vegetable mixture, stir the lentils, ginger, ground black pepper, cinnamon, chili powder, paprika, and vegetable broth. Bring the soup to a boil over high heat, then reduce the heat to medium-low, cover and simmer for about 30 minutes until the lentils and vegetables are soft.

3. Pour the soup into a blender, working in batches, filling the pitcher no more than halfway full. With a folded kitchen towel, keep the blender's lid down and start the blender carefully, using a few short pulses to transfer the soup before leaving it to puree. Purée until smooth and pour into a clean pot in batches. Alternately, right in the cooking pot, you should use a stick blender to puree the broth.

4. Place the pureed soup back in the cooking pot. Bring back over medium-high heat, around 10 minutes, to a simmer. To thin the soup to your desired consistency, add water as needed. For garnish, serve with yogurt.

5. Instead of yogurt as a garnish, this soup is also well served with crumbled feta cheese.

Instant Pot® Hamburger Soup

(Ready in 1 Hour and 10 Minutes, Serve 8, Difficulty: Normal)

Nutrition per Serving:

Calories 112, Protein 18.7 g, Carbohydrates 17.8 g, Fat 11.2 g, Cholesterol 51.7mg, Sodium 950.4mg.

Ingredients:

- 680 g of ground beef
- 1 medium onion, finely chopped
- 3(14.5 ounces) cans of beef consommé
- 1(28 ounces) can of diced tomatoes
- 2 cups of water
- 1(10.75 ounces) can of condensed tomato soup
- 4 carrots, finely chopped
- 3 stalks of celery, finely chopped
- 4 tablespoons of pearl barley
- ½ teaspoon of dried thyme
- 1 bay leaf

Instructions:

1. Switch on a multi-functional pressure cooker and select the cook mode (such as Instant Pot®). Cook and stir until browned, 5-10 minutes, with the beef and onion. Pour the beef, onions, water, and tomato soup into the mixture. Add some celery, onions, barley, thyme, and bay leaf.

2. Cover the lid and lock it. Pick "Feature Soup," set the timer to 30 minutes. Allow pressure to build for 10-15 minutes.

3. The release pressure is about 10 minutes using the natural-release method as instructed by the manufacturer.

Hearty Italian Meatball Soup

(Ready in 30 Minutes, Serve 8, Difficulty: Easy)

Nutrition per Serving:

Calories 127, Protein 16.7 g, Carbohydrates 30.8 g, Fat 8.9 g, Cholesterol 49.3mg, Sodium 498.1mg.

Ingredients:

- 3 cups of water
- 2(14 ounces) cans diced tomatoes with onion and garlic, undrained
- 2(14 ounces) cans of beef broth
- 1 teaspoon of Italian seasoning
- 1(16 ounces) package of frozen cooked Italian-style meatballs
- 2 cups of frozen Italian-blend vegetables
- 1 cup of small star-shaped dried pasta
- ¼ cup of grated parmesan cheese

Instructions:

1. Stir together the water, onions, beef broth, and Italian seasoning in a large pot and bring to a boil. Cover the oven with meatballs, Italian-blended vegetables, and pasta.

2. Return the broth to a boil, reduce the heat to medium-low, and cook for around 10 minutes until the meatballs are hot and the pasta is tender. Garnish with parmesan cheese and ladle broth in bowls.

Beef Noodle Soup

(Ready in 50 Minutes, Serve 6, Difficulty: Normal)

Nutrition per Serving:

Calories 377, Protein 25.5 g, Carbohydrates 24.8 g, Fat 19.4 g 3, Cholesterol 89.3mg 3, Sodium 1039.7mg.

Ingredients:

- 453 g of cubed beef stew meat
- 1 cup of chopped onion
- 1 cup of chopped celery
- ¼ cup of beef bouillon granules
- ¼ teaspoon of dried parsley
- 1 pinch of ground black pepper
- 1 cup of chopped carrots
- 5 ¾ cups of water
- 2 ½ cups of frozen egg noodles

Instructions:

1. Sauté the stew beef, onion, and celery in a large saucepan over medium-high heat for 5 minutes or until the meat is browned on all sides.

2. Add the bouillon, parsley, carrots, ground black pepper, and pasta with water and eggs. Bring it to a boil, bring it to low heat, and cook for 30 minutes.

California Italian Wedding Soup

(Ready in 25 Minutes, Serve 6, Difficulty: Easy)

Nutrition per Serving:

Calories 159, Protein 11.5 g, Carbohydrates 15.4 g, Fat 5.6 g, Cholesterol 55.3mg, Sodium 98.6mg.

Ingredients:

- 226 g of extra-lean ground beef
- 1 egg, lightly beaten
- 2 tablespoons of Italian-seasoned breadcrumbs
- 1 tablespoon of grated parmesan cheese
- 2 tablespoons of shredded fresh basil leaves
- 1 tablespoon of chopped Italian flat-leaf parsley (Optional)
- 2 green onions, sliced (Optional)
- 5 ¾ cups of chicken broth
- 2 cups of finely sliced escarole (spinach may be substituted)
- 1 lemon, zested
- ½ cup of orzo (rice-shaped pasta), uncooked

For Topping:

- Grated parmesan cheese

Instructions:

1. The meat, egg, parsley, bread crumbs, cheese, basil, and green onions are mixed to form 3/4-inch balls.

2. Over high heat, pour the broth into a large saucepan. Drop into meatballs while boiling. Stir in escarole, orzo, and lemon zest. Return to a boil and reduce to medium heat. Cook for 10 minutes on a slow boil or until the orzo is tender, stirring frequently. Serve with cheese.

Vegetarian Kale Soup

(Ready in 55 Minutes, Serve 8, Difficulty: Normal)

Nutrition per Serving:

Calories 277, Protein 9.6 g, Carbohydrates 50.9 g, Fat 4.5 g, Cholesterol 0mg, Sodium 372.2mg.

Ingredients:

- 2 tablespoons of olive oil
- 1 yellow onion, chopped
- 2 tablespoons of chopped garlic
- 1 bunch of kale, stems removed and leaves chopped
- 8 cups of water
- 6 cubes of vegetable bouillon (such as Knorr®)
- 1(15 ounces) can of diced tomatoes
- 6 white potatoes, peeled and cubed
- 2(15 ounces) cans of cannellini beans (drained if desired)
- 1 tablespoon of Italian seasoning
- 2 tablespoons of dried parsley
- Salt and pepper, to taste

Instructions:

1. In a large soup pot, heat the olive oil and cook the onion and garlic until soft. Stir in the kale and cook for about 2 minutes, until wilted. Stir in the water, stir up the water

2. Tomatoes, potatoes, beans, vegetable bouillon, Italian seasoning, and parsley. Simmer the soup for 25 minutes on medium heat or until the potatoes are fully cooked. To taste, season with salt and pepper.

Thai Red Curry Chicken Soup

(Ready in 45 Minutes, Serve 6, Difficulty: Normal)

Nutrition per Serving:

Calories 130, Protein 16.4 g, Carbohydrates 16.8 g, Fat 23.1 g, Cholesterol 36.8mg, Sodium 662.9mg.

Ingredients:

- 2 tablespoons of red curry paste
- 1 red bell pepper, thinly sliced
- 1 small onion, chopped
- 1(14 ounces) can of coconut milk
- 1 tablespoon of fish sauce
- 3 cups of homemade chicken stock
- 2 cups of shredded cooked chicken
- 1 ½ cups of cooked basmati rice
- 4 tablespoons of chopped fresh cilantro

Instructions:

1. Cook the curry paste over medium-high heat in a large, heavy saucepan until the oils are set to release, 1-2 minutes. Add the red pepper and onion and cook for about 5 minutes, stirring, until tender. Stir in coconut milk until mixed well. Add the fish sauce, and then the stock of chicken.

2. Lower the heat and simmer for 15 minutes. Add cooked rice and chicken. Stir over heat until thoroughly warmed. Right before serving, add chopped cilantro.

Ukrainian Red Borscht Soup

(Ready in 1 Hour and 5 Minutes, Serve 10, Difficulty: Normal)

Nutrition per Serving:

Calories 257, Protein 10.1 g, Carbohydrates 24.4 g, Fat 13.8 g, Cholesterol 31mg, Sodium 626.3mg.

Ingredients:

- 1(16 ounces) package of pork sausage
- 3 medium beets, peeled and shredded
- 3 carrots, peeled and shredded
- 3 medium baking potatoes, peeled and cubed
- 1 tablespoon of vegetable oil
- 1 medium onion, chopped
- 1(6 ounces) can of tomato paste
- ¾ cup of water
- ½ medium head cabbage, cored and shredded
- 1(8 ounces) can of diced tomatoes, drained
- 3 cloves of garlic, minced
- Salt and pepper, to taste
- 1 teaspoon of white sugar, or to taste

For Topping:

- ½ cup of sour cream

For Garnish:

- 1 tablespoon of chopped fresh parsley

Instructions:

1. Crumble (if using the sausage over medium-high heat into a skillet. Cook and stir until it is not pink anymore. Remove and set aside from the heat.

2. Fill a large pot with water halfway (about 2 quarts) and bring it to a boil. Stir in the sausage, then cover the pot. Return to a boil. Add the beets, and cook until their color is gone. Add the carrots and potatoes, and cook for about 15 minutes, until tender. Add the cabbage, the diced tomatoes, and the can.

3. Over medium heat, heat the oil in a skillet. Add the onion, then cook until it's tender. Combine the tomato paste and water until well mixed. To the pot, transfer. To the soup, add the raw garlic, cover, and turn the heat off. Let them stand for 5 minutes. Taste, and then season with salt, sugar, and pepper.

4. Ladle it into serving bowls and if desired, garnish it with sour cream and fresh parsley.

Coconut Curry Pumpkin Soup

(Ready in 50 Minutes, Serve 6, Difficulty: Normal)

Nutrition per Serving:

Calories 217, Protein 2 g, Carbohydrates 12 g, Fat 13.5 g, Cholesterol mg, Sodium 600.6mg.

Ingredients:

- ¼ cup of coconut oil
- 1 cup of chopped onions
- 1 clove of garlic, minced
- 3 cups of vegetable broth
- 1 teaspoon of curry powder
- ½ teaspoon of salt
- ¼ teaspoon of ground coriander
- ¼ teaspoon of crushed red pepper flakes
- 1(15 ounces) can 100% pure pumpkin
- 1 cup light of coconut milk

Instructions:

1. Heat the coconut oil over medium to high heat in a large bath. Add the onions and garlic and simmer for around 5 minutes until the onions are translucent.

2. Combine the vegetable broth, curry powder, cinnamon, cilantro, and flakes of red pepper. Cook and whisk for about 10 minutes before the mixture comes to a gentle boil. Cover and simmer for an additional 15 to 20 minutes, stirring regularly.

3. Whisk in the coconut milk and pumpkin and roast for another 5 minutes.

4. Pour the soup into a blender, fill just halfway and if necessary, work in batches, heat until smooth. Return to a pot and reheat briefly before serving, over medium heat.

Avocado Soup with Chicken and Lime

(Ready in 30 Minutes, Serve 6, Difficulty: Easy)

Nutrition per Serving:

Calories 129, Protein 16.5 g, Carbohydrates 24.9 g, Fat 15.3 g, Cholesterol 37.3mg, Sodium 1047.6mg.

Ingredients:

- 4(6 inches) of corn tortillas, julienned
- 1 ½ tablespoon of olive oil
- 1 white onion, sliced thinly
- 8 cloves of garlic, thinly sliced
- 4 fresh jalapeno peppers, sliced
- 8 ounces of skinless, boneless chicken breast halves, cut into thin strips
- 1 quart of chicken broth
- ¼ cup of fresh lime juice
- 1 tomato, seeded and diced
- Salt and ground black pepper, to taste
- 1 avocado, peeled, pitted, and diced
- ¼ cup of chopped fresh cilantro

Instructions:

1. Preheat the oven to 400 degrees Fahrenheit (204 degrees Celsius). On a baking sheet, arrange the tortilla strips.

2. Bake in the preheated oven for 3-5 minutes, until finely browned.

3. Heat oil over low heat in a large saucepan. In oil, fry the onion, garlic, and jalapenos for 4-5 minutes until lightly browned.

4. Stir in the chicken, lime juice, chicken broth, onion, salt, and pepper. Simmer gently for about 10 minutes until the chicken is no longer pink.

5. Stir in the cilantro and avocado and heat for 3-5 minutes. Change the seasonings according to taste.

6. Sprinkle with tortilla strips to serve. Ladle broth into cups.

Vegan Red Lentil Soup

(Ready in 55 Minutes, Serve 4, Difficulty: Normal)

Nutrition per Serving:

Calories 130, Protein 13 g, Carbohydrates 34.2 g, Fat 14.6 g, Cholesterol 0mg, Sodium 80.9mg.

Ingredients:

- 1 tablespoon of peanut oil
- 1 small onion, chopped
- 1 tablespoon of minced fresh ginger root
- 1 clove of garlic, chopped
- 1 pinch of fenugreek seeds
- 1 cup of dry red lentils
- 1 cup of butternut squash, peeled, seeded, and cubed
- ⅓ cup of finely chopped fresh cilantro
- 2 cups of water
- ½ (14 ounces) of can coconut milk
- 2 tablespoons of tomato paste
- 1 teaspoon of curry powder
- 1 pinch of cayenne pepper
- 1 pinch of ground nutmeg
- Salt and pepper, to taste

Instructions:

1. Heat the oil and cook the ginger, garlic, onion, and fenugreek in a large pot over medium heat until the onion is tender.

2. Mix in the pot with the lentils, squash, and cilantro. Add the water, coconut milk, and tomato paste and stir. Use curry powder, nutmeg, cayenne pepper, salt, and pepper to season.

3. Bring to a boil, reduce heat to low, and simmer for 30 minutes or until tender with lentils and squash.

Spicy Chipotle Sweet Potato Soup

(Ready in 55 Minutes, Serve 8, Difficulty: Normal)

Nutrition per Serving:

Calories 113, Protein 5.2 g, Carbohydrates 48.7 g, Fat 15.7 g, Cholesterol 33mg, Sodium 501.9mg.

Ingredients:

- 2 tablespoons of olive oil
- 1 large yellow onion, chopped
- 1587 g of sweet potatoes, peeled and cut into 2-inch chunks
- 4 ½ cups of vegetable broth, or as needed
- 1(7 ounces) can of chipotle peppers in adobo sauce, drained
- ½ cup of heavy cream
- 2 limes, juiced
- Salt, to taste
- 1 cup of sour cream
- ½ cup of chopped fresh cilantro, or to taste

Instructions:

1. Heat the olive oil over medium heat in a large saucepan or Dutch oven, cook and stir the onion in the hot oil until softened, for 3-5 minutes.

2. Add the sweet potatoes, bring to a boil, and enough vegetable broth to cover the sweet potatoes. Reduce the heat, cover the saucepan partially, and boil until the sweet potatoes are soft enough for a fork to pierce easily around 30 minutes.

3. Stir in the sweet potato mixture with the chipotle peppers.

4. Using an immersion blender to process the sweet potato mixture until the soup is smooth. Whisk in the broth with heavy cream and lime juice until smooth and cooked through, and season with salt.

5. Serve each serving of soup served with 2 teaspoons of sour cream and a cilantro sprinkle.

Copycat Panera® Broccoli Cheddar Soup

(Ready in 1 Hour and 5 Minutes, Serve 8, Difficulty: Normal)

Nutrition per Serving:

Calories 230, Protein 14.3 g, Carbohydrates 10.7 g, Fat 23 g, Cholesterol 70.5mg, Sodium 624mg.

Ingredients:

- 1 tablespoon of butter
- ½ onion, chopped
- ¼ cup of melted butter
- ¼ cup of flour
- 2 cups of milk
- 2 cups of chicken stock
- 1 ½ cup of coarsely chopped broccoli florets
- 1 cup of matchstick-cut carrots
- 1 stalk of celery, thinly sliced
- 2 ½ cups of shredded sharp cheddar cheese
- Salt and ground black pepper, to taste

Instructions:

1. In a skillet over medium-high heat, melt one tablespoon of butter. Cook the onion in hot butter for around 5 minutes until it is translucent. Only put aside.

2. In a large saucepan, stir together 1/4 cup of melted butter and flour over medium-low heat, simmer until the flour loses its granular structure, and add 1 to 2 tablespoons of milk, if necessary, 3-4 minutes to keep the flour from burning.

3. Pour milk into the flour mixture gradually by continuously whisking. Stir the chicken stock into a mixture of milk. Bring to a boil, cook for about 20 minutes until the flour flavor is gone and the mixture thickens. Add the broccoli, carrots, sautéed onion, and celery and boil for about 20 minutes until the vegetables are soft.

4. Stir in the vegetable mixture with the cheddar cheese before the cheese melts. To taste, season with salt and pepper.

Green Tomato and Bacon Soup

(Ready in 1 Hour and 10 Minutes, Serve 6, Difficulty: Normal)

Nutrition per Serving:

Calories 212, Protein 7.1 g, Carbohydrates 12.1 g, Fat 5.7 g, Cholesterol 13.4mg, Sodium 655mg.

Ingredients:

- 8 slices of bacon, cut into bite-size pieces
- 1 small red onion, chopped, or to taste
- 3 cloves of garlic, minced, or to taste
- 5 cups of chopped green tomatoes

- 3 cups of vegetable broth
- ½ teaspoon of celery salt, or to taste
- 1 bay leaf, or to taste
- Freshly ground black pepper, to taste

Instructions:

1. Place the bacon over medium-low heat in a stockpot, cook and stir until the bacon starts to brown, around 5 minutes. Stir in the bacon with the onion and garlic cloves

2. Cook and stir for about 10 minutes, until the onion is tender. Mix the bacon-onion combination with green tomatoes, celery salt, vegetable broth, bay leaf, and black pepper.

3. Bring it to a boil. Reduce the heat and simmer for about 40 minutes, until the tomatoes are tender.

Hearty Corn and Pumpkin Soup

(Ready in 50 Minutes, Serve 8, Difficulty: Normal)

Nutrition per Serving:

Calories 288, Protein 7.1 g, Carbohydrates 44.3 g, Fat 11.1 g, Cholesterol 7.2mg, Sodium 1819.6mg.

Ingredients:

- 1/3 cup of olive oil
- 2 leeks, white and light green parts only, thinly sliced
- 2 carrots, peeled and diced
- 9 cups of chicken broth
- 5 small red potatoes, diced
- 1½ teaspoons of salt
- ¼ teaspoon of ground cloves
- Ground black pepper, to taste
- 2(16 ounces) cans of pumpkin puree
- 1(16 ounces) package of frozen whole-kernel corn
- ½ cup of whole milk
- 1 tablespoon of minced fresh parsley, or to taste

Instructions:

1. Over medium heat, heat the olive oil in a large pot. In hot oil, cook and stir the leeks and carrots until softened, for 5-10 minutes.

2. Stir the chicken broth into the leek mixture and bring it to a boil. Add the potatoes, salt, cloves, and pepper, and cook for about 15 minutes, until the potatoes are tender.

3. In a large bowl, pour in the pumpkin puree. Stir 1 cup of the mixed broth and potatoes into the pumpkin.

4. In a large pot, pour the pumpkin mixture, corn, and milk into the chicken broth mixture. Stir to combine and simmer, at least 5 minutes, until

heated through and flavors blend. Sprinkle with parsley on individual servings.

Butternut and Acorn Squash Soup

(Ready in 1 Hour and 20 Minutes, Serve 8, Difficulty: Hard)

Nutrition per Serving:

Calories 266, Protein 5.1 g, Carbohydrates 33.8 g, Fat 14.5 g, Cholesterol 42.2mg, Sodium 139.3mg.

Ingredients:

- 1 butternut squash, halved and seeded
- 1 acorn squash, halved and seeded
- 3 tablespoons of butter
- ¼ cup of chopped sweet onion
- 1 quart of chicken broth
- 1 cup of packed brown sugar
- 1(8 ounces) package of cream cheese, softened
- ½ teaspoon of ground black pepper
- ½ teaspoon of ground cinnamon to taste
- Fresh parsley, for garnish

Instructions:

1. Preheat the oven to 350 degrees Fahrenheit (176 degrees Celsius). Place the side-cut squash halves in a baking dish. Bake until tender or 45 minutes. Remove from the heat and slightly cool. Scoop the skins with the pulp and discard.

2. Melt the butter over medium heat in a skillet, and sauté the onion until it is tender.

3. Mix the squash pulp, onion, cream cheese, broth, brown sugar, pepper, and cinnamon in a blender or food processor until smooth. This can be carried out in several batches.

4. Transfer the soup over medium heat to a pot and cook, occasionally stirring, until thoroughly heated. Garnish with parsley and warm to serve.

Chef John's Butternut Bisque

(Ready in 50 Minutes, Serve 6, Difficulty: Normal)

Nutrition per Serving:

Calories 213, Protein 3.2 g, Carbohydrates 27.1 g, Fat 13.7 g, Cholesterol 45.8mg, Sodium 1058.9mg.

Ingredients:

- 3 tablespoons of butter
- 1 large onion, diced
- 1 teaspoon of kosher salt, plus more to taste, divided
- 1(907 g) butternut squash
- 2 tablespoons of tomato paste
- 1 quart of chicken broth
- 1 pinch of cayenne pepper

- 2 tablespoons of maple syrup, or to taste
- ½ cup of heavy cream or crème fraiche
- Pomegranate seeds

For Garnish:

- Some heavy cream or crème fraiche
- Chopped fresh chives.

Instructions:

1. Over medium-low pressure, melt butter in a pot. Put in the onions and a huge pinch of salt. Cook and stir until the onions, around 10-15 minutes, have softened but not taken on any color.

2. Cut off the squash ends. Carefully cut the squash lengthwise in ½ and remove the seeds. Using a potato peeler, peel the squash. Slice into chunks.

3. Raise the heat to medium-high below the pot. In the tomato paste, stir, simmer, and stir until the mixture starts to caramelize and brown for about 2 minutes. Add the potato, 1 teaspoon of salt, chicken broth, and cayenne pepper. Bring to a boil, reduce heat to medium-low, and simmer, 15-25 minutes, until the squash is very tender. Reduce heat to low levels. Blend until very creamy with an immersion blender. Add the cream and maple syrup and if needed, add more salt.

4. Ladle into bowls for serving. garnish with a cream swirl and a scattering of pomegranate seeds and chives.

Butternut Squash Soup

(Ready in 1 Hour, Serve 6, Difficulty: Normal)

Nutrition per Serving:

Calories 230, Protein 6.9 g, Carbohydrates 59.7 g, Fat 6.8 g, Cholesterol 20.9mg, Sodium 1151.4mg

Ingredients:

- 2 tablespoons of butter
- 1 small onion, chopped
- 1 stalk of celery, chopped
- 1 medium carrot, chopped
- 2 medium potatoes, cubed
- 1 medium butternut squash, peeled, seeded, and cubed
- 1(32 fluid ounces) container of chicken stock
- Salt and freshly ground black pepper, to taste

Instructions:

1. In a large pot, melt the butter and fry the onion, potatoes, celery, carrot, and squash for 5 minutes, or until lightly browned. To cover the vegetables, add plenty of chicken stock. Bring it to a boil. Reduce the flame, cover the pot, and simmer for 40 minutes or until all the vegetables are tender.

2. In a blender, pass the soup and blend until creamy.

3. To achieve the desired consistency, return to the pot and blend in any remaining stock. With salt and pepper, season.

Carrot and Ginger Soup

(Ready in 55 Minutes, Serve 6, Difficulty: Normal)

Nutrition per Serving:

Calories 246, Protein 3.5 g, Carbohydrates 33.8 g, Fat 12.8 g, Cholesterol 20.4mg, Sodium 171.7mg.

Ingredients:

- ½ medium butternut squash
- 2 tablespoons of olive oil
- 1 onion, diced
- 453 g of carrots, peeled and diced
- 3 cloves of garlic, crushed or to taste
- 1(2 inches) piece of fresh ginger, peeled and thinly sliced
- 4 cups of water
- Salt and pepper, to taste
- 1 pinch of ground cinnamon
- ¼ cup of heavy cream (Optional)

Instructions:

1. The oven should be preheated to 350 degrees Fahrenheit (176 degrees Celsius). Scoop the seeds from ½ of the butternut squash and place the cut side down on a greased baking sheet. Bake in the oven for 30-40 minutes or until tender. Allow to cool, then with a large spoon, scoop the squash flesh out of the skin and set aside. Discard the skin.

2. Over medium heat, heat the olive oil in a large saucepan or soup pot. Add the chopped onion and garlic and cook until the onion is translucent, stirring well. Add the squash, carrots, and ginger and pour in the water. Bring to a boil and cook until the carrots and ginger are tender, for at least 20 minutes or until tender.

3. In a mixer, or with an immersion blender, purée the mixture. If necessary, add boiling water to thin it but keep in mind that this is meant to be a thick creamy soup. Send the soup back to the tub, and heat through it. Use salt, pepper, and cinnamon to season.

4. Ladle into serving bowls and as a garnish, if desired, pour a small swirl of cream over the end.

Creamy Italian White Bean Soup

(Ready in 50 Minutes, Serve 4, Difficulty: Normal)

Nutrition per Serving:

Calories 124, Protein 12 g, Carbohydrates 38.1 g, Fat 4.9 g, Cholesterol 2.4mg, Sodium 1014.4mg.

Ingredients:

- 1 tablespoon of vegetable oil

- 1 onion, chopped

- 1 stalk of celery, chopped

- 1 clove of garlic, minced

- 2(16 ounces) cans of white kidney beans, rinsed and drained

- 1(14 ounces) can of chicken broth

- ¼ teaspoon of ground black pepper

- ⅛ teaspoon of dried thyme

- 2 cups of water

- 1 bunch of fresh spinach, rinsed and thinly sliced

- 1 tablespoon of lemon juice.

Instructions:

1. Heat the oil in a large saucepan. In olive oil, fry the onion and celery for 5-8 minutes or until tender. Add the garlic and fry, constantly stirring, for 30 seconds. Add the rice, chicken broth, pepper, thyme, and 2 cups of water and blend well. Bring to a boil, reduce the heat and cook for 15 minutes, then simmer.

2. Remove 2 cups of the bean and vegetable mixture from the soup with a slotted spoon and set it aside.

3. Combine remaining soup in small batches in the blender at low speed until smooth (it helps remove the centerpiece of the blender cover to allow steam to escape.) Until blended, pour soup back into the stockpot and mix in the reserved beans.

4. Bring it to a boil, stirring regularly. Add the spinach and simmer for 1 minute or until the spinach wilts. Remove from heat and serve on top of fresh grated parmesan cheese. Stir in lemon juice.

Geneva's Ultimate Hungarian Mushroom Soup

(Ready in 50 Minutes, Serve 6, Difficulty: Normal)

Nutrition per Serving:

Calories 14, Protein 7 g, Carbohydrates 16.2 g, Fat 7 g, Cholesterol 18.9mg, Sodium 573.1mg.

Ingredients:

- 2 tablespoons of unsalted butter

- 2 cups of chopped onions

- 680 g of fresh mushrooms, thickly sliced

- 4 ½ teaspoons of chopped fresh dill

- 1 tablespoon of Hungarian sweet paprika

- 1 tablespoon of soy sauce

- 2 cups of low-sodium chicken broth

- 1 cup of skim milk

- 3 tablespoons of all-purpose flour

- ½ ripe tomato

- ½ Hungarian wax pepper

- 1 teaspoon of salt

- Ground black pepper, to taste

- ½ cup of light sour cream.

Instructions:

1. In a large pot over medium heat, melt the butter. In the butter, cook and stir the onions until fragrant, about 5 minutes. Add the mushrooms and continue to cook for about 5 more minutes until the mushrooms are tender. Mix the mushroom mixture with the dill, paprika, soy sauce, and chicken broth, reduce the heat to low, cover and simmer for 15 minutes.

2. In a small bowl, whisk the milk and the flour together. In the soup, stir the mixture. Add the Hungarian wax and tomato pepper. Return the cover to the pot and simmer, occasionally stirring, for another 15 minutes. With salt and pepper, season.

3. In the soup, combine the sour cream and continue to cook and stir until the soup has thickened, 5-10 more minutes. Remove the pepper and tomato from the Hungarian wax and discard them before serving the soup.

Winter Root Vegetable Soup

(Ready in 1 Hour and 35 Minutes, Serve 6, Difficulty: Normal)

Nutrition per Serving:

Calories 132, Protein 5.2 g, Carbohydrates 40.7 g, Fat 18 g, Cholesterol 22.7mg, Sodium 1786.4mg.

Ingredients:

- 3 parsnips, peeled and cut into ½-inch pieces

- 3 carrots, peeled and cut into ½-inch pieces

- 1 celery root, peeled and cut into ½-inch pieces

- 2 turnips, quartered

- 1 sweet potato, peeled and cut into ½-inch pieces

- 1(907 g) butternut squash, peeled and cut into ½-inch pieces

- ¼ cup of olive oil

- 1 teaspoon of kosher salt

- ½ teaspoon of ground black pepper

- 3 tablespoons of butter

- 1 stalk of celery, diced

- ½ sweet onion, diced

- 1 quart of vegetable broth

- ½ cup of half-and-half cream

- Salt and ground black pepper, to taste

Instructions:

1. Preheat the oven to 425 degrees Fahrenheit (218 degree Celsius).

2. In a large roasting pan, combine the turnips, carrots, turnips, sweet potato, celery root, and

butternut squash. Season with one teaspoon of kosher salt and 1/2 teaspoon of pepper and spray with olive oil. Toss vegetables to spread seasonings equally.

3. Roast in the preheated oven for 30-45 minutes, stirring after 15 minutes until the vegetables are easily pierced with a fork.

4. Meanwhile, over medium heat, melt the butter in a big pot or Dutch oven. Stir in the onion and celery, cook and stir until the onion is tender and translucent, about 5 minutes. Pour in the bouillon of vegetables and put to a boil, uncovered.

5. Combine the roasted vegetables and begin to cook for 10 minutes. Use an immersion blender to puree the broth.

6. Add half and half, and if necessary, season with salt and pepper. Add more vegetable broth if the soup gets too thick.

Ham and Split Pea Soup Recipe-A Great Soup

(Ready in 1 Hour and 50 Minutes, Serve 8, Difficulty: Hard)

Nutrition per Serving:

Calories 237, Protein 25.1 g, Carbohydrates 37 g, Fat 14.4 g, Cholesterol 39.8mg, Sodium 1186.7mg.

Ingredients:

- 2 tablespoons of butter
- ½ onion, diced
- 2 ribs of celery, diced
- 3 cloves of garlic, sliced
- 453 g of diced ham
- 1 bay leaf
- 453 g of dried split peas
- 1 quart of chicken stock
- 2 ½ cups of water
- Salt and ground black pepper, to taste

Instructions:

1. Place the butter over medium-low heat in a large soup pot. Add the cabbage, celery, and sliced garlic and stir. Slowly cook until the onions, 5-8 minutes, are translucent but not brown.

2. Mix the ham, bay leaf, and split peas together. Sprinkle with chicken stock and water. Stir to mix, and cook gently, about 1 hour and 15 minutes, until the peas are soft and the soup is thick. Occasionally stir.

3. To serve, season with salt and black pepper.

African Peanut Soup

(Ready in 1 Hour and 10 Minutes, Serve 10, Difficulty: Normal)

Nutrition per Serving:

Calories 122, Protein 7.4 g, Carbohydrates 23.5 g, Fat 12.2 g, Cholesterol mg, Sodium 558.5mg.

Ingredients:

- 2 tablespoons of olive oil
- 2 medium onions, chopped
- 2 large red bell peppers, chopped
- 4 cloves of garlic, minced
- 1(28 ounces) can of crushed tomatoes, with liquid
- 8 cups of vegetable broth or stock
- ¼ teaspoon of pepper
- ¼ teaspoon of chili powder
- ⅔ cup of extra crunchy peanut butter
- ½ cup of uncooked brown rice

Instructions:

1. Heat oil over medium to high heat in a large stockpot. Cook the onions and bell peppers until well browned and tender. When almost cooked, stir in the garlic to avoid burning.

2. Stir in the onions, vegetable stock, chili powder, and pepper. Reduce fire to medium heat and boil for 30 minutes, uncovered.

3. Add the rice, cover, and cook for another 15 minutes or until the rice is tender. Introduce peanut butter when well combined, then serve.

Slow Cooker Creamy Chicken and Dumplings

(Ready in 5 Hours and 15Minutes, Serve 8, Difficulty: Hard)

Nutrition per Serving:

Calories 238, Protein 17.3 g, Carbohydrates 37.9 g, Fat 18.3 g, Cholesterol 37.6mg, Sodium 1294mg.

Ingredients:

- 4 skinless, boneless chicken breast halves
- 2(10.75 ounces) cans of condensed cream of mushroom soup
- 1 onion, minced
- 2 tablespoons of butter
- 2 tablespoons of rosemary
- Ground black pepper, to taste
- 1 cup of vegetable broth, or as needed
- 2(10 ounces) packages of refrigerated biscuit dough, torn into pieces

Instructions:

1. In a slow cooker, mix the chicken, mushroom soup cream, rosemary, onion, butter, and black pepper and add enough vegetable broth to fully cover the ingredients.

2. Cook for 4 ½-5 ½ hours, on high.

3. On top of the chicken mixture, arrange torn biscuit dough, continue cooking until the dough is cooked through about 30 minutes more.

Caramelized Butternut Squash Soup

(Ready in 50 Minutes, Serve 1, Difficulty: Normal)

Nutrition per Serving:

Calories 189, Protein 2.9 g, Carbohydrates 24.9 g, Fat 10.3 g, Cholesterol 22.9mg, Sodium 788.4mg.

Ingredients:

- 3 tablespoons of extra-virgin olive oil
- 1360 g of butternut squash, peeled and cubed
- 1 large onion, sliced
- 3 tablespoons of butter
- 1 tablespoon of sea salt
- 1 teaspoon of freshly-cracked white pepper
- 4 cups of chicken broth, or more as needed
- ¼ cup of honey
- ½ cup of heavy whipping cream
- 1 pinch of ground nutmeg, or more to taste
- Salt, to taste
- Ground white pepper, to taste

Instructions:

1. In a large pot, heat olive oil over high heat. Cook and stir the squash until thoroughly browned, about 10 minutes, in hot oil. Stir in the squash onion, sugar, sea salt, and cracked white pepper, cook and stir until the onions are fully tender and begin to brown for about 10 minutes.

2. Over the mixture, add chicken broth and honey, bring to a boil, reduce heat to medium-low and simmer for around 5 minutes until the squash is tender.

3. Pour the mixture no more than half full into a blender. Cover and keep the lid in place and pulse a few times before mixing. In batches, purée until smooth.

4. Stir in the soup to serve with the milk, nutmeg, cinnamon, and ground white pepper.

Pho Ga Soup

(Ready in 30 Minutes, Serve 6, Difficulty: Easy)

Nutrition per Serving:

Calories 162, Protein 13.5 g, Carbohydrates 32 g, Fat 5.4 g, Cholesterol 27.5mg, Sodium 148.9mg.

Ingredients:

- 1 tablespoon of vegetable oil
- 1 small yellow onion, chopped
- 1(8 ounces) package of baby Bella mushrooms, chopped
- 4 cloves of garlic, minced
- 8 cups of water
- 1(6.75 ounces) package of rice stick noodles
- 8 teaspoons of chicken bouillon
- 2 cooked chicken breasts, shredded
- 4 green onions, chopped
- ⅓ cup of fresh cilantro, chopped
- 2 cups of bean sprouts
- 1 lime, sliced into wedges
- 1 dash of Sirach hot sauce, or to taste.

Instructions:

1. Heat the vegetable oil over medium-high heat in a large saucepan and cook the onion, mushrooms, and garlic until tender, 5-10 minutes. Add the onion mixture to the broth, rice noodles, and chicken bouillon and bring to a boil. Reduce heat to low levels.

2. In chili, combine grilled chicken, green onions, and cilantro and cook for another 5 minutes.

3. Top with bean sprouts, a squeeze of lime juice, and Sirach hot sauce and transfer soup to serving bowls.

Absolutely Ultimate Potato Soup

(Ready in 50 Minutes, Serve 8, Difficulty: Normal)

Nutrition per Serving:

Calories 129, Protein 12.6 g, Carbohydrates 44 g, Fat 41.5 g, Cholesterol 91.2mg, Sodium 879.4mg.

Ingredients:

- 453 g of bacon, chopped
- 2 stalks of celery, diced
- 1 onion, chopped
- 3 cloves of garlic, minced
- 8 potatoes, peeled and cubed
- 4 cups of chicken stock, or enough to cover potatoes
- 3 tablespoons of butter
- ¼ cup of all-purpose flour
- 1 cup of heavy cream
- 1 teaspoon of dried tarragon
- 3 teaspoons of chopped fresh cilantro
- Salt and pepper, to taste

Instructions:

1. Cook the bacon in a Dutch oven over medium heat until done. Take the bacon out of the grill, and set it aside. Drain the bacon fat from all but ¼ cup.

2. In the reserved bacon drippings, cook the celery and onion until the onion is translucent, about 5 minutes. Add the garlic, and proceed to cook for 1-2 minutes. To coat, add the cubed potatoes and toss.

3. Cook for between 3-4 minutes. Place the bacon back in the pan and add more chicken stock to cover the potatoes. Cover and boil until tender, then cook the potatoes.

4. Melt the butter over medium heat in a separate pan. Whisk the flour in. Cook for 1-2 minutes, continuously stirring. Heavy cream, tarragon, and cilantro are whisked in. Bring the cream mixture to a boil, and simmer until it thickens, stirring continuously. Into the potato mixture, stir the cream mixture.

5. Mash about 1/2 of the soup and return to the pan. Adjust the seasonings according to taste.

Healing Cabbage Soup

(Ready in 1 Hour and. 15 Minutes, Serve 8, Difficulty: Normal)

Nutrition per Serving:

Calories 228, Protein 1.5 g, Carbohydrates 8.6 g, Fat 5.2 g, Cholesterol 0mg, Sodium 435.9mg.

Ingredients:

- 3 tablespoons of olive oil
- ½ onion, chopped
- 2 cloves of garlic, chopped
- 2 quarts of water
- 4 teaspoons of chicken bouillon granules
- 1 teaspoon of salt, or to taste
- ½ teaspoon of black pepper, or to taste
- ½ head of cabbage, cored and coarsely chopped
- 1(14.5 ounces) can of Italian-style stewed tomatoes, drained and diced

Instructions:

1. Heat olive oil over medium heat in a large stockpot. Stir in the onion and garlic and simmer for about 5 minutes until the onion is clear.

2. Add sugar, bouillon, salt, and pepper and stir. Bring it to a boil, and add the cabbage. Simmer for about 10 minutes before the cabbage wilts.

3. Stir the tomatoes in. Return to the boil and simmer for 15-30 minutes, stirring regularly.

Ukrainian Red Borscht Soup

(Ready in 1 Hour and 5 Minutes, Serve 18, Difficulty: Normal)

Nutrition per Serving:

Calories 257, Protein 10.1 g, Carbohydrates 24.4 g, Fat 13.8 g, Cholesterol 31mg, Sodium 626.3mg.

Ingredients:

- 1(16 ounces) package of pork sausage
- 3 medium beets, peeled and shredded
- 3 carrots, peeled and shredded
- 3 medium baking potatoes, peeled and cubed
- 1 tablespoon of vegetable oil
- 1 medium onion, chopped
- 1(6 ounces) can of tomato paste
- ¾ cup of water
- ½ medium head cabbage, cored and shredded
- 1(8 ounces) can of diced tomatoes, drained
- 3 cloves of garlic, minced
- Salt and pepper, to taste
- 1 teaspoon of white sugar, or to taste

For Topping:

- ½ cup of sour cream

For Garnish:

- 1 tablespoon of chopped fresh parsley

Instructions:

1. Crumble (if using the sausage over medium-high heat into a pan. Cook and stir until it is not pink anymore.

2. Remove and set aside from the heat.

3. Fill a large pot with water halfway (about 2 quarts) and bring it to a boil. Stir in the bacon, then cover the oven. Return to the boil. Add the beets, and cook until their color is gone. Add the carrots and potatoes, and simmer for about 15 minutes, until tender. Add the cabbage, the sliced tomatoes, and the can.

4. Over medium heat, heat the oil in a pan. Add the onion, then roast until it's tender. Add the tomato paste and water until well combined. Transfer the pot to the broth, add the raw garlic, cover, and turn the heat off. Let stand for 5 minutes. Taste, and then season with salt, sugar, and pepper.

5. Ladle it into serving bowls and if desired, garnish it with sour cream and fresh parsley.

Fresh Asparagus Soup

(Ready in 30 Minutes, Serve 4, Difficulty: Easy)

Nutrition per Serving:

Calories 167, Protein 9.7 g, Carbohydrates 18.7 g, Fat 6.7 g, Cholesterol 15mg, Sodium 966.8mg.

Ingredients:

- 453 g of fresh asparagus
- ¾ cup of chopped onion
- ½ cup of vegetable broth
- 1 tablespoon of butter
- 2 tablespoons of all-purpose flour
- 1 teaspoon of salt
- 1 pinch of ground black pepper
- 1 ¼ cups of vegetable broth
- 1 cup of soy milk
- ½ cup of yogurt
- 1 teaspoon of lemon juice
- ¼ cup of grated parmesan cheese

Instructions:

1. In a saucepan with 1/2 cup vegetable broth, put the asparagus and onion. Bring the broth to a boil, reduce the heat, and let the vegetables cook until tender.

2. For garnish, reserve a few asparagus tips. In an electric mixer, put the remaining vegetable mixture and puree until smooth.

3. In the pan that was used for simmering the asparagus and onions, melt the butter. While the starch, salt, and pepper are sprinkled into the sugar, whisk. Do not let the flour brown. Let the mixture cook for only 2 minutes. Increase the heat and stir the remaining 1 ¼ cup of vegetable broth. When the mixture comes to a boil, begin stirring.

4. In the saucepan, stir the vegetable puree and milk. Whisk the yogurt, followed by the lemon juice, into the mixture. Stir until fully heated, then ladle into bowls. With reserved asparagus tops, garnish. If needed, sprinkle with parmesan cheese.

Southwestern Turkey Soup

(Ready in 45 Minutes, Serve 8, Difficulty: Normal)

Nutrition per Serving:

Calories 218, Protein 13.5 g, Carbohydrates 11.9 g, Fat 9.8 g, Cholesterol 32.5mg, Sodium 632mg.

Ingredients:

- 1 ½ cups of shredded cooked turkey
- 4 cups of vegetable broth
- 1(28 ounces) can of whole peeled tomatoes
- 1(4 ounces) can of chopped green Chile peppers
- 2 Roman (plum) tomatoes, chopped
- 1 onion, chopped
- 2 cloves of garlic, crushed
- 1 tablespoon of lime juice
- ½ teaspoon of cayenne pepper
- ½ teaspoon of ground cumin
- Salt and pepper, to taste

- 1 avocado, peeled, pitted, and diced
- ½ teaspoon of dried cilantro
- 1 cup of shredded Monterey Jack cheese.

Instructions:

1. Combine the turkey, broth, dried tomatoes, fresh tomatoes, green chilies, ginger, garlic, and lime juice in a large pot over medium heat. Use cayenne, cinnamon, and pepper to season. Bring it to a boil, reduce the flame, and simmer for 15 to 20 minutes.

2. Add the cilantro and avocado and boil for 15 to 20 minutes, until lightly thickened. Spoon into bowls for cooking, then finish with melted cheese.

Cheese Soup with Broccoli

(Ready in 1 Hour and 5 Minutes, Serve 7, Difficulty: Normal)

Nutrition per Serving:

Calories 349, Protein 20.8 g, Carbohydrates 22.8 g, Fat 19.5 g, Cholesterol 38.4mg, Sodium 1538.3mg.

Ingredients:

- 1 onion, chopped
- 6 tablespoons of margarine
- ⅓ cup of all-purpose flour
- Salt and pepper, to taste
- 4 cups of milk
- 3 cups of chicken broth
- 1 carrot, shredded
- 1 cup of broccoli florets
- ½ cup of chopped celery
- 453 g of processed cheese food (e.g., Velveeta®), cubed

Instructions:

1. Cook the onions in the butter or margarine until tender in a large saucepan over medium-high heat. Stir in the flour, salt, and pepper to taste.

2. Until smooth, blend. Slowly add the cream until the mixture is thick and bubbling.

3. Bring the chicken broth to a boil in a smaller saucepan. Add the carrot, broccoli, and celery. Cook for approximately 5 minutes, or until tender. Combine the mixture of the broth with the mixture of the milk and whisk until thoroughly mixed.

4. Put some cheese. Allow the soup to heat until the cheese is melted over medium heat. Important: Do not let the soup boil because the soup becomes separated and curdled by the cheese. Serve warm and enjoy it!

Cabbage Fat-Burning Soup

(Ready in 45 Minutes, Serve 1, Difficulty: Normal)

Nutrition per Serving:

Calories 290, Protein 4 g, Carbohydrates 20.7 g, Fat 0.5 g, Cholesterol 0mg, Sodium 483.1mg.

Ingredients:

- 5 carrots, chopped
- 3 onions, chopped
- 2(16 ounces) cans of whole peeled tomatoes, with liquid
- 1 large head cabbage, chopped
- 1(1 ounce) envelope of dry onion soup mix
- 1(15 ounces) can of cut green beans, drained
- 2 quarts of tomato juice
- 2 green bell peppers, diced
- 10 stalks of celery, chopped
- 1(14 ounces) can of beef broth

Instructions:

1. Place the chicken breasts in a stockpot or Dutch oven with the broth. Bring to a boil and simmer for 20 minutes or until the chicken is fully cooked. To cool, remove the chicken from the broth and set it aside.

2. In the pot, place the leeks and carrots and simmer for 10 minutes, or until tender. Into bite-sized bits, shred the cooled chicken and return it to the pot.

3. Add the noodles to the cabbage and egg and simmer for another 5 minutes or until the noodles are tender. Like a stew, the broth should be thick.

4. Serve hot with Thai chili sauce and season to taste.

Spanish Garlic Soup

(Ready in 35 Minutes, Serve 6, Difficulty: Easy)

Nutrition per Serving:

Calories 118, Protein 2.4 g, Carbohydrates 10.9 g, Fat 7.9 g, Cholesterol 1.1mg, Sodium 1053.2mg.

Ingredients:

- 2 tablespoons of olive oil
- 1 head garlic, peeled and lightly crushed
- 6 cups of chicken stock
- 2 carrots, cut into matchsticks
- 1 red bell pepper, thinly sliced
- Salt and pepper, to taste

Instructions:

1. Heat oil over low heat in a large saucepan. Stir in the garlic and simmer for about 5 minutes, until lightly browned. Pour in 1 cup of chicken stock, cover, and allow to simmer for about 10 minutes until the garlic is soft.

2. Mash the garlic into a coarse paste with a fork. Pour in the remaining chicken stock, bring to a boil and increase the heat to medium-high.

3. Add the carrots and cook for 1 minute, then add the red pepper and cook until the vegetables are tender.

4. Before eating, season with salt and pepper to taste.

Chicken Sotanghon

(Ready in 1 Hour and 45 Minutes, Serve 10, Difficulty: Easy)

Nutrition per Serving:

Calories 210, Protein 8.9 g, Carbohydrates 24.2 g, Fat 8.4 g, Cholesterol 29.8mg, Sodium 736.8mg.

Ingredients:

- 2 ½ cups of water
- 1 teaspoon of salt
- 453 g of chicken legs
- 1-ounce of dried shiitake mushrooms
- 8 ounces of bean thread noodles (cellophane noodles)
- 3 tablespoons of olive oil
- 1 onion, chopped
- 2 cloves of garlic, minced
- 1 ½ teaspoon of achiote powder
- 1 tablespoon of fish sauce
- Salt and pepper, to taste
- 2(14.5 ounces) cans of chicken broth
- Green onions, chopped

Instructions:

1. Bring 2 cups of water to a boil in a pot with one teaspoon of salt, cook the chicken in the boiling water until the middle is no longer pink and the juices are transparent, for about 10 minutes. A center-inserted instant-read thermometer can read at least 165 degrees F (74 degrees Celsius). Reserve the liquid, remove the chicken and cook until the meat is separated from the bones and two forks are shredded. Discard the bones and skin.

2. Allow soaking until pliable, around 30 minutes, while the chicken cools, put the shiitake mushrooms in a bowl and pour enough warm water over them to fully cover. Remove and slice from the water and set aside. Place the bean thread noodles in the water and if needed, add more warm water to cover. Allow soaking for about 10 minutes until tender. Drain. If needed, cut the noodles.

3. Heat the olive oil over medium heat in a pan, cook and stir until the onion and garlic are tender about 5 minutes. Add the achiote powder and begin boiling and stirring until the red-orange color is well covered with the mixture. Stir in the mixture of shredded

chicken meat, sliced shiitake mushrooms, fish sauce, and season to taste with salt and pepper.

4. Cook the mixture for about 5 minutes before adding the reserved liquid from the frying of the chicken and the chicken broth. Bring it to a 5-minute boil. Add the noodles and cook for an extra 5 minutes. Garnish with the green onion that will be eaten.

Curried Zucchini Soup

(Ready in 45 Minutes, Serve 6, Difficulty: Normal)

Nutrition per Serving:

Calories 227, Protein 1.8 g, Carbohydrates 6.3 g, Fat 5.2 g, Cholesterol 0.5mg, Sodium 536.9mg

Ingredients:

* 2 tablespoons of extra virgin olive oil
* 1 large onion, halved and thinly sliced
* 1 tablespoon of curry powder
* Sea salt, to taste
* 4 small zucchinis, halved lengthwise and cut into 1-inch slices
* 1 quart of chicken stock

Instructions:

1. In a large pot, heat the oil. Stir in the onion, then add the curry powder and salt. Until the onion is tender, cook and stir. Stir in the zucchini mixture, then cook until tender. Pour the chicken stock into it.

2. Bring it to a boil. Cover, reduce heat to a low level and simmer for 20 minutes.

3. Remove soup from heat. Using a hand blender or transfer it to a blender in batches, then blend until almost smooth.

Portuguese Chicken Soup II

(Ready in 40 Minutes, Serve 6, Difficulty: Normal)

Nutrition per Serving:

Calories 159, Protein 16.8 g, Carbohydrates 6.8 g, Fat 7.1 g, Cholesterol 49.1mg, Sodium 63.2mg.

Ingredients:

* 1 whole bone-in chicken breast, with skin
* 1 onion, cut into thin wedges
* 4 sprigs fresh parsley
* ½ teaspoon of lemon zest
* 1 sprig fresh mint
* 6 cups of chicken stock
* ⅓ cup of thin egg noodles
* 2 tablespoons of chopped fresh mint leaves
* Salt, to taste

* ¼ teaspoon of freshly ground white pepper

Instructions:

1. Simmer the chicken breast in stock in a large saucepan with the onion, lemon zest, parsley, and mint sprig until cooked, about 35 minutes.

2. Cool, remove the breast, then peel the meat off and cut it into julienne.

3. Strain the broth, bring it back to the pot, and bring it to a boil. Pasta and chopped mint are included. Season with salt and white pepper to taste. Heat before the al dente pasta is cooked.

4. Stir in the lemon juice and chicken julienne, and remove from the heat. Ladle it into soup dishes and cover it with lemon and mint leaf pieces.

Quick and Easy Chicken Noodle Soup

(Ready in 30 Minutes, Serve 6, Difficulty: Easy)

Nutrition per Serving:

Calories 216, Protein 13.4 g, Carbohydrates 12.1 g, Fat 6.1 g Cholesterol 46.4mg, Sodium 1356.8mg.

Ingredients:

* 1 tablespoon of butter
* ½ cup of chopped onion
* ½ cup of chopped celery
* 4(14.5 ounces) cans of chicken broth
* 1(14.5 ounces) can of vegetable broth
* 226 g of chopped cooked chicken breast
* 1 ½ cup of egg noodles
* 1 cup of sliced carrots
* ½ teaspoon of dried basil
* ½ teaspoon of dried oregano
* Salt and pepper, to taste

Instructions:

1. Melt the butter in a big pot over medium heat. Cook the onion and celery in the butter for 5 minutes, until just tender. Pour in the broths of meat and vegetables and stir in the chicken, carrots, noodles, basil, salt, pepper, and oregano.

2. Bring to a boil and simmer for 20 minutes before serving, then reduce the heat.

Curry Red Lentil Soup

(Ready in 50 Minutes, Serve 6, Difficulty: Normal)

Nutrition per Serving:

Calories 300, Protein 20.5 g, Carbohydrates 54.7 g, Fat 12.9 g, Cholesterol 0mg, Sodium 136.9mg.

Ingredients:

* 2 teaspoons of olive oil
* 1 head of cauliflower, chopped into small florets
* 2 carrots, chopped

* 2 cups of boiling water
* 1 cube of vegetable bouillon
* 1(14 ounces) can of reduced-fat coconut milk
* 1 cup of red lentils
* 1 teaspoon of garlic powder
* 1 teaspoon of dried onion flakes
* 1 teaspoon of curry powder
* 1 teaspoon of paprika
* 1 teaspoon of ground turmeric
* ½ teaspoon of ground cumin
* 1 bunch of kale leaves, stems, and inner ribs discarded, leaves coarsely chopped.

Instructions:

1. Heat the olive oil over medium-high heat in a large pot. Add the carrots and cauliflower and cook until softened, 7-8 minutes.

2. Pour in a cup of hot water and vegetable bouillon and whisk until it is dissolved. Add the cauliflower mixture to the broth and coconut milk. Bring it to a boil.

3. In a dish, combine the lentils, onion flakes, garlic powder, curry, paprika, turmeric, and cumin.

4. Cover and leave to boil for about 20 minutes until the lentils are fully cooked and tender. Stir in the kale and let sit for 5 minutes under low pressure. Remove from the heat and serve.

Egg Drop Soup

(Ready in 20 Minutes, Serve 6, Difficulty: Easy)

Nutrition per Serving:

Calories 211, Protein 7.5 g, Carbohydrates 4.8 g, Fat 6.7 g, Cholesterol 191mg, Sodium 1395.7mg.

Ingredients:

* 1 cup of chicken broth
* ¼ teaspoon of soy sauce
* ¼ teaspoon of sesame oil
* 1 teaspoon of cornstarch (Optional)
* 2 teaspoons of water (Optional)
* 1 egg, beaten
* 1 drop of yellow food coloring (Optional)
* 1 teaspoon of chopped fresh chives
* ⅛ teaspoon of salt (Optional)
* ½ teaspoon of ground white pepper (Optional)

Instructions:

1. Combine the chicken broth, soy sauce, and sesame oil in a small saucepan. Bring it to a boil. To dissolve the cornstarch, stir the cornstarch and water together and pour into the boiling broth.

2. If used, whisk gently before mixing in the egg and yellow food coloring. Before eating, season it with chives, salt, and pepper.

Chunky Chicken Noodle Soup

(Ready in 25 Minutes, Serve 1, Difficulty: Easy)

Nutrition per Serving:

Calories 210, Protein 8.8 g, Carbohydrates 13.2 g, Fat 1.6 g, Cholesterol 26.5mg, Sodium 1233.5mg.

Ingredients:

* 3 quarts of water
* 1(32 fluid ounces) container of chicken stock
* 8 cubes of chicken bouillon
* 3 skinless, boneless chicken breast halves, cut into 1-inch pieces
* 4 cups of egg noodles
* 1 cup of frozen peas and carrots
* 2 carrots, chopped
* 2 stalks of celery, chopped
* ¼ cup of chopped onion
* 1 teaspoon of salt
* 1 teaspoon of ground black pepper
* ¼ teaspoon of dried basil
* ⅛ teaspoon of crushed bay leaf
* ⅛ teaspoon of dried oregano

Instructions:

1. In a large stockpot, put the water, chicken stock, and chicken bouillon to a boil. Put in the chicken breast, the egg noodles, the peas and vegetables, the sliced carrots, the celery, the onion, the garlic, the black pepper, the basil, the bay leaves, and the oregano.

2. Continue to simmer for 20 minutes, uncovered. Reduce the heat to mild and cook until the chicken in the center is no longer pink and the noodles are soft, 5-10 more minutes.

Avgolemono

(Ready in 30 Minutes, Serve 4, Difficulty: Easy)

Nutrition per Serving:

Calories 150, Protein 8.4 g, Carbohydrates 21.8 g, Fat 4.2 g, Cholesterol 139.5mg, Sodium 54.6mg.

Ingredients:

* 1 ¾ quart of chicken broth
* ½ cup of uncooked orzo pasta
* 3 eggs
* 1 lemon, juiced
* 1 tablespoon of cold water
* Salt and pepper, to taste

Instructions:

1. In a large saucepan, pour the chicken broth, and bring it to a boil. Stir in the pasta, then simmer for 5 minutes.

2. Add the lemon juice and 1 tablespoon of cold water, then beat the eggs until frothy. Stir the hot chicken stock slowly into a ladleful, then add one or 2 more. Be alert not to scramble through the eggs!

3. Bring this mixture back into the pan, put it off the flame, and stir well. Season with salt and pepper and serve with lemon slices garnished at once. If the eggs have been added, do not let the soup boil, or it will curdle!

Excellent Broccoli Cheese Soup

(Ready in 45 Minutes, Serve 18, Difficulty: Normal)

Nutrition per Serving:

Calories 363, Protein 17.3 g, Carbohydrates 15.2 g, Fat 26.3 g, Cholesterol 80.5mg, Sodium 1180.6mg.

Ingredients:

- ¾ cup of butter
- ¾ cup of all-purpose flour
- 9 cups of chicken stock
- 9 cups of milk
- 1 teaspoon of salt
- 1 ½ teaspoon of white pepper
- 5 cups of fresh broccoli florets
- 680 g of processed cheese, shredded
- 3 cups of shredded cheddar cheese

Instructions:

1. Over medium heat, melt the butter in a big pot and add in the flour. Reduce the heat to a minimum, and simmer for about 2 minutes, stirring constantly.

2. Combine the milk and the chicken stock and season with salt and white pepper. Bring to a boil, bring to low heat, and simmer for about 10 minutes.

3. Bring a pot of lightly salted water to a boil. In the boiling water, put the broccoli and cook for 2 minutes, or until just tender. Remove and set aside from the heat, drain, and set aside.

4. Mix the processed cheese and cheddar cheese gradually into the big pot until it is melted. Mix the broccoli in. Continue to cook for another 5 minutes.

Cajun Scallop Chowder

(Ready in 30 Minutes, Serve 4, Difficulty: Easy)

Nutrition per Serving:

Calories 235, Protein 37.1 g, Carbohydrates 32.7 g, Fat 9.5 g, Cholesterol 91.1mg, Sodium 1398.1mg.

Ingredients:

- 1(16 ounces) package mixed frozen vegetables (broccoli, corn, red pepper)
- 2 tablespoons of butter
- ¾ cup of chopped onion
- 1 clove of garlic, minced

- 1(4 ounces) package of sliced fresh mushrooms
- 1 tablespoon of Cajun seasoning
- 2 tablespoons of all-purpose flour
- 1 ½ cups of milk
- 453 g of scallops, rinsed, drained, and cut in ½
- 1 teaspoon of salt
- ⅛ teaspoon of ground black pepper

Instructions:

1. Place in a pot with enough water to cover the mixed vegetables and bring to a boil until the vegetables are tender around 5 minutes. Drain and set aside.

2. Over medium-low heat, melt the butter in a pot, cook and stir in the melted butter the onion, garlic, mushrooms, and Cajun seasoning until the onion is tender but not yet browned, around 5 minutes. Stir the flour in.

3. Pour in the milk, boil, and stir until the mixture thickens and begins to bubble. Add the scallops, salt, and pepper and continue to cook for 5-7 minutes until the scallops are opaque. Fold the vegetables into the mixture and simmer for-3 minutes before the vegetables are reheated. Immediately serve.

Chicken Tortilla Soup I

(Ready in 40 Minutes, Serve 8, Difficulty: Normal)

Nutrition per Serving:

Calories 377, Protein 23.1 g, Carbohydrates 30.9 g, Fat 19.1 g, Cholesterol 46.1mg, Sodium 943.2mg.

Ingredients:

- 1 onion, chopped
- 3 cloves of garlic, minced
- 1 tablespoon of olive oil
- 2 teaspoons of chili powder
- 1 teaspoon of dried oregano
- 1(28 ounces) can of crushed tomatoes
- 1(10.5 ounces) can of condensed chicken broth
- 1 ¼ cup of water
- 1 cup of whole corn kernels, cooked
- 1 cup of white hominy
- 1(4 ounces) can of chopped green Chile peppers
- 1(15 ounces) can of black beans, rinsed and drained
- ¼ cup of chopped fresh cilantro
- 2 boneless chicken breast halves, cooked and cut into bite-sized pieces
- Crushed tortilla chips
- 1 avocado, sliced
- Shredded Monterey jack cheese
- Green onions, chopped

Instructions:

1. Heat oil over low heat in a medium-sized stockpot. Cook the garlic and onion in the oil until tender.

2. Stir in the chili powder, onions, oregano, broth, and water. Bring it to a boil and let it simmer for 5-10 minutes.

3. Stir in the corn, chilies, beans, chicken, and cilantro. Simmer for 10 minutes.

4. Cover with crushed tortilla chips, avocado strips, cheese, and sliced green onion. Ladle soup into separate serving cups.

Curried Pumpkin Soup

(Ready in 1 Hour and 10 Minutes, Serve 6, Difficulty: Normal)

Nutrition per Serving:

Calories 221, Protein 4.7 g, Carbohydrates 22.6 g, Fat 3.4 g, Cholesterol 5.1mg, Sodium 696.5mg.

Ingredients:

- 4 Macintosh apples, peeled, cored, and chopped
- 1 tablespoon of butter
- 1 onion, finely chopped
- 2 cloves of garlic, crushed
- 1 tablespoon of curry powder
- 1 teaspoon of ground cumin
- 1(15 ounces) can of pumpkin puree
- 4 cups of chicken broth
- 1 cup of water
- 1 teaspoon of white sugar

Instructions:

1. Over medium pressure, melt the butter in a big saucepan. Add the onion, garlic, curry, and cook until the onion is soft and fragrant, stirring regularly.

2. Stir in the pumpkin, apples, broth, water, and sugar. Bring it to a boil, stirring regularly. Cover, and reduce to low heat. Simmer for 25 minutes, occasionally stirring.

3. In a food processor or a blender, blend the soup.

4. Return soup to saucepan, reheat, covered, over low heat.

Lentil and Buckwheat Soup

(Ready in 1 Hour and 55 Minutes, Serve 6, Difficulty: Normal)

Nutrition per Serving:

Calories 122, Protein 7.2 g, Carbohydrates 28.9 g, Fat 10 g, Cholesterol 0mg, Sodium 191.7mg.

Ingredients:

- 1 cup of brown lentils
- 1 tablespoon of olive oil
- 1 small onion, grated
- 1 small carrot, grated
- 2 bay leaves
- 4 ½ cups of low-sodium vegetable broth, divided
- ¾ cup of raw buckwheat groats
- 1(9 ounces) package of fresh baby spinach
- 3 tablespoons of extra-virgin olive oil

Instructions:

1. Soak the lentils for 1 hour in a bowl of cold water. Drain and set aside.

2. Heat oil over medium heat in a Dutch oven or heavy-bottomed stew pot.

3. Add the grated onion and carrot and sauté for 3 to 5 minutes, until tender. Add the lentils and bay leaves and mix until they are oil-coated. Pour 3 cups of vegetable broth into the mixture, stir and bring to a boil. Leave it for 10 minutes at a slow boil.

4. To a boil, reduce heat and add buckwheat. Simmer until soft but not mushy lentils and buckwheat is cooked over 25 minutes, if necessary, adding remaining broth. Remove from the heat and fold until wilted with fresh spinach. Remove the bay leaves.

5. Serve hot on top of each part with a 1/2 tablespoon of olive oil.

Spicy Shrimp Tortilla Soup with Zucchini Noodles

(Ready in 35 Minutes, Serve 6, Difficulty: Easy)

Nutrition per Serving:

Calories 131, Protein 22.4 g, Carbohydrates 10 g, Fat 1.6 g, Cholesterol 174.3mg, Sodium 583.3mg.

Ingredients:

- 1 zucchini
- 2(14.5 ounces) cans of petite diced tomatoes
- 1(14.5 ounces) can of low-sodium chicken broth
- 2 teaspoons of chili powder
- 1 teaspoon of crushed red pepper flakes
- ½ teaspoon of dried Mexican oregano
- ¼ teaspoon of ground black pepper
- 453 g of uncooked medium shrimp, peeled and deveined

Instructions:

1. Cut the zucchini in two and make a ¼-inch deep cut lengthwise on both sides.

2. Cut with a spiralizer into small noodles.

3. In a large saucepan, mix the onion, broth, red pepper flakes, chili powder, oregano, and black pepper over medium-high heat. Simmer the broth, reduce the heat, and cook for 15 minutes.

4. Add the shrimp and the amount of zucchini required. Simmer for 3-5 minutes, until the shrimp is pink. Ladle into soup bowls.

Six Can Chicken Tortilla Soup

(Ready in 20 Minutes, Serve 6, Difficulty: Easy)

Nutrition per Serving:

Calories 221, Protein 17.2 g, Carbohydrates 27.2 g, Fat 4 g, Cholesterol 32mg, Sodium 1482.5mg.

Ingredients:

- 1(15 ounces) can of whole kernel corn, drained
- 2(14.5 ounces) cans of chicken broth
- 1(10 ounces) can of chunk chicken
- 1(15 ounces) can of black beans
- 1(10 ounces) can of diced tomatoes with green Chile peppers, drained

Instructions:

1. Open the cans of rice, chicken broth, black beans, chunk chicken, green chilies, and sliced tomatoes.

2. In a big saucepan or stockpot, pour everything. Simmer until chicken is cooked over medium heat.

Creamy Chicken and Wild Rice Soup

(Ready in 25 Minutes, Serve 8, Difficulty: Easy)

Nutrition per Serving:

Calories 236, Protein 12 g, Carbohydrates 22.6 g, Fat 36.5 g, Cholesterol 135.1mg, Sodium 996.9mg.

Ingredients:

- 4 cups of chicken broth
- 2 cups of water
- 2 cooked, boneless chicken breast halves, shredded
- 1(4.5 ounces) package of quick-cooking long grain and wild rice with seasoning packet
- ½ teaspoon of salt
- ½ teaspoon of ground black pepper
- ¾ cup of all-purpose flour
- ½ cup of butter
- 2 cups of heavy cream

Instructions:

1. Combine the broth, water, and chicken in a large pot over medium heat. Only bring it to a boil, then stir in the rice and reserve the seasoning packet. Cover and Remove from the heat.

2. Combine the salt, pepper, and flour in a small bowl. Melt the butter in a medium saucepan over medium heat. Stir in the contents of the packet of seasoning until the mixture is bubbly.

3. Reduce the heat to low, then whisk in the tablespoons of the flour mixture to form a roux. Whisk in the cream, a little at a time, until smooth and fully incorporated. Cook for 5 minutes until it thickens.

4. Stir the mixture of milk into the broth and rice. Cook for 10-15 minutes over medium heat until thoroughly cooked.

Hungarian Mushroom Soup

(Ready in 50 Minutes, Serve 6, Difficulty: Normal)

Nutrition per Serving:

Calories 20, Protein 7.5 g, Carbohydrates 14.8 g, Fat 13.5 g, Cholesterol 32mg, Sodium 828.7mg.

Ingredients:

- 4 tablespoons of unsalted butter
- 2 cups of chopped onions
- 453 g of fresh mushrooms, sliced
- 2 teaspoons of dried dill weed
- 1 tablespoon of paprika
- 1 tablespoon of soy sauce
- 2 cups of chicken broth
- 1 cup of milk
- 3 tablespoons of all-purpose flour
- 1 teaspoon of salt
- Ground black pepper, to taste
- 2 teaspoons of lemon juice
- ¼ cup of chopped fresh parsley
- ½ cup of sour cream

Instructions:

1. In a big pot over medium heat, melt the butter. Cook the onions for 5 minutes in the butter.

2. Add the mushrooms and cook for another 5 minutes. Stir in the dill, paprika, broth, and soy sauce. Lower the heat, cover it and simmer for 15 minutes.

3. Whisk the milk and flour together in a separate small bowl. Pour this into the broth and whisk to mix. Cover and boil, stirring regularly, for 15 more minutes.

4. At last, add cinnamon, lemon juice, ground black pepper, parsley, and sour cream to taste. Combine and allow to heat over low heat for approximately 3-5 minutes. Do not boil. Serve Immediately.

Thai Chicken Cabbage Soup

(Ready in 45 Minutes, Serve 6, Difficulty: Normal)

Nutrition per Serving:

Calories 227, Protein 20.8 g, Carbohydrates 42.3 g, Fat 3.1 g Cholesterol 61.3mg, Sodium 118.3mg.

Ingredients:

- 3 skinless, boneless chicken breast halves

- 8 cups of chicken broth
- 2 leeks, sliced
- 6 carrots, cut into 1-inch pieces
- 1 medium head cabbage, shredded
- 1(8 ounces) package of uncooked egg noodles
- 1 teaspoon of Thai Chile sauce

Instructions:

1. Place the chicken breasts in a stockpot or Dutch oven with the broth. Bring to a boil and simmer for 20 minutes or until the chicken is fully cooked. To cool, remove the chicken from the broth and set it aside.

2. In the pot, place the leeks and carrots and simmer for 10 minutes, or until tender. Into bite-sized bits, shred the cooled chicken and return it to the pot.

3. Add the noodles to the cabbage and egg and simmer for another 5 minutes or until the noodles are tender. Like a stew, the broth should be thick.

4. Serve hot with Thai chili sauce and season to taste.

Old-Fashioned Potato Soup

(Ready in 45 Minutes, Serve 6, Difficulty: Normal)

Nutrition per Serving:

Calories 338, Protein 10.1 g, Carbohydrates 51.6 g, Fat 10.8 g, Cholesterol 31.3mg, Sodium 857.5mg.

Ingredients:

- ¼ cup of butter
- 1 large onion, chopped
- 6 potatoes, peeled and diced
- 2 carrots, diced
- 3 cups of water
- 2 tablespoons of chicken bouillon powder
- Ground black pepper to taste
- 3 tablespoons of all-purpose flour
- 3 cups of milk
- 1 tablespoon of dried parsley
- ¼ teaspoon of dried thyme

Instructions:

1. Melt butter over medium heat in a casserole bowl. Stir in the onion, cook and stir for about 5 minutes until the onion has softened and become translucent.

2. Place the diced potatoes, carrots, water & chicken soup base in another pot and bring to a boil while the onions are frying. Cook for about 10 minutes, until the vegetables are tender. Do not overcook. Season it to taste with ground black pepper.

3. To create a paste, add the flour to the fried onions. Cook, constantly stirring, for 2 minutes. Add the milk steadily and stir well.

4. Cook continuously until cooked through, stirring over low heat. Add the combination of potatoes and carrots. Stir in the thyme and parsley and heat up. Serve hot.

Spaetzle and Chicken Soup

(Ready in 2 hrs. 20 Minutes, Serve 8, and Difficulty: Hard)

Nutrition per Serving:

Calories 126, Protein 36.3 g, Carbohydrates 45.3 g, Fat 25.2 g, Cholesterol 222.7mg, Sodium 648mg.

Ingredients:

- 1(1360 g) of a whole chicken
- 2(14.5 ounces) of cans chicken broth
- 2 medium yellow onions, quartered
- 1 bunch of celery with leaves, cut into pieces
- 1(16 ounces) package of baby carrots
- Salt and ground black pepper, to taste
- ½ teaspoon of garlic salt, or to taste
- 5 eggs
- ½ cup of water
- 1 teaspoon of salt
- 3 cups of all-purpose flour
- ½ teaspoon of parsley flakes

Instructions:

1. Place the chicken and add enough water to cover it in a stockpot. Pour in the chicken broth and add the onions and celery. Add salt, pepper, and garlic salt to the seasoning. Bring it to a boil and simmer for 1 hour or so to get a healthy broth.

2. Remove it to a plate when the chicken is cooked and tender, and let sit until it is cool enough to treat. Strain the broth and discard the onions and celery. Take the broth back to the stockpot. Strip the chicken meat from the bones, slice it or break it into bits, and add it to the oven. Boil the broth and add the carrots.

3. Then stir together the eggs, water, and salt in a medium dish. Add flour gradually until the dough is firm enough for a ball to form. You can need more flour or less. On a flat plate, pat the dough out. Cut slices of dough from the side of the plate with a butter knife until they are around 2-3 inches long. Allow them to fall straight into the broth that is boiling.

4. The soup is ready until the carrots are tender. Sprinkle with flakes of parsley and serve.

Cheeseburger Soup I

(Ready in 50 Minutes, Serve 8, Difficulty: Normal)

Nutrition per Serving:

Calories 121, Protein 18.9 g, Carbohydrates 18.6 g, Fat 18.3 g, Cholesterol 80.9mg, Sodium 595.6mg.

Ingredients:

- 226 g of ground beef
- ¾ cup of chopped onion
- ¾ cup of shredded carrots
- ¾ cup of chopped celery
- 1 teaspoon of dried basil
- 1 teaspoon of dried parsley
- 4 tablespoons of butter
- 3 cups of chicken broth
- 4 cups of cubed potatoes
- ¼ cup of all-purpose flour
- 2 cups of cubed Cheddar cheese
- 1 ½ cup of milk
- ¼ cup of sour cream

Instructions:

1. In a large pot, melt one tablespoon butter or margarine over medium heat: cook and stir vegetables and beef until beef is brown.

2. Stir in basil and parsley. Add broth and potatoes. Bring to a boil, then simmer until potatoes are tender, about 10-12 minutes.

3. Melt the remainder of butter and stir in flour. Add the milk, stirring until smooth.

4. Gradually add milk mixture to the soup, stirring constantly. Bring to a boil and reduce heat to simmer. Stir in cheese.

5. When cheese is melted, add sour cream and heat through. Do not boil.

Classic Jewish Chicken Soup

(Ready in 4 Hours and 15 Minutes, Serve 1, and Difficulty: Hard)

Nutrition per Serving:

Calories 200, Protein 18.5 g, Carbohydrates 21.2 g, Fat 4.7 g, Cholesterol 48mg, Sodium 283.3mg.

Ingredients:

- 1 whole chicken, giblets removed
- 2 large onions, chopped
- Water to cover
- 2 tablespoons of dried dill weed (Optional)
- 2 tablespoons of dried parsley (Optional)
- Salt and ground black pepper, to taste
- 4 large carrots, peeled and cut into cubes
- 2 potatoes, peeled and cut into cubes
- 2 leeks, diced
- 3 stalks of celery, diced
- 1 large kohlrabi bulb, peeled and diced
- 3 parsnips, peeled and cut into cubes
- 2 tablespoons of chicken bouillon granules (Optional)
- Salt and ground black pepper, to taste.

Instructions:

1. Simmer the chicken breast in stock in a large saucepan with the onion, lemon zest, parsley, and mint sprig until cooked, about 35 minutes.

2. Cool, remove the breast, then peel the meat off and cut it into julienne.

3. Strain the broth, bring it back to the pot, and bring it to a boil. Pasta and chopped mint are included. Season with salt and white pepper to taste. Heat before the al dente pasta is cooked.

4. Stir in the lemon juice and chicken julienne, and remove from the heat. Ladle it into soup plates and cover it with lemon and mint leaf pieces.

Roasted Pumpkin Soup

(Ready in 1 Hour and 25 Minutes, Serve 8, Difficulty: Hard)

Nutrition per Serving:

Calories 357, Protein 4.8 g, Carbohydrates 25.3 g, Fat 28.2 g, Cholesterol 3mg, Sodium 867mg.

Ingredients:

- 1 large sweet potato
- 1 small pumpkin or buttercup squash, peeled and cut into 1-inch cubes (4 cups)
- 3 large carrots, peeled and cut in ½
- 2 large red onions, halved
- ¼ cup of cold-pressed extra-virgin olive oil
- 1 teaspoon of flaked sea salt, or to taste
- ½ teaspoon of ground allspice
- 1 pinch of ground white pepper
- 1 teaspoon of ground nutmeg
- 1 teaspoon of ground cumin
- 1 teaspoon of ground coriander
- 1 teaspoon of ground ginger
- 1 pinch of ground black pepper
- 4 cups of chicken stock
- 2(13.5 ounces) cans of coconut milk

Instructions:

1. Preheat the oven to 350 degrees Fahrenheit (176 degrees Celsius). Wrap sweet potato in aluminum foil, put on an oven-safe dish to collect drips.

2. Bake until smooth in the preheated oven, about 45 minutes.

3. While roasting the sweet potato, put the pumpkin, carrots, and onions in a baking pan. Sprinkle with cinnamon, allspice, and white pepper. Coat with olive oil.

4. Bake in the preheated oven for 30-40 minutes, until tender.

5. When cold enough to handle, peel the sweet potato and squash.

6. Add the carrots, tomatoes, nutmeg, cilantro, garlic, salt, and pepper to a big saucepan. Stir in the chicken stock and milk with the coconut. Bring the soup to a boil, reduce the heat and simmer for about 20 minutes, until fragrant. Remove from the heat.

7. Using an immersion blender, blend until the soup is creamy.

Simple and Delicious Kale Soup

(Ready in 30 Minutes, Serve 6, Difficulty: Easy)
Nutrition per Serving:

Calories 288, Protein 14.7 g, Carbohydrates 43.9 g, Fat 7.5 g, Cholesterol 20.3mg, Sodium 1054.3mg.

Ingredients:
- 1 tablespoon of butter
- 1 small onion, chopped
- 2 cups of chicken broth
- 1 small tomato, chopped
- 3 cups of loosely packed chopped kale
- 1 cup of canned white beans, rinsed and drained

Instructions:

1. Over medium-high heat, melt butter in a pot. Cook the onion in hot butter for 5-10 minutes, until soft. Stir in the onion with the chicken broth and tomato.

2. To near-boil, heat broth mixture and stir kale into liquid before fully submerged. Cook for 3-5 minutes before the kale wilts.

3. Stir the beans into the soup and simmer for another 2-3 minutes, until heated.

Martha's Vegetable Beef Soup

(Ready in 30 Minutes, Serve 6, Difficulty: Easy)
Nutrition per Serving:

Calories 118, Protein 9.1 g, Carbohydrates 14.8 g, Fat 10.5 g, Cholesterol 32.2mg, Sodium 582.9mg.

Ingredients:
- 226 g of ground beef
- 1(14.5 ounces) can stewed tomatoes
- 1(8 ounces) can of tomato sauce
- 2 cups of water
- 1(10 ounces) package of frozen mixed vegetables
- ¼ cup of dry onion soup mix
- 1 teaspoon of white sugar

Instructions:

1. Cook the ground beef for around 5 minutes, or until browned, in a large pot over medium-high heat. Drain out the excess Fat.

2. Stir in the tomatoes, vegetables, sauce, water, blended broth, and honey.

3. Bring it to a boil and bring it to low heat. Cover and simmer for 20 minutes.

Quick Black Bean Soup

(Ready in 25 Minutes, Serve 6, Difficulty: Easy)
Nutrition per Serving:

Calories 223, Protein 16.7 g, Carbohydrates 61.8 g, Fat 4.4 g, Cholesterol 9.9mg, Sodium 2176.5mg.

Ingredients:
- 2(15 ounces) cans of black beans
- 1(15 ounces) can of diced tomatoes with green Chile peppers, drained
- 2(15 ounces) cans of chicken broth, divided
- 1 ½ teaspoon of ground cumin
- 1 teaspoon of salt
- 1 teaspoon of ground black pepper
- ¼ teaspoon of cayenne pepper
- 1(15 ounces) can of black beans
- 3 cups of hot cooked rice
- 6 tablespoons of sour cream, for topping

Instructions:

1. Drain some of the liquid from 2 cans of black beans.

2. In a blender, add two cans of black beans, diced tomatoes with green chili peppers, 1 cup of chicken broth, cinnamon, black pepper, and cayenne pepper, and combine until creamy, then pour into a saucepan.

3. Add the remaining broth of the chicken and one can of black beans. Over medium heat, place the saucepan, bring the mixture to a boil, and cook for 15 minutes.

4. In each of the 6 cups, put ½ cup of hot rice in. Over sugar, ladle soup, and top with 1 tablespoon sour cream.

Amazing Gnocchi Soup

(Ready in 30 Minutes, Serve 6, Difficulty: Easy)
Nutrition per Serving:

Calories 127, Protein 18.1 g, Carbohydrates 33.2 g, Fat 9.4 g, Cholesterol 42.4mg, Sodium 490.6mg.

Ingredients:
- 3 cups of water

- 1 ¼ cups of potato gnocchi
- 1 cooked chicken breast, chopped
- 1 small tomato, diced
- ⅓ onion, diced
- ½ cup of corn
- 1 green onion, chopped
- 2 teaspoons of chicken bouillon granules
- 3 broccoli stalks
- ¼ teaspoon of dried thyme
- ⅛ teaspoon of ground black pepper
- ⅛ teaspoon of salt
- 1 pinch of dried basil

Instructions:

1. Bring to a boil, combine water, gnocchi, ham, tomato, cabbage, maize, green onion, pepper, salt, chicken bouillon, broccoli, thyme, and basil.

2. Reduce heat and boil for about 15 minutes until gnocchi is cooked through and flavors are blended.

Italian Wedding Soup I

(Ready in 50 Minutes, Serve 6, Difficulty: Normal)

Nutrition per Serving:

Calories 216, Protein 27.3 g, Carbohydrates 13.3 g, Fat 14.2 g, Cholesterol 86.8mg, Sodium 1211mg.

Ingredients:

- 226 g of extra-lean ground beef
- 1 egg, lightly beaten
- 2 tablespoons of dry bread crumbs
- 1 tablespoon of grated Parmesan cheese
- ½ teaspoon of dried basil
- ½ teaspoon of onion powder
- 5 ¾ cups of chicken broth
- 2 cups of thinly sliced escarole
- 1 cup of uncooked orzo pasta
- ⅓ cup of finely chopped carrot

Instructions:

1. Combine the beef, bacon, bread crumbs, cheese, and the basil and onion powder in a medium bowl.

2. Shape into 3/4-inch balls.

3. Heat the boiling broth in a large saucepan, stir in the escarole, orzo pasta, diced carrot, and meatballs. Return to boil, then reduce heat to medium. Cook for 10 minutes at a slow boil, or until the pasta is al dente. To prevent sticking, stir frequently.

Cream of Fennel Soup

(Ready in 30 Minutes, Serve 6, Difficulty: Easy)

Nutrition per Serving:

Calories 128, Protein 4.9 g, Carbohydrates 30.8 g, Fat 16.1 g, Cholesterol 56mg, Sodium 835.7mg.

Ingredients:

- 3 tablespoons of butter
- 2 heads fennel, bulbs, and stalks diced into ¼-inch pieces
- 2 leeks, halved, rinsed, and diced into ¼-inch pieces
- 4 potatoes, peeled and diced into ¼-inch pieces
- 6 cups of chicken broth
- 2 carrots, diced (Optional)
- 1 red bell pepper, diced (Optional)
- 1 cup of heavy whipping cream
- 2 tablespoons of anise-flavored liqueur (such as Pernod®)
- Salt and white pepper, to taste

Instructions:

1. In a large pot over medium heat, melt the butter. Add fennel, cook, and stir for about 5 minutes, until fragrant. Stir in the leeks and cook for 3-5 minutes, until slightly softened.

2. Add the broth and potatoes. Bring the soup to a boil, reduce the heat, and cook for about 15 minutes until the vegetables are very tender.

3. Mash the soup until creamy with an immersion blender. Add the carrots and red bell pepper and simmer for about 5 minutes, until softened. Remove from heat. Stir in heavy cream and liqueur flavored with anise.

4. Season with white pepper and salt.

Joe's Homemade Mushroom Soup

(Ready in 20 Minutes, Serve 20, Difficulty: Easy)

Nutrition per Serving:

Calories 227, Protein 8.7 g, Carbohydrates 16.5 g, Fat 15 g, Cholesterol 41.5mg, Sodium 314.8mg.

Ingredients:

- 1 ¼ cup of butter
- 1 large onion, chopped
- 2268 g of sliced fresh mushrooms
- 1 ¼ cup of all-purpose flour
- 2 ½ teaspoons of ground black pepper
- 1 ½ teaspoon of salt
- 10 cups of milk
- 10 cups of chicken broth
- ½ cup of minced fresh parsley
- 1 pinch ground nutmeg, or to taste

- ¼ cup of sour cream, or as needed

Instructions:

1. Over medium heat, melt the butter in a large saucepan. In hot butter, cook and stir the onion and mushroom for about 3 minutes until the onion is tender. Stir in the onion mixture with flour, pepper, and salt.

2. Stream milk and chicken broth into the mixture steadily when stirring.

3. Bring the liquid to a boil and simmer for about 2 minutes, until it thickens. Remove the saucepan from the heat. Stir in the broth with parsley and nutmeg. Bowls of ladle soup and top each with a dollop of sour cream.

Brussels Sprouts Soup with Caramelized Onions

(Ready in 1 Hour and 10 Minutes, Serve 4, Difficulty: Normal)

Nutrition per Serving:

Calories 112, Protein 7.2 g, Carbohydrates 31.5 g, Fat 10.5 g, Cholesterol 13.4mg, Sodium 801.3mg.

Ingredients:

- 1 tablespoon of olive oil
- 3 onions, thinly sliced
- 1 tablespoon of sugar
- 453 g of Brussels sprouts, trimmed and halved
- 1 teaspoon of fresh thyme
- 4 cups of chicken stock
- Salt and ground black pepper, to taste
- ½ cup of sour cream
- 4 dashes hot pepper sauce (such as Frank's Red-Hot®), or to taste

Instructions:

1. Combine the oil and onions over low heat in a pot. Cover and cook for 30-40 minutes, until very tender and smooth. Remove the cover and sprinkle the onions with sugar. Cook, uncovered, 10-15 minutes longer until the onions are light brown.

2. Stir the Brussels sprouts and thyme into the pot. Pour in the stock and add salt and pepper to the soup for seasoning. Bring to a boil, reduce the heat, and cook for around 10 minutes until the sprouts are just tender.

3. Allow the broth to cool. Blend with an immersion blender to a perfect consistency.

4. Reheat gently for about 2 minutes and if necessary, adjust the seasoning.

5. Using a spoonful of sour cream and a hot pepper sauce dash to finish the soup.

Pasta Fazoolander

(Ready in 30 Minutes, Serve 4, Difficulty: Easy)

Nutrition per Serving:

Calories 278, Protein 14.4 g, Carbohydrates 34.9 g, Fat 9.6 g, Cholesterol 18.7mg, Sodium 199mg.

Ingredients:

- 1 ½ tablespoon of olive oil
- 1 teaspoon of tomato paste
- 1 anchovy fillet, chopped
- 4 cups of chicken broth
- 1 cup of dry cheese tortellini
- 1(15 ounces) can of white beans, rinsed and drained
- Salt and ground black pepper, to taste
- 1 pinch of red pepper flakes
- 1 pinch of dried oregano
- 2 cups of baby spinach leaves
- ¼ cup of grated parmesan cheese
- 1 pinch of red pepper flakes, or to taste

Instructions:

1. Heat oil over low heat in a large saucepan. Introduce tomato paste and anchovy fillet and cook for 2-3 minutes, until fragrant and color deepens.

2. Place the chicken broth in it and get it to a boil. Stir in tortellini and beans, cook for about 10 minutes until tortellini is cooked through but still strong to the bite.

3. Add cinnamon, black pepper, one pinch of red pepper, and oregano. Add spinach, cook, and stir for 2-3 minutes, until only wilted.

4. Remove from heat. Garnish with red pepper flakes and grated parmesan cheese and ladle into cups.

Creamy Sweet Potato with Ginger Soup

(Ready in 1 Hour, Serve 8, Difficulty: Normal)

Nutrition per Serving:

Calories 219, Protein 3.6 g, Carbohydrates 22 g, Fat 10.7 g, Cholesterol 37.7mg, Sodium 90.7mg.

Ingredients:

- 2 tablespoons of olive oil
- 680 g of peeled raw sweet potatoes, cut into 1-inch chunks
- 1 large onion, cut into large dice
- 1 tablespoon of butter
- 1 pinch of sugar
- 3 large cloves of garlic, thickly sliced
- 1 ½ teaspoon of ground ginger
- ½ teaspoon of ground nutmeg
- ⅛ teaspoon of cayenne pepper

- 3 cups of chicken broth, homemade or from a carton or can
- 1 ½ cup of half-and-half (or whole milk)
- Salt and freshly ground pepper, to taste
- Garnish, chopped, honey-roasted peanuts

Instructions:

1. Heat the oil in a large deep-frying pan over medium-high heat until it shimmers.

2. Add the sweet potatoes, the onion, then cook, stirring very little at first, and more often, 7 to 8 minutes, until the vegetables begin to turn golden brown.

3. Reduce heat to low and add butter, sugar, and garlic, continue cooking until all vegetables are about 10 minutes long and have a rich spotty caramel color.

4. Add the ginger, nutmeg, and cayenne pepper and cook until fragrant, for a further 30 seconds to 1 minute.

5. Add the broth and, over medium-high heat, bring to a simmer. Reduce heat to low and boil until sweet potatoes are soft, partly covered, 10 minutes.

6. Blend it until very smooth, 30 seconds-1 minute, using an immersion blender or traditional blender.

7. Add enough half-and-a-half to return to the pan (or a soup pot) so that the mixture is soup-like yet moist enough to float the garnish. Taste, and if needed, add salt and pepper. Ladle into bowls, heat through, garnish and serve.

Turkish Soup

(Ready in 15 Minutes, Serve 1-2, Difficulty: Easy)

Nutrition per Serving:

Calories 331, Protein 19 g, Carbohydrates 17 g, Fat 9 g, Fiber 10 g

Ingredients:

- 1 cup red lentils
- 1 chopped carrot
- 1 chopped potato
- 1 chopped onion
- ½ cup celery
- 3 minced garlic cloves
- ½ tablespoon rice
- 3 teaspoons olive oil
- ½ teaspoon paprika
- ½ teaspoon coriander
- Salt to taste

Instructions:

1. Turn "sauté" on your pressure cooker and add oil.

2. While it's heating up, prepare your veggies.

3. Cook the garlic for a few minutes when the oil is hot until it is fragrant.

4. Rinse off the lentils and rice, then put them in the pressure cooker.

5. Add the water, paprika, salt, and veggies to 2 1/2 cups.

6. Close the lid and seal it.

7. Select the "manual" and cook for 10 minutes at high pressure.

8. Hit "cancel," and quick-release when time is up.

9. Let the mixture cool in a blender for a little while before blending.

10. serve!

Pumpkin Chipotle Soup

(Ready in 30 Minutes, Serve 8, Difficulty: Easy)

Nutrition per Serving:

Calories 214, Protein 3.4 g, Carbohydrates 13.3 g, Fat 9.5 g, Cholesterol 24.4mg, Sodium 790.5mg.

Ingredients:

- 2 tablespoons of butter
- 2 tablespoons of all-purpose flour
- 4 cups of vegetable stock
- 1(29 ounces) can of pumpkin puree
- 2 chipotle peppers in adobo sauce, minced
- 1 ½ cups of half-and-half cream
- 2 tablespoons of "sofrito"
- 1 tablespoon of Worcestershire sauce
- 1 teaspoon of salt
- 1 teaspoon of paprika

Instructions:

1. In a large saucepan over medium heat, melt the butter. Stir in the flour and simmer for about 3 minutes before the flour turns golden brown.

2. Whisk and bring to a boil over high heat in the vegetable supply. Whisk until no lumps remain in the pumpkin puree, then add the chipotle peppers, half-and-a-half milk, "sofrito," cinnamon, Worcestershire sauce paprika. Return to a simmer, then reduce the heat to medium-low, and cook until hot and thickened for 8 minutes.

Potato-Parsnip Soup with Crème Fraiche and Bacon

(Ready in 1 Hour and 35 Minutes, Serve 6, Difficulty: Hard)

Nutrition per Serving:

Calories 277, Protein 7.8 g, Carbohydrates 46.4 g Fat 30.9 g, Cholesterol 81.7mg, Sodium 617.8mg.

Ingredients:

- 680 g of potatoes, peeled and cut into chunks
- 453 g of parsnips, peeled and cut into chunks
- 1 onion, cut into large chunks
- 3 cloves of garlic, quartered
- 3 tablespoons of extra-virgin olive oil
- 1 teaspoon of smoked paprika
- 1 teaspoon of salt
- Freshly ground black pepper, to taste
- 1(32 ounces) of carton low-sodium vegetable broth
- 1 pint of half-and-half
- 1 pinch of salt, to taste

For Garnish:

- 1(7 ounces) of container crème Fraiche
- 4 slices of bacon strips, cooked and crumbled
- ¼ cup of chopped fresh chives

Instructions:

1. The oven should be preheated to 425 degrees Fahrenheit (218 degrees Celsius). With parchment paper, cover a rimmed baking sheet.

2. On the prepared baking sheet, spread the potatoes, parsnips, onions, and garlic cloves drizzle the top with olive oil. Use paprika, salt, and pepper to season. Toss until evenly coated and spread back out into an even layer.

3. Roast in the preheated oven for about 40 minutes, until browned in spots.

4. Place the roasted vegetables in a large pot. Cover with vegetable broth. Cook until the vegetables are very tender, about 30 minutes. Bring to a simmer. Remove from the heat.

5. Use an immersion blender to gently blend the hot soup until smooth. Stir in half-and-a-half when well-integrated. Season with salt.

6. Soup with a ladle into bowls. With dollops of crème Fraiche, bacon bits, and chives, garnish each bowl.

Chapter 6: Dinner Recipes

In this chapter, we are going to give you some delicious and mouthwatering recipes on Octavia Dinner recipes.

Citrusy Shrimp-Stuffed Avocados

(Ready in 15 Minutes, Serve 4, Difficulty: Easy)

Nutrition per Serving:

Calories 420, Protein 31 g, Carbohydrates 13 g, Fat 29 g, Saturated Fat5 g, Sodium 430 mg, Fiber 7 g.

Ingredients:

- 1 small shallot, finely chopped
- ¼ cup of mayonnaise
- 3 tablespoon of sour cream
- 3 tablespoons of lime juice
- 2 tablespoons of orange juice
- 453 gramsof chopped cooked shelled shrimp
- 1 cup of grape tomatoes, halved
- 1 Serrano of Chile, thinly sliced
- 2 ripe avocados, halved, pits removed

For Garnish:

- Cilantro

For Serving:

- Sweet potato chips

Instructions:

1. Whisk the shallot, mayonnaise, orange juice, sour cream, lime juice, and half a teaspoon of salt in a small bowl.

2. Put the shrimp, onions, chili, and half of the dressing in a big bowl. Keep it in the fridge for 20 minutes or up to 2 hours.

3. Spoon in the avocado halves to serve and drizzle with the remaining dressing. Garnish with cilantro, then serve with some chips of sweet potato.

Steak Salad with Charred Green Onions and Beets

(Ready in 35 Minutes, Serve 4, Difficulty: Easy)

Nutrition per Serving:

Calories 312, Protein 29 g, Carbohydrates 9 g, Fat 18 g, Sodium 735mg, Fiber 3 g.

Ingredients:

- 1(2" thick) of boneless top loin beefsteak (453 grams)
- 1 tablespoon of vegetable oil
- ½ bunch of green onions, halved
- ¾ teaspoon of flaky sea salt
- 1 ½ ounce of container mixed greens
- ½ small head radicchio, leaves separated and torn
- 4 cooked beets, quartered
- ¼ cup of red-wine vinegar
- 1 tablespoon of extra virgin olive oil
- 2 ounces of blue cheese, crumbled

Instructions:

1. Set up the sous vide unit in the 8-quart saucepot as the package directs. Add water and set the device's temperature to 130 degrees Celsius (266 degree F).

2. Place the steak in a reseal able plastic bag of a gallon size, seal tightly, push out excess air. Place your bag in hot water. Cook for 2 hours. Remove the bag from the water. Take the steak out of the bag and pat it dry.

3. Heat oil to medium-high until very hot in a 10-inch skillet. Add the green onions and cook for 2 minutes or until lightly charred. Add steak to skillet. Cook 2 minutes, turning frequently. Transfer to a cutting board, sprinkle with ½ teaspoon flaky sea salt, and thickly slice.

4. Toss the greens, radicchio, olive oil, beets, vinegar, and 1/4 teaspoon each of the flaky sea salt and pepper into a large cup. Transfer to a tray. Place the steak, onions, and blue cheese on top.

Creamy Corn Chowder

(Ready in 15 Minutes, Serve 4, Difficulty: Easy)

Nutrition per serving:

Calories 224, Protein 14 g, Carbohydrates 66 g, Fat 15 g, Saturated Fat5 g, Sodium 510mg, Fiber 6 g.

Ingredients:

- Roasted vegetables from mustard glazed pork chops
- 4 cup of low-sodium chicken broth
- 453 grams of thawed frozen corn
- ¼ cup of heavy cream
- 2 tablespoon of fresh lemon juice
- ½ teaspoon of salt
- ½ teaspoon of pepper
- Crumbled bacon and thinly sliced scallions, if desired

Instructions:

1. Thyme from reserved roasted vegetables is discarded, and ½ of them are transferred to a large pot. Low-Sodium chicken broth should be added and brought to a boil. Mash until smooth, using an immersion blender (or regular blender).

2. Add to the pot the frozen maize (thawed) and remaining roasted vegetables and bring to a simmer. Stir in fresh lemon juice, heavy cream, salt, and pepper. If desired, serve topped with crumbled bacon and thinly sliced scallions.

Instant Pot Chicken Soup

(Ready in 30 Minutes, Serve 6, Difficulty: Easy)

Nutrition per serving:

Calories 230, Protein 28 g, Carbohydrates 11 g, Fat 16 g Saturated 4.5 g, Sodium 345 mg, Fiber 2 g.

Ingredients:

- One 1360 g-1587 g of chicken, including neck (discard giblets), skin removed
- 2 large carrots, halved
- 1 onion, quartered
- 1 clove of garlic, smashed
- 1 bay leaf
- 4 sprigs of parsley
- Kosher salt
- 1 ½ cup of egg noodles

For Serving:

- Chopped dill
- 2 stalks of celery, halved, plus celery leaves

Instructions:

1. In the electric pressure cooker, put the chicken in a pot, add the carrots, celery, bay leaf, onion, garlic, parsley, 3/4 teaspoon of salt, and 6 cups of water. Lock and cook the lid for 15 minutes at high pressure (12.0). To relieve pressure, use the rapid-release process, then open the lid. Move the chicken to the tub, then the carrots and celery to the cutting board, and let it cool.

2. Through a fine-mesh sieve, strain broth in a pot, discard any remaining solids, move back to the pot, press Cook and carry the mixture to a simmer. Add the noodles and cook for 5-6 minutes, until tender. Then press cancel.

3. Carrots and celery, meanwhile, are sliced into small chunks, and chicken is shredded into large bits, discarding skin and bones. Stir in the broth and serve, if needed, soup sprinkled with dill and celery leaves.

Pan-Fried Chicken with Lemony Roasted Broccoli

(Ready in 35 Minutes, Serve 6, Difficulty: Easy)

Nutrition per Serving:

Calories 316, Protein 44 g, Carbohydrates 15 g, Fat 15.5 g, Saturated Fat 2.5 g, Sodium 375mg, Fiber 5 g.

Ingredients:

- 680 grams of broccoli, cut into florets
- 2 cloves of garlic, thinly sliced
- 3 tablespoon of olive oil
- Kosher salt and pepper
- 4 6-0unces of skinless-boneless chicken breast
- 1 cup of all-purpose flour
- 1 lemon, cut into ½-inch pieces
- 2 tablespoon of lemon juice

Instructions:

1. Heat the oven to 425 degrees Fahrenheit (218 degree Celsius). Toss the broccoli and garlic with 1 tablespoon of oil on the rimmed baking sheet. Roast for 10 minutes and add 1/4 teaspoon of salt and pepper each.

2. Meanwhile, season with 1/4 teaspoon of salt and pepper, chicken breasts to even thickness, then coat in flour. Heat 1 tablespoon of oil in a large skillet over medium-high heat and cook 3-5 minutes per side of chicken until golden brown. Nestle chicken in the center of broccoli and roast for about 6 minutes until chicken is cooked through and broccoli is golden brown and tender.

3. Return the skillet to medium heat, add the remaining tablespoons of oil, then the lemon bits, and cook for 3 minutes, stirring, until golden. Add lemon juice and 1/3 cup water and cook any browned pieces, stirring and scraping. Spoon and serve with broccoli over chicken.

4. Prepare and store the broccoli and lemons for up to 2 days before cooking.

Rustic Smoky Glazed Chicken & Veggie Bake

(Ready in 45 Minutes, Serve 6, Difficulty: Easy)

Nutrition per Serving:

Calories 270, Protein 18 g, Carbohydrate 23 g, Total Fat 13 g, Saturated Fat 3 g, Sodium 440mg.

Ingredients:

- 2 teaspoons of smoked paprika
- 2 teaspoons of ground cumin
- ½ teaspoon of pepper
- Extra-virgin olive oil
- Kosher salt
- 453 gramsof potatoes
- ½ pound of carrots
- 113 grams of Brussels sprouts
- 113 grams of onion
- 113 grams of halved mushrooms
- 113 grams of asparagus, cut up
- 113 grams of whole green beans
- 680 grams of chicken pieces

- Chopped parsley, for serving.

For Serving:

- Lemon wedges

Instructions:

1. Preheat the oven to 450 degrees Fahrenheit (232 Celsius). Combine the paprika, and pepper.

2. Combine 2 tablespoons of olive oil, 1/3 rub, and 1/2 teaspoon of salt with potatoes, Brussels sprouts, carrots, and onion on a large rimmed baking sheet. Roast for 10 min.

3. Toss 2 teaspoons of olive oil and one-third of the asparagus, mushrooms, and green beans into another baking dish. Push the pan to one side. Arrange the chicken bits on the other hand. Sprinkle with the rub that remains.

4. Season the Protein and veggies with 1/2 teaspoon of salt. Roast both pans for 20-35 minutes or until all vegetables are softened, and the chicken is cooked (transfer chicken from pan to platter if cooked before veggies are tender). Garnish it with parsley and a squeeze of lemon to serve.

Chicken Souvlaki Skewers

(Ready in 25 Minutes, Serve 6, Difficulty: Easy)

Nutrition per Serving:

Calories 231, Protein 30 g, Carbohydrates 42 g, Fat 14 g, Saturated Fat 2 g, Sodium 750 mg, Fiber 5 g.

Ingredients:

- 453 gramsof skinless, boneless chicken breasts, cut into 1" chunks
- 3 tablespoon of olive oil
- ½ teaspoon of ground coriander
- ½ teaspoon of. dried oregano
- 1 pot of grape tomatoes
- 2 cloves of garlic, chopped
- 3 tablespoons of fresh lemon juice
- ½ head of romaine lettuce, shredded
- 4 green onions, thinly sliced
- ½ cup of chopped dill
- 4 pitas, warmed

For Serving:

- Lemon wedges

Instructions:

1. Heat grill on medium-high. Toss chicken with one tablespoon of oil, then kosher salt and pepper with coriander, oregano, and 1/4 teaspoon each. Onto the skewers with thread.

2. On a large piece of heavy-duty foil, put the tomatoes and garlic cloves Sprinkle each with 1/4 teaspoon of kosher salt and pepper and one tablespoon oil. To shape a pouch, fold and crimp the foil.

3. Place pouch and skewers on the grill. Cook for 8-10 minutes, turning the pouch and turning the skewers periodically until the chicken is cooked. Brush the chicken with one tablespoon of lemon juice just before removing it from the grill.

4. Meanwhile, toss the broccoli, onions, and dill in the bowl with the remaining two tablespoons of lemon juice, one tablespoon of oil, and 1/4 teaspoon of kosher salt and pepper each.

5. Serve pitas and lemon with chicken, tomatoes, and salad.

Chicken Bolognese

(Ready in 20 Minutes, Serve 6, Difficulty: Easy)

Nutrition per Serving:

Calories 326, Protein 6 g, Carbohydrates 68 g, Fat 17 g, Saturated Fat 5 g, Sodium 510 mg, Fiber 4 g.

Ingredients:

- 12 ounces of mezze rigatoni
- 1 tablespoon of olive oil
- 2 cloves of garlic, pressed
- 453 gramsof ground chicken
- ½ teaspoon of red pepper flakes
- Kosher salt and pepper
- ½ cup of dry white wine
- ½ cup of low-sodium chicken broth
- 1 tablespoon of finely grated lemon zest
- ½ cup of finely grated Parmesan cheese
- ¾ cup of chopped flat-leaf parsley
- 1 tablespoon of chopped tarragon
- ¼ cup of chopped chives
- 2 tablespoon of cold unsalted butter (optional)

For Serving:

- Finely grated Parmesan cheese

Instructions:

1. As per package instructions, cook pasta. Set aside 1 cup of pasta water, drain the pasta, and place it back in the pot.

2. Meanwhile, in a broad skillet, heat the oil to medium. Add the garlic and cook until it begins to sizzle, for about 1 minute.

3. Add chicken, season with red pepper flakes and 1/2 teaspoon of salt and pepper, and cook for 4-5 minutes, breaking into very small bits, until almost cooked through. Add the wine and boil until almost evaporated, 2 minutes or so.

4. To mix, add broth and toss, and then bring to a simmer. Fold in the lemon zest, spices, and Parmesan cheese. Remove from heat and if used, add butter, stir and toss until melted.

5. Toss with rigatoni and 1/2 cup of pasta water reserved, adding more if the pasta looks dry. If necessary, top with additional Parmesan.

Salmon with Grilled Eggplant and Chickpea Croutons

(Ready in 1 Hour and 15 Minutes, Serve 4, Difficulty: Normal)

Nutrition per Serving:

Calories 330, Protein 37 g, Carbohydrates 29 g, Fat 19 g, Saturated Fat 3.5 g, Sodium 400 mg, Fiber 9 g.

Ingredients:

- 3 tablespoons plus 1 teaspoon of olive oil, divided
- 1 small onion, finely chopped
- 2 cloves of garlic, pressed, divided
- Kosher salt
- 1 cup of chickpea flour
- 1 tablespoon of lemon zest plus 2 teaspoons of lemon juice
- 2 medium eggplants (about 12 ounces each)
- 567 grams of skinless salmon fillet, cut into 4 pieces
- ¼ cup of plain full-fat yogurt
- 1 cup of mint leaves, torn
- 2 tablespoons of chopped chives

Instructions:

1. Line 4 1/2 with an 8 1/2-inch parchment loaf pan, leaving the overhang on 2 long sides. Heat 1 tablespoon of oil in a medium saucepan.

2. Add the onion, ½ the garlic, and ¼ teaspoon of salt, and cook until soft, occasionally stirring, for 5 minutes. Stir in 2 cups of water and bring it to a boil. Slowly stream in the chickpea flour when whisking and whisk vigorously, off the heat, until mostly lump-free.

3. Transfer the mixture with the lemon zest and puree to the food processor, gradually adding one tablespoon of oil until absolutely smooth. Transfer immediately to the prepared smooth top and pan. Cover and push with a heavy item with another sheet of parchment and another loaf pan. Refrigerate for 30 minutes to 1 hour until it is solid.

4. Meanwhile, heat a medium-high grill. Break the mixture of chickpeas into 1/2-inch cubes. In a small skillet, heat 1 teaspoon of oil and cook for 2-3 batches, occasionally turning, until browned, 3-5 minutes. Transfer to the paper towel to drain.

5. Slice the eggplants 1/2 inch thick lengthwise. Brush the remaining tablespoon of oil with the eggplant slices, season with a pinch of salt, and grill until tender and lightly charred, 3-4 minutes.

Season salmon with ¼ teaspoon of salt and pepper each, add to grill along with eggplant, and grill 3-5 minutes per side until opaque throughout. Transferring to plates.

6. Whisk together the yogurt, lemon juice, remaining garlic, and a pinch of salt in a small bowl. Drizzle the eggplant with the yogurt sauce and sprinkle with the chickpea croutons, mint, and chives.

7. Serve with grilled salmon.

Roasted Tomato & Chive Pizza

(Ready in 35 Minutes, Serve 8, Difficulty: Easy)

Nutrition per Serving:

Calories 335, Protein 17 g, Carbohydrate 45 g, Fat 14 g, Saturated Fat 5 g, Sodium 895mg.

Ingredients:

- Non-stick cooking spray
- 1 large pre-baked pizza crust
- ½ cup of olive tapenade
- 1 cup of shredded Gruyere
- 1 ¾ cup of grape tomatoes
- ¼ cup of mushrooms
- Snipped chives

Instructions:

1. Spray with cooking spray on a large baking sheet. Place the crust on the pizza pan.

2. Using olive tapenade to spread the crust.

3. Gruyere, grape tomatoes, and mushrooms on top.

4. Spray the cooking spray on the top of the pizza. Bake for 20-25 minutes at 425 degrees Fahrenheit (218 degree Celsius), or until the bottom is deeply golden brown.

5. Chives on top.

Grilled Chicken with Smoky Corn Salad

(Ready in 30 Minutes, Serve 4, Difficulty: Easy)

Nutrition per Serving:

Calories 235, Protein 21 g, Carbohydrates 21 g, Fat 13 g, Saturated Fat 3.5 g, Sodium 315mg, Fiber 2 g.

Ingredients:

- 4 6-ounce of boneless, skinless chicken-breast halves
- Salt
- Pepper
- 2 limes, halved
- 4 ears corn, shucked
- ¼ cup of chopped cilantro
- 2 tablespoons of chopped green olives
- 1 ounce of finely grated manchego cheese

- Salt
- Pepper
- 1 ½ teaspoon of olive oil
- 1 teaspoon of smoked paprika

Instructions:

1. To cook through, season skinless chicken-breast halves, boneless, with salt and pepper and grill on medium-high, 5-6 minutes per hand.

2. Meanwhile, grill limes, cut downsides, and charred corn, for 6-8 minutes.

3. Cut the cob corn, toss two lime halves of juice in a bowl, chop the cilantro, chop the green olives, chop the Manchego cheese, and pinch the salt and pepper together.

4. Serve the chicken and the remaining lime halves with the corn and drizzle with the olive oil and smoked paprika mixture.

Red Curry Shrimp and Cilantro Rice

(Ready in 30 Minutes, Serve 4, Difficulty: Easy)

Nutrition per Serving:

Calories 130, Protein 24 g, Carbohydrates 51 g, Fat 11 g, Saturated Fat 6.5 g, Sodium 570mg, Fiber 4 g.

Ingredients:

- 1 cup of long-grain white rice
- 1 teaspoon of grated lime zest
- 2 tablespoons of fresh lime juice
- 1 cup of chopped cilantro
- 1 tablespoon of canola oil
- 1 1-inch piece of ginger (cut into matchsticks)
- 2 cloves of garlic, thinly sliced
- 2 tablespoons of Thai red curry paste
- 1 13.5-ounce of can light coconut milk
- 1 tablespoon of fish sauce
- 680 grams of baby bok choy (4 to 6 heads, trimmed and leaves separated, large leaves halved lengthwise)
- 453 gramsof peeled and deveined shrimp

Instructions:

1. Cook white long-grain rice. Fluff with a fork and fold with cilantro and grated lime zest.

2. Heat the canola oil in a big, medium skillet. Add the garlic and ginger and sauté for 2 minutes.

3. Add the red Thai curry paste and cook for 2 minutes. Add light coconut milk and fish sauce and cook for 3 minutes.

4. Stir in the baby bok Choy and the peeled and deveined shrimp and cook for 3-4 minutes until the shrimp is opaque. Stir in the juice of fresh lime. If desired, serve over rice with additional coriander, sliced red chilies, and lime wedges.

Roasted Garlic-Parmesan Zucchini, Squash, and Tomatoes

(Ready in 40 Minutes, Serve 6, Difficulty: Normal)

Nutrition per Serving:

Calories 152.7, Protein 12.9 g, Carbohydrate 16.8 g, Total Fat 11.7 g, Sodium 442.9mg, Potassium 810.1 mg.

Ingredients:

- 2 small zucchinis (453 grams), cut into 1/2-inch-thick slices
- 2 small yellow squashes (453 grams), cut into 1/2-inch-thick slices
- 14 ounces of flavor-in or small Campari tomatoes, sliced into halves
- 3 tablespoons of olive oil
- 4 cloves of garlic, minced (1 1/2 tablespoon)
- 1 1/4 teaspoon of Italian seasoning
- Salt and freshly ground black pepper
- 1 cup (2.4 ounces) of finely shredded Parmesan cheese

For Garnish (optional):

- Fresh or dried parsley

Instructions:

1. Preheat the oven to 400 degrees F (204 Celsius). Line a sheet of parchment paper or aluminum foil with an 18x13-inch rimmed baking sheet.

2. Whisk together the olive oil, garlic, and Italian seasoning in a small bowl (if possible, let rest 5-10 minutes to allow flavors to infuse into oil). In a large mixing bowl, put the zucchini, squash, and tomatoes together. Pour the mixture of olive oil over the top and toss it gently with your hands to cover evenly.

3. Spread onto a prepared baking dish and spread into an even layer. With salt and pepper, season. Sprinkle the top of each one with parmesan. Roast 25-30 minutes in a preheated oven until the veggies are tender and the parmesan cheese is golden brown. If desired, garnish with parsley and serve warm.

Crunchy Chickpea Kale Caesar

(Ready in 35 Minutes, Serve 6, Difficulty: Easy)

Nutrition per Serving:

Calories 141, Protein 14 g, Carbohydrate 43 g, Fat 22 g, Saturated Fat 3 g, Sodium 870mg.

Ingredients:

- 2(15-ounce) cans of chickpeas, rinsed and drained
- 2 tablespoons of extra-virgin olive oil
- Kosher salt
- Freshly ground black pepper

- ¼ pot of mayonnaise
- 2 tablespoons of lemon juice
- 2 tablespoons of finely grated parmesan cheese
- 1 tablespoon of Dijon mustard
- 2 cloves of garlic, finely chopped
- 1 teaspoon of anchovy paste
- 1 large bunch of kale (tough stems removed), chopped
- 2 small peppers, seeded and thinly sliced

Instructions:

1. Pat a chickpea very dry with paper towels. Toss with olive oil, 1/4 teaspoon of salt, and 1/2 teaspoon of pepper on a rimmed baking sheet. Roast for 30 minutes in an oven at 425 degrees Fahrenheit (218 degree Celsius). Shake periodically, and leave to cool.

2. Whisk the parmesan cheese, Dijon, mayonnaise, lemon juice, garlic, anchovy paste, and 1/4 teaspoon salt in a large bowl. Combine the kale and peppers, then toss to cover. Top the salad with chickpeas to serve.

Roasted Shrimp & Poblano Salad

(Ready in 35 Minutes, Serve 6, Difficulty: Easy)

Nutrition per Serving:

Calories 201, Protein 17 g, Carbohydrate 9 g, Fat 12 g, Saturated Fat 2 g, Sodium 940mg.

Ingredients:

- 2 medium shallots
- 3 poblano peppers
- 1 tablespoon of canola oil
- 2 teaspoons of chili powder
- 4 radishes
- 1 lime
- 1 avocado
- 453 gramsof large shelled, deveined shrimp
- 1 5-ounce of container mixed greens

Instructions:

1. Heat the oven to 450 degrees Fahrenheit (232 Celsius). Medium shallots in slice 2. Remove the three poblano peppers from the seeds, then slice them.

2. Mix the shallots and poblano peppers with 1 tablespoon of canola oil and 2 teaspoons of chili powder on the baking sheet. 20 minutes to roast.

3. Slice 4 radishes and slice 1 avocado thinly. Only set aside. Squeeze 3 tablespoons of juice out of 1 lime and set it aside.

4. Add 453 g of large shelled, deveined shrimp to the baking sheet after the peppers have been in the oven for 20 minutes. Place it back in the oven and roast for 5 minutes. Slightly cool.

5. Combine the shrimp mixture with the sliced radishes, lime juice, 1/2 teaspoon salt, and 1/5-ounce container of mixed greens when ready to serve. On top, add the sliced avocado.

Smoky Vegan Black Bean Soup

(Ready in 4 Hours 50 Minutes, Serve 6, Difficulty: Hard)

Nutrition per Serving:

Calories 132, Protein 14 g, Carbohydrates 51 g, Fat 11 g, Saturated Fat 1 g, Fiber 19 g, Sodium 535mg.

Ingredients:

- 2 tablespoon of extra virgin olive oil
- 2 medium carrots, chopped
- 2 stalks of celery, sliced
- 1 medium onion, finely chopped
- ¼ cup of tomato paste
- 3 cloves of garlic, crushed with press
- 1 ½ teaspoon of ground cumin
- 1 teaspoon of smoked paprika
- 3 cups of lower-sodium vegetable or chicken broth
- 3 cans (15 oz. each) of lower-sodium black beans, undrained
- 1 cup of frozen corn

For Serving:

- Avocado chunks and cilantro leaves

Instructions:

1. In a 12-inch skillet, heat oil on medium-high. Add the carrots, onion, and celery. Cook for 6-8 minutes or until the browning begins, stirring occasionally.

2. Add the tomato paste, garlic, and paprika, all smoked. Cook, stirring, until the garlic is golden and the tomato paste is browned, or 1-2 minutes. Stir in half a cup of broth and scrape off any brown bits.

3. Skillet contents are transferred to the 6-8-quart slow-cooker bowl and beans, maize, and remaining broth. Cover and cook for 4 hours on high or 6 hours on low. Using avocado and cilantro to serve.

4. **Instant Pot Instructions**: As outlined in the step, select the cooking feature and cook vegetables. Add beans, maize, and broth, then. Select the slow cooking function and cook for 4 hours on high or 6 hours on low.

Teriyaki Chicken with Vegetables

(Ready in 25 Minutes, Serve 5, Difficulty: Easy)

Nutrition per Serving:

Calories 139, Proteins 51.4 g, Carbohydrates 25.5 g, Fat 10.4 g, Cholesterol 130 mg, Sodium 1120 mg.

Ingredients:

- 2-3 pound of chopped organic chicken breast

- 12-16 ounces of organic fresh broccoli
- 2 cloves of garlic, you can also use ginger
- 4-5 large organic carrots, sliced
- Pepper flakes, (Optional)
- 2 tablespoons of olive oil

For Teriyaki Sauce:

- 2 tablespoons of chopped ginger
- 1/3 cup of gluten-free, reduced-sodium soy sauce
- 1/3 cup of cold water
- 3-4 teaspoons of arrowroot powder, (or cornstarch)
- 1/4 cup of honey, (or unrefined sugar)

Instructions:

1. The Teriyaki sauce ingredients are combined in a small tub. If you only make the sauce for future use. In a small saucepan, heat the sauce until it thickens, stirring periodically, over medium to low heat. About 5 minutes. Let the sauce cool and store it in the refrigerator in an airtight glass jar.

2. In a large skillet, add olive oil over medium to high heat. Add the chicken and carrots and cook, occasionally stirring, for about 6-8 minutes, until almost tender. Add the garlic, then proceed to cook for another minute.

3. Place the broccoli on a healthy microwave platter and microwave for 6-7 minutes while the chicken is cooking. You can need less time, depending on how good your microwave is. My microwave isn't too strong, so I use 7 minutes, but 3-4 minutes might be enough in yours.

4. Stir in the chicken and carrots with the Teriyaki sauce from the bowl and stir for around 1-2 minutes or until it thickens. Turn off the heat and when used, add the broccoli and pepper flakes. Stir to combine.

5. Serve over brown rice or knobs of rice.

Wild-Salmon Cakes with Quinoa Salad

(Ready in 55 Minutes, Serve 6, Difficulty: Normal)

Nutrition per Serving:

Calories 250, Protein 33 g, Carbohydrate 52 g, Fat 18 g, Saturated Fat 3 g, Sodium 340mg.

Ingredients:

- 453 gramsof skinless wild salmon, cut into small chunks
- 2 green onions, sliced
- ½ teaspoon of grated orange zest
- Kosher salt
- 2 teaspoons of extra-virgin olive oil
- ¼ cup of chopped fresh basil
- 3 tablespoon of orange juice

- 3 tablespoon of sherry vinegar
- Extra-virgin olive oil
- Freshly ground black pepper
- 5 cup of cooked quinoa
- 5 cup of packed mixed greens

For Serving:

- Orange wedges.

Instructions:

1. Pulse the salmon, green onion, and orange zest in the food processor until finely chopped. Shape into eight cookies. Freeze for 10 minutes. Season with 1/4 teaspoon of salt. Heat 2 teaspoons of olive oil in a medium 12-inch non-stick skillet. Add the cakes, then cook on each side for 4 minutes.

2. Meanwhile, whisk the basil, orange juice, sherry vinegar, 2 tablespoons olive oil, and 1/4 teaspoon of salt and pepper in a large bowl. Add the quinoa and the mixed greens and toss to mix.

3. If needed, serve with salmon cakes and orange wedges.

Mediterranean Baked Cod

(Ready in 20 Minutes, Serve 4, Difficulty: Easy)

Nutrition per Serving (without rolls):

Calories 220, Protein 32 g, Carbohydrate 8 g, Fat 5 g, Saturated Fat 1 g, Sodium 115mg.

Ingredients:

- 1 medium onion, thinly sliced
- 6 ounces of mini sweet peppers
- Salt
- 1 tablespoon of extra-virgin olive oil
- 1 pot of grape tomatoes, halved
- 8 sprigs fresh thyme
- 680 grams of cod fillets
- ¼ cup of water
- Pepper

For Serving:

- Whole-grain rolls

Instructions:

1. Cook onions, peppers, and 1/4 teaspoon salt in olive oil in a 7-8-quart wide-bottomed oven-safe medium-high saucepan for 5 minutes or until onions are almost tender, stirring occasionally.

2. Add the tomatoes and thyme and cook for 2 minutes. Add the cod fillets and broth, and add 1/4 teaspoon of salt and pepper to the cod. Cover and bake for 15 minutes, or until the cod is baked, at 450 degrees Fahrenheit (232 Celsius). Discard the thyme sprigs. Serve with whole-grain rolls.

Grilled Pork Tenderloin with Grainy Mustard Vinaigrette

(Ready in 35 Minutes, Serve 8, Difficulty: Easy)

Nutrition per Serving:

Calories 290, Protein 32 g, Carbohydrates 11 g, Fat 13 g, Saturated Fat 3 g, Sodium 595 mg, Fiber 5 g.

Ingredients:

- 12 ounces of green beans
- 2 tablespoon of olive oil, divided
- 567 gramsof pork tenderloin
- 3 tablespoons of no-salt-added grainy mustard
- 2 tablespoons of red wine vinegar
- 1 small shallot, finely chopped
- 1 teaspoon of mayonnaise
- 6 cups of baby kale
- 453 gramsof grape tomatoes, cut into halves

Instructions:

1. Add 1 teaspoon of olive oil and 1/4 teaspoon of salt to the green beans and place on half of a large sheet of heavy-duty foil. Fold the foil over and crimp firmly to seal. Grill, sealed, for 20 minutes on average.

2. Brush the pork tenderloin with two teaspoons of olive oil and season with ½ teaspoon of salt and pepper. Grill, sealed, medium to cooked 145 degrees Fahrenheit, occasionally turning, for around 18-20 minutes. Let rest for 5 minutes and slice.

3. Mix the mustard, shallot, and red wine vinegar, 1 tablespoon of olive oil, mayonnaise, and 1/4 teaspoon salt.

4. Toss the grape tomatoes and baby kale with ½ of the vinaigrette. Use pork, beans, and remaining vinaigrette to serve.

Lemon Garlic Dump Chicken

(Ready in 50 Minutes, Serve 8, Difficulty: Normal)

Nutrition per Serving:

Calories 255, Protein 36 g, Fat 11 g, Sodium 197mg, Potassium 632mg.

Ingredients:

- 2 teaspoons of minced garlic
- 1/4 cup of olive oil
- 1 tablespoon of parsley flakes
- 2 tablespoons of lemon juice or the juice of 1 whole lemon
- 6 chicken breasts or 8-10 chicken tenders

Instructions:

1. In a 1-gallon freezer bag, put all of the ingredients. I used ½ gallon mason jar with a large mouth to keep the bag upright as I filled it with the chicken and other ingredients.

2. Turn the bag over several times after sealing the bag until everything is mixed and the chicken is well coated. Freeze flat.

3. At the same time, I wanted to make some of these meals to store them in my freezer to be used later. This is my stack of ready-made dump chicken dinners all ready for the freezer!

Option 1–Bake:

Thaw chicken. Pour chicken and marinade into a baking dish, turn chicken to coat. Bake at 350 degrees Fahrenheit (176 Celsius) for 35 minutes.

Option 2–Grill:

Thaw and grill in a cast-iron skillet on the stove, or outside on the barbecue grill, until no longer pink inside.

Option 3–Slow Cooker:

Place the frozen chicken in your slow cooker and cook on low for 6-8 hours (or high for 4-6 hours.)

Insanely Easy Vegetarian Chili

(Ready in 55 Minutes, Serve 8, Difficulty: Normal)

Nutrition per Serving:

Calories 215, Protein 6.8 g, Carbohydrates 29 g, Fat 3 g, Cholesterol 0mg, Sodium 423.3mg.

Ingredients:

- 1 tablespoon of vegetable oil
- 1 cup of chopped onions
- ¾ cup of chopped carrots
- 3 cloves of garlic, minced
- 1 cup of chopped green bell pepper
- 1 cup of chopped red bell pepper
- ¾ cup of chopped celery
- 1 tablespoon of chili powder
- 1 ½ cups of chopped fresh mushrooms
- 1(28 ounces) can of whole peeled tomatoes with liquid, chopped
- 1(19 ounces) can of kidney beans with liquid
- 1(11 ounces) can of whole kernel corn, undrained
- 1 tablespoon of ground cumin
- 1 ½ teaspoon of dried oregano
- 1 ½ teaspoon of dried basil

Instructions:

1. Heat oil over medium heat in a large saucepan. Sauté the carrots, onions, and garlic until tender. Add the red pepper, green pepper, celery, and chili powder and mix properly. Cook for about 6 minutes, until the vegetables are tender.

2. Add the mushrooms and cook for 4 minutes. Stir in the onions, corn, and kidney beans. Use oregano, and basil to season. Bring to a boil, and reduce to medium heat. Cover and simmer, stirring periodically, for 20 minutes.

Caribbean Chicken and "Rice"

(Ready in 30 Minutes, Serve 6, Difficulty: Easy)

Nutrition per serving:

Calories 370, Protein 37 g, Carbohydrates 37 g, Fat 9 g, Saturated Fat 4 g, Sodium 990 mg, Fiber 10 g.

Ingredients:

- 4 cup of riced cauliflower
- ¼ cup of water
- 4 skinless, boneless chicken-breast cutlets
- 2 teaspoon of olive oil
- ¼ cup of sweetened cream of coconut
- 2 tablespoon of hot sauce
- 2 limes, halved
- 1(15-ounces) can of black beans, rinsed and drained

For Garnish:

- Chopped Cilantro

Instructions:

1. Combine rice cauliflower and water on high for 6 minutes, cover with vented plastic wrap, and microwave.

2. Meanwhile, brush the chicken with olive oil and season with 1/2 teaspoon of salt and pepper all over. Grill for 5 minutes on average, turning over once halfway through. Whisk together the coconut sweetened cream and the hot sauce, then brush on the chicken. Grill until cooked through (165 degrees Fahrenheit), brushing and turning 2 more times, about 5 minutes longer. Grill 2 limes, halved, for 2-3 minutes until lightly charred.

3. Toss the black beans and 1/4 teaspoon of salt with the cooked cauliflower. Serve chicken with limes over cauliflower, garnished with chopped cilantro.

Grilled Asparagus and Shiitake Tacos

(Ready in 20 Minutes, Serve 6, Difficulty: Easy)

Nutrition per serving:

Calories 350, Protein 7 g, Carbohydrate 36 g, Fat 21 g, Saturated Fat 2 g, Sodium 445mg.

Ingredients:

- 3 tablespoons of canola oil
- 4 gloves of garlic, crushed with press
- 1 teaspoon of ground chipotle chile
- ½ teaspoon of kosher salt
- 8 ounces of shiitake mushrooms, stems discarded
- 1 bunch green onions, trimmed
- 8 corn tortillas, warmed
- 1 cup of homemade or prepared guacamole
- Lime wedges
- Cilantro sprigs

For Serving:

- Hot sauce

Instructions:

1. Heat grill on medium. Mix the oil, garlic, chipotle, and salt in a large baking dish. Toss to coat with asparagus, shiitakes, and green onions. Grill asparagus for 5-6 minutes until tender and lightly charred, turning occasionally. Grill the shiitakes and green onions for 4-5 minutes until lightly charred, turning occasionally. Place the vegetables on the cutting board.

2. "Cut 2" lengths of asparagus and green onions and sliced shiitakes. Serve with tortillas of maize, guacamole, and wedges of lime, cilantro, and hot sauce.

Cauliflower Chowder

(Ready in 45 Minutes, Serve 6, Difficulty: Normal)

Nutrition per Serving:

Calories 129, Protein 5.4 g, Carbohydrates 16 g, Fat 5.5 g, Sodium 408mg, Potassium 418mg, Sugars 4.1 g.

Ingredients:

- 4 slices of bacon, diced
- 2 tablespoons of unsalted butter
- 2 cloves of garlic, minced
- 1 onion, diced
- 2 carrots, peeled and diced
- 2 stalks of celery, diced
- 1/4 cup of all-purpose flour
- 4 cups of chicken broth
- 1 cup of 2% milk
- 1 head of cauliflower, roughly chopped
- 1 bay leaf
- Kosher salt and freshly ground black pepper, to taste
- 2 tablespoons of chopped fresh parsley leaves

Instructions:

1. Over medium heat, heat a big stockpot or Dutch oven. Add bacon and cook for around 6-8 minutes, until brown and crispy. Transfer to a paper towel-lined tray set aside.

2. In the stockpot, melt the butter. Add the onion, garlic, carrots, and celery. Cook for around 3-4 minutes, stirring periodically, until tender. Stir in the

bay leaf and cauliflower. Cook for about 3-4 minutes, stirring periodically, until barely crisp-tender.

3. Whisk in the flour for around 1 minute, until lightly browned. Gradually whisk in the chicken broth and milk and cook for around 3-4 minutes, whisking continuously, until slightly thickened.

4. Bring to a boil, reduce heat and simmer until tender, around 12-15 minutes, and season to taste with salt and pepper. If the chowder is too thick, add more milk until the desired consistency is achieved, if necessary.

5. Serve immediately, garnished, if desired, with bacon and parsley.

Tuna Poke Bowl Recipe

(Ready in 20 Minutes, Serve 6, Difficulty: Easy)
Nutrition per Serving:
Calories 200, Protein 29 g, Carbohydrate 7 g, Fat 5 g, Saturated Fat 1 g, Sodium 905 mg.

Ingredients:
- 1 tablespoon plus 1 teaspoon of low-sodium soy sauce
- 1 tablespoon plus 1 teaspoon of toasted sesame oil
- ¼ sweet onion, thinly sliced
- 3 scallions, thinly sliced
- Kosher salt
- 453 grams of fresh sushi-grade ahi tuna, cut into 1-inch cubes
- 1 Persian cucumber, thinly sliced
- 1 tablespoon of rice vinegar
- ¼ teaspoon of sugar
- 1 teaspoon of black sesame seeds, plus more for sprinkling
- 1 ripe avocado, quartered

For Serving:
- Cooked rice

Instructions:
1. Combine the soy sauce, onion, sesame oil, scallions, and a pinch of salt in a large bowl. Toss and refrigerate with tuna until ready for use.

2. Toss the cucumbers with sugar, vinegar, sesame seeds, and a pinch of salt in a small cup. Let the 5 minutes stand.

3. When needed, marinated cucumbers, serve tuna and avocado over rice. If needed, sprinkle with extra black sesame seeds.

Salmon Burger

(Ready in 30 Minutes, Serve 4, Difficulty: Easy)
Nutrition per Serving:
Calories: 170, Protein: 20 g Carbohydrates: 2 g, Fat: 9 g.

Ingredients:
- 1 large egg
- 453 gramsof finely chopped skinless salmon fillet
- 2 scallions, chopped
- 3 tablespoons of chopped fresh dill, divided
- 3 tablespoons of chopped flat-leaf parsley, divided
- Kosher salt and pepper
- 1 tablespoon of olive oil
- ½ cup of Greek yogurt
- 1 teaspoon of lemon zest plus 2 tablespoons of juice
- 4 brioche buns, toasted
- 8 bibb lettuce leaves
- 2 Persian cucumbers or ½ English cucumber, shaved lengthwise
- 2 cup of broccoli or radish sprouts

Instructions:
1. Beat the egg in a medium bowl until frothy. Fold in the salmon, scallions, 2 teaspoons of parsley and dill, and 1/4 teaspoon of salt and pepper each.

2. Heat 1 tablespoon of oil in a medium skillet. Spoon 4 mounds (approximately 1/2 cup each of salmon mixture into the skillet and flatten into 1/2-inch-thick patties. Cook the patties, 2 minutes per hand, until golden brown.

3. Meanwhile, mix the yogurt, lemon zest, and juice in a bowl with the remaining tbsp. Parsley and dill, and ½ teaspoon of salt and pepper each.

4. Spread the yogurt sauce on the bottom buns (about 2 ½ tablespoons each and add the top buns, lettuce, cucumber, salmon patties, and sprouts.

Soba Salad with Grilled Tofu

(Ready in 15 Minutes, Serve 3, Difficulty: Easy)
Nutrition per Serving:
Calories 360, Protein 18 g, Carbohydrates 51 g, Fat 10 g, Saturated Fat 1 g, Fat 6 g, Sodium 775 mg.

Ingredients:
- 12 ounces of extra-firm tofu
- Kosher salt
- Black pepper
- 8 ounces of soba noodles
- 5 ounces of baby spinach

- ¼ cup of Ponzu sauce
- 6 radishes, thinly sliced
- ¼ cup of chopped peanuts

Instructions:

1. Cut the tofu into 1/2-inch-thick slices, dry with paper towels, and press. With salt and pepper, season. Medium-high grill for 10-15 minutes, rotating once covered. Cut into bite-size pieces.

2. In the meantime, cook noodles with soba. Place baby spinach in the colander in the sink, drain directly over the spinach with hot noodles. Rinse and drain well with cold water. Toss in a sauce of radishes, ponzu, and grilled tofu. Nice with peanuts.

Fish Tacos

(Ready in 50 Minutes, Serve 6, Difficulty: Easy)
Nutrition per Serving (fish only):

Calories 300, Protein 24 g, Carbohydrates 22 g, Fat 13 g, Saturated Fat 1 g, Sodium 480 mg Fiber 1 g,

Ingredients:

- ¼ cup of corn-starch
- 1 teaspoon of chili powder
- ½ teaspoon of baking powder
- 1 ¼ cup of all-purpose flour
- 1 cup of lager beer or seltzer
- 680 grams of skinless mahi-mahi or tilapia fillets (or skinless, boneless chicken breasts) cut into 2"-long strips
- Small (6") flour tortillas

For Frying:

- Canola or vegetable oil

Instructions:

1. Combine the corn-starch, chili powder, baking powder, 1 cup of flour, and 1 teaspoon of salt in a medium bowl. Only when mixed, stir in beer and 1/2 cup of ice cubes (some small lumps are OK), let the batter stand for 10 minutes.

2. Place a large wire rack on top of the baking sheet with foil.

3. Heat 2 inches of oil on medium-high in a 5-quart heavy-bottomed pot until it reaches 176 degrees Celsius(350 degrees Fahrenheit) on a deep-fry thermometer.

4. Working in batches of 1 piece at a time, toss the remaining 1/4 cup of flour with the fish, then dip in the batter, letting the excess drip off. Place thoroughly in hot oil. Depending on the size, repeat with 3-6 more fish pieces, making sure not to crowd the pot.

5. Fry for around 3 minutes, turning periodically (and adjusting the heat as required to retain the temperature), until deep golden brown.

6. Transfer the cooked fish to the rack with a slotted spoon. Sprinkle with a pinch of salt. With the remaining fish, flour and batter, repeat.

7. Serve on flour tortillas with pineapple and Romaine slaw, quick pickled onions, citrusy radishes, or cabbage and corn slaw.

Quinoa with Broccoli Pesto

(Ready in 30 Minutes, Serve 6, Difficulty: Easy)
Nutrition per Serving:

Calories 359, Protein 12 g, Carbohydrates 16 g, Fat 23 g, Sodium 406mg, Potassium 509mg.

Ingredients:

- 1 cup of quinoa rinsed
- 2 cups of water
- 5 cups of fresh broccoli cut into small florets (about 2 good size broccoli crowns)
- 4 cloves of garlic
- 2/3 cup of freshly grated parmesan, divided
- 2/3 cup of sliced or slivered almonds toasted, divided
- 1/2 teaspoon of salt
- Juice from 1 fresh lemon (2 tablespoons)
- 1/4 cup of olive oil
- 1/4 cup of heavy cream

Optional Toppings:

- Chopped basil red Chile oil (recipe below)
- Sliced avocado
- To make this dish vegan substitute the heavy cream with coconut milk. For the parmesan cheese, you can use Parma, or add about ¼ cup of sesame seeds in place of the parmesan cheese.

Instructions:

1. Heat the quinoa with 2 cups of water in a medium saucepan until it boils. Reduce flame, cover, and simmer until all the water and quinoa fluffs are absorbed, for about 15 minutes. When the seeds have sprouted, quinoa is done. Set aside.

2. Heat a large pot of water to boiling and add the broccoli. Only cook long enough to bring out the raw taste and until the broccoli is bright green. Roughly 90 seconds. Drain the broccoli and rinse with cold water to prevent further cooking of the broccoli. Set aside.

3. Mash 2 cups of cooked broccoli, garlic, 1/3 cup of almonds, 1/3 cup of parmesan cheese, salt, and lemon juice in a food processor to make the broccoli pesto. Drizzle in the cream and olive oil and pulse until almost smooth.

4. Toss the quinoa and remaining broccoli florets with the broccoli pesto just before serving. Taste, and at this point, you might decide to add more

lemon juice or salt. Add and taste the remaining 1/3 cup of parmesan cheese. When you like, add more.

5. On serving dishes or bowls, spoon the mixture. Add your chosen toppings. Sliced avocado and liberal quantities of red chili oil are strongly recommended.

Red Chile Oil:

1. In a small saucepan, heat 1/2 cup of extra-virgin olive oil until heated, but not so hot that it smokes.

2. Stir in 1 1/2 teaspoon of crushed red pepper flakes and turn off the heat.

3. Put aside and let it cool down. It is well prepared the day before and stored overnight in the refrigerator.

4. Before using it, return to room temperature again.

Double Crunch Honey Garlic Pork Chops

(Ready in 30 Minutes, Serve 4, Difficulty: Normal)

Nutrition per Serving:

Calories 336, Protein 33 g, Carbohydrates 55 g, Total Fat 22 g, Cholesterol 131mg, Sodium 251mg, Fiber 2 g, Sugar 47 g.

Ingredients:

- 6 center loin pork chops, well-trimmed
- 1 cup of flour
- 2 teaspoon of salt
- 1 1/2 tablespoon of ground ginger
- 2 teaspoons of black pepper
- 1 tablespoon of ground nutmeg
- 1 teaspoon of ground thyme
- 1/2 teaspoon of cayenne pepper
- 1 teaspoon of ground sage
- 1 tablespoon of paprika
- 2 eggs
- 4 tablespoons of water

For the Honey Garlic Sauce:

- 2 tablespoons of olive oil
- 3–4 cloves of garlic, minced
- 1 cup of honey
- ¼ cup of soy sauce (Low-sodium version is best)
- 1 teaspoon of ground black pepper

Instructions:

1. Sift the rice, salt, black pepper, ground ginger, thyme, nutmeg, sage paprika, and cayenne pepper together.

2. By whisking the eggs and water together, make an egg wash.

3. Season salt and pepper with the pork chops, then dip the meat into the flour and spice mixture. Dip the chop into the egg wash and then into the flour and spice mix for the final time, squeezing the mix into the meat to make good contact.

4. On the stove, heat a skillet with around half an inch of canola oil covering the bottom. Here, you want to carefully monitor the temperature so that the chops do not brown too fast.

5. Before dipping the cooked pork chops into the honey garlic sauce, drain for a few minutes on a wire rack. With noodles or rice, serve.

To make the Honey Garlic Sauce:

1. Add 2 tablespoons of olive oil and sliced garlic to a medium saucepan. To soften the garlic, cook over medium heat, but do not let it brown.

2. Add the honey, black pepper, and soy sauce.

3. For 5-10 minutes, boil together, remove from the heat and allow to cool for a few minutes. Watch this cautiously as it simmers because it can very easily foam up over the pot.

Herb and Citrus Oven Roasted Chicken

(Ready in 1 hr. 10 Minutes, Serve 6, Difficulty: Hard)

Nutrition per Serving:

Calories 268, Protein 18 g, Carbohydrates 12 g, Fat 17 g, Sodium 74mg, Potassium 39mg, Fiber: 2 g.

Ingredients:

- 1/4 cup of olive oil
- 4 cloves of garlic, minced
- 2 tablespoons of sugar
- 2 whole lemons, one juiced and 1 sliced
- 2 whole oranges, one juiced and 2 sliced
- 1 tablespoon of Italian seasoning
- 1/2 teaspoon of paprika
- 1 teaspoon of onion powder
- 1/4 teaspoon of crushed red pepper flakes
- Kosher salt and freshly ground pepper, to taste
- 10-12 pieces (about 4 226 grams) of bone-in chicken parts (thighs and legs are best), pat dry
- 1 medium onion, thinly sliced
- 1 teaspoon of dried thyme (or fresh chopped)
- 1 tablespoon of dried rosemary (or fresh chopped)

For Garnish (optional):

- Chopped fresh herbs (rosemary, thyme, parsley)

Instructions:

1. Preheat the oven to 400 degrees Fahrenheit (204 Celsius).

2. Combine the olive oil, garlic, orange juice, Italian seasoning, sugar, lemon juice, paprika, onion powder, red pepper, salt, and pepper in a small cup.

3. Place the chicken on a 13x9-inch dish for baking. Place the skin parts upside down and spread them uniformly in the tub. Pour the mixture of olive oil all over the chicken, rotating the pieces to cover all sides. Around and under the chicken, place slices of lemon, orange, and onion. Sprinkle thyme, rosemary, salt, and pepper all over generously.

4. Bake for around 1 hour uncovered, or until the chicken is cooked and the juices run clear. Remove the pieces from the serving dish and garnish, if desired, with additional chopped fresh herbs.

Grilled Chicken with Herbed Corn Salsa
(Ready in 20 Minutes, Serve 6, Difficulty: Easy)
Nutrition per Serving:

Calories 249, Protein 39 g, Carbohydrate 17 g, Fat 31 g, Saturated Fat 8 g, Sodium 690mg.

Ingredients:

- 2 113 grams of skin-on, bone-in chicken thighs
- Salt
- Pepper
- 2 large ears corn, shucked
- 1 cup of packed fresh basil leaves
- ½ cup of packed fresh mint leaves
- ¼ cup of grated parmesan cheese
- 1 clove of garlic
- ¼ cup of lemon juice
- 2 tablespoons of extra-virgin olive oil

Instructions:

1. Season the chicken thighs with ½ teaspoon of salt and pepper. Grill the chicken for 15-20 minutes on medium, covered, or until the chicken is cooked (165 degrees Fahrenheit), turning once.

2. Grill the corn for 10 minutes on average, turning periodically. Pulse the basil, mint, parmesan cheese, garlic, and 1/4 teaspoon of salt in the food processor until finely chopped.

3. Add the lemon juice and olive oil, then pulse until mixed. Cut the kernels off the cobs, whisk in the sauce with the herbs.

4. Serve chicken with a mixture of maize.

Zucchini Lasagna
(Ready in 2 Hours, Serve 8, Difficulty: Hard)
Nutrition per Serving:

Calories: 275, Protein 26 g Carbohydrates 13 g, Fat 13 g, Saturated Fat 7 g, Cholesterol 84mg, Sodium 648mg, Fiber 2.5 g, Sugar 5 g.

Ingredients:

- 453 gramsof 93% lean ground beef
- 1 1/2 teaspoons of kosher salt
- 1 teaspoon of olive oil
- 1/2 large onion, chopped
- 3 cloves of garlic, minced
- 1 28-ounce can of crushed tomatoes
- 2 tablespoons of chopped fresh basil
- Black pepper, to taste
- 3 (8 ounces each) medium zucchinis, sliced 1/8" thick
- 1 1/2 cups of part-skim ricotta
- 1/4 cup of parmesan cheese
- 1 large egg
- 4 cups (16 ounces) of shredded part-skim mozzarella cheese

Instructions:

1. Place the brown meat in a medium saucepan and season with salt. Drain in the colander when cooked to remove any fat.

2. Add the olive oil to the pan and cook for 2 minutes with the garlic and onions. Put the meat back in the pan, then add the tomatoes, basil, salt, and pepper. Simmer for at least 30-40 minutes on the low, covered. The sauce should be thick, so do not add extra water.

3. In the meantime, slice zucchini into 1/8" thick slices, add salt gently and set aside for 10 minutes. When cooked, zucchini has a lot of water, salting it takes a lot of moisture out. Blot excess moisture with a paper towel after 10 minutes.

4. Preheat to medium-high a gas grill or grill pan, and grill 2-3 minutes per side, until slightly browned. To soak up excess moisture, put on paper towels.

5. Preheat oven to 375 degrees Fahrenheit.

6. Combine the ricotta cheese, parmesan cheese, and egg in a medium bowl. Stir well.

7. Spread ½ cup of sauce on the bottom and layer the zucchini to cover in a 9x12 casserole. Spread ½ cup of the mixture of ricotta cheese, then top with 1 cup of mozzarella cheese and repeat the process until all the ingredients are used up. Top the last layer with remaining zucchini and sauce, cover with foil and bake for 30 minutes. Uncover the foil and bake for 20 minutes (to dry the sauce).

8. Let stand before serving for around 5-10 minutes.

Skinny Broccoli Cheese Soup Recipe
(Ready in 25 Minutes, Serve 6, Difficulty: Normal)
Nutrition per Serving:

Calories 200, Protein 16 g, Carbohydrates 15 g, Fat 10 g.

Ingredients:

- 1 tablespoon of butter
- 1 small yellow onion roughly chopped
- 1 stalk of celery, roughly chopped
- 2 cloves of garlic, minced
- 1 teaspoon of salt plus, (or to taste)
- 1/2 teaspoon of nutmeg
- 1/4 teaspoon of fresh pepper
- 3 1/2 cups of vegetable broth more as needed to thin out to desired consistency
- 1 cup of skim milk
- 1(16 ounces) bag of frozen cauliflower florets
- 1 medium carrot shredded
- 1(16 ounces) bag of frozen broccoli florets
- 1 1/2 (6-8 ounces) cup of reduced-fat shredded sharp cheddar

Instructions:

1. Melt butter over medium/medium-high heat in a large soup pot.

2. Add the chopped onion, celery, garlic, and spices and cook for 5 minutes or so.

3. Bring to a boil and add the broth, milk, and cauliflower.

4. Simmer until the cauliflower is tender with a fork, around 3-5 minutes.

5. To mix, use an immersion blender.

6. Add the carrots and broccoli and simmer until the broccoli, about 5 minutes, is cooked to your taste.

7. To mix, use an immersion blender.

8. Add the cheese until it is melted.

9. Re-season and taste, if necessary, and serve!

Pumpkin & Kale Lasagna

(Ready in 1 Hour and 20 Minutes, Serve 1, Difficulty: Hard)

Nutrition per Serving

Calories 390, Protein 18 g, Carbohydrates 10 g, Fat 31 g, Sodium 790mg, Potassium 300mg, Sugars 3 g.

Ingredients:

- 2 cans of pumpkin puree (15 ounces each 100% pure)
- 2 eggs
- 1/4 teaspoon of cayenne
- 3/4 teaspoon of salt
- 1/2 teaspoon of ground black pepper
- 16 ounces of lasagna noodles
- 3 tablespoons of virgin olive oil extras
- 4 cloves of garlic, minced
- 1/2 bunch of kale stems removed, leaves coarsely chopped
- 1/2 teaspoon of red pepper flakes
- 3 tablespoons of unsalted butter
- 3 tablespoons of all-purpose flour
- 3 cups of whole milk
- 1 tablespoon of chopped fresh sage finely
- 1 pinch of ground nutmeg
- Nonstick spray
- 1/4 cup of couscous dry, uncooked
- 10 ounces of cheese slices mozzarella
- 1/2 cup of grated parmesan cheese

For Garnish (Optional):

- Fresh parsley, chopped

Instructions:

1. Preheat the oven to 375 degrees F (190 degree Celsius). Lightly oil a 11x7 or 9x13-inch baking dish with softened butter only, and put aside. Start by blending the pumpkin-ricotta mixture. Whisk the ricotta, squash, parmesan, egg, garlic, dried sage, dried basil, cinnamon, pepper, and nutmeg together in a medium bowl until smooth. Only put aside.

2. Make the kale. Heat a nonstick skillet over medium to medium-high heat. Add the olive oil. Once hot, add the garlic and cook for 30 seconds to 1 minute or until fragrant (you don't want it to be brown). Add the kale and cook for 1-2 minutes until wilted. Season to taste with salt and pepper. Set aside.

3. Make the sauce from cheese. Over low heat, heat a big pot or Dutch oven. Add some butter. Whisk in the flour until it is melted, stirring continuously to mix, and simmer for 1 minute. Add the milk steadily, whisking continuously, and raising the heat to high. Continue to whisk for about 5 minutes before the milk comes to a boil and thickens. To mix, add the nutmeg and cinnamon and whisk. Lower the heat to medium-low and add the mozzarella and fontina cheeses steadily, stirring well after each addition, until the cheeses are fully melted. Add the pepper and salt. Reduce the heat to low when the lasagna is being prepared.

4. Into the bottom of the baking bowl, spoon ¼ of the cheese sauce. Next, on top, put a layer of lasagna noodles. Next, on top of the noodles, spread ¼ of the pumpkin-ricotta mixture uniformly. Sprinkle on top with 1/3 of the kale. Repeat with 2 more layers of cheese sauce, pasta, ricotta, spinach, or before the ingredients have run out. Sprinkle the surface generously with the mozzarella and parmesan to finish. Bake for 45 minutes or until golden brown on the top and sides.

5. Make the crispy sage leaves while the lasagna is baking. Melt the butter in a medium skillet over

medium to medium-high heat. Add the sage leaves and fry for 30 seconds to 1 minute after melting and starting to bubble, reducing the heat if the butter begins to get too brown. Remove the pan's sage leaves and let them soak on paper towels.

6. Let cool for 15 minutes before cutting after the lasagna is done baking. Serve it on top of crispy fried sage leaves! "Fully cooked chicken & apple 12 ounce-sausage links, sliced crosswise into 1/4" bits, optional.

Garlic Mushroom Quinoa
(Ready in 35 Minutes, Serve 6, Difficulty: Normal)

Nutrition per Serving:

Calories 152.7, Protein 12.9 g. Carbohydrate 16.8, Fat 11.7 g, Sodium 442.9mg, Potassium 810.1mg.

Ingredients:

- 1 cup of quinoa
- 1 tablespoon of olive oil
- 453 g of cremini mushrooms, thinly sliced
- 5 cloves of garlic, minced
- 1/2 teaspoon of dried thyme
- Kosher salt and freshly ground black pepper, to taste
- 2 tablespoons of grated parmesan cheese

Instructions:

1. Cook quinoa in a large saucepan with 2 cups of water, set aside as per package instructions.

2. Heat the olive oil over medium-high heat in a large skillet. Add the mushrooms, garlic, and thyme, and cook until tender, occasionally stirring around 3-4 minutes and seasoning with salt and pepper. Stir in the quinoa before it mixes well.

3. If desired, serve immediately, garnished with parmesan cheese.

Low Carb Cauliflower Pizza Crust Recipe (Crispy + 3 Ingredients)
(Ready in 45 Minutes, Serve 8, Difficulty: Normal)

Nutrition per Serving:

Calories 106, Protein: 10 g, Carbohydrates 5 g, Net Carbs 3 g, Fat 6 g, Fiber 2 g, Sugar 2 g.

Ingredients:

- 1 226 grams of cauliflower (florets only-about one large head)
- 1 1/2 cup of grated parmesan cheese
- 1 large egg
- 1/2 tablespoon of Italian seasoning (Optional)
- 1/2 teaspoon of garlic powder (optional)

Instructions:

1. The oven should be preheated to 400 degrees Fahrenheit (204 degrees Celsius). If you plan on using a pizza stone (recommended) or a pizza pan, place a piece of parchment paper on a pizza peel.

2. In a food processor, blend the cauliflower florets until they are the consistency of rice.

3. Stir fry the cauliflower for about 10 minutes in a sauté pan on the stove, until the cauliflower is very soft. (This is important! If it's still crisp, the texture is off, so keep cooking until nice and soft.)

4. Meanwhile, whisk the egg in a large bowl. Stir in the cheese with parmesan cheese. Stir those in as well when using Italian seasoning and garlic powder.

5. When the cauliflower rice is thoroughly cooked and soft.

Option 1(more effort-recommended if making one large pizza): Place the cauliflower rice into a kitchen towel and squeeze over the sink.

Option 2(easier-better for making 2 smaller pizzas): Stir the cauliflower rice directly into the egg/cheese mixture.

With both options, make sure it's mixed very well. You may need to press with a spatula.

1. Spread the "dough" with your hands on the parchment paper, to about 1/4" thick. Depending on which option you chose in the previous step, you can make one large pizza or 2 smaller pizzas."

2. Use the pizza peel to transfer the parchment paper to the stone in the oven when using a pizza stone (recommended for best results). Otherwise, place the pan in the oven. Bake for about 20 minutes, until the top is dry and firm and the edges are a little golden.

Serving size: 1 slice of a large pizza, 2 slices of 2 smaller pizzas, or 1/8 of the entire recipe.

Creamy Pumpkin Soup
(Ready in 15 Minutes, Serve 4, Difficulty: Easy)

Nutrition per Serving:

Calories 162, Protein 5 g, Carbohydrates 18 g, Fat 9 g, Sodium 987mg, Potassium 373mg, Fiber 5 g, Sugar 7 g.

Ingredients:

- 2 cups of pumpkin puree
- 1 1/4 cup of vegetable broth
- 1 cup of reduced-fat coconut milk
- 1 small yellow onion
- 1 tablespoon of minced garlic
- 1 teaspoon of thyme
- 1/2 teaspoon of salt
- 1/4 teaspoon of pepper
- 4 tablespoon of pumpkin seeds

Instructions:

1. Chop the onion and garlic and sauté with 1/4 cup of vegetable stock in a medium saucepan.

2. To make a saucepan, add pumpkin puree, 1 cup of vegetable broth, coconut milk, thyme, salt, and pepper. To combine the ingredients, stir. Heat for 5 minutes, or until heated through on medium heat.

3. Transfer the soup to the blender and mix until all the ingredients are mixed.

4. Pour 4 bowls in. Use pumpkin seeds and black pepper to sprinkle.

Roasted Butternut Squash and Chickpea Curry

(Ready in 55 Minutes, Serve 6, Difficulty: Normal)

Nutrition per Serving:

Calories 243, Protein 8.3 g, Fat 5.5 g, Sodium 399.7mg, Potassium ,076.7mg, Sugars 4.6 g,

Ingredients:

- 1 medium (about 3-4 cups) butternut squash, cubed
- 2 tablespoons of coconut oil
- 1 red onion
- 4 cloves of garlic
- 1 thumb-sized piece of ginger
- 1 tablespoon of curry powder
- 1 teaspoon of garam masala
- 1/2 teaspoon of ground cumin
- 1/2 teaspoon of cumin seeds
- 1/4 teaspoon of turmeric
- 1/4 teaspoon of hot chili powder
- 1 tin(400ml) of chopped tomatoes
- 1 tin(400ml) of coconut milk
- 200ml of vegetable stock
- 1 tin(400 g) of chickpeas
- Salt and pepper

To serve:

- Chopped coriander
- Basmati rice

Instructions:

1. Preheat oven to 400 degrees Fahrenheit (204 Celsius). Cut the squash from both sides, slice it and cut it lengthwise in half. Cut into cubes of approximately equal size, around 1 cm.

2. Place on a large baking tray, drizzle with salt and pepper oil, toss and place for 35-40 minutes in the oven until soft and brown on the edges.

3. In the meantime, start the curry. On medium heat, add coconut oil to a large pan, and once melted, add the finely chopped onion. For a few minutes, stir and fry, then add crushed garlic and grated ginger. Leave it for another minute to cook.

4. All the spices are added: curry powder, garam masala, and seeds of turmeric, and chili powder. Cook for 30 seconds until fragrant. If necessary, add a little more oil so that it does not burn.

5. Mix in the chopped tomatoes, coconut milk, and stock of vegetables. Simmer gently and let cook for 10 minutes. Transfer to a bowl and blend until smooth with a hand mixer or a food processor. Transfer to the pan again.

6. Add the chickpeas and cook for another 5-10 minutes. It should be thickened and sweet, creamy, and orange in color. Taste the sauce and add salt and pepper to the seasoning. You should add some additional chili powder if you like it spicy.

7. Add the butternut squash roast, stir, and serve. Top with some chopped fresh cilantro and serve with your favorite sides and basmati rice, like onion bhajis.

Mediterranean Chicken Bowls

(Ready in 20 Minutes, Serve 6, Difficulty: Normal)

Nutrition per Serving:

Calories 237, Protein 43 g, Carbohydrate 53 g, Fat 9.5 g, Saturated Fat 1.5 g, Sodium 425mg, Fiber 5 g.

Ingredients:

- 453 grams of boneless, skinless chicken breasts, cut into 1 ½-in pieces
- 1 tablespoon of olive oil
- 1 teaspoon of dried oregano
- 1 teaspoon of ground sumac
- Kosher salt and pepper
- 1 pint of grape or cherry tomatoes
- 1 medium onion, roughly chopped
- 1 cup of couscous
- 1 teaspoon of grated lemon zest plus
- 1 tablespoon of lemon juice
- ¼ cup of fresh dill, divided

For Serving:

- Crumbled feta
- Lemon wedges

Instructions:

1. Toss the chicken with the oil in a large bowl, then add the oregano, sumac, and ½ teaspoon of salt and pepper. Add the onion and tomatoes and toss to mix.

2. Arrange an even layer in the air fryer basket and fry at 400 degrees Fahrenheit (204 Celsius), shaking the basket occasionally, 15-20 minutes, until chicken is golden brown and cooked through.

3. In the meantime, toss couscous with lemon zest and prepare the directions per box. Fork and fold the fluff with lemon juice and 2 teaspoons of dill.

4. Serve over couscous chicken and vegetables, spooning over the top of any juices collected at the bottom of the air fryer. If desired, sprinkle with the remaining dill and feta and serve with lemon wedges.

"Flush the Fat Away" Lentil and Vegetable Soup

(Ready in 45 Minutes, Serve 10, Difficulty: Normal)

Nutrition per Serving:

Calories 72, Protein 1 g, Carbohydrates 11 g, Fat 3 g, Sodium 633mg, Potassium 272mg, Fiber 3 g.

Ingredients:

- 2 cups of dry lentils rinsed
- 1 cup of dry quinoa rinsed
- 2 carrots shredded
- 1 sweet potato cut into bite-size pieces
- 1 yellow onion diced
- 2 cloves of garlic minced
- 5 cups of vegetable broth low-sodium (no sugar added)
- 4 ounces of diced green chiles
- 2 teaspoon of chili powder
- 1 teaspoon of cumin
- 1/4 teaspoon of crushed red pepper flakes
- 1 teaspoon of black pepper
- 1/2 teaspoon of sea salt (or to taste)
- 2 cups of chard torn and packed, center stem removed
- 1 avocado, chopped
- 1/2 cup of chopped fresh cilantro

Instructions:

1. In a big pot, add all the ingredients, except the last three (chard, avocado, and cilantro). Bring to a boil, reduce the heat to a low boil, cover and leave the lid slightly.

2. Cook for about 30 minutes, until the lentils and quinoa are tender.

3. Add a torn Swiss card and cook for about 5 minutes, until wilted.

4. Use diced avocado and chopped cilantro to serve and top.

Stuffed Green Peppers with Brown Rice, Italian Sausage, And Parmesan

(Ready in 1 Hour and 5 Minutes, Serve 4, Difficulty: Hard)

Nutrition per Serving:

Calories 134, Protein 27 g, Carbohydrates 23, Fat 15 g, Saturated Fat 5 g, Unsaturated Fat 8 g, Cholesterol 84mg, Sodium 597mg, Fiber 3 g, Sugar 5 g.

Ingredients:

- 1 Cup of uncooked long-grain brown rice (I used Uncle Ben's® Brown Rice, but any long-grain rice will work.)
- 4 large green bell peppers, bottom trimmed, cap end cut off and diced, and seeds removed
- 1 large onion, diced
- 1 tablespoon of olive oil
- 8 ounces of Turkey sweet or Italian sausage (see notes)
- 1/2 teaspoon of ground fennel
- 1/2 teaspoon of dried Greek or Turkish oregano
- 1/2 cup of grated parmesan cheese
- Salt and fresh ground black pepper, to taste
- 1/4 cup of grated mozzarella cheese

Instructions:

1. Cook rice according to the package instructions, or use a cooker for rice.

2.Preheat the oven to 375 degrees Fahrenheit (190 degrees Celsius).

3. Trim the bottom of the bell peppers so that they have to stand on a flat surface. Cut off the stem end of the peppers with a relatively generous amount, then remove the seeds.

4. In a baking dish that you have sprayed with non-stick spray or olive oil, place the hollowed-out peppers. (A dish that's close to the peppers in size will work best.)

5. Remove the stem part from the pepper caps and cut any white membrane off, then dice the caps of the pepper and the onion into rather small dices.

6. Heat two teaspoons of olive oil. In a large skillet, cook the diced pepper and onion for 3-4 minutes until the olive oil begins to soften but does not brown.

7. Remove the pepper-onion mixture and add 1 tsp to a bowl. Then squeeze the sausage out of the casing and cook until the sausage is lightly browned, breaking it apart with the back of the turner.

8. To blend the flavors, put the onion-pepper mixture back in the pan with the sausage, add the dried spices, and cook for 2-3 minutes.

9. Then add cooked rice and parmesan cheese, season the mixture to taste with salt and fresh

ground black pepper, and cook for about 1-2 minutes, just long enough to warm.

10. Use a spoon to press the mixture down so that it is tightly packed into the pepper shell, stuff the filling mixture into the hollowed-out peppers. (I stopped pre-cooking the peppers a few years ago before stuffing them, and now I prefer raw stuffed peppers.) If you have any extra filling, you can put it in a small ramekin and bake it with the peppers.

11. Bake the peppers for 30 minutes, remove from the oven and top each pepper with a generous pinch of rubbed mozzarella. Return the peppers to the oven and cook for another 10-15 minutes, until the cheese is melted and lightly browned. Serve it warm.

12. Leftover peppers can be frozen for 1 month or 2, although the frozen peppers will be a little softer (but still very tasty) in texture. Before freezing, I cut them in half top-to-bottom and freeze 2 halves in a small baking dish with a snap-on lid.

Mushroom-Stuffed Cabbage Rolls

(Ready in 1 Hour and 50 Minutes, Serve 1, Difficulty: Hard)

Nutrition per Serving:

Calories 167, Protein 4.9 g, Carbohydrates 23.7 g, Fat 7.6 g, Cholesterol 0mg, Sodium 218mg.

Ingredients:

* 1 large head cabbage, cored
* 2 tablespoons of olive oil, divided
* 1 medium onion, minced
* ¼ cup of fresh thyme leaves, divided
* 3 cloves of garlic, chopped
* 340 g of finely chopped mushrooms
* ½ cup of raisins
* 1 teaspoon of ground cinnamon
* ¾ cup of roughly chopped walnuts
* 1 teaspoon of sea salt, or to taste, divided
* ½ cup of uncooked brown rice
* 1(16 ounce) can of crushed tomatoes, divided
* Ground black pepper to taste

Instructions:

1. To a boil, put a big pot of lightly salted water. Drop the cabbage into the pot and immerse it completely in the wine. For 10 minutes, cook. Remove from the water and allow for about 10 minutes to cool enough to manage. Carefully pull the leaves off.

2. The oven should be preheated to 350 degrees Fahrenheit (176 degrees Celsius).

3. Heat 1 tablespoon of oil over medium to high heat in a large skillet. Add the onion, 1/3 of the garlic, and the thyme. Cook for about 5 minutes, until the onions are translucent. Add the mushrooms, cinnamon, and raisins and cook for about 3 minutes. Stir in the walnuts and add 1/3 of the sea salt to season. Transfer the mixture to a large bowl and incorporate the rice into a uniform mixture, stirring the stuffing.

4. Grease a baking dish with the remaining olive oil and use a thin layer of tomatoes to line the rim. Sprinkle 1/3 of the thyme, 1/3 of the sea salt, and pepper lightly to taste.

5. Scoop into a cabbage leaf around a heaping tablespoon of stuffing and first fold into the sides, then roll and put in the prepared pan. Repeat with the leaves, and the stuffing left. To close up any broken rolls, use any torn leaves. Top the remaining tomatoes with the rest of the thyme. Season with the remaining pepper and salt.

6. Use aluminum foil or a sheet to cover the baking dish.

7. Bake until tender in the preheated oven, about 45 minutes.

Greek Yogurt Mac and Cheese

(Ready in 30 Minutes, Serve 10, Difficulty: Easy)

Nutrition per Serving:

Calories 367, Protein 15 g Carbohydrates 43.8 g, Fat 16 g, Potassium 21mg, Fiber 4.6 g, Sugar 4.2 g.

Ingredients:

Macaroni and Cheese:

8 ounces of Eat Banza Elbow Macaroni® (or other gluten-free pasta)

* 2 tablespoons of tapioca flour
* ½ teaspoon of onion powder
* ¼ teaspoon of garlic powder
* ¾ teaspoon of sea salt
* ¼ teaspoon of freshly ground black pepper
* 2 tablespoons of butter
* 1 cup of 2% milk
* 1 cup of plain Greek yogurt
* 2 cups of shredded cheddar cheese

For Topping:

* 2 tablespoons of grated parmesan cheese
* ½ cup of shredded cheddar cheese
* ¼ cup of almond meal/flour
* ¼-½ teaspoon of garlic salt
* ¼ teaspoon of freshly ground black pepper

Instructions:

1. Preheat oven to 375 degrees Fahrenheit (190 degree Celsius). Grease an 8x8-inch baking dish (or 2-quart casserole dish), set aside.

2. Cook pasta according to package instructions.

3. Drain and rinse pasta with cold water, transfer to a large bowl, and set aside.

4. Measure out dry ingredients (tapioca flour, onion powder, garlic powder, salt and pepper) into a small bowl. Set aside.

5. Add butter to a medium saucepan. Heat over medium heat until melted.

6. Once butter is melted, add dry ingredients and whisk until combined.

7. Cook on medium-high heat for 30 seconds or until it forms a paste-like consistency and becomes light brown.

8. Add milk and whisk until ingredients are combined.

9. Add Greek yogurt and whisk until combined.

10. Cook the mixture over medium-high heat until it begins to thicken (but does not boil).

11. Once the mixture is thick, turn heat to low and add 2 cups of cheese. Stir until the cheese is melted.

12. Add cheese sauce to the cooked and drained pasta and stir to combine.

13. Pour mixture into prepared baking dish.

14. In a small bowl, combine topping ingredients.

15. Sprinkle topping over pasta.

16. Bake in preheated oven for 15-20 minutes or until the cheese on the top is melted and slightly browned.

17. Serve warm!

Easy Burrito Bowl

(Ready in 25 Minutes, Serve 4, Difficulty: Normal)

Nutrition per Serving:

Calories 319, Protein 23.8 g, Carbohydrates 18.6 g, Fat 18.3 g, Sugar 1.8 g, Sodium 308 mg, Fiber 6.1 g.

Ingredients:

- 1 boneless, skinless chicken breast
- 2 cups of roughly chopped romaine lettuce
- ⅔ cup of cooked quinoa
- ½ avocado, sliced
- 1 lime
- 1 dash of chili powder
- ½ cup of cherry tomatoes, sliced in ½
- 4 tablespoon of low-fat shredded cheddar cheese
- Hot sauce (optional)

Instructions:

1. Sprinkle all sides of the chicken breast with chili powder.

2. Bake the chicken breast in the oven for 30-40 minutes at 400 degrees F (204 Celsius), until the chicken is fully cooked.

3. Slice it up into bite-sized chunks when the chicken is cooked.

4. Spread out 1/2 cup of quinoa, 1 cup of lettuce, and 1/4 cup of tomatoes to assemble each bowl.

5. To the cups, add the chicken, top with the avocado slices, and squeeze ½ lime of juice over each dish.

6. Finally, over each bowl, sprinkle 2 tablespoons of cheese and add hot sauce, if desired.

Steak Chimichurri

(Ready in 25 Minutes, Serve 6, Difficulty: Easy)

Nutrition per Serving:

Protein 0 g, Carbohydrates 1 g, Fat 8 g, Cholesterol 0mg, Sodium 15mg, Sugars 0 g.

Ingredients:

- 16 ounces of mixed baby peppers
- 3 tablespoon of olive oil, divided
- 2 12 ounces of strip steaks (about 1 ½ in. thick), trimmed
- 2 tablespoons of red wine vinegar
- 2 scallions, finely chopped
- 1 small garlic glove, grated
- ½ large red chili(seeded), finely chopped
- ½ cup of chopped flat-leaf parsley
- ½ cup of chopped cilantro

Instructions:

1. Heat grill to medium. Toss the peppers in a wide bowl with one tablespoon of oil and 1/4 teaspoon of salt and pepper. Season the steak with ½ teaspoon of salt and pepper.

2. Grill steak and peppers, wrapped, sometimes turning peppers until lightly charred and tender, 5-7 minutes. Add the steak and cook until needed, 5-8 minutes on both sides. Transfer the peppers to the bowl and steak to the cutting board and leave for at least 5 minutes to rest before cutting.

3. Meanwhile, mix the vinegar, scallions, garlic, chili, and the remaining 2 tablespoons of oil in a small bowl and pinch each of the salt and pepper. Stir in the parsley and cilantro, add the steak and peppers and serve.

Salmon with Grapefruit and Lentil Salad

(Ready in 15 Minutes, Serve 4, Difficulty: Easy)

Nutrition per Serving:

Calories 330, Protein 36 g, Carbohydrate 22 g, Fat 10.5 g, Saturated Fat 2 g, Sodium 275mg, Fiber 9 g.

Ingredients:

* 2 tablespoon of olive oil, divided
* 567 gramsof skinless salmon fillet
* Kosher salt and pepper
* 2 tablespoons of red wine vinegar
* 1 15-ounce can of lentils, rinsed
* 1 small English cucumber, cut into pieces
* 1 pink grapefruit, peel and pith removed, cut into pieces
* 4 small radishes, thinly sliced
* 6 cups of arugula

Instructions:

1. Heat 1 tablespoon of oil in a medium-sized non-stick skillet. Slice the salmon into 4 parts and season each with 1/4 teaspoon of salt and pepper. Cook for approximately 7 minutes, until golden brown. Turn over the salmon and continue to cook until just opaque, about 2 more minutes.

2. Meanwhile, whisk together the vinegar and the remaining tablespoon of oil in a large bowl. Add lentils and coat with a flip.

3. Then mix the grapefruit, cucumber, and radishes. Using arugula to fold and serve with salmon.

Sloppy Joes II

(Ready in 40 Minutes, Serve 6, Difficulty: Normal)

Nutrition per Serving:

Calories 189, Protein 15.1 g, Carbohydrates 11.2 g, Fat 9.4 g, Cholesterol 49.6mg, Sodium 416.3mg.

Ingredients:

* 453 g of lean ground beef
* ¼ cup of chopped onion
* ¼ cup of chopped green bell pepper
* ½ teaspoon of garlic powder
* 1 teaspoon of prepared yellow mustard
* ¾ cup of ketchup
* 3 teaspoons of brown sugar
* Salt, to taste
* Ground black pepper, to taste

Instructions:

1. Brown the ground beef, carrot, and green pepper in a medium skillet over medium heat and rinse off the liquids.

2. Add the garlic powder, ketchup, mustard, and brown sugar, and blend well. Reduce the fire and cook for 30 minutes. Season with salt and pepper.

Spinach and Feta Quiche with Sweet Potato Crust

(Ready in 1 Hour and 10 Minutes, Serve 4, Difficulty: Normal)

Nutrition per Serving:

Calories 220, Protein 13 g, Carbohydrate 18 g, Fat 8.7 g, Fiber 3 g, Sugars 6 g, Sodium 393mg.

Ingredients:

* Cooking spray
* 2 medium sweet potatoes, peeled and cut into 1/8-in.-thick slices
* 1 teaspoon of canola oil
* 1/2 cup of sliced onion
* 1(5-ounces) bag of fresh baby spinach
* 1/2 cup of 1% low-fat milk
* 1/4 teaspoon of kosher salt
* 1/4 teaspoon of freshly ground black pepper
* 1/4 teaspoon of crushed red pepper
* 4 large eggs
* 2 large egg whites
* 1.5ounces of feta cheese, crumbled (about 1/3 cup)

Instructions:

1. Preheat the oven to 350 degrees Fahrenheit (176 Celsius)..

2. Use a cooking spray to coat a 9-inch pie plate. Layer sweet potatoes on the bottom and the plate edges in somewhat overlapping concentric circles, cutting slices in half to fit around the sides (rounded side up). Use the cooking spray to coat potatoes. Bake for 20 minutes in a preheated oven, or until the potatoes are tender. Place a pan on a rack with metal. Increase the temperature of the oven to 375 degrees Fahrenheit (190 degree Celsius).

3. Heat a large, medium-sized non-stick skillet. Add the onion and oil and cook for 3 minutes. Add the spinach and cook for 3 minutes. Remove from heat, refrigerate.

4. In a medium cup, combine the milk and the next five ingredients (egg whites) and stir with a fork. Arrange the spinach mixture in the crust and pour the mixture of eggs over the spinach. Sprinkle feta over it. Bake for 35 minutes or until the egg mixture is set at 375 degrees Fahrenheit (190 degree Celsius). Let stand for 5 minutes. Cut into 8 wedges.

Hawaiian Meatballs

(Ready in 50 Minutes, Serve 4, Difficulty: Normal)

Nutrition per Serving:

Calories 336, Protein 18.8 g, Carbohydrates 28 g, Fat 16.5 g, Cholesterol 68.1mg, Sodium 278.9mg.

Ingredients:

- 453 g of ground beef
- ½ teaspoon of ground ginger
- ¼ teaspoon of garlic powder
- ¼ teaspoon of ground black pepper
- 1(8 ounces) can of pineapple chunks, juice reserved
- ⅓ cup of water, or as needed

Sauce:

- ¼ cup of brown sugar
- 2 tablespoons of cornstarch
- ¼ cup of white vinegar
- 1 tablespoon of soy sauce
- 1 green bell pepper, chopped

Instructions:

1. Mix the ground beef, ginger, garlic powder, and pepper until well mixed. Using one 1/2-inch meatball to shape.

2. Cook the meatballs over medium-high heat in a large frying pan until browned, for about 10 minutes. Remove the meatballs from a plate and save the drippings for the pan.

3. Pour the juice from the canned pineapple into a liquid measuring cup while the meatballs are frying, then add enough water to produce 1 cup. In a shallow bowl, mix the brown sugar and cornstarch.

4. Add the combination of pineapple juice and brown sugar to the warm pan drippings. Add the soy sauce and vinegar and get it to a boil. Cook for 2-3 minutes before the sauce thickens. Add the meatballs, slices of pineapple, and green pepper. Simmer for about 10 minutes until the meatballs are no longer pink on the inside.

Skinny Shrimp Alfredo Pasta Bake

(Ready in 40 Minutes, Serve 8, Difficulty: Normal)

Nutrition per Serving:

Calories 193, Protein 41.9 g, Fat 21.5 g, Sodium 583.9mg, Sugars 4.9 g.

Ingredients:

- 453 g of medium shrimp, peeled and deveined
- 2 tablespoons of olive oil, divided
- Kosher salt and freshly ground black pepper, to taste
- 8 ounces of whole wheat penne pasta
- 1(14.5-ounce) can of petite diced tomatoes, drained
- 1/2 cup of reduced-fat mozzarella cheese
- 1/2 teaspoon of crushed red pepper flakes, (Optional)

- 2 tablespoons of freshly grated parmesan cheese
- 2 tablespoons of chopped fresh parsley leaves

For the Alfredo Sauce:

- 2 tablespoons of unsalted butter
- 4 cloves of garlic, minced
- 1 tablespoon of all-purpose flour
- 1(6-ounce) can of 2% evaporated milk
- 1-ounce of light cheese cream
- 1/4 cup of chicken broth, or to taste
- Kosher salt and freshly ground black pepper, to taste

Instructions:

1. Melt the butter in a large skillet over medium-high heat to make the Alfredo sauce. Add garlic and cook, frequently stirring, for about 1-2 minutes, until fragrant.

2. Whisk in the flour for around 1 minute, until lightly browned. Gradually whisk in the milk, and cook for around 1-2 minutes, whisking continuously, until slightly thickened. Stir in the cream cheese and chicken broth until smooth, around 1 minute, then season to taste with salt and pepper. As needed, add more chicken broth until the desired consistency is reached.

3. Preheat the oven to 400 degrees Fahrenheit (204 Celsius). Oil a baking sheet thinly or brush with non-stick spray.

4. On the prepared baking sheet, put the shrimp. To taste, add 1 tablespoon of olive oil, salt, and pepper, and toss gently to blend. Put in the oven and roast for 6-8 minutes, only until pink, firm, and cooked. Take it out of the oven and set it aside.

5. Cook pasta according to package instructions in a big pot of boiling salted water. Drain well.

6. Lower the temperature of the oven to 350 degrees Fahrenheit (176 Celsius). Cover an 8x8-inch baking dish lightly with non-stick spray.

7. Combine the seafood, pasta, onions, mozzarella cheese, flakes of red pepper, and Alfredo sauce in a big tub. To the prepared baking dish, add the pasta mixture and cover with parmesan.

8. Place in the oven and bake until the cheese is melted and golden brown, about 10 minutes.

9. Serve right away, garnished, if desired, with parsley.

Skinny Teriyaki Pork Chops with Pineapple

(Ready in 3 Hours and 10 Minutes, Serve 6, and Difficulty: Hard)

Nutrition per Serving:

Calories 201, Protein 25 g, Carbohydrates: 9.4 g, Fat 6.7 g, Saturated Fat 2.3 g, Fiber 0.5 g, Sugar 8 g.

Ingredients:

- ⅓ cup of Tropicana® Trop50® orange juice or canned pineapple juice
- 2 tablespoons of less-sodium soy sauce
- 1 tablespoon of rice vinegar
- 1 tablespoon of brown sugar
- ½ teaspoon of ground ginger
- ½ teaspoon of onion powder
- ½ teaspoon of garlic powder
- 4(4-ounces) boneless pork chops, trimmed of fat
- 2 teaspoons of corn-starch
- 4 thickly sliced fresh pineapple rings

Instructions:

1. Mix the orange juice, ground ginger, soy sauce, rice vinegar, brown sugar, onion powder, and garlic powder in a small bowl to make a marinade.

2. In a large reseal able container, place the pork chops and add the marinade to cover. Seal the bag and place it in the refrigerator overnight for at least 2 hours. To coat the pork chops uniformly with the marinade, turn the bag every hour or so, if possible.

3. To a shallow dish, transfer the pork chops. In a small saucepan, pour the marinade into it.

4. Dissolve the corn-starch in a small bowl into 2 teaspoons of cold water to form a slurry. Place the marinade casserole over medium heat and bring it to a boil. Lower the heat to a low level and whisk in the slurry. Cook for about 2 minutes, whisking, until the sauce thickens. Remove from the heat and set aside to use as a base for the pineapple and grilled pork chops.

5. Preheat the medium-high heat of an outdoor grill, grill pan, or outdoor grill. Cover lightly with cooking spray on the grill rack of the indoor grill or grill pan.

6. Place the pork chops on the grill and cook until the inner temperature reaches 145 degrees Fahrenheit, 4-5 minutes on each side, sometimes brushing as you grill with the baste.

7. Add the pineapple slices to the grill and cook on both sides for 1-2 minutes.

8. Right before serving, let the pork chops rest for 2-4 minutes.

9. To serve, on top of each pork chop, place 1 grilled pineapple slice and serve with any remaining marinade sauce.

Santa Fe Stuffed Peppers

(Ready in 1 hr., Serve 6, Difficulty: Normal)

Nutrition per Serving:

Calories 268, Protein 18 g, Carbohydrates 44 g, Fat 5 g, Saturated Fat 1 g, Sodium 218mg, Fiber 8 g, Sugar 11 g.

Ingredients:

- 6 bell peppers, tops sliced off and seeded (any color)
- 2 teaspoons of extra virgin olive oil
- 1 onion, diced
- 1 jalapeño pepper, seeded and diced (keep seeds for more heat)
- 226 g of fat-free ground turkey
- 1 teaspoon of ground cumin
- 1 teaspoon of chili powder
- Salt, to taste
- Black pepper, to taste
- 1(15 ounces) can of reduced-sodium black beans, drained and rinsed
- 1 cup of canned or frozen no-salt-added sweet corn, drained and rinsed
- 1(15 ounces) can of no-salt-added diced tomatoes, drained
- juice of 1 lime (about 2 tablespoons)
- 2 tablespoons of finely chopped fresh cilantro
- 1 cup of cooked brown rice
- 6 tablespoons of reduced-fat Monterey Jack cheese

Instructions:

1. Preheat the oven to 350 degrees Fahrenheit (176 Celsius).. Set up a 9x13-inch baking dish and put the peppers in the dish to match nicely, cut-side-up.

2. Over medium heat, heat a large skillet, add the oil, onion, and jalapeño, cooking for 2-4 minutes until the onions become translucent.

3. Season the meat with the chili powder, salt, and pepper, add the turkey and split it with a wooden spoon until it is all white, about 4-6 minutes.

4. To the skillet, add the black beans, maize, diced tomatoes, lime juice, cilantro, and cooked rice. Remove from the heat and stir to combine.

5. Fill each pepper evenly with around 3/4 of a cup of the skillet mixture. Pour enough water into the bottom of the baking dish to cover up to around 1 centimeter of the peppers' bottom. As they are in the oven, this will steam the peppers to render them tender.

6. Cover the dish with foil and bake it for 40-45 minutes, until the peppers are tender.

7. Uncover each pepper and top it with 1 tablespoon of cheese and bake for 5 minutes, until the cheese is melted.

8. Add a dollop of optional light sour cream or plain Greek yogurt and extra chopped cilantro and lime to each pepper.

Slow Cooker Quinoa Chicken Chili
(Ready in 5 Hours and 10 Minutes, Serve 6, and Difficulty: Hard)
Nutrition per Serving:

Calories 331, Protein 21 g, Fat 2.5 g, Saturated Fat 1 g, Sugar 4.5 g, Sodium 282mg, Fiber 11 g

Ingredients:

- 1 cup of quinoa, uncooked
- 28 ounces of can crushed tomatoes
- 1 14 ounces of can diced tomatoes
- 1 can, (15 ounces) of black beans*
- 1 can (15 ounces) of kidney beans*
- 2 chicken breasts
- 3 cups of vegetable stock*
- 1 large bell pepper, chopped
- 1 teaspoon of cumin
- 1 teaspoon of chili powder

Instructions:

1. Put all the ingredients in a 6-quart slow cooker and cook for 5-7 hours on low heat.

2. Remove the chicken out of the slow cooker, shred it, pull the chicken apart using two forks, and return it to the slow cooker.

3. Keep the slow cooker warm until you're ready to serve it.

4. Grab a dollop of Greek yogurt or low-Fat cheese and enjoy

Chicken Romano
(Ready in 40 Minutes, Serve 4, Difficulty: Normal)
Nutrition per Serving:

Calories 236, Protein 41.4 g, Carbohydrates 34.2 g, Sugars 5.5 g, Fat 6 g, saturated Fat 1.2 g.

Ingredients:

- 4 (907 g) skinless, boneless chicken breast halves
- 1 egg white
- 1 tablespoon of water
- 1 ¼ cup of cornflakes, crushed (about 1/2 cup)
- 2 tablespoons of grated Romano cheese

- ½ teaspoon of dried, crushed Italian seasoning, basil or oregano
- 4 ounces of dried multi-grain spaghetti
- 1 ⅓ cups of low-sodium tomato-base pasta sauce
- 453 g of shaved or grated Romano cheese
- 1 bunch od snipped fresh Italian parsley, flat-leaf

Instructions:

1. Preheat the oven to 400 degrees Fahrenheit (204 Celsius). Set aside, lightly coat a 15x10-inch baking sheet with nonstick cooking spray or line with foil and coat with cooking spray. Place between two pieces of plastic wrap with each piece of chicken. Pound the chicken lightly until about 1/2-inch-thick, using the flat side of a meat mallet. Remove the plastic wrap. Just set aside.

2. Use a fork to beat the white egg and the water together in a shallow dish. Combine the crushed cornflakes, two tablespoons of grated cheese, the Italian seasoning, and 1/8 teaspoon of ground black pepper in another shallow dish. Dip pieces of chicken, one at a time, into a mixture of eggs, dip into a mixture of cornflakes, turn to coat. In the prepared baking pan, place the coated chicken in it.

3. Bake until the chicken is tender and no longer pink, or about 18 minutes. In the meantime, according to package instructions, cook spaghetti, drain. Cook the pasta sauce in a small saucepan until heated, stirring occasionally.

4. Divide the cooked spaghetti between four serving plates to serve. Top with pasta sauce and chicken. Sprinkle with additional cheese or parsley if desired.

Healthy Spinach Lasagna Rolls
(Ready in 30 Minutes, Serve 9, Difficulty: Hard)
Nutrition per Serving:

Calories 216, Fat 15.9 g, Polyunsaturated Fat 0.4 g, Monounsaturated Fat 2.5 g, Sodium 1,188.6mg.

Ingredients:

- 9 Lasagna noodles, cooked
- 1(10 ounces) package of frozen chopped spinach thawed and completely drained
- 1(15 ounces) container of ricotta cheese
- 1/2 cup of grated parmesan cheese
- 1 egg
- 1/2 teaspoon of minced garlic
- 1/2 teaspoon of dried Italian seasonings
- Salt and fresh pepper
- 1 chicken breast cooked and diced (Optional)
- 32 ounces of marinara sauce
- 9 tablespoons of shredded, part-skim mozzarella cheese

Instructions:

1. Preheat the oven to 350 degrees Fahrenheit (176 Celsius).

2. Make sure the spinach drains well.

3. In a medium cup, mix the spinach, parmesan cheese, ricotta, egg, garlic, chicken, Italian seasonings, and salt and pepper. On the bottom of a 9x13-inch baking platter, add around 1 cup of sauce.

4. On the table, put a piece of wax paper and lay out the lasagna noodles. By patting them with a paper towel, make sure the noodles are dry. Take 1/3 cup of the mixture of ricotta and spread it evenly on a noodle. Place seam side down on the baking dish and roll carefully. Repeat with the noodles that remain.

5. In the baking dish, ladle sauce over the noodles and top each one with 1 tablespoon of mozzarella cheese. Tightly cover the baking dish with aluminum foil and cook for 40 minutes, or until the cheese is melted. Makes nine rolls.

6. Place a little sauce on the plate to serve and top with a lasagna roll

Skinny Three-Cheese Manicotti

(Ready in 1 Hour and 10 Minutes, Serve 6, Difficulty: Hard)

Nutrition per Serving:

Calories 360, Protein 22 g, Total Carbohydrate 39 g, Fat 13 g, Sodium 370mg, Sugars 6 g.

Ingredients:

- 8 dried manicotti shells
- Non-stick cooking spray
- 1 cup of chopped fresh mushrooms
- ¾ cup of purchased shredded carrots
- 3 or 4 cloves of garlic, minced
- 1 cup of light ricotta cheese or low-fat, cottage-style cheese cream
- ¾ cup of shredded reduced-fat mozzarella cheese (3 ounces)
- 2 eggs, lightly beaten
- ¼ cup of grated parmesan cheese
- 2 teaspoons of dried Italian seasoning, crushed
- 1(14.5 ounces) can of Muir Glen™ organic no-salt-added diced tomatoes, undrained
- 1 cup of bottled roasted red sweet peppers, drained and chopped

Instructions:

1. Preheat the furnace to 350 degrees Fahrenheit (176 Celsius). Cook manicotti shells according to the instructions for the box, drain. Using cool water to clean and drain again. Only put aside.

2. Meanwhile, brush an unheated major non-stick skillet with non-stick cooking spray for filling. Preheat over medium heat. To the hot skillet, add the mushrooms, carrots, and garlic cloves Cook for 3-5 minutes or until soft, stirring periodically. Remove from heat, slightly cool. Stir in ricotta cheese, 1/2 cup mozzarella cheese, eggs, parmesan cheese, and season with Italian cheese. Filling a spoon of fried manicotti shells.

3. For the sauce, put undrained tomatoes in a food processor or blender. Cover until smooth, and blend or process. Stir in the red and roasted peppers. In four 12- to 16-ounce ungreased individual baking dishes or a 2-quarter rectangular baking dish, scatter about 1/3 cup of the sauce into the bottoms. Arrange stuffed shells of manicotti in individual baking dishes or large baking dishes, slightly overlapping shells if necessary. Over the manicotti, pour the remaining sauce.

4. For individual baking dishes, bake, covered, for 20-25 minutes, or large baking dishes, for 35-40 minutes or until heated. Uncover the remaining 1/4 cup mozzarella cheese and sprinkle with it. Bake for an extra 5 minutes. Before serving, let it rest for 10 minutes.

Healthy Crockpot Pulled Pork

(Ready in 6 Hour and 10 Minutes, Serve 6, Difficulty: Hard)

Nutrition per Serving:

Calories 346, Protein 41 g, Carbohydrates 13 g, Fat 13 g, Sodium 404mg, Potassium 893mg, Sugar 8 g.

Ingredients:

- 2.5 pound of pork tenderloin (approximately 2 medium pork tenderloins)
- 1/4 cup of extra virgin olive oil
- 1 tablespoon of paprika
- 1 tablespoon of garlic powder
- 1 teaspoon of pepper
- 1/2 teaspoon of onion powder
- 1/2 teaspoon of cinnamon
- 1/4 teaspoon of ginger
- 1 cups chicken of stock

1/2 cup of barbecue sauce of choice (We like Tessamae's®)

Instructions:

Crockpot Instructions:

1. Clean the 'silver skin' off the tenderloin pork.

2. Whisk together the olive oil and spices in a bowl. If possible, in a zip lock bag, marinate the pork in olive oil plus spices overnight, otherwise, place tenderloins in a crockpot and cover with oil/spice marinade. Make sure that all pork areas have some marinade on them.

3. On top of the marinated tenderloin, pour the chicken stock.

4. Cook for 6-8 hours in the crockpot on low or 4-6 hours on high.

5. Use tongs or a fork to pull the tenderloins apart (it'll fall apart when finished cooking. Allow it to soak the juices in the pulled pork.

6. Toss up and enjoy your favorite barbecue sauce!

Instant Pot Instructions:

1. Clean the 'silver skin' off the tenderloin pork. Split into 5–6-inch pieces of pork tenderloin. You might keep the tenderloins whole, so it's going to take longer for the pressure to come in.

2. Whisk together the olive oil and spices in a bowl. If possible, in a zip lock container, marinate the pork in olive oil plus spices overnight, otherwise, put tenderloins in an instant pot and cover with oil/spice marinade. Make sure that all pork areas have a marinade on them.

3. On top of the marinated tenderloin, pour the chicken stock.

4. Set an instant pot for 18 minutes for sealing, pressure cook. Allow the pressure to release gradually for at least 15 minutes when the instant pot is finished, then fast release.

5. Use tongs or a fork to tear the tenderloins apart (it'll break apart while cooking. Allow it to soak the juices in the pulled pork.

6. Toss-up and use your favorite barbecue sauce!

White Beans with Spinach and Sausage

(Ready in 35 Minutes, Serve 6, Difficulty: Normal)

Nutrition per Serving:

Calories 230, Protein 14 g, Carbohydrate 20 g, Fat 9 g, Fiber 6 g, Sodium 890 mg.

Ingredients:

- 8 ounces of turkey or chicken kielbasa sausage
- 2 cups of reduced-sodium chicken broth
- 2 cloves of garlic, minced
- 1 teaspoon of dried oregano
- 1 tablespoon of olive oil
- 1(15 ounces.) can of cannellini beans, drained and rinsed
- 6 cup of baby spinach leaves
- Pepper, to taste

Instructions:

1. Use non-stick cooking spray to spray a medium skillet. Cook the sausage and the juices are drained. Split into 1/4-1/2-inch rounds, and set aside.

2. In a big pot, add in the chicken broth and garlic cloves Place and bring to a boil on medium-high heat.

3. Add the oil, oregano, cooked sausage, and beans. Heat the beans until they are tender.

4. Once the leaves are wilted, add the spinach and cook. Stir and sprinkle on top with pepper.

Mashed Potatoes with Pine Nuts

(Ready in 25 Minutes, Serve 6, Difficulty: Easy)

Nutrition per Serving:

Calories 325, Protein 8 g, Carbohydrates 60 g, Fat 6 g, F

Ingredients:

- 4 pounds peeled and rinsed potatoes
- 1 ½ cups water + ½ cup
- ⅛ Cup pine nuts
- 2 tablespoons olive-oil
- Earth Balance 1 teaspoon salt
- Unsweetened soy milk

Instructions:

1. Put 11/2 cups of water in the pressure cooker.

2. Lower down in the potato steamer basket.

3. Cover the lid and lock it up.

4. Knock on the steam and simmer for 15 minutes.

5. Meanwhile, combine the pine nuts with half a cup of sugar.

6. "Hit "cancel" and quick-release when the pressure cooker beeps.

7. Pull the potatoes out slowly and stab them with a knife.

8. Mash potatoes in a mixer of 1/4 cup of pine nut soy milk combination, Earth Harmony, and salt. In 1/4 cup increments, add soy milk as needed.

9. Enjoy.

Slow Cooker Beef and Broccoli

(Ready in 4 Hour and 30 Minutes, Serve 6, Difficulty: Hard)

Nutrition per Serving:

Calories 126, Protein 48 g, Carbohydrates 35 g, Fat 34 g, Fiber 2 g, Sugar 12 g.

Ingredients:

- 2 pound of sirloin steak (905 g), or boneless beef chuck roast, sliced thin
- 1 cup (240 ml) of beef broth
- ½ cup (120 ml) of low Sodium soy sauce
- ¼ cup (55 g) of brown sugar
- 1 tablespoon of sesame oil
- 4 cloves of garlic, minced
- 4 tablespoons of cornstarch
- 4 tablespoons of water
- 1 head broccoli, cut into florets

For Serving:

* white rice, cooked,

Instructions:

1. Whisk the beef broth, soy sauce, minced garlic, sesame oil, and brown sugar together in the crockpot insert.

2. Place the beef slices in the liquid and toss to coat them.

3. Cover with a lid and cook for 4 hours over low heat.

4. After 4 hours, whisk the cornstarch and water together in a small bowl. Pour the broccoli into a crockpot, add the broccoli and stir gently to combine.

5. Cover with a lid and cook the broccoli and thicken the sauce for 30 minutes.

6. Use warm white rice to serve.

7. Enjoy!

Chicken Cordon Bleu Casserole–Low Carb

(Ready in 45 Minutes, Serve 8, Difficulty: Normal)

Nutrition per Serving:

Calories 232, Protein 34 g, Carbohydrates 2 g, Fat 34 g, Sodium 916mg, Potassium 348mg, Sugar 1 g.

Ingredients:

* 6 cups of shredded cooked chicken (From about 2 pound of chicken)
* 6 ounces of ham cut into bite-size pieces
* 4 ounces of butter melted
* 6 ounces of softened cheese cream
* 1 tablespoon of Dijon mustard
* 1 tablespoon of white wine (optional)
* 1 ounces of lemon juice
* 1/2 teaspoon of salt
* 5 ounces of Swiss cheese

Instructions:

1. Preheat the oven to 350 degrees Fahrenheit (176 Celsius). Put the chicken in a 9x13-inch baking dish at the bottom of the pan. Layer the pieces on top of the ham.

2. Combine melted butter, white wine (if used), softened cream cheese, mustard, lemon juice, and salt in a large bowl with an electric mixer. Blend until it forms a thick sauce. In the baking dish, spread this sauce over the chicken and ham.

3. Place the Swiss cheese slices on top of the sauce. Bake until sweet, for 30-40 minutes.

4. At the end, I broiled it for 2 minutes so that the cheese will become bubblier and more golden. Do not leave it unattended if you have agreed to do so. The cheese topping is easy to burn.

Parmesan and Spinach Orzo

(Ready in 30 Minutes, Serve 6, Difficulty: Easy)

Nutrition per Serving:

Calories 309.8, Carbohydrate 42.3 g, Fat 9.1 g, Sodium 231.7mg.

Ingredients:

* 1 cup of orzo pasta
* 1 tablespoon of olive oil
* 2 cloves of garlic, minced
* 1 onion, diced
* 1 tablespoon of all-purpose flour
* 1 cup of milk
* 1 1/2 cup of roughly chopped spinach
* 1/2 cup of grated parmesan cheese
* Kosher salt and freshly ground black pepper, to taste

Instructions:

1. Cook pasta according to package instructions in a large pot of boiling salted water. Drain well.

2. Over medium heat, heat the olive oil in a saucepan. Add the garlic and onions and cook for around 2-3 minutes, frequently stirring, until the onions are translucent.

3. Whisk in the flour for around 1 minute, until lightly browned. Gradually whisk in the milk, and cook for around 3-4 minutes, whisking continuously, until slightly thickened.

4. Add spinach and cook for around 2-3 minutes, until wilted. Stir in the parmesan until melted, 1 minute or so. To mix, add orzo and gently toss, season with salt and pepper to taste.

5. Immediately serve.

Baked Cod and Asparagus in Garlic Lemon Caper Sauce

(Ready in 30 Minutes, Serve 2, Difficulty: Easy)

Nutrition per Serving:

Calories 278, Protein 33 g, Carbohydrates 8 g, Fat 12 g, Sodium 498mg, Potassium 980mg, Fiber 3 g, Sugar 2 g.

Ingredients:

* 4 fillets cod (I used pacific cod)
* 453 gramsof asparagus (ends trimmed)
* Salt and pepper
* 1 teaspoon of Italian seasoning (thyme, oregano)
* 4 cloves of garlic, minced
* 1 lemon, thinly sliced
* 1/4 cup of capers, drained
* 4 tablespoons of butter

Instructions:

1. Preheat the oven to 400 degrees Fahrenheit (204 Celsius).

2. Make four separate foil pieces (large enough to completely cover each fish fillet, when folded).

3. In the center of each foil, place equal portions of asparagus (end trimmed). Season the asparagus with pepper and salt. Set each fillet of fish on top of the asparagus. With a pinch of Italian herbal seasoning, salt, and pepper, season each fillet and sprinkle minced garlic over each fillet and asparagus.

4. Put a thin lemon slice on top of each cod fillet. Sprinkle each fillet with 1 tablespoon of caper. Thinly sliced, top each fillet with 1 tablespoon butter.

5. To fully enclose it, wrap the foil ends above the top of the cod, but do not wrap too tightly or too close to the fish, leave some space.

6. Place fillets of foil-wrapped fish on a baking sheet. Bake at 400 degrees Fahrenheit (204 Celsius) for 20 minutes, until the cod is cooked and flaky. Depending on your oven and the cod fillet's thickness, it might be ready in 15 minutes.

Broccoli Cheese and Potato Soup

(Ready in 30 Minutes, Serve 8, Difficulty: Easy)

Nutrition per Serving:

Calories 327, Protein 18 g, Carbohydrates 23 g, Fat 19 g, Sodium 922mg, Potassium 822mg, Fiber 4 g, Sugar 7 g.

Ingredients:

- 1 tablespoon of butter
- 1 medium yellow onion chopped
- 3 large white potatoes cubed, about 4 cups
- 4 cups of chicken broth
- 1/2 teaspoon of kosher salt
- 6 cups of broccoli florets*
- 3 cups of whole milk
- 3 cups of shredded medium cheddar cheese
- 2 tablespoons of flour
- 1 teaspoon of freshly ground black pepper

Instructions:

1. In a big Dutch oven over medium heat, melt the butter. Add the onion and simmer for 4-5 minutes, stirring regularly, until softened.

2. Bring to a boil, then reduce the heat to a rolling simmer and cook the potatoes for around 8 minutes or until tender and easily pierced with a fork. Add the cubed potatoes, chicken broth, and kosher salt. Whiz the potatoes and broth to the consistency you want with an immersion blender (I want to leave some bits of potato), or mash with a potato masher.

3. Include the broccoli florets and milk and bring to a boil, cook for 5-7 minutes or until the broccoli is dent, then reduce to a simmer.

4. Toss the flour with the cheese and add 1 cup at a time to the broth, stirring until it is melted, before adding the next batch of cheese. To taste, season with black pepper and more salt.

Recipe Notes: I used fresh broccoli in this soup, but frozen will work in a pinch.

Broiled Tilapia Parmesan

(Ready in 15 Minutes, Serve 8, Difficulty: Easy)

Nutrition per Serving:

Calories 22, Protein 25.4 g, Carbohydrates 0.8 g, Fat 12.8 g, Cholesterol 63.3mg, Sodium 220.5mg.

Ingredients:

- ½ cup of parmesan cheese
- ¼ cup of softened butter
- 3 tablespoons of mayonnaise
- 2 tablespoons of fresh lemon juice
- ¼ teaspoon of dried basil
- ¼ teaspoon of ground black pepper
- ⅛ teaspoon of onion powder
- ⅛ teaspoon of celery salt
- 907 g of tilapia fillets

Instructions:

1. Preheat the broiler in your oven. Grease a broiling pan with aluminum foil or line pan.

2. Blend the parmesan cheese, butter, mayonnaise, and lemon juice in a small cup. Use dried basil, mustard, onion powder, and celery salt to season. Mix thoroughly and put aside.

3. Arrange fillets on a prepared pan in a single sheet. Broil for 2-3 minutes, a few inches from the heat. For a few more minutes, turn the fillets over and broil. Take the fillets from the oven and coat them with the top side of the parmesan cheese mixture. Broil for another 2 minutes or until browned and fish flakes quickly with a fork on the topping. Be alert that the fish is not overcooked.

Best Turkey Meatloaf

(Ready in 1 Hour and 15 Minutes, Serve 8, Difficulty: Hard)

Nutrition per Serving:

Calories 296, Protein 19.7 g, Carbohydrates 25.2 g, Fat 13.2 g, Cholesterol 84.5mg, Sodium 880.8mg.

For Meatloaf:

- 680 g of ground turkey
- ¾ cup of crushed buttery round crackers
- ½ cup of milk
- 1 small onion, chopped
- 1 egg
- 1 ½ teaspoon of salt

- 2 cloves of garlic, minced
- ¼ teaspoon of ground black pepper

For Topping:
- ½ cup of ketchup
- ¼ cup of brown sugar
- 1 tablespoon of Worcestershire sauce

Instructions:

1. Preheat the oven to 350 degrees Fahrenheit (176 degrees Celsius). Grease a jelly roll pan lightly.

2. In a bowl, combine ground turkey, milk, onion, egg, salt, buttery round cracker crumbs, garlic, and black pepper, shape into a loaf, and place on the rolling pan of jelly.

3. In a separate bowl, combine brown sugar, ketchup, and Worcestershire sauce. Set aside.

4. Cook the meatloaf in a preheated oven for 30 minutes, remove the liquid from the oven, and drain. Meatloaf top with ketchup topping. Return the loaf to the oven and continue to bake until the center is no longer pink, about an extra 30 minutes. A center-inserted instant-read thermometer should read at least 160 degrees Fahrenheit (70 degrees Celsius).

Chili Pasta Bake

(Ready in 40 Minutes, Serve 6, Difficulty: Normal)

Nutrition per Serving:

Calories 102, Protein 29.5 g, Fat 25.5 g, Saturated Fat 12.6 g, Sodium 1248.3mg, Sugars 6.9 g.

Ingredients:
- 10 ounces of penne pasta
- 453 gramsof ground beef
- 1 medium onion, chopped
- 2 tablespoons of chili powder
- 1(14 1/2 ounces) can of canned tomatoes, diced cut
- 1(8 ounces) can of tomato sauce
- 1 cup of sauce
- 1(7 ounces) can of diced green chilies, drained
- 2 cups of shredded longhorn cheddar cheese

Instructions:

1. According to package instructions, prepare the pasta, drain.

2. Spray, set aside, a 13x9-inch pan with cooking spray.

3. Preheat the oven to 350 F (176 Celsius).

4. In a large saucepan, cook the meat and onion and drain.

5. To the meat mixture, add the chili powder, tomato sauce, undrained tomatoes, salsa, and chilies.

6. Cook for five more minutes, add the cooked pasta to the mixture and mix well.

7. Pour into the prepared dish, top with the cheese, and bake for 20 minutes in a preheated oven or until thoroughly melted and bubbly.

Spinach and Tortellini Soup

(Ready in 20 Minutes, Serve 6, Difficulty: Easy)

Nutrition per Serving:

Calories 16, Protein 7 g, Carbohydrate 15 g, Fat 5 g, Saturated Fat 2 g, Cholesterol 18mg, Sodium 799mg, Sugars 4 g, Fiber 2 g.

Ingredients:
- 1 teaspoon of olive oil
- 2 cloves of garlic, minced
- 1 can (14-1/2 ounces) of no-salt-added diced tomatoes, undrained
- 3 cans (14-1/2 ounces each) of vegetable broth
- 2 teaspoons of Italian seasoning
- 1 package (9 ounces) of refrigerated cheese tortellini
- 4 cups of fresh baby spinach
- Shredded parmesan cheese
- Freshly ground pepper

Instructions:

1. Heat oil over low heat in a large saucepan. Add the garlic, simmer for 1 minute, and stir. Carry to a boil, stir in the onions, broth, and Italian seasoning. Add the tortellini and carry it to a mild boil. Cook, uncovered, for 7-9 minutes, until the tortellini is tender.

2. Stir the spinach in. Sprinkle cheese and pepper on the servings.

Italian Stuffed Flank Steak

(Ready in 35 Minutes, Serve 3, Difficulty: Easy)

Nutrition per Serving:

Calories 299, Protein 59 g, Carbohydrates 2 g, Fat: 37 g, Sodium 558mg, Potassium 909mg.

Ingredients:
- 3-4 cloves of garlic minced or pressed through garlic press
- 1 small shallot minced
- 2 tablespoons of fresh parsley finely minced
- 1 teaspoon of sage leaves finely minced
- 1 teaspoon of basil minced
- 2 tablespoons of olive oil
- Two 907 g flank steak
- 4 ounces of thinly sliced prosciutto
- 4 ounces of thinly sliced provolone cheese
- Toothpicks-soaked water for 10 minutes

* Salt and pepper, to taste

Instructions:

1. In a small bowl, mix the garlic, shallot, parsley, basil, sage, and olive oil.

2. Sliced horizontally into two thin rectangles around the beef, butterfly, and 907 g flank steak. Spread the herb mixture evenly over the steak's surface so that the grain runs parallel to the edge of the counter.

3. Lay the prosciutto evenly over the steak, leaving the top edge with a 1-inch border.

4. Cover the prosciutto with an even layer of cheese, leaving the top edge with a 1-inch border.

5. Roll steak into tight log and place on cutting board seam-side down, starting from the bottom edge and rolling up away from you, towards the top.

6. Tie a piece of kitchen twine to secure the steak, starting from the middle of the steak roll. Working outward from the center, place more kitchen twine ties at intervals of 1 inch until the entire steak roll is tied up.

7. Slice the pieces of twine into 1-inch-thick pinwheels using a sharp knife. Lightly season the pinwheels with salt and black pepper.

8. With a toothpick, skewer each pinwheel.

9. Preheat the furnace to 350 F (176 Celsius).

10. Over medium-high heat, heat a cast-iron skillet. Place the pinwheels in the pan and brown for about three minutes. For 2 minutes, flip over and brown on the other side.

11. Slide the skillet into a preheated oven and cook for about 8-10 minutes or until the steak achieves the desired doneness.

12. Take the aluminum foil tent from the oven and let it rest for 5 minutes.

13. Remove the toothpicks and enjoy!

Cheesy Chicken Rolls

(Ready in 30 Minutes, Serve 6, Difficulty: Easy)

Nutrition per Serving:

Calories 177, Protein 59.9 g, Carbohydrates 30.9 g, Fat 43.5 g, Cholesterol 171.4mg, Sodium 1723.8mg.

Ingredients:

* 1(8 ounces) can of refrigerated crescent roll dough
* 4 slices of processed American cheese, cut in ½
* 4 cups of cooked, boneless chicken breast halves, shredded
* 1(10.5 ounce) can of condensed cream of chicken soup
* 1 cup of milk
* 1 cup of shredded cheddar cheese

Instructions:

1. Preheat the oven to 375 degrees Fahrenheit (190 degrees Celsius). Grease a 9x13-inch baking dish.

2. Unroll the dough and divide it into eight triangles. Place 1/2 cup of American cheese and 1/2 cup of shredded chicken on the large end of the triangle. Roll and seal the edges with the dough. Placed the prepared dish in place.

3. Mix the broth, milk, and cheddar cheese in a small bowl and spill over the stuffed rolls.

4. Bake for 12-15 minutes in a preheated oven, or until golden brown.

Stuffed Pepper Casserole

(Ready in 1 Hour, Serve 6, Difficulty: Normal)

Nutrition per Serving:

Calories 390, Protein 25 g, Carbohydrate 36 g, Fat 16 g, Sodium 1490mg, Potassium 600mg, Sugars 5 g

Ingredients:

* 453 gramsof ground beef (at least 90% lean)
* 2 cups of diced bell peppers
* ½ cup of diced yellow onion
* 1 teaspoon of Italian seasoning
* ½ teaspoon of salt
* ¼ teaspoon of pepper
* 3 cloves of garlic, finely chopped
* 2 cups of Progresso™ beef flavored broth (from 32-oz carton)
* 1 can (14.5 ounces) of Muir Glen™ organic diced tomatoes, undrained
* 1 can (8 ounces) of tomato sauce
* 1 tablespoon of soy sauce
* 1 cup of uncooked white basmati rice
* 1 ½ cup of shredded cheddar cheese or cheddar cheese blend (6 ounces)

Instructions:

1. Cook the beef, Italian seasoning, bell peppers, onion, salt, and pepper in a 5-quart Dutch oven over medium-high heat for 8-10 minutes, stirring regularly, until the beef is brown and the vegetables are tender.

2.Add garlic cloves, mix and cook for an additional minute.

3. Add the broth, onions, tomato sauce, and soy sauce and reduce the heat to mild. Stir once mixed properly. Bring to boil.

4. Add the uncooked rice. Return to boiling and reduce the heat to medium. Cover and cook for about 25 minutes or until tender.

5. Stir in 1 cup of the shredded cheese, and remove from the heat. Sprinkle with 1/2 of the remaining

cup of cheese. Cover and let stand for 3 to 5 minutes or until the cheese melts.

Honey Lime Shrimp

(Ready in 20 Minutes, Serve 4, Difficulty: Easy)

Nutrition per Serving

Calories 224, Protein 29 g. Carbohydrates 14 g, Fat 8 g, Sodium 226mg, Potassium 127mg, Sugar 13 g.

Ingredients:

- 3 tablespoons of honey
- 3 tablespoons of fresh lime juice plus 1 teaspoon lime zest
- 2 tablespoons of butter
- 1 113 grams of large or extra-large raw shrimp, peeled and deveined, dabbed dry with paper towels
- 1 large clove of garlic, minced (1 1/2 teaspoon)
- Salt and pepper

Instructions:

1. Whisk the honey and lime juice together in a small mixing bowl.

2. Melt butter over medium heat in a 12-inch non-stick pan. Stir in the garlic and cook for 30 seconds.

3. Add the shrimp, season with salt and pepper, and pour in the mixture of honey and lime. Spread out the shrimp in an even layer.

4. Cook on the bottom until pink and opaque, about 1 1/2 minutes, then turn and continue to cook until shrimp have cooked through, about 1 1/2 minutes longer.

5. Using lime zest to sprinkle. If spooning sauce over shrimp is required, serve warm over rice.

Notes: Optionally top shrimp with 2 tablespoons of minced cilantro after cooking for more flavor.

Chapter 7: Salad Recipes

In this chapter we are going to give you some delicious and mouthwatering recipes on Lean & Green Salad recipes.

No-Cook Cranberry Salad

(Ready in 1 Hour, Serve 8, Difficulty: Normal)

Nutrition per Serving:

Calories 142, Protein 1.3 g, Carbohydrates 24.2 g, Fat 5.3 g, Cholesterol 0mg, Sodium 15.2mg.

Ingredients:

- 1(14.5 ounces) can of whole cranberry sauce, such as Ocean Spray®
- 6 seedless green grapes, halved
- ¼ (11 ounces) can of mandarin oranges, drained and quartered
- 2 tablespoons of sweetened flaked coconut
- ½ teaspoon of vanilla extract
- ½ cup of chopped walnuts
- 1 red apple diced

Instructions:

1. In a bowl, add cranberry sauce, grapes, coconut, mandarin oranges, vanilla, walnuts, and apple.

2. Allow it to set before serving for 30 minutes.

Cranberry Jell-O® Salad

(Ready in 40 Minutes, Serve 12, Difficulty: Normal)

Nutrition per Serving:

Calories 209, Protein 2.6 g, Carbohydrates 36.7 g, Fat 7.2 g, Cholesterol 0mg, Sodium 51.3mg.

Ingredients:

- 2 cups of fresh cranberries
- 1(15 ounces) can of mandarin oranges, drained and chopped
- 1 cup of pecans
- 1(15 ounces) can of crushed pineapple, drained
- 2(3 ounces) packages of cranberry-flavored gelatin mix (such as Jell-O®)
- ¾ cup of white sugar
- 1 cup of boiling water
- 1 cup of cold water

Instructions:

1. Place cranberries, mandarin oranges, and pecans into a food processor and pulse several times to chop, process mixture until finely ground, about 30 seconds. Transfer mixture into a large bowl.

2. Mix pineapple, gelatin, sugar, boiling water, and cold water in a separate bowl until gelatin and sugar dissolve. Pour gelatin mixture into cranberry mixture and stir.

3. Pour into a gelatin mold and refrigerate 8 hours or overnight before serving.

Spinach Pomegranate Salad

(Ready in 40 Minutes, Serve 4, Difficulty: Normal)

Nutrition per Serving:

Calories 273, Protein 9.5 g, Carbohydrates 14.9 g, Fat 21.4 g, Cholesterol 28mg, Sodium 584.6mg.

Ingredients:

- 1(10 ounces) bag of baby spinach leaves, rinsed and drained
- ¼ red onion, sliced very thin
- ½ cup of walnut pieces
- ½ cup of crumbled feta
- ¼ cup of alfalfa sprouts (Optional)
- 1 pomegranate, peeled and seeds separated
- 4 tablespoons of balsamic vinaigrette

Instructions:

1. Place the spinach in a bowl with the salad. Place the red onion, walnuts, feta, and sprouts on top.

2. Sprinkle the top with pomegranate seeds, and sprinkle with the vinaigrette.

Mom G's Cranberry Jell-O® Salad

(Ready in 4 Hours and 35 Minutes, Serve 8, and Difficulty: Normal)

Nutrition per Serving:

Calories 260, Protein 3.4 g, Carbohydrates 54.3 g, Fat 4.9 g, Cholesterol 0mg, Sodium 127.9mg.

Ingredients:

- 2(3 ounces) packages of lemon-flavored gelatin mix (such as Jell-O®)
- 1½ cup of boiling water
- 2 cups of cold water
- 1(12 ounces) package of fresh cranberries
- 1 cup of white sugar
- 1 cup of crushed pineapple, drained
- ¾ cup of chopped celery
- ½ cup of chopped walnuts

Instructions:

1. In a bowl of boiling water, dissolve the lemon gelatin and stir in cold water. Chill in the refrigerator for 30-40 minutes, before slightly thickened.

2. In a food processor, chop cranberries and blend sugar into cranberries, pulsating once or twice to

combine. Let the cranberry mixture rest for a few minutes to remove the sugar.

3. Stir the mixture of cranberries, pineapple, celery, and walnuts into the jelly. Pour into a mold of gelatin or a serving bowl. Refrigerate for about 4 hours before fully set.

Winter Fruit Salad with Lemon Poppy seed Dressing

(Ready in 35 Minutes, Serve 12, Difficulty: Normal)

Nutrition per Serving:

Calories 277, Protein 4.9 g, Carbohydrates 21 g, Fat 20.6 g, Cholesterol 8.7mg, Sodium 201.3mg.

Ingredients:

- ½ cup of white sugar
- ½ cup of lemon juice
- 2 teaspoons of diced onion
- 1 teaspoon of Dijon-style prepared mustard
- ½ teaspoon of salt
- 1 cup of vegetable oil
- 1 tablespoon of poppy seeds
- 1 head of romaine lettuce, torn into bite-size pieces
- 4 ounces of shredded Swiss cheese
- 1 cup of cashews
- ¼ cup of dried cranberries
- 1 apple, peeled, cored, and diced
- 1 pear, peeled, cored, and sliced

Instructions:

1. Put the sugar, mustard, lemon juice, onion, and salt together in a blender or food processor. Blend properly. Add oil in a slow process with the machine still running.

2. Steady flow until the mixture is dense and smooth. Add the poppy seeds and blend them for just a few more seconds.

3. Toss together the romaine lettuce, sliced Swiss cheese, dried cranberries, cashews, apple, and pear in a large serving dish. Just before eating, pour the dressing over the salad and toss to coat.

Roasted Beet Salad

(Ready in 40 Minutes, Serve 4, Difficulty: Normal)

Nutrition per Serving:

Calories 66, Protein 2 g, Carbohydrates 15.1 g, Fat 0.2 g, Cholesterol 0mg, Sodium 136.9mg.

Ingredients:

- 6 medium beets, trimmed and scrubbed
- 2 tablespoons of aged balsamic vinegar

- 2 teaspoons of real maple syrup
- Salt and ground black pepper, to taste

Instructions:

1. The oven should be preheated to 400 degrees Fahrenheit (204 degrees Celsius). Loosely cover the beets in aluminum foil and place them on a rimmed baking sheet.

2. Roast in the preheated oven for 50-60 minutes before quickly pierced with a knife or skewer. Unwrap and cool for about 10 minutes until it is comfortable to handle.

3. Peel and slice the beets into chunks.

4. Stir together the vinegar and maple syrup and season with salt and pepper. Pour the beets over. Refrigerate for at least 1 hour until the beets absorb the flavors. Serve it cold.

Autumn Salad with Caramel-Sesame Dressing

(Ready in 40 Minutes, Serve 1, Difficulty: Normal)

Nutrition per Serving:

Calories 223, Protein 4.5 g, Carbohydrates 52 g, Fat 2.6 g, Cholesterol 0.2mg, Sodium 140.1mg.

Ingredients:

- 1 ½ cup of chopped fresh spinach
- 1 ½ cup of chopped romaine lettuce
- ½ ripe Bartlett pear, skinned, cored, and diced into medium chunks
- ½ Fuji apple, skin on, cored, and diced into medium chunks
- ¼ cup of halved seedless red grapes (Optional)
- 3 tablespoons of rice vinegar
- 1 tablespoon of caramel topping, such as Hershey's®
- ¼ teaspoon of sesame oil
- ¼ teaspoon of toasted sesame seeds

Instructions:

1. Place on a plate of spinach, pear, romaine lettuce, apple, and grapes.

2. In a bowl, combine the vinegar, sesame oil, caramel topping, and sesame seeds.

3. Pour the salad over the dressing.

Cranberry Jell-O® Salad with Walnuts

(Ready in 3 Hours, Serve 20, Difficulty: Hard)

Nutrition per Serving:

Calories 131, Protein 1.7 g, Carbohydrates 24.2 g, Fat 3.8 g, Cholesterol 0mg, Sodium 47.7mg.

Ingredients:

- 1(6 ounces) package of cherry-flavored gelatin mix (such as Jell-O®)
- 1½ cup of boiling water
- 2(14.5 ounces) cans of whole berry cranberry sauce
- 2 oranges, peeled and chopped
- 1 cup of diced apple
- 1 cup of chopped walnuts.

Instructions:

1. In a bowl, melt the cherry gelatin blend in hot water, and add the cranberry sauce and oranges to the gelatin. Refrigerate until the mixture is thickened, about 45 minutes, to the consistency of egg whites.

2. Mix the apple and walnuts in the gelatin, transfer to a serving dish or mold, and cook for another 2 hours until firm.

Fresh Cranberry Salad with Celery

(Ready in 40 Minutes, Serve 8, Difficulty: Normal)

Nutrition per Serving:

Calories 265, Protein 3.1 g, Carbohydrates 55.8 g, Fat 5.1 g, Cholesterol 0mg, Sodium 48.3mg.

Ingredients:

- 2 cups of orange juice
- 1(12 ounces) package of fresh cranberries
- 1 cup of white sugar
- 1(3 ounces) package of orange-flavored gelatin (such as Jell-O®)
- 2 bananas, diced
- 1 Granny Smith apple, diced
- 2 stalks of celery, finely chopped
- ½ cup of chopped walnuts

Instructions:

1. In one 1/2-quart pot over medium heat, add orange juice, cranberries, and sugar. Cook for about 5 minutes until the sugar dissolves, and the cranberries start to pop.

2. Remove from the heat and stir in the orange gelatin.

3. Let it cool for at least 20 minutes at room temperature. Stir in the bananas, apples, walnuts, and celery. Refrigerate for 4 hours to overnight, until set.

Maple Cannellini Bean Salad with Baby Broccoli and Butternut Squash

(Ready in 40 Minutes, Serve 8, Difficulty: Normal)

Nutrition per Serving:

Calories 283, Protein 6 g, Carbohydrates 23.8 g, Fat 7 g, Cholesterol 3.7mg, Sodium 323.2mg.

Ingredients:

- 2(15 ounces) cans of cannellini beans, drained and rinsed
- 1 tablespoon of olive oil
- 1 red onion, chopped
- 1 tablespoon of maple syrup
- 1 tablespoon of olive oil
- 1 cup of peeled, seeded, and diced butternut squash
- 1 tablespoon of maple syrup
- 1 tablespoon of olive oil
- 1 cup of chopped baby broccoli
- ¼ cup of chicken stock
- 1 tablespoon of maple syrup
- ½ teaspoon of dried thyme leaves
- 3 slices of bacon, cooked and crumbled

Instructions:

1. Heat the cannellini beans in a saucepan over low heat.

2. Over medium heat, heat one tablespoon of olive oil in a skillet. Add the red onion, cook and stir until the onion is tender and translucent about 5 minutes. Add one tablespoon of maple syrup, reduce heat to medium-low, cook and stir until very tender and dark brown, about 15 more minutes. Remove from the pan and stir in the beans.

3. Heat one additional tablespoon of olive oil over medium heat in a skillet. Add the butternut squash, cook and stir for about 8 minutes, until tender.

4. Add 1 tablespoon of maple syrup and simmer for about 5 minutes, stirring to coat. Remove the bean mixture from the skillet and add the squash.

5. Over medium heat, heat the remaining one tablespoon of olive oil in a skillet. Add the baby broccoli, cook and stir for about 7 minutes, until tender and bright green. Combine the bean mixture with the broccoli.

6. Pour the chicken stock into the bean mixture, raise the heat to medium-low, and add 1 tablespoon of the remaining maple syrup and thyme to the mixture. Carry to a boil and cook until thoroughly cooked, stirring to combine gently before serving, top with crumbled bacon.

Warm Bok Choy, Beet and Feta Salad

(Ready in 40 Minutes, Serve 3, Difficulty: Normal)

Nutrition per Serving:

Calories 212, Protein 5.5 g, Carbohydrates 12.5 g, Fat 16.5 g, Cholesterol 20.2mg, Sodium 333.7mg.

Ingredients:

- 4 small beets, trimmed, leaving 1 inch of stems Added
- 4 cloves of garlic, chopped, divided
- 1 teaspoon of olive oil
- 3 heads of baby bok Choy, chopped
- 2 tablespoons of peanut oil
- 1 ½ teaspoon of butter
- ⅓ cup of crumbled feta cheese

Instructions:

1. Preheat the oven to 425 degrees Fahrenheit (218 degrees Celsius). On a piece of heavy aluminum foil, put the beets, ¼ of the chopped garlic, and the olive oil, and fold the foil into a sealed packet around the beets.

2. Roast the beets in the preheated oven for 40 minutes to 1 hour before they are easily pierced with a fork.

3. Only let the beets cool so they can be treated, then rub to loosen the skin with a paper towel. Set aside to slice into ½-inch squares.

4. In a heavy skillet over medium-high pressure, heat the peanut oil and butter. Cook and stir together Bok Choy and the remaining garlic until bok Choy, about 5 minutes, is slightly softened but still crunchy. Stir in the beets and feta, and remove from the heat. Serve it hot.

Healthier Cranberry Salad

(Ready in 40 Minutes, Serve 9, Difficulty: Normal)

Nutrition per Serving:

Calories 109, Protein 1.6 g, Carbohydrates 18.3 g, Fat 4.4 g, Cholesterol 0mg, Sodium 1.4mg.

Ingredients:

- 1(12 ounces) package of fresh cranberries
- 2 large oranges, peeled and seeded
- 2 apples, cored and chopped
- ½ cup of chopped walnuts
- 2 tablespoons of honey

Instructons:

1. MIx the cranberries and oranges in a food processor. Coarsely chop when combined, then place in a bowl of salad.

2. To the food processor, add apples and chop coarsely. Mix the apples with the orange and cranberry blend.

3. Add the chopped nuts to the fruit mixture, stir to taste, and sweeten. Serve chilled and refrigerated.

Sour Cream Cranberry Jell-O® Salad

(Ready in 40 Minutes, Serve 24, Difficulty: Normal)

Nutrition per Serving:

Calories 94, Protein 1.3 g, Carbohydrates 14.1 g, Fat 4 g, Cholesterol 8.3mg, Sodium 47.8mg.

Ingredients:

- 1(16 ounces) can of jellied cranberry sauce
- 2(3 ounces) packages of black cherry-flavored gelatin mix (such as Jell-O®)
- 1¾ cups of boiling water
- 1(16 ounces) carton of sour cream

Instructions:

1. In a 3-quart dish, mash the jellied cranberry sauce. Mix the gelatin thoroughly with the cranberry sauce. Pour the boiling water into the mixture and stir for about 3 minutes until the gelatin has fully dissolved.

2. Chill until softly set in the refrigerator, 2-3 hours. Fold the sour cream softly onto the gelatin mixture, leaving the sour cream and gelatin blend in the marbled streaks.

3. Return to the refrigerator until firmly fixed, overnight for 4 hours.

4. Store the leftovers in the fridge.

Warm Brussels Sprout Salad with Hazelnuts and Cranberries.

(Ready in 40 Minutes, Serve 6, Difficulty: Normal)

Nutrition per Serving:

Calories 295, Protein 7.1 g, Carbohydrates 31.1 g, Fat 18.3 g, Cholesterol 5mg, Sodium 123.7mg.

Ingredients:

- 453 g of Brussels sprouts, trimmed and quartered
- 2 tablespoons of olive oil
- Salt and ground black pepper, to taste
- 1 cup of chopped hazelnuts
- 3 slices of thick-cut bacon, chopped
- 2 tablespoons of maple syrup
- 2 tablespoons of chopped fresh rosemary
- 1 cup of dried cranberries
- ¼ cup of grated Pecorino-Romano cheese

Instructions:

1. Preheat the oven to 425 degrees Fahrenheit (218 degrees Celsius).

2. Toss the Brussels sprouts together in a bowl of olive oil, salt, and pepper until they are covered. Transfer the coated sprouts to a tray for baking.

3. Bake in the preheated oven for about 15 minutes, until the sprouts are tender.

4. Cook and mix the hazelnuts in a skillet over medium-low heat for about 5 minutes, until lightly toasted and fragrant. Transfer the hazelnuts to a saucepan.

5. In the same pan, cook and stir the bacon over medium heat until crisp, for around 10 minutes. Add the maple syrup and rosemary and cook until the bacon and maple syrup begins to thicken and stick to the back of the spoon, often stirring, for about 10 minutes.

6. In a wide cup, combine the cooked Brussels sprouts with the bacon mixture and toss until the sprouts are filled with maple syrup sauce.

7. Sprinkle with Pecorino-Romano cheese, hazelnuts, cranberries, and toss well. It's best to serve this dish warm.

Roasted Yam and Kale Salad

(Ready in 40 Minutes, Serve 6, Difficulty: Normal)

Nutrition per Serving:

Calories 274, Protein 5 g, Carbohydrates 49.2 g, Fat 7.5 g, Cholesterol 0mg, Sodium 46.3mg.

Ingredients:

- 2 jewel yams, cut into 1-inch cubes
- 2 tablespoons of olive oil
- Salt and freshly ground black pepper, to taste
- 1 tablespoon of olive oil
- 1 onion, sliced
- 3 cloves of garlic, minced
- 1 bunch of kale, torn into bite-sized pieces
- 2 tablespoons of red wine vinegar
- 1 teaspoon of chopped fresh thyme

Instructions:

1. Preheat the oven to a temperature of 400 degrees Fahrenheit (204 degrees Celsius). In a cup, toss the yams with 2 teaspoons of olive oil. Season with salt and pepper to taste, and spread it uniformly on a baking dish.

2. Bake until the yams are tender, 20-25 minutes in the preheated oven.

3. Cool in the refrigerator to room temperature.

4. Meanwhile, over medium heat, heat the remaining one tablespoon of olive oil in a large skillet. Cook and stir in the onion and garlic until the onion is golden brown, about 15 minutes. Stir in the kale and simmer until tender and wilted. Transfer the kale mixture to a bowl, then cool in the refrigerator at room temperature.

5. Combine the yams, spinach, red wine vinegar, and fresh thyme in a bowl until all the ingredients have cooled. With salt and pepper, season to taste, and mix gently to combine.

Cranberry Salad II

(Ready in 20 Minutes, Serve 7, Difficulty: Easy)

Nutrition per Serving:

Calories 315, Protein 4.3 g, Carbohydrates 54.5 g, Fat 11 g, Cholesterol 0mg, Sodium 60.7mg.

Ingredients:

- 2 cups of cranberries
- 1 large orange
- 1 cup of white sugar
- 1 cup of finely chopped walnuts
- 1 cup of chopped celery
- 1 cup of crushed pineapple, drained
- 1(3 ounces) package of raspberry flavored Jell-O® mix
- 2 cups of hot water

Instructions:

1. Combine the gelatin (do not make it stand) with hot water. Mix cranberries with orange (including rind) and sugar. Stir in the almonds, pineapple, and celery.

2. Mix and chill with prepared gelatin.

Sour Cream Cranberry Jell-O® Salad

(Ready in 30 Minutes, Serve 24, Difficulty: Normal)

Nutrition per Serving:

Calories 94, Protein 1.3 g, Carbohydrates 14.1 g, Fat 4 g, Cholesterol 8.3mg, Sodium 47.8mg.

Ingredients:

- 1(16 ounces) can of jellied cranberry sauce
- 2(3 ounces) packages of black cherry-flavored gelatin mix (such as Jell-O®)
- 1 ¾ cup of boiling water
- 1(16 ounces) carton of sour cream

Instructions:

1. In a 3-quart bowl, mash the jellied cranberry sauce. Mix the gelatin thoroughly with the cranberry sauce. Pour the boiling water into the mixture and stir for about 3 minutes until the gelatin has fully dissolved.

2. Chill before gently placed in the refrigerator, 2-3 hours. Fold the sour cream softly onto the gelatin mixture, leaving the sour cream and gelatin blend in the marbled streaks.

3. Return to the refrigerator until firmly fixed, overnight for 4 hours. Store the leftovers in the fridge.

Fall Salad with Cranberry Vinaigrette

(Ready in 40 Minutes, Serve 8, Difficulty: Normal)

Nutrition per Serving:

Calories 214, Protein 6.2 g, Carbohydrates 16.2 g, Fat 15.1 g, Cholesterol 11.2mg, Sodium 171.5mg.

Ingredients:

* ½ cup of cider vinegar
* ¼ cup of cranberries
* ¼ cup of olive oil
* 2 teaspoons of white sugar
* 1 teaspoon of kosher salt
* 1 pinch of freshly ground black pepper
* 2 heads of romaine lettuce, rinsed, dried, and torn into bite-size pieces
* 2 medium heads of Belgian endive, washed, dried, and chopped
* 2 red Anjou pears
* ½ cup of toasted walnuts, chopped
* ½ cup of crumbled Gorgonzola cheese

Instructions:

1. Combine the vinegar and cranberries in a saucepan. Cook until the cranberries soften over medium heat. Add the olive oil, butter, salt, and pepper and remove from the heat.

2. Place the mixture in the blender and stir until creamy. Until chilled, refrigerate.

3. Cut 1 pear, core and julienne, and the other core and dice.

4. Combine the Romaine lettuce, endives, chopped pears, walnuts, and gorgonzola in a large dish. Toss and drizzle to coat with enough dressing.

5. Divide into plates of salad and garnish with pear julienne. Top it with some extra walnuts as well.

Autumn Apple Salad II

(Ready in 40 Minutes, Serve 4, Difficulty: Normal)

Nutrition per Serving:

Calories 202, Protein 5.1 g, Carbohydrates 38.9 g, Fat 4.1 g, Cholesterol 2.8mg, Sodium 40.8mg.

Ingredients:

* 4 tart of green apples, cored and chopped
* ¼ cup of toasted, blanched slivered almonds
* ¼ cup of dried cranberries
* ¼ cup of chopped dried cherries
* 1(8 ounces) container of vanilla yogurt

Instructions:

1. Stir the strawberries, nuts, cranberries, cherries, and yogurt together in a medium bowl.

2. Until uniformly coated.

Fabulous Fruit Salad

(Ready in 20 Minutes, Serve 4, Difficulty: Normal)

Nutrition per Serving:

Calories 243, Protein 5.8 g, Carbohydrates 37.4 g, Fat 9.8 g, Cholesterol 0.9mg, Sodium 55.3mg.

Ingredients:

* 1 red apple, cored and chopped
* 1 Granny Smith apple, cored and chopped
* 1 nectarine, pitted and sliced
* 2 stalks of celery, chopped
* ½ cup of dried cranberries
* ½ cup of chopped walnuts
* 1(8 ounce) container of non-fat lemon yogurt

Instructions:

1. Combine the red apple, Granny Smith apple, nectarines, celery, dried cranberries, and walnuts in a large dish.

2. Mix in yogurt. Chill until ready to serve.

Autumn Waldorf salad

(Ready in 40 Minutes, Serve 2, Difficulty: Normal)

Nutrition per Serving:

Calories 312, Protein 3.2 g, Carbohydrates 70.3 g, Fat 5.5 g, Cholesterol 0mg, Sodium 54.8mg.

Ingredients:

* ¼ cup of plain yogurt
* 1½ teaspoon of brown sugar
* 1 pear, diced
* 1 apple, diced
* 1 cup of sliced celery (Optional)
* ½ cup of raisins
* ¼ cup of dried cranberries
* 2 tablespoons of chopped walnuts
* 1 dash of ground cinnamon (optional)
* 1 dash of ground nutmeg (optional)

Instructions:

1. To make a dressing, blend the yogurt and brown sugar in a bowl.

2. In a cup, blend the peach, apple, cranberries, celery, raisins, and walnuts.

3. To mix, add dressing and toss properly. Sprinkle the end with cinnamon and nutmeg.

4. Before serving, cool the salad for at least 30 minutes.

Healthier Cranberry Salad

(Ready in 40 Minutes, Serve 9, Difficulty: Normal)

Nutrition per Serving:

Calories 109, Protein 1.6 g, Carbohydrates 18.3 g, Fat 4.4 g, Cholesterol 0mg, Sodium 1.4mg.

Ingredients:

- 1(12 ounces) package of fresh cranberries
- 2 large oranges, peeled and seeded
- 2 apples, cored and chopped
- ½ cup of chopped walnuts
- 2 tablespoons of honey

Instructions:

1. Mix the cranberries and oranges in a food processor. Coarsely chop when combined, then place in a bowl of salad.

2. To the food processor, add apples and chop coarsely.

3. Mix the apples with the orange and cranberry blend.

4. Combine the chopped nuts to the fruit mixture, whisk to taste, and sweeten. Serve chilled.

Pear and Pomegranate Salad

(Ready in 40 Minutes, Serve 2, Difficulty: Normal)

Nutrition per Serving:

Calories 153, Protein 1.6 g, Carbohydrates 23.5 g, Fat 7.1 g, Cholesterol 0mg, Sodium 88mg.

Ingredients:

- 3 cups of green leaf lettuce, rinsed and torn
- 1 Bartlett or Anjou pear
- 1 cup of pomegranate seeds
- 1 tablespoon of vegetable oil
- 2 tablespoons of pomegranate juice
- 1 tablespoon of lemon juice
- 1 teaspoon of prepared Dijon-style mustard
- ½ tablespoon of honey
- Ground black pepper, to taste

Instructions:

1. Divide between two bowls of broccoli. Halve the pear and core it, then cut each ½ of it into slices. Divide and gently combine the pear slices and pomegranate seeds in the two bowls.

2. In a saucepan, blend the vegetable oil, pomegranate juice, lemon juice, mustard, sugar, and pepper. Carry it over high heat to a boil.

3. Reduce the heat and boil until the dressing thickens slightly, stirring regularly for around 2 minutes. Over the salads, pour the warm dressing and serve.

Mango Pineapple Salad with Mint

(Ready in 40 Minutes, Serve 6, Difficulty: Normal)

Nutrition per Serving:

Calories 79, Protein 0.5 g, Carbohydrates 18.7 g, Fat 1 g, Cholesterol 0mg, Sodium 10.2mg.

Ingredients:

- 2 cups of peeled, diced ripe mango
- 1 cup of chopped fresh pineapple
- ¼ cup of dried cranberries
- ¼ cup of flaked coconut
- ¼ sprig of chopped fresh mint

Instructions:

1. Toss the mango, pineapple, cranberries, and coconut together in a medium bowl. Garnish with mint. Cover.

2. And cool before serving in the fridge.

Deviled Egg Salad

(Ready in 10 Minutes, Serve 6, Difficulty: Easy)

Nutrition per Serving:

Calories 146, Protein 6.5 g, Carbohydrates 1.3 g, Fat 12.6 g, Cholesterol 215.5mg 7, Sodium 216.6mg.

Ingredients:

- ¼ cup of mayonnaise
- ¼ cup of finely chopped green onion
- ½ teaspoon of prepared yellow mustard
- ¼ teaspoon of salt
- ¼ teaspoon of garlic powder
- ¼ teaspoon of paprika
- ⅛ teaspoon of ground black pepper
- 6 hard-boiled eggs, peeled and chopped

Instructions:

1. In a bowl, stir together the mayonnaise, green onion, mustard, cinnamon, garlic powder, paprika, and black pepper until smooth.

2. Add the eggs, then carefully pour in the mayonnaise mixture to coat them.

Strawberry and Feta Salad II

(Ready in 20 Minutes, Serve 4, Difficulty: Normal)

Nutrition per Serving:

Calories 286, Protein 8 g, Carbohydrates 42.2 g, Fat 11.5 g, Cholesterol 28mg, Sodium 812.3mg.

Ingredients:

- 1(10 ounces) package of romaine lettuce
- 1 ½ cups of sliced fresh strawberries
- ½ cup of crumbled feta cheese
- ⅓ cup of dried cranberries
- 1(3 ounces) package of dried Golden Delicious apples
- ¼ cup of pine nuts
- ½ cup of raspberry vinaigrette salad dressing

Instructions:

1. Combine the Roman lettuce, tomatoes, dried cranberries, feta cheese, dried apples, and pine nuts in a large bowl.

2. Toss with the dressing for the raspberry vinaigrette salad to eat.

Arugula Salad with Bacon and Butternut Squash

(Ready in 40 Minutes, Serve 1, Difficulty: Normal)

Nutrition per Serving:

Calories, 211 Protein 13.1 g, Carbohydrates 10.3 g, Fat 14.1 g, Cholesterol 32.3mg, Sodium 368mg.

Ingredients:

- 1 slice of bacon, cut into small pieces
- 2 mushrooms, sliced, or to taste
- ¼ cup of cooked butternut squash cubes
- 2 cups of arugula
- 1-ounce of crumbled goat cheese
- 1 teaspoon of pine nuts
- ¼ teaspoon of cracked black pepper, or to taste

Instructions:

1. Cook the bacon in a skillet over medium-high heat for 2 to 3 minutes, before some of the Fat returns to the pan. Add the mushrooms, cook and stir together for about 5 minutes, until the mushrooms are tender.

2. In the bacon mixture, stir squash cubes and continue cooking until the squash is hot and the bacon is crisp, 3-5 minutes more.

3. Place the arugula in a bowl and cover it with a mixture of bacon, mushroom, and squash. Sprinkle on top of the salad with goat cheese and top with pine nuts. Use crushed black pepper to sprinkle.

Crisp Apples with Citrus Dressing

(Ready in 40 Minutes, Serve 1, Difficulty: Normal)

Nutrition per Serving:

Calories 258, Protein 1.4 g, Carbohydrates 33.6 g, Fat 14.4 g, Cholesterol 11.6mg, Sodium 88.3mg.

Ingredients:

- 1 apple, cored and cut into chunks

- 2 tangerines, juiced, divided
- 1 tablespoon of sour cream
- 1 tablespoon mayonnaise
- 1 teaspoon of white sugar, or more to taste
- 1 pinch of salt

Instructions:

1. In a bowl, mix the apple chunks with 2 teaspoons of tangerine juice. In a cup, mix the remaining tangerine juice, sour cream, mayonnaise, sugar, and spice until the salt and sugar dissolve.

2. Pour over the apple dressing and toss.

Cranberry Salad

(Ready in 15 Minutes, Serve 10, Difficulty: Easy)

Nutrition per Serving:

Calories 157, Protein 1.4 g, Carbohydrates 25.8 g, Fat 6.1 g, Cholesterol 0.6mg, Sodium 17.1mg.

Ingredients:

- 1(12 ounces) package of fresh cranberries, finely chopped
- ½ cup of white sugar
- 2 cups of chopped apples
- 1 cup of miniature marshmallows
- ½ cup of chopped pecans
- ½ cup of vanilla yogurt
- 1 cup of frozen whipped topping (such as Cool Whip®), thawed

Instructions:

1. In a large, non-reactive bowl, combine the chopped cranberries and sugar. Toss well.

2. For 3 hours cover and refrigerate.

Jicama, Carrot, and Green Apple Slaw

(Ready in 40 Minutes, Serve 8, Difficulty: Normal)

Nutrition per Serving:

Calories 98, Protein 1.2 g, Carbohydrates 16.8 g, Fat 3.6 g, Cholesterol 0mg, Sodium 63.9mg.

Ingredients:

- 2 cups of shredded Napa cabbage
- 1(453 g) jicama, peeled and shredded
- 2 cups of shredded daikon radish
- 2 Granny Smith apples, peeled, cored, and shredded
- 2 large carrots, shredded
- 1 firm pear, shredded
- ¼ cup of finely chopped cilantro
- 2 tablespoons of olive oil
- 3 tablespoons of orange juice
- 1 tablespoon of lime juice

- Sea salt and pepper, to taste

Instructions:

1. Place the cabbage, jicama, radish, apple, carrot, pear, and cilantro into a mixing bowl. Sprinkle with olive oil, orange juice, lime juice, salt, and pepper.

2. Toss until evenly blended and serve.

Fluffy Cranberry Salad

(Ready in 60 Minutes, Serve 10, Difficulty: Normal)

Nutrition per Serving:

Calories 306, Protein 1.1 g, Carbohydrates 76 g, Fat 1.5 g, Cholesterol 4.6mg, Sodium 27.3mg.

Ingredients:

- 453 g of fresh or frozen cranberries
- 8 ounces of miniature marshmallows
- 2 cups of white sugar
- 1(20 ounces) can of crushed pineapple with juice
- 1 banana, peeled and sliced
- 1 cup of whipped cream

Instructions:

1. Allow it to thaw before using frozen cranberries. Grind the cranberries in a food processor or blender. Add the cinnamon, marshmallows, and crushed pineapple.

2. Let the mixture stand overnight.

3. Stir in the sliced banana and the whipped cream just before serving.

Quinoa-Cranberry Salad with Pecans

(Ready in 30 Minutes, Serve 6, Difficulty: Normal)

Nutrition per Serving:

Calories 222, Protein 4.7 g, Carbohydrates 27.9 g, Fat 11 g, Cholesterol 0mg, Sodium 8.4mg.

Ingredients:

- 1 cup of quinoa, rinsed and drained
- 2 cups of water
- ½ cup of chopped toasted pecans
- ½ cup of dried cranberries
- 1 tablespoon of olive oil
- 2 tablespoons of lemon juice
- Salt and pepper, to taste

Instructions:

1. In a saucepan, put the quinoa and water to a boil over high heat. Reduce the heat to medium-low, cover, and simmer for around 15-20 minutes until the quinoa is tender and the water is absorbed. Scrape into a mixing bowl, and cool to warm for about 20 minutes.

2. Stir in the pecans, olive oil, cranberries, and lemon juice until the quinoa has cooled, season to taste with salt and to taste with pepper.

3. Let it stand for 1 hour at room temperature before serving.

Winter Fruit and Pasta Salad

(Ready in 40 Minutes, Serve 5, Difficulty: Normal)

Nutrition per Serving:

Calories 160, Protein 2 g, Carbohydrates 33.3 g, Fat 3.5 g, Cholesterol 0mg, Sodium 5.6mg.

Ingredients:

- 1 cup of mini farfalle pasta
- 2 mandarin oranges, peeled and segmented
- 2 kiwi fruits, peeled, sliced, and quartered
- 1 medium apple, diced
- 1 medium Bartlett pear, cored and diced
- ¼ cup of sweetened dried cranberries, (such as Ocean Spray® Craisins®)
- 2 tablespoons of pomegranate arils
- 2 tablespoons of minced celery

For Dressing:

- 2 tablespoons of lime juice
- 1 tablespoon of honey
- 1 tablespoon of olive oil
- 1 teaspoon of poppy seeds

Instructions:

1. To a simmer, put a big pot of mildly salted water. At a boil, cook farfalle, stirring regularly, until the bite is soft but strong, around 7 minutes. Rinse and rinse well in cold spray.

2. Meanwhile, in a wide cup, mix orange, mandarin sections, apple, kiwi, peach, pomegranate arils, dried cranberries, and celery.

3. To the fruit salad, add the pasta, blending until well mixed.

4. In a small cup, whisk together the lime juice, sugar, olive oil, and poppy seeds.

5. Place the pasta salad over and stir until mixed. Put in the refrigerator for about 30 minutes, until the flavors have mixed.

Chef John's Green Goddess Dressing

(Ready in 40 Minutes, Serve 16, Difficulty: Normal)

Nutrition per Serving:

Calories 124, Protein 0.7 g, Carbohydrates 1.3 g, Fat 13.2 g 2, Cholesterol 10.2mg, Sodium 103.5mg.

Ingredients:

- 1 cup of mayonnaise

- ¾ cup of sour cream
- 1 cup of chopped fresh flat-leaf parsley
- 1 cup of chopped fresh tarragon
- ¼ cup of chopped fresh chives
- 2 tablespoons of fresh lemon juice, or more to taste
- 1 tablespoon of rice vinegar
- 1 anchovy fillet
- 1 clove of garlic, chopped
- 1 pinch of cayenne pepper, or to taste
- Salt and freshly ground black pepper, to taste

Instructions:

1. Mix the mayonnaise, the sour cream, the parsley, the tarragon, the chives, the lemon juice, the rice vinegar, the anchovy fillet, the garlic, the cayenne pepper, and the salt.

2. And black pepper, blend until creamy, in a blender.

Cherry Cranberry Salad

(Ready in 50 Minutes, Serve 16, Difficulty: Normal)

Nutrition per Serving:

Calories 170, Protein 2.3 g, Carbohydrates 31.9 g, Fat 4.8 g, Cholesterol 0mg, Sodium 49.6mg.

Ingredients:

- 3 cups of cranberries
- 2 cups of water
- 1 cup of white sugar
- 1(6 ounces) package of cherry-flavored gelatin mix (such as Jell-O®)
- 1(20 ounces) can of crushed pineapple, undrained
- 1 ½ cup of diced apples
- 1 cup of chopped walnuts

Instructions:

1. In a saucepan, combine the cranberries and water. Bring the water to a boil, reduce the heat and simmer until medium.

2. Remove from the heat to cool slightly until all the cranberries have softened and popped for 5 to 7 minutes.

3. Stir in the cranberry mixture with sugar and gelatin until completely dissolved. Add pineapple with juice, almonds, and walnuts and pour in a 2-quart serving dish in the cranberry mixture.

4. Cover the bowl with plastic wrap and refrigerate for 3-4 hours until chilled and firm.

Fall Harvest Fruit Salad

(Ready in 35 Minutes, Serve 12, Difficulty: Normal)

Nutrition per Serving:

Calories 183, Protein 1.9 g, Carbohydrates 36 g, Fat 4.7 g, Cholesterol 0mg, Sodium 5mg.

Ingredients:

- 4 medium ripe pears, peeled, cored, and cubed
- 4 medium apples, peeled, cored, and cubed
- 1 tablespoon of lemon juice
- 1 cup of sweetened dried cranberries (such as Craisins ®)
- ½ cup of chopped walnuts
- ½ cup of granola
- ½ cup of brown sugar
- 1 teaspoon of ground cinnamon
- ½ teaspoon of ground nutmeg

Instructions:

1. Coat the lemon juice on pears and apples.

2. In a big cup, mix the dried cranberries, granola, brown sugar, walnuts, cinnamon, and nutmeg.

3. In the mixture, toss the pears and apples.

Warm Green Bean and Potato Salad with Goat Cheese

(Ready in 40 Minutes, Serve 8, Difficulty: Normal)

Nutrition per Serving:

Calories 252, Protein 9.2 g, Carbohydrates 28.6 g, Fat 9.6 g, Cholesterol 22.4mg, Sodium 404.1mg.

Ingredients:

- 907 g of red potatoes, cut into bite-size pieces
- 1 serving olive oil cooking spray
- 226 g of frozen French-style green beans, thawed
- 1 cup of chopped red onion
- 4 cloves of garlic, minced
- ½ cup of reduced-fat balsamic vinaigrette dressing
- 1 cup of jarred roasted red peppers, drained and chopped
- ¼ cup of chopped fresh basil
- 1(8 ounces) package of goat cheese, crumbled

Instructions:

1. Place the potatoes and cover them with salted water in a big jar. Bring over high heat to a boil, reduce heat to medium-low, cover and simmer for 8-10 minutes until tender.

2. Drain and allow to dry for 1 minute or 2 while steaming. Place the potatoes in a big bowl.

3. Heat a large skillet over medium-high heat, cooking spray oil. Cook and mix the green beans and onion for about 5 minutes, until tender. Add the garlic, cook, and stir until the garlic is fragrant, about an additional 1 minute.

4. Move the mixture of green beans to the potatoes in a large dish. Lightly toss in the roasted red peppers, balsamic vinaigrette, and basil. Stir in the cheese for the goats.

Orange, Fig, and Gorgonzola Salad

(Ready in 40 Minutes, Serve 4, Difficulty: Normal)

Nutrition per Serving:

Calories 141, Protein 6.8 g, Carbohydrates 14.6 g, Fat 6.6 g, Cholesterol 22.5mg, Sodium 468.1mg.

Ingredients:

- 2 heads of romaine lettuce, chopped
- 2 oranges, peeled, pith removed, and cut into segments
- ½ cup of crumbled Gorgonzola cheese
- 2 fresh figs, cut into 1-inch cubes
- ¼ cup of vinaigrette dressing, or to taste

Instructions:

1. In a large bowl, combine the spinach, grapes, Gorgonzola cheese, and figs.

2. Drizzle the dressing over the salad and coat it with a toss.

Warm Swiss chard and Mushroom Salad

(Ready in 40 Minutes, Serve 2, Difficulty: Normal)

Nutrition per Serving:

Calories 179, Protein 8 g, Carbohydrates 18.5 g, Fat 10.1 g, Cholesterol 6.3mg, Sodium 380.3mg.

Ingredients:

- 1 tablespoon of olive oil
- 2 cloves of garlic, minced
- 1 bunch of Swiss chard, cut into thin strips
- 10 Cremini mushrooms, sliced
- ¼ cup of chopped onion
- 3 tablespoons of balsamic vinegar
- 12 grape of tomatoes, quartered
- 2 tablespoons of crumbled blue cheese
- 1 pinch of salt and ground black pepper to taste

Instructions:

1. Heat olive oil over medium-low heat in a skillet. Cook the garlic in the oil for about 1 minute until it is just fragrant.

2. Add the garlic to the Swiss chard and cook until wilted, 3-5 minutes, place the garlic and chard in a cup, reserve some liquid in the skillet and bring it back to heat.

3. Cook the mushrooms and onion in the skillet until warm, 2-3 minutes, with the reserved oil. Pour the balsamic vinegar over the mushroom and onion mixture, cook and stir for another 2-3 minutes, and add the chard mixture and tomatoes to the dish. Blend gently to combine. Toss the blue cheese with it. To serve, season with salt and pepper.

Cranberry Fluff

(Ready in 40 Minutes, Serve 4, Difficulty: Normal)

Nutrition per Serving:

Calories 275, Protein 1.7 g, Carbohydrates 45 g, Fat 10.4 g, Cholesterol 20.4mg, Sodium 103mg.

Ingredients:

- 3 cups of miniature marshmallows
- 2 cups of ground cranberries
- ¾ cup of white sugar
- 2 cups of diced apple
- ½ cup of seedless grapes, halved
- ½ cup of chopped walnuts (optional)
- ¼ teaspoon of salt
- ½ cup of heavy whipping cream

Instructions:

1. Stir together the marshmallows, cranberries, and sugar over low heat in a saucepan, cook and stir until the marshmallows are fully melted, for about 15 minutes.

2. Transfer the marshmallow mixture to a bowl and leave to refrigerate overnight for 4 hours.

3. Stir in the marshmallow blend of apples, oranges, walnuts, and salt.

4. Using an electric mixer to beat whipping cream in a chilled bowl until stiff peaks develop, fold into the marshmallow mixture.

Easy Caramel Apple Salad

(Ready in 40 Minutes, Serve 12, Difficulty: Normal)

Nutrition per Serving:

Calories 181, Protein 3.2 g, Carbohydrates 20 g, Fat 10.8 g, Cholesterol 0mg, Sodium 227.7mg.

Ingredients:

- 1(8 ounces) container of frozen whipped topping, thawed
- 1(8 ounces) can of crushed pineapple
- 1(3-4 ounces) package of instant butterscotch pudding mix

- 2 cups of chopped apples
- 1 cup of skinless peanuts

Instructions:

1. In a bowl, mix the whipped cream, pineapple, and butterscotch pudding until creamy. In a pudding mixture, fold the apples and peanuts until the salad is well combined.

2. Refrigerate the salad for at least 30 minutes, until fully chilled.

Cranberry Salad V

(Ready in 30 Minutes, Serve 9, Difficulty: Normal)

Nutrition per Serving:

Calories 167, Protein 2.3 g, Carbohydrates 32.3 g, Fat 4.3 g, Cholesterol 0mg, Sodium 62.9mg.

Ingredients:

- 1(3 ounces) package of lemon-flavored Jell-O® mix
- 1 cup of boiling water
- ½ cup of white sugar
- 1(12 ounces) package of cranberries
- 1 cup of chopped celery
- ½ cup of chopped walnuts
- 1(15 ounces) can of crushed pineapple

Instructions:

1. In a food processor, gently cut the cranberries, celery, and walnuts.

2. Combine the gelatin, sugar, and water.

3. Combine cranberry, gelatin, and pineapple (with juice) and blend thoroughly. Pour into the mold and chill until set.

4. Serve with a dollop of mayonnaise on a piece of lettuce.

Warm Thai Kale Salad

(Ready in 40 Minutes, Serve 4, Difficulty: Normal)

Nutrition per Serving:

Calories 176, Protein 5.1 g, Carbohydrates 15 g, Fat 12.1 g, Cholesterol 0mg, Sodium 321.6mg.

Ingredients:

- 2 tablespoons of olive oil
- ½ red onion, thinly sliced
- 5 cloves of garlic, minced
- 1 tablespoon of minced fresh ginger root
- 2 teaspoons of red pepper flakes
- 4 carrots, thinly sliced
- 3 stalks of celery, thinly sliced
- 8 leaves of kale, stemmed and torn into pieces

- 5 sprigs of fresh cilantro, roughly chopped
- 1 lime, juiced
- 2 teaspoons of fish sauce
- ½ teaspoon of lime zest, or to taste
- 1 small cucumber, cut into matchstick-size pieces (Optional)
- ¼ cup of roasted peanuts (Optional)
- 4 sprigs of fresh mint, roughly chopped (Optional)

Instructions:

1. Over medium, prepare, heat a heavy-bottom skillet, add olive oil and swirl in the skillet. Cook and mix the onion in the hot oil for 3 to 4 minutes, until softened.

2. Combine the flakes of garlic, ginger, and red pepper, cook and stir until slightly browned and fragrant with the garlic and ginger, about 1 minute.

3. Stir in the onion mixture with the carrots and celery, cook and stir for 1 minute. Cook and mix until the kale is mildly wilted, about 45 seconds, and add the kale and cilantro. Stir in the kale mixture, lime juice, fish sauce, and lime zest until the kale is evenly covered in the lime juice.

4. Serve the cucumber, popcorn, mint, and kale salad.

Easy Broccoli Bacon Salad

(Ready in 20 Minutes, Serve 8, Difficulty: Easy)

Nutrition per Serving:

Calories 231, Protein 2.9 g, Carbohydrates 28 g, Fat 13.5 g, Cholesterol 5.2mg, Sodium 94.7mg.

Ingredients:

- 1 large head broccoli, cut into florets
- 1 small red onion, chopped
- 12 slices of cooked bacon, crumbled
- 1 cup of raisins
- ¼ cup of sunflower seeds

For Dressing:

- ½ cup of mayonnaise
- 1 cup of white sugar
- 3 tablespoons of red wine vinegar

Instructions:

1. In a dish, add the broccoli, cabbage, bacon, oranges, and Sunflower seeds.

2. In a bowl, blend the mayonnaise, butter, and red wine vinegar until the dressing is smooth.

3. Pour over the mixture of broccoli and stir to coat.

Maple-Dijon Brussels Leaf Salad

(Ready in 20 Minutes, Serve 12, Difficulty: Easy

Nutrition per Serving:

Calories 174, Protein 5.1 g, Carbohydrates 22.1 g, Fat 8.6 g, Cholesterol 0mg, Sodium 61.4mg.

Ingredients:

- 907 g of Brussels sprouts, trimmed
- ¼ cup of maple syrup
- 2 tablespoons of extra-virgin olive oil
- 4 teaspoons of Dijon mustard
- 4 teaspoons of apple cider vinegar
- 1 cup of sweetened dried cranberries
- 1 cup of cinnamon-roasted almonds

Instructions:

1. Using a paring knife to hack cores out of Brussels sprouts. Place leaves in a wide cup, peeling layers apart to remove individual leaves.

2. In a small bowl, mix the maple syrup, Dijon mustard, olive oil, and apple cider vinegar. Drizzle sprout leaves over Brussels, add cranberries, and cover with a flip.

3. Add the almonds and before serving, toss again.

My Favorite Chicken Salad

(Ready in 1 Hour and 15 Minutes, Serve 6, Difficulty: Normal)

Nutrition per Serving:

Calories 287, Protein 11 g, Carbohydrates 5.5 g, Fat 25.5 g, Cholesterol 31.4mg, Sodium 384.3mg.

Ingredients:

- 2 cooked skinless, boneless chicken breast halves, cut into cubes
- 3 stalks of celery, finely diced
- ¾ cup of chopped pecans
- ½ cup of mayonnaise
- 2 tablespoons of minced yellow onion
- 1½ tablespoons of sweet pickle relish
- 2 teaspoons of prepared mustard
- 1 ½ teaspoon of ground black pepper
- 1 ½ teaspoon of minced fresh dill
- 1 teaspoon of lemon juice
- ½ teaspoon of white sugar
- ½ teaspoon of salt
- ½ teaspoon of garlic powder
- ½ teaspoon of paprika

Instructions:

1. In a dish, add the chicken, celery, yellow onion, pecans, mayonnaise, relish, mustard, seasoning, dill, lemon juice, cinnamon, salt, ground garlic, and paprika until well mixed.

2. Before serving, refrigerate for at least 1 hour.

Autumn Waldorf Salad

(Ready in 40 Minutes, Serve 2, Difficulty: Normal)

Nutrition per Serving:

Calories 312, Protein 3.2 g, Carbohydrates 70.3 g, Fat 5.5 g, Cholesterol 0mg, Sodium 54.8mg.

Ingredients:

- ¼ cup of plain yogurt
- 1 ½ teaspoons of brown sugar
- 1 pear, diced
- 1 apple, diced
- 1 cup of sliced celery (Optional)
- ½ cup of raisins
- ¼ cup of dried cranberries
- 2 tablespoons of chopped walnuts
- 1 dash of ground cinnamon (optional)
- 1 dash of ground nutmeg (optional)

Instructions:

1. To make a dressing, blend the yogurt and brown sugar in a cup.

2. In a cup, blend the peach, apple, cranberries, celery, raisins, and walnuts.

3. To mix, add dressing and toss properly. Sprinkle the end with cinnamon and nutmeg.

4. Before serving, cool the salad for at least 30 minutes.

Pomegranate Ambrosia Salad

(Ready in 40 Minutes, Serve 12, Difficulty: Normal)

Nutrition per Serving:

Calories 167, Protein 1.5 g, Carbohydrates 27.1 g, Fat 7.3 g, Cholesterol 2.1mg, Sodium 41.4mg.

Ingredients:

- 2 cups of pomegranate seeds
- 1(15 ounces) can of pineapple tidbits, drained
- 4 bananas, peeled and sliced
- 3 cups of peeled, cored, and chopped tart apple
- ½ cup of chopped pecans
- 3 tablespoons of mayonnaise
- 2 tablespoons of creamy salad dressing, e.g., Miracle Whip ™

Instructions:

1. Combine the pomegranate seeds, bananas, pineapple, apples, and pecans in a large dish. Stir in the sauce with mayonnaise and lettuce until finely coated.

2. Before serving, cover and refrigerate overnight.

Roasted Lettuce, Radicchio, and Endive

(Ready in 40 Minutes, Serve 6, Difficulty: Normal)

Nutrition per Serving:

Calories 192, Protein 6.3 g, Carbohydrates 16.7 g, Fat 12.9 g, Cholesterol 2.6mg, Sodium 1108.6mg.

Ingredients:

- 2 heads of radicchio, halved lengthwise
- 2 heads of Belgian endive, halved lengthwise
- 1 head of chicory (curly endive), halved lengthwise
- 1 head of romaine lettuce, halved lengthwise
- 3 tablespoons of olive oil, divided
- ¾ cup of pitted Greek olives
- ½ cup of capers
- 1 tablespoon of dried oregano
- 1 ½ teaspoon of ground thyme
- 1 teaspoon of salt
- 1 teaspoon of ground black pepper
- 1 teaspoon of ground dried Chile pepper (Optional)
- 2 tablespoons of grated Romano cheese (Optional)

Instructions:

1. Preheat the oven to 375 degrees Fahrenheit (190 degrees Celsius). Line a parchment paper baking bowl.

2. On the baking sheet, put the radicchio, chicory, Belgian endive, and Romaine lettuce halves in a single layer. Drizzle the end of 2 tablespoons of olive oil.

3. Combine the olives in a small bowl and the capers.

4. To produce the spice mixture, blend the oregano, salt, black pepper, thyme, and chili pepper in a small dish.

5. Using your fingers to stuff the inner leaves with olives, capers, and seasoning mixture. To avoid stuffing from coming out, wrap the halves together with kitchen string. Drizzle on top of the remaining one tablespoon of olive oil.

6. Bake in a preheated oven for 10-15 minutes, until crispy and wilted. Cut the kitchen string off and sprinkle on top of Romano cheese before serving.

Buffalo Chicken Pasta Salad

(Ready in 1 Hour and 30 Minutes, Serve 12, Difficulty: Hard)

Nutrition per Serving:

Calories 379, Protein 13.6 g, Carbohydrates 34.6 g, Fat 21.1 g, Cholesterol 40.2mg, Sodium 1051.5mg.

Ingredients:

- 1(16 ounces) package of uncooked rotini pasta
- ½ cup of mayonnaise
- 1 cup of chunky blue cheese dressing
- ½ cup of buffalo wing sauce
- 1 teaspoon of salt
- ½ teaspoon of black pepper
- 453 g of frozen cooked chicken strips, defrosted and diced
- ½ cup of red bell pepper, diced
- ½ cup of green bell pepper, diced
- 1 cup of red onion, diced

Instructions:

1. Fill a large pot with thinly salted water and bring it over high heat to a rolling boil. That's when the water is boiling.

2. Stir in the rotini, and bring to a boil again. Cook uncovered until the pasta has cooked through but is still firm to the bite, stirring regularly around 8 minutes. Drain well in a colander set in the sink.

3. In a big cup, whisk together the blue cheese dressing, mayonnaise, buffalo wing sauce, salt, and pepper. Add the chicken, bell peppers, cooked pasta, and red onion and mix to cover with the dressing. Cover and cook for at least 1 hour before serving in the refrigerator.

Hot Fruit Salad

(Ready in 40 Minutes, Serve 12, Difficulty: Normal)

Nutrition per Serving:

Calories 149, Protein 0.7 g, Carbohydrates 37.7 g, Fat 0.1 g, Cholesterol 0mg, Sodium 15.3mg.

Ingredients:

- 1(20 ounces) jar of chunky applesauce
- 1(21 ounces) can of cherry pie filling
- 1(15 ounces) can of sliced peaches, drained
- 1(11 ounces) can of mandarin orange segments, drained
- 1(8 ounces) can of pineapple chunks
- ½ cup of brown sugar
- 1 teaspoon of ground cinnamon

Instructions:

1. In a slow cooker, pour the applesauce, cherry pie filling, peaches diced, pineapple, mandarin oranges, brown sugar, and cinnamon.

2. On a low setting, cover and cook for 90 minutes.

Really, Truly Gorgeous Dried Fruit Salad

(Ready in 40 Minutes, Serve 12, Difficulty: Normal)

Nutrition per Serving:

Calories 211, Protein 2.7 g, Carbohydrates 51.6 g, Fat 1.9 g, Cholesterol 0mg, Sodium 9mg.

Ingredients:

* 8 ounces of dried figs
* 8 ounces of dried apricots
* 8 ounces of pitted prunes
* ½ cup of dried cranberries
* ½ cup of raisins
* ½ cup of golden raisins
* ¼ cup of pine nuts
* 1 tablespoon of honey

Instructions:

1. In a cup, mix the figs, apricots, raisins, prunes, cranberries, and golden raisins. Only dump enough water in to cover it. Cover the bowl and soak for at least 8 hours overnight.

2. Pour the fruits into a saucepan with the soaking water. Stir in the honey and pine nuts.

3. Bring to a boil, roast, stirring regularly, around 30 minutes, until the fruit is tender but still retains its form. Remove the fruit and liquid from the heat and add it to the cup, taking care not to split the fruit. Cool to room temperature.

Fennel and Watercress Salad

(Ready in 40 Minutes, Serve 20, Difficulty: Normal)

Nutrition per Serving:

Calories 178, Protein 3.1 g, Carbohydrates 8.9 g, Fat 15.4 g, Cholesterol 0mg, Sodium 201.8mg.

Ingredients:

* ½ cup of chopped dried cranberries
* ¼ cup of red wine vinegar
* ¼ cup o balsamic vinegar
* 1 tablespoon of minced garlic
* 1¼ teaspoons of salt
* 1 cup of extra virgin olive oil
* 6 bunches of watercress, rinsed, dried, and trimmed
* 3 bulbs fennel, trimmed, cored, and thinly sliced
* 3 small heads radicchio, cored and chopped
* 1 cup of pecan halves, toasted

Instructions:

1. Mix the cranberries, balsamic vinegar, red wine vinegar, garlic, and salt in a cup. In the olive oil, whisk.

2. Combine the fennel, watercress, radicchio, and pecans in a large salad dish. Stir in the vinaigrette and pour the salad over it.

3. Toss well at once and serve.

Almond Chicken Salad

(Ready in 15 Minutes, Serve 4, Difficulty: Easy)

Nutrition per Serving:

Calories 323, Protein 26.3 g, Carbohydrates 19.7 g, Fat 15.1 g, Cholesterol 53.9mg, Sodium 236.8mg.

Ingredients:

* 4 green onions, thinly sliced
* 1 large carrot, shredded
* 1 red bell pepper, cut into 1/2-inch pieces
* 226 g of sugar snap peas, halved
* 2 cups of chopped, cooked chicken breast meat
* ½ cup of fresh cilantro leaves
* ½ cup of blanched slivered almonds, toasted
* 2 tablespoons of white sugar
* 2 tablespoons of distilled white vinegar
* 1 ½ tablespoon of sesame oil
* 1 tablespoon of teriyaki sauce
* 1 tablespoon of ground dry mustard

Instructions:

1. Mix the onions, carrot, red pepper, peas, chicken, cilantro, and almonds in a big dish. Set aside.

2. Whisk together the sugar, vinegar, sesame oil, teriyaki sauce, and dried mustard in a small bowl until smooth. Pour over the mixture of salad and toss until covered.

3. Serve in pockets of pita or on a lettuce bed.

Ham Salad Spread

(Ready in 15 Minutes, Serve 12, Difficulty: Easy)

Nutrition per Serving:

Calories 230, Protein 7.5 g, Carbohydrates 1.4 g, Fat 21.7 g, Cholesterol 56.9mg, Sodium 578.7mg.

Ingredients:

* 3 cups of ground fully cooked ham
* 2 hard-cooked eggs, chopped
* 2 tablespoons of finely chopped celery
* 4 teaspoons of sweet pickle relish
* 2 teaspoons of finely chopped onion
* 1 cup of mayonnaise
* 1 tablespoon of prepared yellow mustard

Instructions:

1. In a mug, mix the ham, eggs, pickle relish, celery, and onion.

2. In a separate dish, combine the mayonnaise and mustard and pour over the ham mixture. To coat, stir. Refrigerate until time for serving.

Healthier Cranberry Salad

(Ready in 40 Minutes, Serve 9, Difficulty: Normal)

Nutrition per Serving:

Calories 109, Protein 1.6 g, Carbohydrates 18.3 g, Fat 4.4 g, Cholesterol 0mg, Sodium 1.4mg.

Ingredients:

* 1(12 ounces) package of fresh cranberries
* 2 large oranges, peeled and seeded
* 2 apples, cored and chopped
* ½ cup of chopped walnuts
* 2 tablespoons of honey

Instructions:

1. Mix the cranberries and oranges in a food processor. Coarsely chop until mixed, then place in a bowl of salad.

2. To the food processor, add apples and chop coarsely.

3. Mix the apples with the orange and cranberry mixture.

4. Add the chopped nuts to the fruit mixture, stir to taste, and sweeten. Serve chilled.

Barbie's Tuna Salad

(Ready in 40 Minutes, Serve 4, Difficulty: Normal)

Nutrition per Serving:

Calories 228, Protein 13.4 g, Carbohydrates 5.3 g, Fat 17.3 g, Cholesterol 23.7mg, Sodium 254.6mg.

Ingredients:

* 1(7 ounces) can of white tuna, drained and flaked
* 6 tablespoons of mayonnaise or salad dressing
* 3 tablespoons of sweet pickle relish
* 1 tablespoon of parmesan cheese
* 2 teaspoon of dried minced onion flakes
* 1 tablespoon of dried parsley
* 1 teaspoon to dried dill weed
* ¼ teaspoon of curry powder
* 1 pinch of garlic powder

Instructions:

Stir together the salmon, mayonnaise, relish, and onion flakes, Parmesan cheese in a medium bowl. Using parsley, curry powder, dill, and garlic powder to season. Mix well and serve with crackers or on a sandwich.

Zesty Apple Salad

(Ready in 40 Minutes, Serve 4, Difficulty: Normal)

Nutrition per Serving:

Calories 236, Protein 4.4 g, Carbohydrates 49.3 g, Fat 3.4 g, Cholesterol 2.8mg, Sodium 67.2mg.

Ingredients:

* 2 Granny Smith apples, diced
* 1(15 ounces) can of mandarin oranges, drained
* 1 ½ cups of miniature marshmallows
* 1 cup of halved seedless red grapes
* 1(8 ounces) container of lemon yogurt
* 2 tablespoons of chopped walnuts

Instructions:

1. In a bowl, combine the strawberries, bananas, grapes, yogurt, marshmallows, and walnuts.

Fabulous Fruit and Yogurt Salad

(Ready in 40 Minutes, Serve 5, Difficulty: Normal)

Nutrition per Serving:

Calories 188, Protein 5 g, Carbohydrates 26 g, Fat 8.7 g, Cholesterol 2.3mg, Sodium 44.4mg.

Ingredients:

* 1 ½ cup of halved seedless grapes
* 2 stalks of celery, chopped
* 1 red apple, cored and chopped
* 1 orange, peeled and sliced
* ½ cup of blackberries
* ½ cup of chopped walnuts
* 1(8 ounces) container of vanilla yogurt

Instructions:

1. In a big cup, combine the grapes, celery, apples, orange slices, blackberries, and walnuts.

2. Add yogurt and stir to coat.

3. Cover the bowl with plastic wrap and refrigerate for at least 30 minutes, until the salad is chilled.

Fruity Curry Chicken Salad

(Ready in 45 Minutes, Serve 8, Difficulty: Normal)

Nutrition per Serving:

Calories 229, Protein 15.1 g, Carbohydrates 12.3 g, Fat 14 g, Cholesterol 44.5mg, Sodium 188mg.

Ingredients:

* 4 skinless, boneless chicken breast halves, cooked and diced

- 1 stalk of celery, diced
- 4 green of onions, chopped
- 1 Golden Delicious apple, peeled, cored, and diced
- ½cup of golden raisins
- 1 cup of seedless green grapes, halved
- ½ cup of chopped toasted pecans
- 1 teaspoon of ground black pepper
- ½ teaspoon of curry powder
- ¾ cup of light mayonnaise

Instructions:

1. Mix the chicken, celery, cabbage, apple, raisins, grapes, pecans, pepper, curry powder, and mayonnaise in a big dish.

2. Mix all together. Serve!

The Best Chicken Salad Ever

(Ready in 30 Minutes, Serve 8, Difficulty: Easy)

Nutrition per Serving:

Calories 103, Protein 7.6 g, Carbohydrates 3.2 g, Fat 6.3 g, Cholesterol 25.6mg, Sodium 141.2mg.

Ingredients:

- 2 boneless chicken breast halves, cooked
- ¼ cup of creamy salad dressing
- 4 tablespoons of Coleslaw dressing
- 1 stalk of celery, chopped
- ¼ onion, chopped
- Salt and pepper, to taste

Instructions:

1. Combine the chicken, the creamy salad sauce, the Coleslaw dressing, onion, celery, salt, and pepper in a food processor.

2. Mix until it's chopped well.

Roasted Beets with Feta

(Ready in 20 Minutes, Serve 4, Difficulty: Easy)

Nutrition per Serving:

Calories 149, Protein 3.9 g, Carbohydrates 11.1 g, Fat 10.3 g, Cholesterol 14mg, Sodium 243mg.

Ingredients:

- 4 beets, trimmed, leaving 1 inch of stems Added
- ¼ cup of minced shallot
- 2 tablespoons of minced fresh parsley
- 2 tablespoons of extra-virgin olive oil
- 1 tablespoon of balsamic vinegar
- 1 tablespoon of red wine vinegar
- Salt and pepper, to taste
- ¼ cup of crumbled feta cheese

Instructions:

1. Preheat the oven to 400 degrees Fahrenheit (204 degrees Celsius). Every beet is separately wrapped in aluminum foil and placed on a baking sheet.

2. Bake the beets in a preheated oven for 45 minutes to 1 hour until they are quickly pierced with a fork. Remove from the oven until done, and allow to cool until you can handle them.

3. Peel and cut the beets into 1/4-inch strips.

4. While the beets are roasting, in a cup, whisk together the shallot, parsley, olive oil, balsamic vinegar, and red wine vinegar until combined, season with salt and pepper taste, and set aside.

5. Place the warm, sliced beets on a serving dish to assemble the dish, pour the vinaigrette over the beets, and sprinkle with feta cheese before serving.

Tuna Fish Salad

(Ready in 15 Minutes, Serve 4, Difficulty: Easy)

Nutrition per Serving:

Calories 240, Protein 8.5 g, Carbohydrates 2.3 g, Fat 22.1 g, Cholesterol 19.9mg, Sodium 251.6mg.

Ingredients:

- 1(5 ounces) can of tuna, drained
- 1 tablespoon of chopped fresh parsley
- ¼ cup of chopped celery
- ½ cup of mayonnaise
- ½ teaspoon of lemon juice
- ¼ cup of chopped onion
- ¼ teaspoon of garlic powder
- 1 teaspoon of salt
- 1 teaspoon of ground black pepper
- Paprika, to taste

Instructions:

1. Combine the salmon, celery, cabbage, mayonnaise, parsley, lemon juice, ground garlic, salt, and pepper in a large dish.

2. Mix when chilled and refrigerate. If necessary, sprinkle with paprika.

Carol's Chicken Salad

(Ready in 20 Minutes, Serve 9, Difficulty: Easy)

Nutrition per Serving:

Calories 293, Protein 19.4 g, Carbohydrates 10.3 g, Fat 19.5 g, Cholesterol 59.9mg, Sodium 278.7mg.

Ingredients:

- ½ cup of mayonnaise
- ½ teaspoon of salt
- ¾ teaspoon of poultry seasoning
- ¼ teaspoon of onion powder
- ¼ teaspoon of garlic powder
- ¼ teaspoon of ground black pepper

- 1 tablespoon of lemon juice
- 3 cups of diced, cooked chicken breast meat
- ½ cup of finely chopped celery
- ½ cup of chopped green onions
- 1(8 ounces) can of water chestnuts, drained and chopped
- 1½ cups of diced Swiss cheese
- 1½ cups of halved green grapes

Instructions:

1. Whisk the mayonnaise, cinnamon, poultry seasoning, onion powder, garlic powder, pepper, and lemon juice together in a medium bowl.

2. Toss the chicken, water chestnuts, celery, green onions, Swiss cheese, and grapes together in a large bowl.

3. Add the paste of mayonnaise, then stir to coat. Chill until serve.

Avocado Salad

(Ready in 15 Minutes, Serve 6, Difficulty: Easy)
Nutrition per Serving:

Calories 126, Protein 2.1 g, Carbohydrates 10.2 g, Fat 10 g, Cholesterol 0mg, Sodium 8.5mg.

Ingredients:

- 2 avocados, peeled, pitted, and diced
- 1 sweet onion, chopped
- 1 green bell pepper, chopped
- 1 large ripe tomato, chopped
- ¼ cup of chopped fresh cilantro
- ½ lime, juiced
- Salt and pepper, to taste

Instructions:

1. Combine the avocados, cabbage, bell pepper, cilantro, tomato, and lime juice in a medium dish. Toss until covered uniformly.

2. Season with salt and pepper.

Becky's Chicken Salad

(Ready in 20 Minutes, Serve 10, Difficulty: Easy)
Nutrition per Serving:

Calories 274, Protein 11 g, Carbohydrates 5 g, Fat 23.6 g, Cholesterol 42.8mg, Sodium 388mg.

Ingredients:

- 2½ cups of diced and chilled, cooked chicken meat
- 1 cup of chopped celery
- 1 cup of sliced, seedless grapes
- ½ cup of sliced almonds
- 2 tablespoons of chopped fresh parsley
- 1 teaspoon of salt

- 1 cup of mayonnaise
- ¼ cup of heavy whipping cream

Instructions:

1. Whip the cream into gentle peaks in a medium bowl.

2. Combine the whipped cream with the beef, celery, almonds, grapes, salt, parsley, and mayonnaise. Refrigerate.

Brussels sprouts with Bacon Dressing

(Ready in 24 Minutes, Serve 8, Difficulty: Easy)
Nutrition per Serving:

Calories 171, Protein 8.2 g, Carbohydrates 19.7 g, Fat 7.7 g, Cholesterol 10.2mg, Sodium 290.8mg.

Ingredients:

- 557 g of Brussels sprouts
- 1 tablespoon of vegetable oil
- 4 ounces of bacon, sliced
- ½ cup of cider vinegar
- 1 lemon, juiced
- 2 tablespoons of brown sugar
- Salt and ground black pepper, to taste
- 1 pinch of cayenne pepper

Instructions:

1. Slice each sprout of Brussels in half, cut each half into strips, and remove the cores. Transfer to a large bowl.

2. Heat the vegetable oil over medium heat in a skillet. Cook and stir the bacon for 8-10 minutes, until browned and crisp. Stir in the lemon juice, cider vinegar, and brown sugar.

3. Season with cinnamon, black pepper, and to taste, cayenne pepper. Boost the heat to strong and cook for 1 minute.

4. Pour over the bowl of Brussels sprouts with hot bacon mixture and toss to coat completely. To taste, season with salt and black pepper.

Easy Apple Coleslaw

(Ready in 40 Minutes, Serve 6, Difficulty: Normal)
Nutrition per Serving:

Calories 137, Protein 1 g, Carbohydrates 25.2 g, Fat 4.5 g, Cholesterol 3.4mg, Sodium 107.6mg.

Ingredients:

- 3 cups of chopped cabbage
- 1 unpeeled red apple, cored and chopped
- 1 unpeeled Granny Smith apple, cored and chopped
- 1 carrot, grated
- ½ cup of finely chopped red bell pepper

- 2 green onions, finely chopped
- 1 cup of mayonnaise
- ½cup of brown sugar
- 1 tablespoon of lemon juice, or to taste

Instructions:

1. Place the cabbage, carrot, red bell pepper, red apple, green apple, and green onions in a wide dish.

2. Mix the mayonnaise, brown sugar, and lemon juice together in a shallow cup.

3. Pour the salad over the dressing.

Green Salad

(Ready in 30 Minutes, Serve 8, Difficulty: Easy)

Nutrition per Serving:

Calories 47, Protein 2.7 g, Carbohydrates 5.3 g, Fat 2.1 g, Cholesterol 3.1mg, Sodium 162.7mg.

Ingredients:

- ½ cup of chopped onion
- ½ cup of chopped green bell pepper
- 2(10 ounces) packages of mixed salad greens
- 4 thinly sliced chicken deli meat, chopped
- 1 tomato, chopped
- ¼ teaspoon of onion powder
- 3 dashes of garlic powder
- 1 pinch of ground black pepper
- 2 pinches of salt
- 3 tablespoons of balsamic vinaigrette salad dressing

Instructions:

1. Set aside to cool. Microwave or cook the onion and bell pepper until tender.

2. Combine the onion, chili, salad greens, deli meat, and tomato in a large salad dish. Sprinkle with onion powder, black pepper, garlic powder, and salt. To combine, toss.

3. To coat, pour on ample salad dressing or vinegar, toss again and serve.

Holiday Chicken Salad

(Ready in 15 Minutes, Serve 12, Difficulty: Easy)

Nutrition per Serving:

Calories 315, Protein 13.9 g, Carbohydrates 15.2 g, Fat 23.1 g, Cholesterol 42mg, Sodium 213.1mg.

Ingredients:

- 4 cups of cubed, cooked chicken meat
- 1 cup of mayonnaise
- 1 teaspoon of paprika
- 1½ cup of dried cranberries
- 1 cup of chopped celery
- 2 green onions, chopped
- ½ cup of minced green bell pepper
- 1 cup of chopped pecans
- 1 teaspoon of seasoning salt
- Ground black pepper, to taste

Instructions:

1. Mix the mayonnaise and paprika with the seasoned salt in a medium dish. Combine the dried cranberries, celery, cabbage, bell pepper, and nuts. Add sliced chicken and blend thoroughly.

2. Season with black pepper. Refrigerate for 1 hour.

Chapter 8: Meat Dishes

In this chapter, we are going to give you some delicious and mouthwatering recipes on Lean & Green Meat Dishes recipes.

Momma's Healthy Meatloaf

(Ready in1 Hour, Serve 4, Difficulty: Normal)

Nutrition per Serving:

Calories 378, Protein 26.4 g, Carbohydrates 24 g, Fat 20.1 g, Cholesterol 157.2mg, Sodium 457.2mg.

Ingredients:

- Cooking spray
- 1 tablespoon of olive oil
- 1 green bell pepper, diced
- ½ cup of diced sweet onion
- ½ teaspoon of minced garlic
- 453 g of extra-lean (95%) ground beef
- 1 cup of whole wheat bread crumbs
- 2 large eggs
- ¾ cup of shredded carrot
- ¾ cup of shredded zucchini
- Salt and ground black pepper, to taste
- ¼ cup of ketchup, or to taste

Instructions:

1. Preheat the oven to 400 degrees Fahrenheit (204 degrees Celsius). Use cooking spray to spray a 9x5-inch loaf pan.

2. Heat the olive oil over medium heat in a saucepan, cook and mix the green bell pepper and the onion in the hot oil for 5-10 minutes until the onion is clear and the bell pepper is softened.

3. Add garlic and simmer for 1-2 minutes until it is fragrant.

4. In a large bowl, add ground beef, zucchini, salt, bread crumbs, eggs, carrot, pepper, & bell pepper mixture, using your hands to blend properly. In the prepared loaf tin, press the meat mixture into it.

5. Bake in the preheated oven for 35-40 minutes until it is no longer pink in the middle. A center-inserted instant-read thermometer can read at least 160 degrees Fahrenheit (70 degrees Celsius). Spread on top of the meatloaf with ketchup and bake until bubbling, about 5 more minutes.

Cheeseburger Meatloaf

(Ready in 1 hour and 20 Minutes, Serve 8, Difficulty: Normal)

Nutrition per Serving:

Calories 310, Protein 31.7 g, Carbohydrates 4 g, Fat 29.1 g, Cholesterol 161.9mg, Sodium 811.3mg.

Ingredients:

- 907 g of ground beef
- ¾ cup of fresh bread crumbs
- ½ cup of minced onion
- 2 eggs, beaten
- 1 ½ teaspoons of salt
- 1 ½ teaspoons of ground black pepper
- 3 cups of shredded cheddar cheese

Instructions:

1. Preheat the oven to 350 degrees Fahrenheit (176 degrees Celsius).

2. Combine the meat, bread crumbs, onion, eggs, salt, and pepper in a big bowl and blend well. Pat out a 14x18-inch rectangle of meat mixture on a sheet of wax paper. Spread cheese over the beef, leaving the edges around a 3/4-inch border.

3. To enclose the filling and shape a pinwheel loaf, roll up the jelly roll mode. To enclose the cheese, press the beef in on both sides. Place in a 10x15-inch baking dish.

4. Bake for 1 hour in a preheated oven or until the inside temperature reaches 160 degrees Fahrenheit (70 degrees Celsius).

Mexican Taco Meatloaf

(Ready in 1 Hour, Serve 8, Difficulty: Normal)

Nutrition per Serving:

Calories 227, Protein 21.6 g, Carbohydrates 7.1 g, Fat 16.6 g, Cholesterol 120.2mg, Sodium 468.4mg.

Ingredients:

- 680 g of lean ground beef
- 1 cup of crushed tortilla chips
- ¾ cup of shredded pepper Jack cheese
- 1 small onion, chopped
- 1(1 ounce) packet of taco seasoning mix
- 2 eggs, beaten
- ½ cup of milk
- ¼ cup of mild red taco sauce, or to taste

Instructions:

1. The oven should be preheated to 350 degrees Fahrenheit (176 degrees Celsius).

2. Combine thoroughly in a bowl, season with beef, pepper Jack cheese, tortilla chips, onion, and taco.

3. In a separate bowl, whisk together the eggs, milk, and taco sauce.

4. Add the mixture of meat and stir until well combined.

5. Squeeze the mixture into a 9x5-inch loaf pan and line the middle with a slice of taco sauce.

6. Bake for 45-60 minutes in the preheated oven until baked and browned on top.

Classic Meatloaf

(Ready in 1 Hour and 5 Minutes, Serve 10, Difficulty: Normal)

Nutrition per Serving:

Calories 128, Protein 21.6 g, Carbohydrates 14.8 g, Fat 14.9 g, Cholesterol 85.3mg, Sodium 755.4mg.

Ingredients:

- 1 carrot, coarsely chopped
- 1 rib of celery, coarsely chopped
- ½ onion, coarsely chopped
- ½ red bell pepper, coarsely chopped
- 4 white mushrooms, coarsely chopped
- 3 cloves of garlic, coarsely chopped
- 1134 g of ground chuck
- 1 tablespoon of Worcestershire sauce
- 1 egg, beaten
- 1 teaspoon of dried Italian herbs
- 2 teaspoons of salt
- 1 teaspoon of ground black pepper
- ½ teaspoon of cayenne pepper
- 1 cup of plain bread crumbs
- 1 teaspoon of olive oil
- 2 tablespoons of brown sugar
- 2 tablespoons of ketchup
- 2 tablespoons of Dijon mustard
- Hot pepper sauce, to taste

Instructions:

1. To 325 degrees F (165 degree Celsius) preheat the oven.

2. In a food processor, put the carrot, celery, onion, red bell pepper, mushrooms, and garlic and pulse until very thinly sliced, almost into a puree.

3. Put the minced vegetables and blend in ground chuck, Worcestershire sauce, and egg in a big mixing cup. Add the Italian spices, garlic, cayenne pepper, and black pepper. Blend the vegetables and egg into the beef, combining gently with a wooden spoon. Pour the bread crumbs into it. Gently mix in the crumbs with your fingertips with your hand only before mixed, around 1 minute.

4. Form a meatloaf into a ball. Place the ball of meat in the bowl and add olive oil into *-the baking dish. Shape the ball into a 6x4-inch loaf.

5. Bake until the meatloaf is hot in the preheated oven, about 15 minutes.

6. Meanwhile, blend the brown sugar, ketchup, Dijon mustard, and hot sauce in a shallow tub. Stir until it has dissolved the brown sugar.

7. In the microwave, cut the meatloaf. Smooth the glaze on top of the meatloaf with the back of a spoon, then force a little bit of glaze down the sides of the meatloaf with the back of the spoon.

8. Put the meatloaf back in the oven and bake for another 30-40 minutes until the loaf is no longer pink on the inside and the glaze is cooked on the loaf. A thermometer for instant reading inserted into the thickest section of the loaf can read at least 160 degrees Fahrenheit (70 degrees Celsius). Cooking time can depend on the meatloaf's form and thickness.

Easy Meatloaf

(Ready in 1 Hour and 10 Minutes, Serve 8, Difficulty: Hard)

Nutrition per Serving:

Calories 237, Protein 18.2 g, Carbohydrates 18.5 g, Fat 24.7 g, Cholesterol 98mg, Sodium 334.6mg.

Ingredients:

- 680 g of ground beef
- 1 egg
- 1 onion, chopped
- 1 cup of milk
- 1 cup of dried bread crumbs
- Salt and pepper, to taste
- 2 tablespoons of brown sugar
- 2 tablespoons of prepared mustard
- ⅓ cup of ketchup

Instructions:

1. Preheat the oven to 350 degrees Fahrenheit (176 degrees Celsius).

1. Combine the meat, egg, cabbage, milk, bread, or cracker crumbs in a large dish.

2. Season to taste with salt and pepper and put in a 9x5-inch lightly greased loaf pan, or shape into a loaf and place in a 9x13-inch lightly greased baking dish.

3. Combine the brown sugar, mustard, and ketchup in a separate, shallow dish. Mix well and spill over the meatloaf.

4. Bake for 1 hour at 350 degrees Fahrenheit (176 degrees Celsius).

Brown Sugar Meatloaf with Ketchup Glaze

(Ready in 1 Hour and 20 Minutes, Serve 8, Difficulty: Hard)

Nutrition per Serving:

Calories 278, Protein 19.1 g, Carbohydrates 22.8 g, Fat 12.2 g, Cholesterol 102.8mg, Sodium 719.9mg.

Ingredients:

- ½ cup of ketchup
- ½ cup of packed brown sugar
- 1 ½ teaspoon of salt
- ½ teaspoon of chili powder
- 680 g of lean ground beef
- 1 ½ cup of croutons, crushed
- 1 small onion, chopped
- 2 eggs
- ¼ cup of milk
- ¼ teaspoon of ground black pepper

Instructions:

1. Preheat the oven to 350 degrees Fahrenheit (176 degrees Celsius). Grease a 9x5-inch loaf pan lightly.

2. In a cup, whisk together the ketchup, brown sugar, salt, and chili powder until smooth.

3. Spread the bottom of the prepared loaf pan with a small amount of the ketchup mixture.

4. In a wide bowl, mix ground beef, croutons, onion, eggs, milk, and black pepper, form a loaf, and position in a prepared pan. Eared over the loaf with the leftover ketchup mixture.

Bake in the preheated oven for about 1 hour until the middle is no longer pink. A center-inserted instant-read thermometer can read at least 160 degrees Fahrenheit (70 degrees Celsius).

Cheesy Meatloaf

(Ready in 1 Hour and 15 Minutes, Serve 8, and Difficulty: Normal)

Nutrition per Serving:

Calories 208, Protein 30.4 g, Carbohydrates 17.6 g, Fat 23.2 g, Cholesterol 135.5mg, Sodium 701.9mg.

Ingredients:

- 453 g of ground beef
- 453 g of ground pork
- 1(1 ounce) envelope of dry onion soup mix
- 2 eggs, beaten
- 1 ½ cups of dry bread crumbs
- Ground black pepper to taste
- ¾ cup of water
- 2 cups of shredded mozzarella cheese, divided

Instructions:

1. Preheat the oven to 350 degrees Fahrenheit (176 degrees Celsius).

2. Combine the meat, pork, soup mixture, eggs, bread crumbs, pepper, and water in a large bowl. Stir in ½ a glass of cheese.

3. Spread half of the mixture into a 9x5 inch loaf pan and blend properly. Layer 1 1/2 cup of leftover cheese over the meatloaf mixture. Cover with the meatloaf mixture for the remaining portion.

4. Bake for 60 minutes in a preheated oven. Until serving, let it cool for 10 to 15 minutes.

Bacon-Wrapped Buffalo Meatloaf

(Ready in 2 Hours. Serve 6, Difficulty: Easy)

Nutrition per Serving:

Calories 348, Protein 35.8 g, Carbohydrates 19.3 g, Fat 13.6 g, Cholesterol 134.5mg, Sodium 1239.3mg.

Ingredients:

- 2 tablespoons of butter
- 2 slices of bacon, chopped
- ½ yellow onion, chopped
- 1 carrot, cubed
- 1 red bell pepper, chopped
- 1 fresh poblano pepper, chopped (Optional)
- 4 button mushrooms, chopped
- 3 cloves of garlic
- ¼ teaspoon of dried rosemary
- 2 cups of fresh bread crumbs
- ¼ cup of milk
- 1 large egg
- 2 teaspoons of kosher salt, or to taste
- 1 teaspoon of Worcestershire sauce
- 1 teaspoon of freshly ground black pepper
- 1 pinch of cayenne pepper
- 907 g of ground buffalo
- 7 slices of thick-cut bacon, or more as needed

For Glaze:

- 2 tablespoons of rice vinegar (optional)
- 2 tablespoons of brown sugar (optional)
- 1 tablespoon of Dijon mustard (optional)

Instructions:

1. Preheat the oven to 350 degrees Fahrenheit (176 degrees Celsius). Grease a 9x13-inch baking dish lightly.

2. Melt butter over medium heat in a large skillet. Cook and stir the chopped bacon in the hot butter for 5-10 minutes, until almost crisp.

3. In a food processor, slice the onion, carrot, poblano pepper, celery, red bell pepper, mushrooms, and garlic until finely chopped.

4. In the skillet, add the vegetable blend and rosemary to the bacon, cook and stir until the vegetables are softened and sweetened, about 5 minutes.

5. In a bowl, combine the vegetable mixture, bread crumbs, and milk. Let the room temperature cool. Stir in the vegetable mixture, egg, salt, Worcestershire sauce, black pepper, and cayenne pepper. Add the buffalo meat to the vegetable mixture and blend until well blended with your hands.

6. Turn the meat mixture into a prepared baking dish and form a 9x5x3-inch meatloaf. Lay bacon strips crosswise over the meatloaf's top, tucking bacon beneath the loaf at the ends.

7. In a bowl, whisk together the rice vinegar, brown sugar, and mustard until the glaze is soft.

8. Bake the meatloaf for 30 minutes in a preheated oven. Brush the glaze over the loaf and continue baking until the center is no longer pink, about 30 more minutes. A center-inserted instant-read thermometer should read at least 155 degrees Fahrenheit (68 degrees Celsius), before slicing, cool for 10 minutes.

Italian Style Turkey Meatloaf

(Ready in 1 Hour and 5 Minutes, Serve 6, Difficulty: Hard)

Nutrition per Serving:

Calories 216, Protein 17.8 g, Carbohydrates 8.1 g, Fat 7 g, Cholesterol 86.8mg, Sodium 651mg.

Ingredients:

* Cooking spray
* 453 g of ground turkey
* 1 egg
* ¼ cup of Italian seasoned bread crumbs
* 1 teaspoon of Italian seasoning
* ½ clove of garlic, minced
* ½ teaspoon of ground black pepper, or to taste
* ¼ teaspoon of salt, or to taste
* 2 cups of tomato sauce, divided

Instructions:

1. Preheat oven to 400 degrees Fahrenheit (204 degrees Celsius). Prepare a baking dish with spray for cooking.

2. In a big cup, blend turkey, egg, bread crumbs, Italian seasoning, garlic, black pepper, salt, form a loaf, and place in a prepared baking dish.

3. Bake for 40 minutes in a preheated oven. Spoon over the loaf with around ½ the tomato sauce and proceed.

4. Bake for 10-15 more minutes, until the meatloaf is no longer pink in the middle. A center-inserted instant-read thermometer can read at least 160 degrees Fahrenheit (70 degrees Celsius). Set aside the meatloaf for 5-10 minutes before serving.

5. Serve with the cut meatloaf as the meatloaf sits, and cook the remaining tomato sauce over medium-low heat in a small saucepan.

Best Ever Meatloaf I

(Ready in 1 Hour and 25 Minutes, Serve 8, Difficulty: Normal)

Nutrition per Serving:

Calories 270, Protein 17.1 g, Carbohydrates 7 g, Fat 18.7 g, Cholesterol 87.1mg, Sodium 216.6mg.

Ingredients:

* 680 g of lean ground beef
* 1 cup of tomato juice
* ¾ cup of rolled oats
* 1 egg
* ¼ cup of chopped onion
* ½ teaspoon of salt
* ¼ teaspoon of ground black pepper

Instructions:

1. Preheat the oven to 350 degrees Fahrenheit (176 degrees Celsius).

2. Combine the beef, tomato juice, oatmeal, egg, chopped onion, salt, and pepper in a large dish.

3. Mix lightly but carefully. Press into the 8x4 inch loaf pan.

4. Bake for 1 hour, or until the meat and juices are no longer pink and transparent. Drain. Let it stand before serving for 5 minutes.

The Best Meatloaf I've ever Made

(Ready in 1 Hour and 25 Minutes, Serve 1, Difficulty: Hard)

Nutrition per Serving:

Calories 221, Protein 17.9 g, Carbohydrates 8.7 g, Fat 11.6 g, Cholesterol 76.1mg, Sodium 648.6mg.

Ingredients:

* 1 tablespoon of butter
* ¼ cup of minced onion
* 2 cloves of garlic, minced
* 1 ½ teaspoon of salt
* 1 ½ teaspoon of freshly ground black pepper
* 907 g of extra-lean ground beef
* 3 slices of bread, toasted and crumbled
* 7 buttery round crackers, crushed
* 1 egg, lightly beaten
* 3 ½ tablespoons of sour cream
* 1 ½ tablespoon of Worcestershire sauce
* 1(15 ounces) can of tomato sauce, divided

- ¼ cup of milk (Optional)
- 3 tablespoons of ketchup

Instructions:

1. Preheat the oven to 350 degrees Fahrenheit (176 degrees Celsius).

2. In a medium-hot saucepan, melt the butter and cook the onion and garlic for 5 minutes, until the onion is tender. Remove from heat, and combine salt and pepper to season.

3. Combine the onion and garlic, meat, crumbled bread, crushed crackers, cheese, sour cream, Worcestershire sauce, and ½ of the tomato sauce in a big tub.

4. Stir in 1 teaspoon of milk at a time until the mixture is sticky but not soggy. Transfer the mixture to a 5x9-inch loaf pan.

5. Bake in a preheated oven for 40 minutes, uncovered. Increase the temperature of the oven to 400 degrees Fahrenheit (204 degrees Celsius) and begin cooking for 15 minutes at an internal temperature of 160 degrees Fahrenheit (70 degrees Celsius).

6. Mix the remaining tomato sauce and ketchup in a small bowl. Pour the meatloaf over the top and begin to bake for 10 minutes.

Beth's Meat Loaf

(Ready in 1 Hour and 20 Minutes, Serve 5, Difficulty: Hard)

Nutrition per Serving:

Calories 388, Protein 28.9 g, Carbohydrates 22.2 g, Fat 20 g, Cholesterol 162.6mg, Sodium 935.1mg.

Ingredients:

- 2 eggs, beaten
- ¾ cup of milk
- ½ cup of dry bread crumbs
- ¼ cup of chopped onion
- 1 teaspoon of salt
- 1 teaspoon of ground black pepper
- ½ teaspoon of crumbled dried sage
- 680 g of ground beef
- ½ cup of ketchup
- 2 tablespoons of brown sugar
- 1 teaspoon of dry mustard powder

Instructions:

1. Preheat the oven to 350 degrees Fahrenheit (176 degrees Celsius). Grease a 9x5-inch loaf pan.

2. Lightly whisk together the beaten eggs, sugar, bread crumbs, onion, cinnamon, black pepper, and sage in a bowl until well mixed.

3. Gently work when mixed in the ground beef and press the meat mixture into the prepared loaf tray.

4. Bake until the loaf is no longer pink inside and the juices are transparent, around 50 minutes, in the preheated oven. At least 160 degrees Fahrenheit (70 degrees Celsius) can be read by an instant-read thermometer inserted into the loaf core

5. Shake together the ketchup, brown sugar, and dry mustard powder in a bowl while the meatloaf is baking, until the sugar has dissolved. Take the loaf from the oven when it's finished, and spread the topping over the loaf. Return to the oven and bake for around ten more minutes before the topping is set.

Super Moist Meatloaf

(Ready in 1 Hour, Serve 8, Difficulty: Normal)

Nutrition per Serving:

Calories 326, Protein 21.9 g, Carbohydrates 8.1 g, Fat 15.4 g, Cholesterol 118.7mg, Sodium 715.4mg.

Ingredients:

- 907 g of ground beef
- ½ onion, chopped
- 2 eggs, beaten
- ¾ cup of small chunks of bread
- ½ cup of milk
- ½ cup of chopped green bell pepper
- 1 ½ teaspoon of salt
- ¼ teaspoon of sage
- ¼ teaspoon of ground black pepper
- ½ cup of ketchup, or to taste

Instructions:

1. Preheat the oven to 350 degrees Fahrenheit (176 degrees Celsius).

2. In a bowl, mix the ground beef, cabbage, eggs, bread, sugar, sage, green bell pepper, salt, and black pepper. Press into the tray of a loaf. Spread over the top of the loaf with ketchup.

3. Bake in the preheated oven for about 45 minutes, until the middle is no longer pink. A center-inserted instant-read thermometer may read at least 160 degrees Fahrenheit (70 degrees Celsius).

Instant Pot® Meatloaf

(Ready in 1 Hour and 25 Minutes, Serve 8, Difficulty: Hard)

Ingredients:

- 907 g of ground beef
- 1 cup of dry bread crumbs
- ½ cup of diced onion
- ½ apple, peeled, cored, and diced
- 2 teaspoons of garlic powder
- ½ teaspoon of salt

- ½ teaspoon of ground black pepper

For Topping:

- ⅓ cup of ketchup
- 2 tablespoons of prepared yellow mustard
- 2 tablespoons of brown sugar

Instructions:

1. In a large bowl, add the meat, bread crumbs, onion, apple, garlic powder, salt, and pepper until finely combined.

2. Shape a loaf with the beef mixture and put it on a large piece of aluminum foil. Fold the foil up and around the meatloaf's edges, producing a makeshift loaf pan.

3. In a multi-functional pressure cooker, pour 1/2 cup water (such as Instant Pot®) and place the steam rack inside with the handles up.

4. On the top of the rack, put the meatloaf. Seal the vent, close the lid, and lock it. According to the manufacturer's instructions, choose high pressure, and set the timer for 25 minutes. Allow pressure to build for 10 to 15 minutes.

5. Set a rack for the oven about 6 inches from the heat source and preheat the oven's broiler.

6. Use the quick-release method according to the manufacturer's instructions to carefully release cooker pressure for about 5 minutes. Unlock the lid and then remove it. Transfer the meatloaf to a baking sheet, still on the rack. Broil the meatloaf in the oven for about 5 minutes, until browned.

7. In a small bowl, combine your ketchup, mustard, and brown sugar. Brush over the meatloaf and broil again for 1-2 minutes, until caramelized.

Lighter Meatloaf

(Ready in 1 Hour and 35 Minutes, Serve 8, Difficulty: Normal)

Nutrition per Serving:

Calories 229, Protein 21.5 g, Carbohydrates 18.5 g, Fat 14.6 g, Cholesterol 71mg, Sodium 466.3mg.

Ingredients:

- Cooking spray
- 453 g of ground sirloin
- 453 g of ground turkey
- 1 cup of quick-cooking oats
- 1 small onion, chopped
- 2 large eggs
- 2 large white eggs
- 7 tablespoons of chili sauce, divided
- 1 tablespoon of dried basil
- 1 teaspoon of minced garlic from a jar
- ½ teaspoon of salt
- ½ teaspoon of coarsely ground black pepper

Instructions:

1. Preheat the oven to 375 degrees Fahrenheit (190 degrees Celsius). Using cooking spray to prepare a glass or stoneware 13x9-inch baking bowl.

2. In a bowl, mix the sirloin, turkey, egg whites, oats, onion, eggs, three tablespoons of chili sauce, basil, garlic, salt, and pepper, turn into a 9x5-inch loaf, and place in the baking dish.

3. Bake for 50 minutes in the preheated oven. Spoon the leftover chili sauce over the top of the meatloaf and continue to bake for about 20 more minutes until the middle is no longer pink.

4. A center-inserted instant-read thermometer can read at least 160 degrees Fahrenheit (70 degrees Celsius). Before slicing, allow the meatloaf to rest for 10 minutes.

Best Turkey Meatloaf

(Ready in 1 Hour and 15 Minutes, Serve 8, Difficulty: Normal)

Nutrition per Serving:

Calories 296, Protein 19.7 g, Carbohydrates 25.2 g, Fat 13.2 g, Cholesterol 84.5mg, Sodium 880.8mg.

Ingredients:

- 680 g of ground turkey
- ¾ cup of crushed buttery round crackers
- ½ cup of milk
- 1 small onion, chopped
- 1 egg
- 1 ½ teaspoon of salt
- 2 cloves of garlic, minced
- ¼ teaspoon of ground black pepper

For Topping:

- ½ cup of ketchup
- ¼ cup of brown sugar
- 1 tablespoon of Worcestershire sauce

Instructions:

1. Preheat the oven to 350 degrees Fahrenheit (176 degrees Celsius). Grease a jelly roll pan lightly.

2. In a bowl, mix ground turkey, egg, salt, garlic, buttery round cracker crumbs, milk, onion, and black pepper, turn into a loaf, and put on the rolling pan of jelly.

3. In a separate bowl, combine brown sugar, ketchup, and Worcestershire sauce. Set aside.

4. Cook the meatloaf in a preheated oven for 30 minutes, remove the liquid from the oven and rinse. Meatloaf finishes with ketchup topping.

5. Return the loaf to the oven and begin to bake until the middle is no longer yellow, around an additional 30 minutes. A center-inserted instant-read

thermometer can read at least 160 degrees Fahrenheit (70 degrees Celsius).

Tennessee Meatloaf

(Ready in 1 Hour and 55 Minutes, Serve 10, Difficulty: Hard)

Nutrition per Serving:

Calories 223, Protein 17.1 g, Carbohydrates 15.9 g, Fat 11.2 g, Cholesterol 92mg, Sodium 324.1mg.

Ingredients:

- cooking spray
- 1 onion, chopped
- ½ green bell pepper, chopped
- 2 cloves of garlic, minced
- 2 large eggs, lightly beaten
- 1 teaspoon of dried thyme
- 1 teaspoon of seasoned salt
- ½ teaspoon of ground black pepper
- 2 teaspoons of prepared mustard
- 2 teaspoons of Worcestershire sauce
- ½ teaspoon of hot pepper sauce (such as Tabasco®)
- ½ cup of milk
- ⅔ cup of quick-cooking oats
- 453 g of ground beef
- 226 g of ground pork
- 226 g of ground veal

For Brown Sugar Glaze:

- ½ cup of ketchup
- ¼ cup of brown sugar
- 2 tablespoons of cider vinegar

Instructions:

1. Combine the brown sugar, ketchup, and cider vinegar in a cup and blend properly.

2. Preheat the oven to 350 degrees Fahrenheit (176 degrees Celsius). For faster cleanup, spray two 9x5-inch loaf pans with cooking spray or line with aluminum foil.

3. In a covered microwave container, add the onion and green pepper.

4. Until softened, cook for 1-2 minutes. Set aside.

5. Combine the garlic, eggs, thyme, seasoning cinnamon, black pepper, vinegar, Worcestershire sauce, chili sauce, milk, and oats in a large mixing cup. Mix thoroughly. Stir in the green pepper and fried onion. Add ground beef, veal, and bacon. Work all ingredients together until fully blended and uniform with gloved hands.

6. Divide 1/2 of the meatloaf mixture into each prepared loaf pan and pat half of the mixture. Brush the loaves with half the glaze and set aside the rest of the glaze.

7. Bake for 50 minutes in a preheated oven. Take the pans from the oven and drain the fat carefully. Brush the loaves with the glaze that remains. Place them back in the oven and bake for ten more minutes. Remove the pans from the oven and allow the meatloaf to stand before slicing for 15 minutes.

Glazed Meatloaf II

(Ready in 1 Hour and 20 Minutes, Serve 8, Difficulty: Hard)

Nutrition per Serving:

Calories 318, Protein 22.4 g, Carbohydrates 18.9 g, Fat 16.8 g, Cholesterol 89.7mg, Sodium 398.2mg

Ingredients:

- ½ cup of ketchup
- 1 cup of brown sugar
- 1 tablespoon of lemon juice
- 1 teaspoon of dry mustard
- 907 g of lean ground beef
- 3 slices of bread, shredded
- ¼ cup of diced onion
- 1 egg, beaten
- 1 cube of beef bouillon, crumbled
- 3 tablespoons of lemon juice

Instructions:

1. Preheat the oven to 350 degrees Fahrenheit (176 degrees Celsius).

2. Combine the ketchup, brown sugar, 1 tablespoon of lemon juice, and the dried mustard in a small bowl until smooth.

3. Combine ground beef, egg, bouillon, shredded bread, onion, 3 tablespoons lemon juice, and 1/3 cup ketchup mixture in a large bowl until well blended. In a 9x5-inch loaf pan, form into a loaf and place.

4. Bake for one hour. Pour the fat away. Pour a mixture of reserved ketchup over the loaf. Bake for an extra 10 minutes.

The Easiest and Delish Meatloaf Ever!

(Ready in1 Hour and 10 Minutes, Serve 8, Difficulty: Hard)

Nutrition per Serving:

Calories 246, Protein 16.5 g, Carbohydrates 10.9 g, Fat 14.9 g, Cholesterol 76.5mg, Sodium 557.6mg.

Ingredients:

- 1 egg
- 680 g of ground beef
- 1(14 ounces) can of diced tomatoes with green Chile peppers, (such as RO*TEL®), undrained

- 1 sleeve buttery round crackers, (such as Ritz®), crushed
- 1 teaspoon of onion flakes (Optional)
- 1 ½ teaspoon of garlic powder, or to taste
- 1 ½ teaspoon of seasoned salt, or to taste
- ½ teaspoon of ground black pepper, or to taste

Instructions:

1. Preheat the oven to 375 degrees Fahrenheit (190 degrees Celsius).

2. In a mixing bowl, beat the egg and then add the ground beef, tomatoes, and crushed crackers. Season with garlic powder, onion flakes, ground salt, and pepper.

3. Mix until combined equally. Pack into a 9x5-inch loaf pan.

4. Bake in the preheated oven for about 1 hour until the middle is no longer pink. A center-inserted instant-read thermometer can read at least 160 degrees Fahrenheit (70 degrees Celsius).

Melt-In-Your-Mouth Meat Loaf

(Ready in 5 Hour and 40 Minutes, Serve 8, and Difficulty: Hard)

Nutrition per Serving:

Calories 328, Protein 24.7 g, Carbohydrates 18.4 g, Fat 16.9 g, Cholesterol 135.6mg, Sodium 841.1mg.

Ingredients:

- 2 eggs
- ¾ cup of milk
- ⅔ cup of seasoned bread crumbs
- 2 teaspoons of dried minced onion
- 1 teaspoon of salt
- ½ teaspoon of rubbed sage
- ½ cup of sliced fresh mushrooms
- 680 g of ground beef
- ¼ cup of ketchup
- 2 tablespoons of brown sugar
- 1 teaspoon of ground mustard
- ½ teaspoon of Worcestershire sauce

Instructions:

1. In a large bowl, combine the eggs, milk, bread crumbs, onion, garlic, sage, and mushrooms. Crumble the ground beef over the mixture and blend to stir properly. Place in a 5-quart slow cooker, then form into a round loaf.

2. Cover and simmer for 5-6 hours before the meat thermometer reads 160 degrees Fahrenheit (71 degrees Celsius).

3. In a shallow bowl, whisk the ketchup, mustard, brown sugar, and Worcestershire sauce with a spoonful of meatloaf sauce. Return to slow cooker and cook on low for around 15 minutes until heated. Let it stand before cutting for 10 minutes.

Turkey and Quinoa Meatloaf

(Ready in 1 Hour and 20 Minutes, Serve 5, Difficulty: Hard)

Nutrition per Serving:

Calories 259, Protein 25.3 g, Carbohydrates 15.2 g, Fat 11 g, Cholesterol 120.8mg, Sodium 967.6mg.

Ingredients:

- ¼ cup of quinoa
- ½ cup of water
- 1 teaspoon of olive oil
- 1 small onion, chopped
- 1 large clove of garlic, chopped
- 1(20 ounces) package of ground turkey
- 1 tablespoon of tomato paste
- 1 tablespoon of hot pepper sauce
- 2 tablespoons of Worcestershire sauce
- 1 egg
- 1 ½ teaspoons of salt
- 1 teaspoon of ground black pepper
- 2 tablespoons of brown sugar
- 2 teaspoons of Worcestershire sauce
- 1 teaspoon of water

Instructions:

1. In a saucepan, put the quinoa and water to a boil over high heat. Reduce the heat to medium-low, cover and simmer for around 15-20 minutes until the quinoa is tender and the water is absorbed. Set to cool aside.

2. Preheat the oven to 350 degrees Fahrenheit (176 degrees Celsius).

3. Over medium melt, heat the olive oil in a skillet. Stir in the onion, cook and stir for about 5 minutes until the onion has softened and become translucent. Add the garlic and roast, then remove from the heat to cook for another minute.

4. In a large bowl, whisk together the turkey, cooked quinoa, onion, tomato paste, hot sauce, 2 tablespoons of Worcestershire, egg, salt, and pepper until well mixed.

5. It would be very sticky in the mixture. Shape it into a loaf on a baking sheet lined with foil. In a small dish, combine the brown sugar,2 teaspoons of Worcestershire, and 1 teaspoon of water. Rub it over the top of the meatloaf with the paste.

6. Bake in the preheated oven for around 50 minutes until the middle is no longer pink. A center-inserted instant-read thermometer can read at least 160 degrees Fahrenheit (70 degrees Celsius). Before

slicing and serving, let the meatloaf cool for 10 minutes.

Mini Meatloaves

(Ready in 1 Hour, Serve 8, Difficulty: Normal)
Nutrition per Serving:

Calories 325, Protein 15.1 g, Carbohydrates 16.6 g, Fat 14.4 g, Cholesterol 73.9mg, Sodium 656mg.

Ingredients:
- 1 egg
- ¾ cup of milk
- 1 cup of shredded cheddar cheese
- ½ cup of quick-cooking oats
- 1 teaspoon of salt
- 453 g of ground beef
- ⅔ cup of ketchup
- ¼ cup of packed brown sugar
- 1 ½ teaspoon of prepared mustard

Instructions:

1. Preheat the oven to 350 degrees Fahrenheit (176 degrees Celsius).

2. Combine the egg, milk, cheese, oatmeal, and salt in a large bowl. Add the ground beef, mix well, and make eight miniature meatloaves to form this mixture.

3. Place these in a 9x13 inch baking dish, which is lightly greased.

4. Combine the ketchup, brown sugar, and mustard in another small bowl. Stir and spread thoroughly over each meatloaf.

5. Bake, uncovered, for 45 minutes at 350 degrees Fahrenheit (176 degrees Celsius).

Old Italian Meat Sauce

(Ready in 4 Hours and 30 Minutes, Serve 20, and Difficulty: Normal)
Nutrition per Serving:

Calories 296, Protein 15.2 g 3, Carbohydrates 15.9 g, Fat 16.8 g, Cholesterol 50.8mg, Sodium 788.1mg.

Ingredients:
- 907 g of lean ground beef
- 453 g of ground pork
- 2 tablespoons of olive oil
- 2 onions, chopped
- 1 clove of garlic, crushed
- 3 cups of red wine
- 907 g of fresh mushrooms, sliced
- ¼ teaspoon of dried rosemary
- 4 tablespoons of chopped fresh oregano
- ¼ teaspoon of chopped fresh thyme
- 3(29 ounces) cans of tomato sauce
- 1(6 ounces) can of tomato paste
- 2 tablespoons of grated parmesan cheese

Instructions:

1. In a large skillet, set aside the brown beef and pork over medium heat until it is no longer pink.

2. Heat the olive oil in a large skillet over medium heat and sauté the onions and garlic until tender.

3. Add about half a bottle of wine and blend well.

4. To the skillet, add the mushrooms, rosemary, oregano, and thyme and add another ½ cup of wine and sauté until tender.

5. Add to the mixture the browned beef, tomato sauce, and tomato paste, boil for 1 hour, and add the remaining 2 cups of wine.

6. Simmer sauce over low heat for 2-3 hours, stirring regularly, then serve.

Charley's Slow Cooker Mexican Style Meat

(Ready in 8 Hours and 50 Minutes, Serve 12, and Difficulty: Hard)
Nutrition per Serving:

Calories 261, Protein 18.4 g, Carbohydrates 3.3 g, Fat 19.1 g, Cholesterol 68.7mg, Sodium 314.7mg.

Ingredients:
- 1(1814 g) chuck roast
- 1 teaspoon of salt
- 1 teaspoon of ground black pepper
- 2 tablespoons of olive oil
- 1 large onion, chopped
- 1 ¼ cups of diced green Chile pepper
- 1 teaspoon of chili powder
- 1 teaspoon of ground cayenne pepper
- 1(5 ounces) bottle of hot pepper sauce
- 1 teaspoon of garlic powder

Instructions:

1. Remove any extra Fat off the roast, and season with salt and pepper. Heat the olive oil over medium-high heat in a large skillet. Put the beef in the hot pan, and on all sides, brown it easily.

2. Transfer the roast and cover it with the sliced onion to a slow cooker. Season with bell peppers, chili powder, sweet pepper sauce, cayenne pepper, and garlic powder. To cover 1/3 of the roast, add enough water.

3. Cover and cook for 6 hours on top, to ensure that at least a small liquid volume is still at the bottom of the cooker.

4. Reduce the heat and continue to cook for 2-4 hours, or until the meat is fully tender and falls apart.

5. Transfer the roast to a bowl and use two forks to shred it (reserve 2 cups of cooking liquid, if desired). Served in burritos or tacos.

Melt-In-Your-Mouth Meat Loaf

(Ready in 5 Hours and 40 Minutes, Serve 6, and Difficulty: Hard)

Nutrition per Serving:

Calories 328, Protein 24.7 g, Carbohydrates 18.4 g, Fat 16.9 g, Cholesterol 135.6mg, Sodium 841.1mg.

Ingredients:

- 2 eggs
- ¾ cup of milk
- ⅔ cup of seasoned bread crumbs
- 2 teaspoons of dried minced onion
- 1 teaspoon of salt
- ½ teaspoon of rubbed sage
- ½ cup of sliced fresh mushrooms
- 680 g of ground beef
- ¼ cup of ketchup
- 2 tablespoons of brown sugar
- 1 teaspoon of ground mustard
- ½ teaspoon of Worcestershire sauce

Instructions:

1. In a large bowl, combine the eggs, milk, bread crumbs, onion, garlic, sage, and mushrooms.

2. Crumble the ground beef over the mixture and blend to stir properly. Place in a 5-quart slow cooker, then form into a round loaf. Cover and simmer for 5-6 hours before the meat thermometer reads 160 degrees Fahrenheit (71 degrees Celsius).

3. In a shallow mug, whisk the ketchup, mustard, brown sugar, and Worcestershire sauce with a spoonful of meatloaf sauce. Return to slow cooker and cook on low for around 15 minutes until heated. Let it stand before cutting for 10 minutes.

Healthy Turkey Loaf

(Ready in 40 Minutes, Serve 5, Difficulty: Normal)

Nutrition per Serving:

Calories 211, Protein 10.3 g, Carbohydrates 6.1 g, Fat 5.1 g, Cholesterol 73mg, Sodium 174.3mg.

Ingredients:

- 226 g of ground turkey
- 1 egg
- ¼ cup of salsa
- ⅛ cup of chopped red bell pepper
- ⅛ cup of chopped yellow bell pepper
- ¼ cup of chopped onion
- ¼ cup of dry bread crumbs
- Lemon pepper, to taste

Instructions:

1. Preheat the oven to 350 degrees Fahrenheit (176 degrees Celsius).

2. Mix the turkey, egg, salsa, yellow bell pepper, red bell pepper, cabbage, bread crumbs, and lemon pepper in a big bowl.

3. Mix well until mixed with your hands. Roll it into a small loaf and put it on a baking sheet lined with foil.

4. Bake for 25 minutes in the preheated oven.

Meatloaf for Tomato Haters

(Ready in 1 Hour and 15 Minutes, Serve 6, Difficulty: Hard)

Nutrition per Serving:

Calories 396, Protein 27.8 g, Carbohydrates 16 g, Fat 23.8 g, Cholesterol 121.9mg, Sodium 978.6mg.

Ingredients:

- 1 cup of diced onion
- 1 cup of diced green bell pepper
- ¾ cup of Italian-style bread crumbs
- ¼ cup of hot pepper sauce
- 1 teaspoon of salt
- 1 teaspoon of ground black pepper
- 907 g of ground beef
- 1(.75 ounces) packet of dry brown gravy mix

Instructions:

1. Preheat the oven to 350 degrees Fahrenheit (176 degrees Celsius).

2. In a large bowl, mix the onion, bell pepper, hot pepper sauce, bread crumbs, egg, salt, and pepper.

3. Add ground beef and combine.

4. Press the mixture of beef into a loaf pan. Sprinkle the beef with the brown gravy blend.

5. Bake in a preheated oven for 1 hour, until baked and browned. Remove from the oven and leave to rest before serving for 10 minutes.

Meat in its Juices

(Ready in 55 Minutes, Serve 6, Difficulty: Normal)

Nutrition per Serving:

Calories 337, Protein 29.2 g, Carbohydrates 27.5 g, Fat 16.3 g, Cholesterol 57.8mg, Sodium 860.2mg.

Ingredients:

- 6 slices of bacon
- 4 fresh tomatillos, husks removed
- 3 serrano Chile peppers, seeded and chopped
- 1 clove of garlic, peeled

- 3 cups of water
- 907 g of flank steak, cut into 1/2-inch squares
- 1 cube of chicken bouillon
- 2(15.5 ounces) cans of pinto beans
- ½ onion, chopped
- 6 tablespoons of chopped fresh cilantro
- Ground black pepper, to taste
- 1 lime, cut into 6 wedges

Instructions:

1. Over medium-high heat, cook the bacon in a large deep skillet until crispy, around 10 minutes. Drain it on a tray lined with paper towels. Crumble and Set aside the bacon.

2. In a small saucepan over medium-high heat, add the tomatillos, serrano peppers, garlic, and water, bring to a boil, cover, and simmer for 10 minutes. Take the pan out of the heat and allow it to cool

3. To a blender, move the contents and blend until smooth. Only put aside. If you like, you can skip the simmering phase and mix all the raw ingredients with a few browned flank steak bits.

4. Over medium-high heat, place the non-stick skillet and cook the flank steak in the hot skillet until fully browned. Pour a combination of tomatillo over the beef and bring to a boil. In the mixture, stir the chicken bouillon and reduce the heat to mild. Cover the skillet and cook for at least 30 minutes and up to 1 hour, until tender.

5. Meanwhile, in a saucepan, heat the pinto beans over medium heat until warm, reduce the heat to a minimum, and remain warm until necessary. In the flank steak mixture, stir the bacon and pinto beans and split the mixture between 6 cups. Garnish each with a slice of onion, coriander, black pepper, and lime.

Turkey-Beef Meatloaf

(Ready in 1 Hour and 30 Minutes, Serve 6, Difficulty: Hard)

Nutrition per Serving:

Calories 341, Protein 28 g, Carbohydrates 25 g, Fat 14.2 g, Cholesterol 115.7mg, Sodium 849.3mg.

Ingredients:

- Cooking spray
- 340 g of ground turkey
- 340 g of lean ground beef
- 1 small onion, chopped
- 1 cup of milk
- 1 cup of seasoned bread crumbs
- 1 large egg
- 1 teaspoon of dried rosemary
- ½ teaspoon of salt

- ¼ teaspoon of ground black pepper
- ⅓ cup of ketchup
- 2 tablespoons of brown sugar
- 2 tablespoons of prepared yellow mustard

Instructions:

1. The oven should be preheated at 350 degrees Fahrenheit (176 degrees Celsius). Use cooking spray to spray a 9x13-inch loaf pan.

2. In a mixing dish, mix the ground turkey, ground beef, carrot, yogurt, bread crumbs, egg, rosemary, salt, and pepper.

3. Into the prepared pan, click.

4. In a separate dish, mix the ketchup, brown sugar, and mustard and whisk them together. Pour over the meatloaf mixture.

5. Bake in the preheated oven until the thermometer inserted in the middle reads at least 165 degrees Fahrenheit (74 degrees Celsius) for approximately 1 hour. It's better to give at least 5 minutes of rest before serving.

BBQ Pork for Sandwiches

(Ready in 4 Hours and 45 Minutes, Serve 12, and Difficulty: Hard)

Nutrition per Serving:

Calories 355, Protein 30.2 g, Carbohydrates 15.2 g, Fat 18.1 g, Cholesterol 82.9mg, Sodium 623.2mg.

Ingredients:

- 1(14 ounces) can of beef broth
- 1360 g of boneless pork ribs
- 1(18 ounces) bottle of barbeque sauce

Instructions:

1. Pour in a slow cooker can of beef broth, and add boneless pork ribs. Cook for 4 hours on high heat or until the meat shreds quickly.

2. Take the beef away and shred it with two forks. It won't seem to work right away, but it will.

3. Preheat the oven to 350 degrees Fahrenheit (176 degrees Celsius). In a Dutch oven or iron pan, pass the shredded pork and whisk in the barbeque sauce.

4. Bake for 30 minutes in a preheated oven or until thoroughly heated.

Spaghetti Squash with Paleo Meat Sauce

(Ready in 1 Hour and 10 Minutes, Serve 8, Difficulty: Normal)

Nutrition per Serving:

Calories 388, Protein 17 g, Carbohydrates 14.5 g, Fat 29.9 g, Cholesterol 52.2mg, Sodium 167.1mg.

Ingredients:

- ¼ cup of water

- 1 spaghetti squash, halved lengthwise and seeded
- 680 g of ground beef
- 1 white onion, diced
- 1 tablespoon of extra-virgin olive oil
- 1 cup of sliced mushrooms
- 1 zucchini, diced
- 1 green bell pepper, chopped
- 1 red bell pepper, chopped
- 1(14.5 ounces) can of crushed tomatoes
- 1(8 ounces) can of crushed tomatoes
- ¼ cup of chopped fresh basil, or to taste
- ¼ cup of chopped fresh oregano, or to taste
- ¼ cup of chopped fresh thyme, or to taste
- 1 tablespoon of red pepper flakes, or to taste
- ½ cup of extra-virgin olive oil, divided

Instructions:

1. Preheat the oven to 400 degrees Fahrenheit (204 degrees Celsius).

2. Onto a baking bowl, add water. Place the squash halves in the baking dish with the cut sides down, roast for 30-40 minutes until tender.

3. Cook and mix the ground beef and onions in a skillet over medium-high heat while the squash is frying, until the beef is crumbly, evenly browned, and no longer pink. Drain some extra grease and discard it. Set aside the beef.

4. Heat 1 tablespoon of olive oil in a medium-hot saucepan, cook and stir in the mushrooms, zucchini, green and red bell peppers, crushed tomatoes, basil, oregano, and thyme.

5. Simmer over medium heat for about 10 minutes, until the vegetables are cooked and tender. Add the ground beef and onions and stir until mixed. Simmer over low heat, stirring regularly, and finish the spaghetti squash preparation.

6. Scrape the hot spaghetti squash halves inside with a fork to shred the squash into strands and divide it into eight plates. Drizzle 1 tablespoon extra-virgin olive oil with each serving of spaghetti squash and top each serving with a generous amount of meat sauce.

Meat-Lover's Slow Cooker Spaghetti Sauce

(Ready in 8 Hour and 40 Minutes, Serve 8, and Difficulty: Normal)

Nutrition per Serving:

Calories 264, Protein 15 g, Carbohydrates 18.8 g, Fat 14.8 g, Cholesterol 45.2mg, Sodium 1025.1mg.

Ingredients:

- 2 tablespoons of olive oil

- 2 small onions, chopped
- 113 g of bulk Italian sausage
- 453 g of ground beef
- 1 teaspoon of dried Italian herb seasoning
- 1 teaspoon of garlic powder
- ½ teaspoon of dried marjoram
- 1(29 ounces) can of tomato sauce
- 1(6 ounces) can of tomato paste
- 1(14.5 ounces) can of Italian-style diced tomatoes
- 1(14.5 ounces) can of Italian-style stewed tomatoes
- ¼ teaspoon of dried thyme leaves
- ¼ teaspoon of dried basil
- ½ teaspoon of dried oregano
- 2 teaspoons of garlic powder
- 1 tablespoon of white sugar

Instructions:

1. Heat the olive oil over medium heat in a pan, cook and stir in the onions and the Italian sausage until browned, about 10 minutes.

2. To a slow cooker, pass the sausage and onions. Cook the ground beef, the Italian seasoning, one teaspoon of garlic powder, and marjoram in the same skillet and mix, breaking the meat as it cooks until the meat is browned, about 10 minutes. Through the slow cooker, pass the ground beef.

3. Stir in the tomato sauce, the tomato paste, the sliced tomatoes, the stewed tomatoes, the thyme, the basil, the oregano, and the garlic powder for 2 teaspoons. Place the cooker on the low side and steam the sauce for 8 hours. Stir in the sugar roughly 15 minutes before serving. Serve it hot.

Meatloaf Muffins

(Ready in 50 Minutes, Serve 6, Difficulty: Normal)

Nutrition per Serving:

Calories 136, Protein 36.9 g, Carbohydrates 26.9 g, Fat 22.7 g, Cholesterol 165.3mg, Sodium 1285.3mg.

Ingredients:

- 907 g of lean ground beef
- 1(10.5 ounces) can of condensed vegetable soup
- ½ cup of chopped onion
- 1 cup of dry bread crumbs
- 2 eggs
- 1 teaspoon of salt
- 1 pinch of ground black pepper
- ¾ cup of ketchup (Optional)

Instructions:

1. Preheat the oven to 350 degrees Fahrenheit (176 degrees Celsius). Grease a 12-cup muffin tin gently.

2. In a bowl, combine the ground beef, soup, carrots, bread crumbs, eggs, salt, and pepper. Scoop equally into lined muffin cups to blend.

3. Bake for 1 hour at a constant temperature of 160 degrees Fahrenheit (70 degrees Celsius). in the preheated oven Remove from the oven after 50 minutes, drizzle with ketchup on top of each muffin, if needed, and return to the oven for another 10 minutes.

Classic and Simple Meat Lasagna

(Ready in 1 Hour and 35 Minutes, Serve 8, Difficulty: Hard)

Nutrition per Serving:

Calories 250, Protein 35.6 g, Carbohydrates 47.1 g, Fat 19.3 g, Cholesterol 114.5mg, Sodium 999mg.

Ingredients:

- 12 whole wheat lasagna noodles
- 453 g of lean ground beef
- 2 cloves of garlic, chopped
- ½ teaspoon of garlic powder
- 1 teaspoon of dried oregano, or to taste
- Salt and ground black pepper, to taste
- 1(16 ounces) package of cottage cheese
- 2 eggs
- ½ cup of shredded parmesan cheese
- 1 ½ (25 ounces) jars of tomato-basil pasta sauce
- 2 cups of shredded mozzarella cheese

Instructions:

1. Preheat the oven to 350 degrees Fahrenheit (176 degrees Celsius).

2. Fill a large pot with thinly salted water and bring it over high heat to a rolling boil. When the water has cooked, add a few lasagna noodles at a time and return to the boil.

3. Cook the uncovered pasta, stirring regularly, until the pasta is thoroughly cooked but still strong to the bite, around 10 minutes. Place the noodles on a tray.

4. Put the ground beef in a medium-hot saucepan and Combine the garlic, garlic powder, oregano, salt, and black pepper to the saucepan. Cook the meat until it's no longer yellow, about 10 minutes, and cut it into small chunks as it cooks. Drain the excess grease.

5. Mix the cottage cheese, eggs, and Parmesan cheese in a bowl until completely mixed.

6. In a 9x13-inch baking pan, put four noodles side by side on the bottom, top with a layer of tomato-basil sauce, a layer of ground beef mixture, and a layer of cottage cheese mixture. Repeat the layers, finish with a layer of sauce, and scatter the mozzarella cheese on top. In aluminum foil, protect the bowl.

7. Bake for about 30 minutes in the preheated oven until the casserole is bubbling and the cheese has melted. Remove the foil and bake for about 10 more minutes before the cheese has started to brown. Allow it to stand before serving for at least 10 minutes.

Restaurant-Style Taco Meat Seasoning

(Ready in 40 Minutes, Serve 10, Difficulty: Normal)

Nutrition per Serving:

Calories 316, Protein 10.6 g, Carbohydrates 2.1 g, Fat 12.4 g, Cholesterol 43.6mg, Sodium 212.1mg.

Ingredients:

- 1 ½ tablespoon of corn flour
- 4 ½ teaspoons of chili powder
- ½ teaspoon of onion powder
- ½ teaspoon of garlic powder
- ½ teaspoon of seasoned salt
- ½ teaspoon of paprika
- ¼ teaspoon of cumin
- ½ teaspoon of garlic salt
- ¼ teaspoon of sugar
- 1 teaspoon of dried minced onion
- ½ teaspoon of beef bouillon granules
- ¼ teaspoon of ground red pepper
- 604 g lean of ground chuck
- 1 cup of water

Instructions:

1. Preheat the oven to 350 degrees Fahrenheit (176 degrees Celsius).

2. Pour a large pot with thinly salted water and bring it to a rolling boil over high heat. Add a few lasagna noodles after the water has cooked, then return to the boil.

3. Cook the uncovered pasta for about 10 minutes, occasionally stirring, until the pasta is thoroughly cooked but still firm to the bite. Place it on a tray with the noodles.

4. In a medium-hot saucepan, put the ground beef and add the garlic, garlic powder, oregano, salt, and black pepper to the saucepan. Cook the meat for about 10 minutes, until it's no longer pink, then cut it into small chunks as it cooks. Drain the grease from the excess.

5. In a bowl, combine the cottage cheese, eggs, and parmesan cheese until thoroughly combined.

6. Place four noodles side by side in a 9x13-inch baking pan on the bottom, top with a layer of

tomato-basil sauce, a layer of ground beef mixture, and a cottage layer cheese mixture. Repeat the layers, combine a layer of sauce to the finish, and spread the mozzarella cheese on top. Cover the bowl with aluminum foil.

7. Bake in the preheated oven for about 30 minutes until the casserole is bubbling and the cheese has melted. Before the cheese begins to brown, cut the foil and bake for about ten more minutes. Allow it to stand for at least 10 minutes before serving.

Good New Orleans Creole Gumbo

(Ready in 3 Hours and 40 Minutes, Serve 20, and Difficulty: Normal)

Nutrition per Serving:

Calories 283, Protein 20.9 g, Carbohydrates 12.1 g, Fat 16.6 g, Cholesterol 142.6mg, Sodium 853.1mg.

Ingredients:

- 1 cup of all-purpose flour
- ¾ cup of bacon drippings
- 1 cup of coarsely chopped celery
- 1 large onion, coarsely chopped
- 1 large green bell pepper, coarsely chopped
- 2 cloves of garlic, minced
- 453 g of Andouille sausage, sliced
- 3 quarts of water
- 6 cubes of beef bouillon
- 1 tablespoon of white sugar
- Salt, to taste
- 2 tablespoons of hot pepper sauce (such as Tabasco®), or to taste
- ½ teaspoon of Cajun seasoning blend (such as Tony Chachere's®), or to taste
- 4 bay leaves
- ½ teaspoon of dried thyme leaves
- 1(14.5 ounces) can of stewed tomatoes
- 1(6 ounces) can of tomato sauce
- 2 teaspoons of gumbo file powder
- 2 tablespoons of bacon drippings
- 2(10 ounces) packages of frozen cut okra, thawed
- 2 tablespoons of distilled white vinegar
- 453 g of lump crabmeat
- 1360 g of uncooked medium shrimp, peeled and deveined
- 2 tablespoons of Worcestershire sauce
- 2 teaspoons of gumbo file powder

Instructions:

1. Create a roux to form a smooth mixture by whisking the flour and 3/4 cup bacon drippings together in a large, heavy saucepan over medium-low heat. Cook the roux until it turns a deep mahogany brown color, whisking vigorously.

2. It will take 20 to 30 minutes, closely watch the heat and continuously whisk or roux can fire. Remove from the heat and whisk until the mixture has finished heating.

3. In the working bowl of a food processor, put the celery, onion, green bell pepper, garlic, and pulse until the vegetables are very finely chopped. In the roux, stir the onions, and pour in the sausage. Bring the mixture to a boil over medium-low heat and cook for 10-15 minutes until the vegetables are tender. Remove and set aside from the heat.

4. In a big Dutch oven or soup pot, put the water and beef bouillon cubes to a boil. Stir and whisk the roux mixture into the hot water until the bouillon cubes dissolve. Mix the cinnamon, salt, hot pepper sauce, Cajun spices, bay leaves, thyme, stewed tomatoes, and tomato sauce and lower the heat to a simmer. Simmer the broth over low heat for 1 hour, blend at the 45-minute stage with 2 teaspoons of file gumbo powder.

5. Meanwhile, in a pan, melt 2 teaspoons of bacon drippings and cook the okra over medium heat for 15 minutes with the vinegar, scrape the okra with the slotted spoon whisk in the gumbo. Mix in the crabmeat, shrimp, and Worcestershire sauce, and simmer for another 45 minutes before the flavors have merged. Stir in 2 more teaspoons of file gumbo powder just before serving.

Stuffing Meatloaf

(Ready in 55 Minutes, Serve 8, Difficulty: Normal)

Nutrition per Serving:

Calories 289, Protein 19.9 g, Carbohydrates 15.5 g, Fat 15.8 g, Cholesterol 83.5mg, Sodium 429.8mg.

Ingredients:

- Cooking spray
- 680 g of ground beef
- 1 small onion, chopped
- ¾ cup o chicken-flavored bread stuffing mix (such as Kraft® Stove Top®)
- 1 egg
- 1 cup of shredded mozzarella cheese, or to taste

Instructions:

1. Preheat the oven to 400 degrees Fahrenheit (204 degrees Celsius). Use cooking spray to spray a 9x5-inch loaf pan.

2. Heat the olive oil over medium heat in a saucepan, cook and mix the green bell pepper and the onion in the hot oil for 5-10 minutes until the onion is clear and the bell pepper is softened.

3. Add garlic and simmer for 1-2 minutes until it is fragrant.

4. In a large bowl, add ground beef, zucchini, salt, bread crumbs, eggs, carrot, pepper, & bell pepper mixture, using your hands to blend properly. In the prepared loaf tin, press the meat mixture into it.

5. Bake in the preheated oven for 35-40 minutes until it is no longer pink in the middle. A center-inserted instant-read thermometer can read at least 160 degrees Fahrenheit (70 degrees Celsius). Spread on top of the meatloaf with ketchup and bake until bubbling, about 5 more minutes.

Kathy's Meat Hot Sauce

(Ready in 1 Hour and 10 Minutes, Serve 24, Difficulty: Normal)

Nutrition per Serving:

Calories 176, Protein 6.7 g, Carbohydrates 1.7 g, Fat 4.6 g, Cholesterol 22.9mg, Sodium 177mg.

Ingredients:

- 907 g of ground beef
- 2 ½ cups of tomato juice
- 1 ½ tablespoon of yellow mustard
- 1 tablespoon of ground black pepper
- 20 dashes of hot pepper sauce (such as Tabasco®)
- 5 teaspoons of chili powder
- 2 teaspoons of red pepper flakes
- ½ teaspoon of salt

Instructions:

1. In a large skillet, cook ground beef over medium heat for about 10 minutes until the meat is crumbly and no longer yellow; remove the excess Fat and move the ground beef to a large saucepan.

2. Mix in the beef with tomato paste, yellow mustard, black pepper, sweet pepper sauce, chili powder, red pepper, and salt.

3. Bring the sauce to a boil, reduce the heat to medium, and cook for 1 hour, stirring regularly.

Carnitas-Pressure Cooker

(Ready in 1 Hour and 35 Minutes, Serve 24, Difficulty: Hard)

Nutrition per Serving:

Calories 154, Protein 11.8 g, Carbohydrates 2.4 g, Fat 10.6 g, Cholesterol 42.7mg, Sodium 470.8mg.

Ingredients:

- 1(3721 g) pork butt roast
- 1 ½ tablespoon of salt
- 1 tablespoon of dried oregano
- 2 teaspoons of ground cumin
- 1 teaspoon of ground black pepper

- ½ teaspoon of Chile powder
- ½ teaspoon of paprika
- 2 tablespoons of olive oil, or more to taste
- 1 cup of orange juice
- 1 onion, coarsely chopped
- 4 cloves of garlic, diced, or more to taste

Instructions:

1. Remove the extra fat from the butt of the pig, cut the pork into 2-inch cubes, and pass it to a bowl.

2. In a bowl, combine the cinnamon, oregano, black pepper, chili powder, and paprika. Rub cubes of pork with a combination of spices. Lightly brush the seasoned pork cubes in olive oil and put them in the pressure cooker. Combine the orange juice, cabbage, and garlic to coat the pork cubes.

3. Place the lid on the pressure cooker and secure it, put it over medium heat to full pressure until the pork is no longer pink in the center, around 60 minutes. Let the pressure drop for around 15 minutes, naturally.

4. Take the pork and shredded beef from the pressure cooker.

Chef John's Italian Meatballs

(Ready in 2 Hours and 15 Minutes, Serve 30, and Difficulty: Hard)

Nutrition per Serving:

Calories 282, Protein 6.2 g, Carbohydrates 1.7 g, Fat 5.5 g, Cholesterol 32.3mg, Sodium 192.1mg.

Ingredients:

- ⅓ cup of plain bread crumbs
- ½ cup of milk
- 2 tablespoons of olive oil
- 1 onion, diced
- 453 g of ground beef
- 453 g of ground pork
- 2 eggs
- ¼ bunch of fresh parsley, chopped
- 3 cloves of garlic, crushed
- 2 teaspoons of salt
- 1 teaspoon of ground black pepper
- ½ teaspoon of red pepper flakes
- 1 teaspoon of dried Italian herb seasoning
- 2 tablespoons of grated parmesan cheese

Instructions:

1. Using foil to protect a baking sheet and brush loosely with cooking spray.

2. Soak the bread crumbs in milk for 20 minutes in a small bowl.

3. Heat olive oil over low heat in a skillet. Cook and mix the onions in hot oil for around 20 minutes, until translucent.

4. In a large tub, combine the beef and pork. Stir in the meat mixture with the rubber spatula once combined: onions, bread crumb mixture, eggs, parsley, garlic, cinnamon, black pepper, red pepper flakes, Italian herb seasoning, and parmesan cheese. Cover for about 1 hour and refrigerate.

5. Preheat the oven to 425 degrees Fahrenheit (218 degrees Celsius).

6. Shape the meat mixture into balls about 1 1/2 inches in diameter using wet hands. Arrange it on a ready baking dish.

7. In the preheated oven, bake for 15-20 minutes until browned and cooked through.

Air Fryer Meatloaf

(Ready in 45 Minutes, Serve 4, Difficulty: Normal)

Nutrition per Serving:

Calories 297, Protein 24.8 g, Carbohydrates 5.9 g, Fat 18.8 g, Cholesterol 125.5mg, Sodium 706.5mg.

Ingredients:

- 453 g of lean ground beef
- 1 egg, lightly beaten
- 3 tablespoons of dry bread crumbs
- 1 small onion, finely chopped
- 1 tablespoon of chopped fresh thyme
- 1 teaspoon of salt
- Ground black pepper, to taste
- 2 mushrooms, thickly sliced
- 1 tablespoon of olive oil, or as needed

Instructions:

1. Preheat an air fryer at 392 degrees Fahrenheit (200 degrees Celsius).

2. In a bowl, mix the ground beef, bread crumbs, egg, cabbage, thyme, salt, and pepper. Thoroughly knead and mix.

3. Move the mixture of beef to a baking pan and smooth out the end.

4. The mushrooms are pressed onto the top and filled with olive oil. Place the pan in the basket for the air fryer and slip it into it.

5. Set the 25-minute air fryer timer and roast the meatloaf until it is nicely browned.

6. Before slicing into wedges and serving, let the meatloaf sit for at least 10 minutes.

Cottage Meatloaf

(Ready in 1 Hour and 5 Minutes, Serve 8, Difficulty: Normal)

Nutrition per Serving:

Calories 326, Protein 18.7 g, Carbohydrates 18.3 g, Fat 19.6 g 3, Cholesterol 110.3mg, Sodium 679.9mg.

Ingredients:

- 680 g of lean ground beef
- ½ cup of ketchup
- ⅓ cup of tomato juice
- ½ teaspoon of salt
- ½ teaspoon of ground black pepper
- ⅛ teaspoon of crushed red pepper
- 2 eggs, beaten
- ¾ cup of fresh bread crumbs
- ¼ cup of diced onion
- 2 teaspoons of prepared mustard

For Topping:

- ½ cup of ketchup
- 1 teaspoon of prepared mustard
- 4 teaspoons of brown sugar

Instructions:

1. Preheat the oven to 400 degrees Fahrenheit (204 degrees Celsius). Use aluminum foil to cover a 9x5-inch loaf tray.

2. Combine the ground beef, ketchup, tomato sauce, salt, vinegar, red pepper, bread crumbs, eggs, onion, and meatloaf mustard in a large bowl until well combined. On a prepared plate, press the meat mixture together.

3. Combine the ketchup, mustard, and brown sugar in a separate dish, until smooth. Spread a mixture of brown sugar over the meatloaf.

4. Bake for 35-45 minutes in a preheated oven until it is no longer pink. Drain out the fat.

5. Let rest 5 minutes before serving.

Barbacoa Meat

(Ready in 4 Hours 20 Minutes, Serve 12, and Difficulty: Normal)

Nutrition per Serving:

Calories 316, Protein 18.2 g, Carbohydrates 1.3 g, Fat 26.2 g, Cholesterol 80mg, Sodium 77.3mg.

Ingredients:

- 1360 g of beef cheek meat
- 1 tablespoon of olive oil
- ¼ cup of salt
- 2 teaspoons of ground cumin
- Ground black pepper, to taste
- 2 cups of water, or more as needed

- ½ yellow onion halved and thickly sliced
- 3 cloves of garlic, chopped

Instructions:

1. Use olive oil to cover beef cheek meat. Rub the beef with garlic, and pepper. Cover the beef in aluminum foil and refrigerate until midnight, for 4 hours.

2. Pour water into a slow cooker

3. Arrange the onion and the garlic in the aluminum foil around the beef cheek meat.

4. Wrap the foil securely around the vegetables and beef. In the slow cooker, put the second sheet of aluminum foil over the meat mixture, covering securely.

5. Cook on medium, if it has evaporated, adding more water until the meat is very tender, 7 to 8 hours. Remove foil packet from slow cooker and shred meat using 2 forks.

Easiest Yummiest Meat Loaf

(Ready in 1 Hour and 10 Minutes, Serve 6, Difficulty: Normal)

Nutrition per Serving:

Calories 265, Protein 18.7 g, Carbohydrates 18.1 g, Fat 12.9 g, Cholesterol 111.2mg, Sodium 495.9mg.

Ingredients:
- 453 g of ground beef
- 1 ½ cups of rolled oats
- 1(10.5 ounces) can of French onion soup (such as Campbell's ®)
- 2 eggs, beaten

Instructions:

1. Preheat the oven to 375 degrees Fahrenheit (190 degrees Celsius). Grease a square 8-inch baking dish.

2. Combine in a bowl the ground beef, rolled oats, French onion soup, and eggs until thoroughly mixed, then transfer to the prepared baking dish.

3. Bake in the preheated oven until the middle of the meatloaf is no longer pink and an instant-read meat thermometer inserted into the center of the loaf reaches 60-75 minutes at least 160 degrees Fahrenheit (70 degrees Celsius).

Classic and Simple Meat Lasagna

(Ready in 1 Hour and 35 Minutes, Serve 8, Difficulty: Hard)

Nutrition per Serving:

Calories 201, Protein 35.6 g, Carbohydrates 47.1 g, Fat 19.3 g, Cholesterol 114.5mg, Sodium 999mg.

Ingredients:
- 12 whole wheat lasagna noodles
- 453 g of lean ground beef
- 2 cloves of garlic, chopped
- ½ teaspoon of garlic powder
- 1 teaspoon of dried oregano, or to taste
- Salt and ground black pepper, to taste
- 1(16 ounces) package of cottage cheese
- 2 eggs
- ½ cup of shredded parmesan cheese
- 1 ½ (25 ounces) jars of tomato-basil pasta sauce
- 2 cups of shredded mozzarella cheese

Instructions:

1. Preheat the oven to 350 degrees Fahrenheit (176 degrees Celsius).

2. Fill a large pot with thinly salted water and bring it over high heat to a rolling boil. When the water has boiled, add a few lasagna noodles at a time and return to the boil. Cook the uncovered pasta, stirring regularly until the pasta is fully cooked but still strong to the bite, around 10 minutes. Place the noodles on a tray.

3. Put the ground beef in a medium-hot saucepan and add the garlic, garlic powder, oregano, salt, and black pepper to the saucepan. Cook the meat until it's no longer pink, about 10 minutes, and cut it into small chunks as it cooks. Drain the excess grease.

4. Mix the cottage cheese, eggs, and parmesan cheese in a bowl until completely mixed.

5. In a 9x13-inch baking pan, put four noodles side by side on the bottom, top with a layer of tomato-basil sauce, a layer of ground beef mixture, and a layer of cottage cheese mixture. Repeat the layers, finish with a layer of sauce, and sprinkle the mozzarella cheese on top.

6. In aluminum foil, cover the dish.

7. Bake for about 30 minutes in the preheated oven until the casserole is bubbling and the cheese has melted. Remove the foil and bake for about 10 more minutes before the cheese has begun to brown. Allow it to stand before serving for at least 10 minutes.

Meat and Spinach Ravioli Filling

(Ready in 40 Minutes, Serve 15, Difficulty: Normal)

Nutrition per Serving:

Calories 107, Protein 6.5 g, Carbohydrates 1.6 g, Fat 8.2 g, Cholesterol 32.8mg, Sodium 124.1mg.

Ingredients:
- 453 g of ground beef
- 1 ½ cups of fresh spinach
- 5 tablespoons of grated Parmesan cheese

- 1 ¼ tablespoon of dried parsley
- ¼ cup of bread crumbs
- ¼ cup of olive oil
- 1 large egg
- ½ teaspoon of garlic salt
- 1 pinch of black pepper

Instructions:

1. Over medium-high prepare, heat a large skillet and stir in the ground beef. Cook and mix until the beef is crumbly, browned uniformly, and not pink anymore.

2. Drain some extra grease and dump it. Stir in the spinach and simmer for around 1-2 minutes, until wilted. Remove from the heat and allow 10 minutes to cool.

3. To a tub, pass the beef mixture. Combine the parmesan cheese, parsley, bread crumbs, egg, garlic salt, olive oil, and pepper and blend well. Run the filling until smooth, via a grinder (or puree in a food processor until smooth).

4. The filling can be stored for up to four days in the refrigerator or up to three months in the freezer.

Salsa Chicken Meatloaf

(Ready in 1 Hour and 45 Minutes, Serve 6, Difficulty: Hard)

Nutrition per Serving:

Calories 393, Protein 31.6 g, Carbohydrates 21.5 g, Fat 19.6 g, Cholesterol 125.7mg, Sodium 897mg.

Ingredients:

- 1 ¼ cup of herb-seasoned croutons
- 1(12 ounces) jar of salsa
- 1 tablespoon of olive oil
- 1 jalapeno pepper, seeded and minced
- 1 cup of finely chopped onion
- 3 cloves of garlic, minced
- 453 g of ground chicken
- 226 g of ground pork
- 1 egg
- 1 ½ tablespoon of taco seasoning mix
- 1 tablespoon of Worcestershire sauce
- 1 cup of shredded pepper jack cheese
- ¼ cup of cilantro, minced
- 2 tablespoons of barbecue sauce
- 2 tablespoons of brown sugar

Instructions:

1. Preheat the oven to 350 degrees Fahrenheit (176 degrees Celsius). Grease a pan with a 5x9-inch loaf.

2. In a large bowl, combine the croutons with the salsa, and set aside to soften for about 15 minutes. Heat the olive oil over medium heat in a skillet and cook the jalapeno pepper, onion, and garlic for 5-8 minutes, until the onion is translucent.

3. In the crouton mixture, blend the ground chicken, taco seasoning, ground pork, egg, Worcestershire sauce, pepper jack cheese, and cilantro, and mash any unbroken croutons.

4. Mix with a combination of fried onions. Into the prepared loaf tray, move the meatloaf. In a cup, blend the barbecue sauce and brown sugar, stirring until the sugar dissolves, and brush the barbecue sauce mixture over the loaf. In a tent, fold a 12-inch-long piece of aluminum foil and bring the foil tent over the loaf.

5. Bake until the juices run clear and the loaf is no longer pink in the center, around 1 hour, in the preheated oven. For the remaining 10 minutes of baking, remove the foil tent. At least 160 degrees Fahrenheit (72 degrees Celsius). It should be read by an instant-read thermometer inserted into the loaf core. Remove from the oven, cover the loaf with foil and allow to stand before serving for 15 minutes.

Sexy Air-Fried Meatloaf

(Ready in 1 Day and 55 Minutes, Serve 4, And Difficulty: Hard)

Nutrition per Serving:

Calories 272, Protein 22.1 g, Carbohydrates 13.3 g, Fat 14.4 g, Cholesterol 123.5mg, Sodium 536.1mg.

Ingredients:

- 226 g of ground pork
- 226 g of ground veal
- 1 large egg
- ¼ cup of chopped fresh cilantro
- ¼ cup of gluten-free bread crumbs
- 2 medium spring onions, diced
- ½ teaspoon of ground black pepper
- ½ teaspoon of Sriracha salt
- ½ cup of ketchup
- 2 teaspoons of gluten-free chipotle chili sauce
- 1 teaspoon of olive oil
- 1 teaspoon of blackstrap molasses

Instructions:

1. Preheat the air fryer to 400 degrees Fahrenheit (204 degrees Celsius)

2. In a nonstick baking dish that fits within the air fryer basket, mix the pork and veal. Add the egg, coriander, bread crumbs, black pepper, spring onions, and 1/2 teaspoon of Sriracha salt and make a well.

3. Using your hands, blend properly. Inside the baking bowl, form a loaf.

4. In a small bowl, blend the ketchup, olive oil, chipotle chili sauce, and molasses and whisk well. Set aside, do not refrigerate.

5. Cook the meatloaf, without opening the basket, in an air fryer for 25 minutes. Remove the meatloaf and line it with the ketchup sauce, completely covering the top. Return the meatloaf to the air fryer and cook for around 7 more minutes before the internal temperature reaches 160 degrees Fahrenheit (71 degrees Celsius).

6. Turn off the air fryer for 5 minutes and let the meatloaf rest inside. Take out the meatloaf and let it sit for 5 more minutes before slicing and serving.

Shelby's Microwave Meat Loaf

(Ready in 45 Minutes, Serve 6, Difficulty: Normal)

Nutrition per Serving:

Calories 382, Protein 29.5 g, Carbohydrates 22.8 g, Fat 18.8 g, Cholesterol 147.6mg, Sodium 664.7mg.

Ingredients:

- 1(8 ounces) can of tomato sauce
- ¼ cup of brown sugar
- 1 teaspoon of prepared mustard
- 2 eggs, lightly beaten
- 1 onion, minced
- ¼ cup of minced green bell pepper
- ¼ teaspoon of garlic powder
- ½ cup of saltine cracker crumbs
- 1 teaspoon of salt
- ¼ teaspoon of ground black pepper
- 907 g of extra lean ground beef

Instructions:

1. Mix the tomato sauce, brown sugar, and mustard in a small bowl and stir until the brown sugar has dissolved.

2. Mix the eggs, chopped onion and garlic powder, green pepper, cracker crumbs, salt, and black pepper in a big mixing bowl, mix in the ground beef and half the tomato mixture sauce, and stir until the meatloaf is fully mixed.

3. In a 2-quart microwave-safe baking dish, put the meat mixture into it. Spread over the meatloaf with the remaining tomato sauce mixture.

4. Cook in the high setting microwave oven until set, the juices run transparent, and the meat inside is no longer pink, 10-15 minutes, depending on the microwave power. 165 degrees Fahrenheit (75 degrees Celsius) can be read by an instant meat thermometer inserted into the middle of the loaf. If the loaf is baked, remove some fat from the dish and rest, uncovered, 10-15 minutes before serving.

Three-Meat Meatloaf

(Ready in 2 Hour, Serve 6, Difficulty: Hard)

Nutrition per Serving:

Calories 305, Protein 25.7 g, Carbohydrates 11.2 g, Fat 17.3 g, Cholesterol 130.4mg, Sodium 728.2mg.

Ingredients:

- 1 large onion, chopped
- 2 carrots, chopped
- 1 cup of beef broth
- 2 eggs
- ½ cup of bread crumbs
- 2 tablespoons of minced fresh basil
- ½ teaspoon of salt
- ½ teaspoon of ground black pepper
- 453 g of ground turkey
- 340 g of ground beef
- 226 g of ground pork sausage
- ½ cup of condensed tomato soup
- 1 tablespoon of balsamic vinegar
- ½ teaspoon of Dijon mustard

Instructions:

1. Preheat the oven to 350 degrees Fahrenheit (176 degrees Celsius). A 9x5-inch loaf pan with oil.

2. In a saucepan, put the onion and carrots, and add the beef broth. Cook, stirring regularly, until the vegetables are tender, around 8 minutes, bring to a boil over medium heat, and reduce heat to a simmer. Place aside the vegetables and broth.

3. Beat the eggs in a big bowl and add the bread crumbs, basil, cinnamon, and black pepper.

4. To moisten the crumbs, allow the mixture to stand for 5 minutes, and lightly blend in the turkey, beef, and pork sausage. Add the fried onions, carrots, and beef broth to the mix. In the prepared loaf pan, put the mixture into it. Mix the tomato soup, balsamic vinegar, and Dijon mustard in a cup and spread the mixture over the meatloaf.

5. Bake until the middle of the loaf is no longer pink and an instant-read meat thermometer reads around 1 ½ hour, at least 160 degrees Fahrenheit (70 degrees Celsius).

Poochie Meat Cakes

(Ready in 2 Hrs. Serve 36, Difficulty: Hard)

Nutrition per Serving:

Calories 309, Protein 14.1 g, Carbohydrates 12.8 g, Fat 22.1 g, Cholesterol 64.3mg, Sodium 73mg.

Ingredients:

- 1 ½ cup of brown rice
- 3 cups of water
- 2 large potatoes, grated

- 4 large carrots, grated
- 2 large stalks of celery, chopped
- 3721 g of ground beef
- 8 eggs
- 1 dash of salt
- ¼ cup of olive oil
- 1 ½ cup of regular rolled oats

Instructions:

1. Preheat the oven to 400 degrees Fahrenheit (204 degrees Celsius). 36 cups in 3 big muffin tins are oiled.

2. Combine the rice in a medium saucepan with water. Cook for 10 minutes and bring to a boil over high pressure, uncovered. Lower the heat, cover it and simmer for 20 minutes. Remove from heat, cool for a few minutes, and then use a fork to fluff and set aside.

3. Combine the potatoes, onions, celery, ground beef, and eggs in a large dish. Using your hands or a strong spoon to blend the ingredients.

4. Mix well with salt, olive oil, rolled oats, and rice.

5. Fill some of the meat mixtures with each muffin cup, then pat it down to make it solid. Bake until the surface feels fixed, or 45 minutes. Cool it on a rack for 10 minutes or more.

6. By flipping the muffin tin upside down above an aluminum foil layer, remove the meat cakes. To release the cake, tap each muffin cup. Refrigerate or freeze in plastic bags that are sealed.

Eileen's Meatloaf

(Ready in 1 Hour and 15 Minutes, Serve 12, Difficulty: Hard)

Nutrition per Serving:

Calories 307, Protein 14.4 g, Carbohydrates 13.3 g, Fat 21.6 g, Cholesterol 76mg, Sodium 616.1mg.

Ingredients:

- 680 g of ground beef
- 1 egg
- 1 cup of sour cream
- 2 tablespoons of Worcestershire sauce
- 1(1 ounce) package of dry onion soup mix
- ½ cup of grated parmesan cheese
- 1 ½ cup of Italian-style dried bread crumbs

Instructions:

1. Preheat the oven to 375 degrees Fahrenheit (190 degrees Celsius).

2. Combine the steak, egg, sour cream, and Worcestershire sauce in a wide bowl. Mix with a combination of soup, cheese, and bread crumbs. Shape the mixture into a loaf and put it in a 9x5 inch pan. Cover with foil.

3. Bake for 45 minutes at 375 degrees Fahrenheit (190 degrees Celsius).

4. Remove the foil and proceed to bake for a further 10 to 15 minutes. For easier slicing, let it stand 5-10 minutes before serving.

Clay Pot Meatloaf and Potatoes

(Ready in 1 Hour and 30 Minutes, Serve 8, Difficulty: Normal)

Nutrition per Serving:

Calories 393, Protein 26.3 g, Carbohydrates 55.8 g, Fat 18.6 g, Cholesterol 115.2mg, Sodium 952.7mg.

Ingredients:

- 453 g of ground beef
- 2 slices of white bread, torn into crumbs
- 1 egg
- 2 tablespoons of milk
- 1(1 ounces) package of onion soup mix, divided
- 4 Yukon-gold potatoes, peeled and cut into eighths
- ¼ cup of ketchup
- 1 sweet onion, sliced
- 4 sprigs of fresh rosemary

Instructions:

1. Soak the clay pot for about 15 minutes in a big bowl of water. Remove the pot from the water.

2. In a large bowl, add the ground beef, bread crumbs, potato, cream, and 1/2 of the onion soup mixture. Mold the mixture into a loaf and put it in a pot of clay. Pour the leftover onion soup mix over the potatoes and layer the potatoes around the loaf.

3. Scatter the onions over the potatoes and add sprigs of rosemary. Place the cover on a pot of clay.

4. Put a pot of clay in a cold oven. Heat the oven to 350 degrees Fahrenheit (176 degrees Celsius).

5. Bake in the oven for around 1 hour, until the meatloaf in the middle is no longer pink. A center-inserted instant-read thermometer can read at least 160 degrees Fahrenheit (70 degrees Celsius).

Tantalizingly Tangy Meatloaf

(Ready in 45 Minutes, Serve 8, Difficulty: Normal)

Nutrition per Serving:

Calories 274, Protein 11.3 g, Carbohydrates 21.1 g, Fat 16.1 g, Cholesterol 71.5mg, Sodium 210.4mg.

Ingredients:

- 453 g of ground beef
- ½ cup of dry bread crumbs
- 1 egg
- Garlic powder, to taste

- 1 dash of Worcestershire sauce
- ⅓ cup of ketchup
- ¼ cup of packed brown sugar
- ¼ cup of pineapple preserves

Instructions:

1. Preheat the oven to 350 degrees Fahrenheit (176 degrees Celsius).

2. Mix the ground beef, egg, bread crumbs, garlic powder, and Worcestershire sauce in a big tub. Mix and put the loaf in a 9x5 inch tub.

3. Bake for 30-50 minutes in a preheated oven.

4. Meanwhile, whisk together the ketchup, brown sugar, and pineapple preserves in a separate medium dish.

5. Pour about 20 minutes over the meatloaf before removing it from the oven.

Onion Meat Relish

(Ready in 35 Minutes, Serve 8, Difficulty: Normal)

Nutrition per Serving:

Calories 248, Protein 0.5 g, Carbohydrates 5.3 g, Fat 2.9 g, Cholesterol 7.6mg, Sodium 240.2mg.

Ingredients:

- 340 g of onion, cut into wedges and separated
- 2 tablespoons of butter
- 2 tablespoons of red wine vinegar
- ¼ tablespoon of salt
- ¼ teaspoon of ground black pepper
- 2 teaspoons of white sugar

Instructions:

1. Cook slowly in a medium saucepan over medium heat and stir in the onions and butter until the onions are tender, for about 10 minutes.

2. With the onions and butter, blend the red wine vinegar, ground black pepper, salt, and white sugar.

3. Continue to cook and stir until the mixture thickens, for about 10 minutes, to a chunky, spreadable consistency. Before serving, refrigerate.

Turkey Meat Loaf: Almost as Good as Mom's Used to Be

(Ready in 1 Hour and 30 Minutes, Serve 12, Difficulty: Hard)

Nutrition per Serving:

Calories 294, Protein 27.2 g, Carbohydrates 18.8 g, Fat 13.1 g, Cholesterol 117.8mg, Sodium 704.4mg.

Ingredients:

- 1(15 ounces) can of tomato sauce
- 1(6 ounces) can of tomato paste
- ½ cup of ketchup
- 2 teaspoons of white sugar
- 1 teaspoon of onion powder
- 1 teaspoon of garlic powder
- 1 teaspoon of dried oregano
- 1 teaspoon of ground black pepper
- 1 teaspoon of Worcestershire sauce
- 1(14.5 ounces) can of Italian-style stewed tomatoes, undrained
- 1360 g of ground turkey
- 1 sleeve roasted vegetable-flavored buttery round crackers, (such as Ritz®), crushed
- 1 onion, diced
- 1 green bell pepper, diced
- 2 eggs, slightly beaten
- 1 tablespoon of dried oregano
- 1 tablespoon of dried thyme
- 2 tablespoons of Worcestershire sauce
- 1 clove garlic, minced
- 2 teaspoons of ground black pepper
- ½ cup of shredded mozzarella cheese (Optional)

Instructions:

1. Preheat the oven to 375°Fahrenheit (190 degrees Celsius). Grease a 9x13-inch baking dish.

2. In a cup, combine the tomato sauce, ketchup, sugar, tomato paste, onion powder, and garlic powder, 1 teaspoon of oregano, one teaspoon of black pepper, and 1 teaspoon of Worcestershire sauce.

3. Put the stewed tomatoes in a wide bowl, using a fork to smash the tomatoes. Add turkey, crushed crackers, green bell pepper, onion, eggs, and 1 tablespoon of oregano, thyme, 1 tablespoons of Worcestershire sauce, garlic, and two tablespoons of black pepper.

4. Mix until combined equally. Spoon the meatloaf mixture into the baking dish you have prepared. Form into a loaf, leaving about ½ inch between the loaf and dish sides.

5. Spoon ½ the topping of the tomato over the loaf.

6. Bake for 45 minutes in the preheated oven. Spoon the rest of the tomato over the loaf and line it with the mozzarella cheese. Bake until the center is no longer pink, for another 15-20 minutes. A center-inserted instant-read thermometer can read at least 160 degrees Fahrenheit (70 degrees Celsius).

Shelby's Microwave Meat Loaf

(Ready in 45 Minutes, Serve 6, Difficulty: Normal)

Nutrition per Serving:

Calories 382, Protein 29.5 g, Carbohydrates 22.8 g, Fat 18.8 g, Cholesterol 147.6mg, Sodium 664.7mg.

Ingredients:

- 1(8 ounces) can of tomato sauce
- ¼ cup of brown sugar
- 1 teaspoon of prepared mustard
- 2 eggs, lightly beaten
- 1 onion, minced
- ¼ cup of minced green bell pepper
- ¼ teaspoon of garlic powder
- ½ cup of saltine cracker crumbs
- 1 teaspoon of salt
- ¼ teaspoon of ground black pepper
- 907 g of extra lean ground beef

Instructions:

1. Mix the tomato sauce, brown sugar, and mustard in a small bowl and stir until the brown sugar has dissolved.

2. Combine the eggs, chopped onion and garlic powder, green pepper, cracker crumbs, salt, and black pepper in a large mixing cup.

3. Mix in the ground beef and ½ the mixture of tomato sauce, stirring until thoroughly mixed with the meat loaf. In a 2-quart microwave-safe baking dish put the meat mixture into it. Spread over the meat loaf with the remaining tomato sauce mixture.

4. Cook in the high setting microwave oven until set, the juices run clear, and the meat inside is no longer pink, 10-15 minutes, depending on the microwave capacity. If the loaf is baked, drain some fat from the dish and rest, uncovered, 10-15 minutes before serving.

My Favorite Pork Turkey Meatloaf

(Ready in 1 Hour and 40 Minutes, Serve 8, Difficulty: Hard)

Nutrition per Serving:

Calories 310, Protein 26 g, Carbohydrates 14.8 g, Fat 16.5 g, Cholesterol 125.1mg, Sodium 783.3mg.

Ingredients:

- 453 g of ground turkey
- 453 g of ground pork
- 1 tablespoon of cooking oil
- 1 carrot, minced
- ½ red bell pepper, minced
- ½ onion, minced
- 2 cloves of garlic, minced
- ⅓ cup of thawed frozen chopped spinach
- ½ cup of bread crumbs
- ½ cup of wheat germ (optional)
- 2 eggs, room temperature
- 2 tablespoons of ketchup

- 2 teaspoons of salt
- 1 teaspoon of black pepper
- 1 tablespoon of honey
- 1 tablespoon of ketchup

Instructions:

1. Preheat the oven to 375 degrees Fahrenheit (190 degrees Celsius). Using aluminum foil to cover a baking sheet.

2. Set out the ground turkey and ground pork to warm slightly at room temperature.

3. Heat the oil over medium heat in a saucepan, cook the carrot, onion, bell pepper, garlic, and spinach in the hot oil until tender, and set aside to cool.

4. In a large bowl, combine the turkey, bacon, wheat germ, bread crumbs, and eggs, 2 teaspoons of ketchup, salt, and pepper. Combine the mixture of vegetables and proceed to blend until mixed evenly. Turn into a loaf and put on the baking sheet.

5. Whisk in a little bowl, spread over the meatloaf, the honey, and 1 tablespoon of ketchup together.

6. Bake in the preheated oven until the center is no longer pink, 60-70 minutes, remove from serving dish and allow to stand 5 minutes before slicing.

Pork Carnitas

(Ready in 6 Hours and 15 Minutes, Serve 12, and Difficulty: Hard)

Nutrition per Serving:

Calories 250, Protein 16.2 g, Carbohydrates 2.3 g, Fat 19.1 g, Cholesterol 62.5mg, Sodium 2072.3mg.

Ingredients:

- ¼ cup of vegetable oil
- 1814 g of pork shoulder, cut into several large pieces
- 3 tablespoons of kosher salt
- 1 onion, chopped
- 1 clove of garlic, crushed
- 3 tablespoons of lime juice
- 1 tablespoon of chili powder
- ½ teaspoon of dried oregano
- ½ teaspoon of ground cumin
- 4(14.5 ounces) cans of chicken broth

Instructions:

1. Heat the vegetable oil over high heat in a big Dutch oven. Season with salt on the pork shoulder, then place the pork in the Dutch oven. Cook for about 10 minutes, until browned on all sides.

2. Put in the onion, garlic, chili powder, lime juice, and oregano. Pour the chicken broth into the mixture and get it to a boil. Reduce the heat to

medium-low, cover, and cook for around 2 ½ hours until the pork is very tender.

3. The oven should be preheated to 400 degrees Fahrenheit (204 degrees Celsius).

4. Transfer the pork shoulder, reserving the cooking liquid, to a large baking dish. Drizzle the reserved cooking liquid with a minimal amount and season gently with salt.

5. In the preheated oven, bake the pork until browned, about 30 minutes. Drizzle the meat every 10 minutes with some of the cooking liquid, then use 2 forks to shred the meat as it browns.

Vegan Lentil Meatloaf

(Ready in 1 Hour, Serve 6, Difficulty: Normal)
Nutrition per Serving:

Calories 360, Protein 15.8 g, Carbohydrates 52.5 g, Fat 10.4 g, Cholesterol 0mg, Sodium 777mg.

Ingredients:

- 1 cooking spray
- 3 tablespoons of olive oil, divided
- 1 onion, diced
- 2 cups of sliced mushrooms
- 2 cloves of garlic, minced
- 3 cups of cooked brown lentils
- 2 cups of bread crumbs
- ½ cup of almond milk
- ¼ cup of ketchup, divided
- 2 tablespoons of flaxseed meal
- 2 tablespoons of soy sauce
- ½ teaspoon of salt
- ½ teaspoon of ground black pepper
- ½ teaspoon of Italian seasoning

Instructions:

1. Preheat the oven to 375 degrees Fahrenheit (190 degrees Celsius). With cooking oil, grease a 9x13-inch loaf pan.

2. In a skillet over medium pressure, heat 1 tablespoon of oil and stir in the onion. Cook and stir for about 4 minutes until the onion has softened and become translucent.

3. Add the mushrooms and garlic, cook and stir for about 3 minutes, until tender.

4. In the bowl of a food processor, combine the remaining 2 tablespoons of olive oil, mushroom mix, cooked lentils, almond milk, bread crumbs, two tablespoons ketchup, salt, pepper, flaxseed meal, soy sauce, and Italian seasoning. Pulse until just blended; if possible, do not over-blend and operate in batches. In the prepared loaf pan, press the mixture together. Brush the end with 2 teaspoons of ketchup left.

5. Bake until golden, about 45 minutes, in the preheated oven.

Meatloaf Cordon Bleu

(Ready in 1 Hour and 30 Minutes, Serve 8, Difficulty: Normal)
Nutrition per Serving:

Calories 376, Protein 33.6 g, Carbohydrates 11.4 g, Fat 20.9 g, Cholesterol 147.9mg, Sodium 877.7mg.

Ingredients:

- 907 g of extra-lean ground beef
- 1 cup of Italian seasoned bread crumbs
- 1 small onion, chopped
- 2 eggs, beaten
- ⅛ teaspoon of garlic powder
- 1 teaspoon of salt
- 1 teaspoon of pepper
- 4 ounces of thinly sliced cooked ham
- 4 ounces of provolone cheese, sliced

Instructions:

1. The oven should be preheated to 350 degrees Fahrenheit (176 degrees Celsius).

2. Mix the ground beef, eggs, bread crumbs, and onion in a medium dish. Garlic powder, salt, and pepper to season with. On a waxed paper sheet, pat the meat mixture out and flatten it to ½ inch thick. On the flattened beef, lime slices of ham and top with cheese slices.

3. To roll the flattened meat into a log, pick up the edge of the waxed paper. Place the loaf in a 9x5 inch loaf pan, remove the waxed paper, seal the ends and seam.

4. Bake in the preheated oven for 1 hour and 15 minutes, or until the loaf is no longer pink inside.

Lemon Barbeque Meatloaf

(Ready in 55 Minutes, Serve 6, Difficulty: Normal)
Nutrition per Serving:

Calories 336, Protein 22.1 g, Carbohydrates 29 g, Fat 15 g, Cholesterol 99.9mg, Sodium 724.3mg.

Ingredients:

- 680 g of ground beef
- ¼ cup of lemon juice
- ½ cup of water
- 1 egg, beaten
- 4 slices of day-old bread, torn into small pieces
- ¼ cup of chopped onion
- 2 teaspoons of seasoning salt
- ½ cup of ketchup
- ⅓ cup of brown sugar

- 1 teaspoon of mustard powder
- ¼ teaspoon of ground allspice
- ¼ teaspoon of ground cloves
- 6 slices of lemon

Instructions:

1. The oven should be preheated to 350 degrees Fahrenheit (176 degrees Celsius). Grease a 9x13 inch baking dish or a similarly-sized dish.

2. Mix the ground beef, onion, lemon juice, water, egg, bread, and salt in a wide bowl until well mixed. I want to turn big balls-shape into six individual loaves. In the prepared baking dish, put them.

3. Bake in the preheated oven for 15 minutes as you are cooking the topping. Stir the ketchup, brown sugar, mustard powder, allspice, and cloves together in a shallow cup. Spoon over the loaves with the sauce, then finish each one with a lemon slice.

4. Return to the oven and simmer for another 30 minutes or until fully baked.

Hidden Veggie Meatloaf

(Ready in 1 Hour and 55 Minutes, Serve 6, Difficulty: Hard)

Nutrition per Serving:

Calories 310, Protein 28.4 g, Carbohydrates 15.6 g, Fat 14.8 g, Cholesterol 118.2mg, Sodium 590mg.

Ingredients:

- 453 g of lean ground beef
- 302 g of ground turkey
- 1 egg
- ¾ cup of finely chopped celery
- ¾ cup of regular rolled oats
- ½ cup of skim milk
- ½ cup of ketchup
- ½ cup of finely chopped onion
- ½ cup of finely chopped green bell pepper
- 1 tablespoon of dried parsley
- 1 teaspoon of dry mustard powder
- ⅔ teaspoon of salt
- ½ teaspoon of minced garlic
- ½ teaspoon of ground black pepper

Instructions:

1. Preheat the oven to 325°Fahrenheit (165 degrees Celsius).

2. In a cup, add celery, rolled oats, ground beef, ground turkey, egg, condensed milk, ketchup, green pepper, onion, parsley, dried mustard, cinnamon, garlic, and black pepper until thoroughly combined, until the mixture is moist. Place the mixture in a 5x9-inch loaf tub.

3. Bake in the preheated oven until the meat thermometer inserted in the middle of the meatloaf registers at least 160 degrees Fahrenheit (70 degrees Celsius) immediately, around 1 1/2 hours. Due to ketchup, the meatloaf can also look pink inside.

Five Meat Habanero Chili

(Ready in 3 Hours and 5 Minutes, Serve 12, and Difficulty: Hard)

Nutrition per Serving:

Calories 309, Protein 26.7 g, Carbohydrates 26.4 g, Fat 21.3 g, Cholesterol 75.9mg, Sodium 1343.8mg.

Ingredients:

- 4 slices of hickory-smoked bacon
- 340 g of ground beef
- 453 g of bulk pork sausage
- 340 g of cubed beef stew meat
- 1 ½ cups of chopped onion
- 2 cloves of garlic, minced
- 1 stalk of celery, chopped
- ½ habanero pepper, seeded and minced, or to taste
- ½ large green bell pepper, chopped
- ½ large red bell pepper, chopped
- 1(28 ounces) can of tomato sauce
- 1 ½ teaspoon of ground cumin
- 2 cups of cubed cooked chicken
- 3(14.5 ounces) cans of fire-roasted diced tomatoes, with juice
- 1(15 ounces) can of cannellini beans, rinsed and drained
- 1(15 ounces) can of pinto beans, rinsed and drained
- 1(15 ounces) can of butter beans, rinsed and drained
- Salt and pepper, to taste
- ¾ cup of sour cream (Optional)

Instructions:

1. Place the bacon in a large pot and cook over medium-high heat for around 10 minutes, stirring periodically, until evenly browned.

2. Drain the bacon slices on a pan that is lined with paper towels. Stir in the ground beef, bacon, and beef stew meat in the same pot. Cook and mix until crumbly, uniformly browned, and no longer yellow, with the ground beef. Drain and set the meat in a bowl aside. Discard any excess grease.

3. Reduce heat to mild, then stir in the same big pot the onion, garlic, habanero pepper, celery, green bell pepper, and red bell pepper, cook and stir until smooth and translucent, around 5 minutes. Stir in

the tomato sauce, then add the mixture of steak, sausage, bacon, and chicken. Stir in the sliced onions, pinto beans, cannellini beans, and butter beans. With salt and pepper, season. Over high heat, bring to a boil, reduce heat to low, and simmer for 2 hours. And use a dollop of sour cream to serve.

Spinach Mozzarella Meatloaf

(Ready in 1 Hour and 15 Minutes, Serve 8, Difficulty: Hard)

Nutrition per Serving:

Calories 333, Protein 27 g, Carbohydrates 17.4 g, Fat 17.1 g, Cholesterol 116.3mg, Sodium 590.2mg.

Ingredients:

- 680 g of ground beef
- 1(10 ounces) package of frozen chopped spinach, thawed and drained well
- 1 ½ cup of Italian seasoned bread crumbs
- 2 cups of shredded mozzarella cheese, divided
- 2 eggs, lightly beaten

Instructions:

1. Preheat the oven to 350 degrees Fahrenheit (176 degrees Celsius). Lightly grease a 5x9 inch loaf pan.

2. In a dish, mix the steak, bread crumbs, spinach, 1 1/2 cups of cheese, and eggs. Switch to the prepared loaf pan.

3. Bake for 1 hour in a preheated oven at an internal mean temperature of 160 degrees Fahrenheit (70 degrees Celsius). For the rest of the cheese to serve, cover it.

Meatloaf Patties

(Ready in 30 Minutes, Serve 4, Difficulty: Easy)

Nutrition per Serving:

Calories 302, Protein 24.7 g, Carbohydrates 15.4 g, Fat 15.5 g, Cholesterol 120.8mg, Sodium 773.3mg.

Ingredients:

- 1 egg, lightly beaten
- 1 slice of soft bread, blended into crumbs
- ½ teaspoon of salt
- ½ teaspoon of ground black pepper
- 453 g of lean ground beef
- 1(8 ounces) can of tomato sauce
- 3 green onions, chopped
- 2 ¼ tablespoons of brown sugar, or to taste
- 2 teaspoons of Worcestershire sauce
- 2 teaspoons of prepared yellow mustard

Instructions:

1. In a large bowl, combine the egg, bread crumbs, salt, and black pepper. Break the ground beef into small bits, blend well with your hands and add to the bowl until the beef is evenly moistened. Shape four patties into the beef mixture.

2. Over medium heat, heat a skillet. In a hot skillet, cook the patties until thoroughly browned, 2-3 minutes per hand, remove to a plate and drain the fat from the skillet.

3. Transfer the skillet back to medium heat. In a skillet, stir together the brown sugar, Worcestershire sauce, tomato sauce, green onions, and yellow mustard. Lie the patties gently in the sauce, bring the liquid to a boil, reduce the heat to medium-low, and simmer for about ten more minutes until the patties are very solid, hot, and grey in the middle.

4. 160 degrees Fahrenheit (70 degrees Celsius). can be read by an instant-read thermometer inserted into the middle

Heavenly Meatloaf with Blue Cheese, Mushrooms, and Spinach

(Ready in 1 Hour, Serve 8, Difficulty: Normal)

Nutrition per Serving:

Calories 257, Protein 23.9 g, Carbohydrates 7 g, Fat 14.2 g, Cholesterol 118.9mg, Sodium 213.1mg.

Ingredients:

- 2 eggs
- 1 cup of finely chopped fresh spinach
- ½ cup of sliced fresh mushrooms
- ½ cup of plain bread crumbs
- ½ small yellow onion, finely chopped
- ⅓ cup of 2% milk
- ⅓ cup of crumbled blue cheese
- 2 tablespoons of reduced-sodium Worcestershire sauce
- 1 tablespoon of minced garlic
- ¼ teaspoon of cayenne pepper
- 1 pinch of dried oregano
- 1 pinch of dried basil
- Salt and ground black pepper, to taste
- 680 g of extra-lean ground beef

Instructions:

1. Preheat the oven to 350 degrees Fahrenheit (176 degrees Celsius). Grease the loaf pan.

2. In a large bowl, combine the eggs, spinach, champagne, bread crumbs, onion, cream, blue cheese, garlic, cayenne pepper, Worcestershire sauce, oregano, basil, cinnamon, and black pepper. Add ground beef and blend thoroughly into the prepared loaf pan with your fingertips.

3. Bake in the preheated oven for 45-60 minutes until it is no longer pink in the middle. A center-

inserted instant-read thermometer can read at least 160 degrees Fahrenheit (70 degrees Celsius).

Never Fail Meatloaf

(Ready in 1 Hour and 45 Minutes, Serve 8, Difficulty: Hard)

Nutrition per Serving:

Calories 302, Protein 28 g, Carbohydrates 68.2 g, Fat 23.6 g, Cholesterol 156.4mg, Sodium 1136.7mg.

Ingredients:

- 1134 g of ground beef
- 3 eggs, beaten
- 1(6 ounces) package of herb-seasoned dry bread stuffing mix
- 1 cup of hickory smoke-flavored barbeque sauce
- 1 onion, finely chopped
- 1 teaspoon of minced garlic
- ½ cup of milk
- 1 cup of barbeque sauce
- 1 cup of packed brown sugar

Instructions:

1. Preheat the oven to 350 degrees Fahrenheit (176 degrees Celsius). Lightly grease a 9x13-inch baking dish.

2. Combine the ground beef, stuffing mix, eggs, hickory smoke-flavored barbeque sauce, garlic, onion, milk in a large mixing bowl.

3. Mix and put thoroughly in the prepared baking dish. Shape yourself into 2 loaves.

4. Combine the barbeque sauce and brown sugar in a small bowl and mix well. Pour over the 2 meatloaves with the glaze.

5. Cover the baking dish and bake for 60-90 minutes in the preheated oven. Uncover the last 15 minutes of baking time. Before slicing, let it rest for 15 minutes.

Meatloaf Cupcakes

(Ready in 1 Hour, Serve 6, Difficulty: Normal)

Nutrition per Serving:

Calories 389, Protein 22.7 g, Carbohydrates 53.7 g, Fat 20.5 g, Cholesterol 100mg, Sodium 1121.5mg.

Ingredients:

- 453 g of ground beef
- 1 cup of crushed saltine crackers
- ½ cup of chopped onion
- ½ cup of chopped green bell pepper
- ⅓ cup of milk
- 1 egg
- 1 tablespoon of Worcestershire sauce
- 2 cloves of garlic, chopped

- 1 teaspoon of ground black pepper
- 1 teaspoon of seasoned salt
- ½ cup of ketchup
- ½ cup of brown sugar
- 4 cups of mashed potatoes
- 1 cup of shredded cheddar cheese

Instructions:

1. Preheat the oven to 350 degrees Fahrenheit (176 degrees Celsius).

2. In a bowl, combine the ground beef, salt crackers, cabbage, green bell pepper, egg, milk, Worcestershire sauce, garlic, black pepper, and salt.

3. In a bowl, stir the ketchup and brown sugar together. Spoon the ketchup mixture from a 6-cup muffin tray onto the bottom of each muffin cup.

4. Cover the beef mixture with muffin cups, leaving ½ inch of space on the top.

5. Bake in the preheated oven for about 30 minutes, until the center is no longer pink.

6. A center-inserted instant-read thermometer can read at least 160 degrees Fahrenheit (70 degrees Celsius). Drain Fat from muffin cups.

7. With mashed potatoes and cheddar cheese, top each 'cupcake'.

8. Continue to bake for another 10 minutes, until the cheese is melted.

Flavored Slow Cooker Meatloaf

(Ready in 6 Hours and 20 Minutes, Serve 4, and Difficulty: Hard)

Nutrition per Serving:

Calories 295, Protein 13.6 g, Carbohydrates 43.2 g, Fat 7.7 g, Cholesterol 67.9mg, Sodium 396.1mg.

Ingredients:

- 1 ground of beef, or more to taste
- 1 small onion, chopped
- ½ cup of bread crumbs
- ¼ cup of beef broth
- 1 egg
- ¼ cup of grated parmesan cheese
- 2 tablespoons of ketchup
- 1 tablespoon of Worcestershire sauce
- ½ teaspoon of Italian seasoning
- ½ teaspoon of dried parsley
- ¼ teaspoon of garlic powder
- ¼ cup of ketchup
- 3 potatoes, coarsely chopped
- ¼ cup of baby carrots

Instructions:

1. In a cup, use your hands to mix ground beef, bread crumbs, onion, broth, egg, and parmesan cheese, 2 tablespoons of ketchup, Worcestershire sauce, parsley, Italian seasoning, and garlic powder. Shape it into a loaf. Center the loaf on a slow cooker's rim, leaving space on the sides.

2. Coat the meatloaf with ¼ cup of ketchup, and the potatoes and carrots surround it. Cook on high for approximately 2 hours. Reduce heat to medium, cook until the meatloaf in the middle is no longer pink and vegetables are tender, 4-6 more hours. A center-inserted instant-read thermometer can read at least 160 degrees Fahrenheit (70 degrees Celsius).

Meatloaf Stuffing

(Ready in 55 Minutes, Serve 6, Difficulty: Normal)

Nutrition per Serving:

Calories 409, Protein 28.3 g, Carbohydrates 44.9 g, Fat 12.5 g, Cholesterol 154.5mg, Sodium 1328.6mg.

Ingredients:

- 680 g of beef, veal, and pork meatloaf meat mix
- 2 green apples, peeled, cored, and diced
- 1 small white onion, diced
- 1 cup of herb-seasoned stuffing mix (such as Pepperidge Farm® Herb-Seasoned Stuffing), crushed
- 3 stalks of celery, diced
- ½ cup of milk
- ¼ cup of water
- 2 eggs
- 1 teaspoon of garlic powder
- ¾ teaspoon of salt
- ¼ teaspoon of ground black pepper
- 1(10.75 ounces) can of cream of mushroom soup

Instructions:

1. Preheat the oven to 350 degrees Fahrenheit (176 degrees Celsius).

2. In a cup, combine the meatloaf beef, apples, onions, stuffing mix, milk, water, celery, potatoes, garlic powder, salt, and black pepper until the ingredients are blended equally.

3. Pour the mushroom soup cream over a 9x5-inch loaf plate. Spoon the meat mixture into the loaf pan and carefully flatten the loaf's top using a spatula.

4. In the preheated oven, bake until the middle is no longer pink, around 1 1/2 hours. A center-inserted instant-read thermometer can read at least 160 degrees Fahrenheit (70 degrees Celsius). Cool in a pan for 5-10 minutes.

5. Flip the meatloaf pan on a serving platter upside down so that the mushroom soup cream is on the top of the loaf

Meatloaf...a Little Southwest Style

(Ready in 1 Hour and 10 Minutes, Serve 8, Difficulty: Normal)

Nutrition per Serving:

Calories 224, Protein 17.2 g, Carbohydrates 11.8 g, Fat 11.7 g, Cholesterol 98.2mg, Sodium 768mg.

Ingredients:

- 680 g of ground beef
- 2 eggs
- ½ cup of chopped onion
- ½ cup of Italian bread crumbs
- ½ cup of salsa
- ¼ cup of ketchup
- ¼ cup of barbeque sauce
- 1 teaspoon of salt
- 1 teaspoon of ground black pepper
- ½ teaspoon of celery salt

Instructions:

1. Preheat the oven to 350 degrees Fahrenheit (176 degrees Celsius).

2. In a bowl, mix the ground beef, bread crumbs, eggs, onion, salsa, ketchup, barbecue sauce, salt, pepper, and celery salt, and move to a loaf tray.

3. Bake in the preheated oven for around 1 hour, until golden brown on top.

Chapter 9: Dessert Recipes

In this chapter, we are going to give you some delicious and mouthwatering recipes
On Lean & Green Dessert recipes.

Tasty Collard Greens

(Ready in 2 Hours and 30 Minutes, Serve 10, and Difficulty: Hard)

Nutrition per Serving:

Calories 142, Protein 9.6 g, Carbohydrates 10.6 g, Fat 7.9 g, Cholesterol 22.7mg, Sodium 688.7mg.

Ingredients:

- ¼ cup of olive oil
- 2 tablespoons of minced garlic
- 5 cups of chicken stock
- 1 smoked turkey drumstick
- 5 bunches collard greens, rinsed, trimmed, and chopped
- Salt and black pepper, to taste
- 1 tablespoon of crushed red pepper flakes (optional)

Instructions:

1. Over medium heat, heat the olive oil in a big jar. Add garlic, then cook gently until light brown. Pour the chicken stock in and add the leg of the turkey. Cover the pot and boil for 30 minutes to boil.

2. To the boiling pot, add the collard greens and turn the heat to medium-high. Let the greens cook, stirring regularly, for about 45 minutes.

3. Reduce the heat to medium and season to taste with salt and pepper. Continue to cook until the greens, 45-60 minutes, are soft and dark green. Drain the greens and reserve the liquid. If desired, add in the red pepper flakes. For reheating leftovers, use the liquid.

Sweet Potato Protein Bars

(Ready in 20 Minutes, Serve 8, Difficulty: Easy)

Nutrition per Serving:

Calories 90, Protein 9 g, Carbohydrates 10 g, Fat 2 g, Fiber: 2 g, Sugar 3 g.

Ingredients:

- 1 cup of cooked, mashed sweet potato (approx. 2 medium)
- 1 teaspoon of vanilla
- 1 teaspoon of cinnamon
- 1/4 cup of maple syrup
- 2 eggs
- 1/3 cup of nut butter
- 1/3 cup of plain yogurt (or whole milk)
- 1/2 teaspoon of baking powder
- 2/3 cup of protein powder (vanilla or chocolate)
- Chocolate chips to melt and drizzle (Optional)

Instructions:

1. In a wide bowl, add the first seven ingredients and mix them well.

2. Add the baking powder and protein powder to blend properly. Pour into the container.

3. Cook for 13-15 minutes at 375 degrees F (190 degree Celsius).

4. Cut into 8 bars and cool before serving.

Black Pepper Blackberry Slush

(Ready in 2 Hours and 30 Minutes, Serve 6, and Difficulty: Hard)

Nutrition per Serving:

Calories 231, Protein 0.4 g, Carbohydrates 7.6 g, Fat 0.1 g, Cholesterol 0mg, Sodium 32.6mg.

Ingredients:

- 3 tablespoons of water
- 2 ½ tablespoons of white sugar
- 1 cup of fresh blackberries
- 1 pinch of ground black pepper
- 1 tiny pinch of salt

Instructions:

1. Combine the water and sugar in a medium-hot saucepan and cook until the sugar melts and the liquid starts to steam. Remove from the heat to room temperature and cool.

2. In a mixer, place the blackberries, the sugar water mixture, the spice, and the salt until the mixture smooth.

3. Onto a shallow bowl, pour through a wire strainer. Tap the dish lightly to scatter the mixture uniformly over the rim. Cover and freeze for at least 2 ½ hours until they are firm.

4. The fork is used to scrape the blackberry mixture into a slush. Cover when ready to serve, and return to the fridge.

Fruity Fun Skewers

(Ready in 15 Minutes, Serve 5, Difficulty: Easy)

Nutrition per Serving:

Calories 61, Protein 0.9 g, Carbohydrates 15.4 g, Fat 0.3 g, Cholesterol 0mg, Sodium 5.1mg.

Ingredients:

- 5 large strawberries, halved

- ¼ cantaloupe, cut into balls or cubes
- 2 bananas, peeled and cut into chunks
- 1 apple, cut into chunks
- 20 skewers

Instructions:

1. Thread the bits of strawberries, cantaloupe, banana, and apple alternately onto skewers, putting on each skewer at least 2 pieces of fruit. On a serving platter, place the fruit skewers decoratively.

Oma's Rhubarb Cake

(Ready in 1 Hour and 15 Minutes, Serve 12, and Difficulty: Normal)

Nutrition per Serving:

Calories 324, Protein 4.4 g, Carbohydrates 57.7 g, Fat 9 g, Cholesterol 49.6mg, Sodium 252.5mg.

Ingredients:

- 1 ¼ cups of white sugar
- 1 teaspoon of baking soda
- ½ teaspoon of salt
- 2 cups of all-purpose flour
- 2 eggs, beaten
- 1 cup of sour cream
- 3 cups of diced rhubarb
- 1 cup of white sugar
- ¼ cup of butter, softened
- ¼ cup of all-purpose flour
- Ground of cinnamon, for dusting

Instructions:

1. The oven must be preheated to 350 degrees Fahrenheit (176 degrees Celsius). A 9x13 inch baking dish has grease and flour.

2. Stir 1 1/4 cups of sugar, baking soda, salt, and 2 cups of flour together in a big dish. Stir in the sour cream and eggs until creamy, then add in the rhubarb. Pour into the dish that has been prepared and scatter uniformly. Stir the remaining 1 cup of sugar and butter together in a smaller bowl until smooth. Till the mixture is crumbly, whisk in 1/4 cup flour. Sprinkle the mixture softly with cinnamon on top of the cake and then sprinkle it lightly.

3. Bake until a toothpick inserted in the middle comes out clean, about 45 minutes, in the preheated oven.

Sarah's Applesauce

(Ready in 30 Minutes, Serve 4, Difficulty: Easy)

Nutrition per Serving:

Calories 121, Protein 0.4 g, Carbohydrates 31.8 g 1, Fat 0.2 g, Cholesterol 0mg, Sodium 2.7mg.

Ingredients:

- 4 apples, peeled, cored, and chopped
- ¾ cup of water
- ¼ cup of white sugar
- ½ teaspoon of ground cinnamon

Instructions:

1. Combine the apples, water, sugar, and cinnamon in a saucepan.

2. Cover and simmer for 15-20 minutes over medium heat, or until the apples are tender. Allow it to cool, then mash it with a potato masher or fork.

Delicious Ham and Potato Soup

(Ready in 45 Minutes, Serve 8, Difficulty: Easy)

Nutrition per Serving:

Calories 195, Protein 6.1 g, Carbohydrates 19.5 g, Fat 10.5 g, Cholesterol 29.9mg,

Sodium 393.7mg.

Ingredients:

- 3 ½ cups of peeled and diced potatoes
- ⅓ cup of diced celery
- ⅓ cup of finely chopped onion
- ¾ cup of diced cooked ham
- 3 ¼ cups of water
- 2 tablespoons of chicken bouillon granules
- ½ teaspoon of salt, or to taste
- 1 teaspoon of ground white or black pepper, or to taste
- 5 tablespoons of butter
- 5 tablespoons of all-purpose flour
- 2 cups of milk

Instructions:

1. In a stockpot, combine the potatoes, ham, celery, onion, and water. Bring to a boil, and simmer until the potatoes are tender, around 10-15 minutes, over medium heat. Stir in the bouillon with the chicken, salt, and pepper.

2. Melt the butter over medium-low heat in a separate saucepan. Whisk in the flour with a fork and cook for about 1 minute, stirring continuously until thick. Slowly stir in the milk until all of the milk has been added so that lumps do not form. Continue to stir until thick, 4-5 minutes, over medium-low heat.

3. In the stockpot, stir the milk mixture and cook the soup until it is sweet. Immediately serve.

Barbequed Pineapple

(Ready in 8 Hours and 30 Minutes, Serve 4, and Difficulty: Easy)

Nutrition per Serving:

Calories 151, Protein 0.8 g, Carbohydrates 30.9 g 1, Fat 0.4 g, Cholesterol 0mg, Sodium 6.1mg.

Ingredients:

- 1 fresh pineapple
- ¼ cup of rum
- ¼ cup of brown sugar
- 1 tablespoon of ground cinnamon
- ½ teaspoon of ground ginger
- ½ teaspoon of ground nutmeg
- ½ teaspoon of ground cloves

Instructions:

1. Peel the pineapple and cut off the middle core, thus leaving it whole. Slice them into 8 rings and place them in a resealable plastic bag or shallow glass dish. Mix the bourbon, brown sugar, cinnamon, ginger, nutmeg, and cloves in a shallow dish. 2. Pour over the pineapple marinade, cover it, and refrigerate for 1 hour or overnight.

Preheat the high-heat barbecue. Slightly grated gasoline.

3. Pineapple rings are grilled for 15 minutes, rotating once or until dried, and char marked around. Serve with the marinade that remains.

Supreme Strawberry Topping

(Ready in 35 Minutes, Serve 4, Difficulty: Easy)

Nutrition per Serving:

Calories 296, Protein 0.6 g, Carbohydrates 23.7 g, Fat 0.3 g, Cholesterol 0mg, Sodium 1mg

Ingredients:

- 1-pint of fresh strawberries
- ⅓ cup of white sugar
- 1 teaspoon of vanilla

Instructions:

1. Wash strawberries and remove stems, cut large berries in ½ or roughly chop them.

2. Combine strawberries, sugar, and vanilla in a saucepan. Cook over medium-high heat, stirring occasionally. The mixture will sizzle for a while, but then the juice will begin to form. Continue stirring, mash a few strawberries with a wooden spoon or heat-proof

3. Remove from heat. In a blender, puree about 1/3 of the sauce, then mix back into remaining topping. Store in refrigerator.

Fried Beans without the Refry

(Ready in 8 Hours and 15 Minutes, Serve 8, and Difficulty: Normal)

Nutrition per Serving:

Calories 135, Protein 8.5 g, Carbohydrates 25.4 g, Fat 0.5 g, Cholesterol 0mg, Sodium 784.7mg.

Ingredients:

- 1 onion, peeled and halved
- 3 cups of dry pinto beans, rinsed
- ½ fresh jalapeno pepper, seeded and chopped
- 2 tablespoons of minced garlic
- 5 teaspoons of salt
- 1 ¾ teaspoon of fresh ground black pepper
- ⅛ teaspoon of ground optional
- 9 cups of water

Instructions:

1. In a slow cooker, put the onion, rinsed beans, jalapeno, garlic, salt, pepper, and cumin together. To mix, pour in the water and stir. Cook for 8 hours on high, adding more water as needed. Note: if during frying, more than 1 cup of water has evaporated, the temperature is too high.

2. Strain them until the beans have fried, and conserve the oil. To achieve the desired consistency, mash the beans with a potato masher, adding the reserved water as needed.

Flaxseed Apricot Bars

(Ready in 35 Minutes, Serve 3, Difficulty: Easy)

Nutrition per Serving:

Calories 178, Protein 5 g, Carbohydrates 21 g, Fat 10 g, Sodium 3mg, Fiber 5 g, Sugar 15 g.

Ingredients:

- 1 ½ cup of raw almonds
- 1 ½ cup of dried apricots
- 1 cup of dates, pitted
- 1/3 cup of unsweetened shredded coconut
- 3 tablespoons of flaxseed meal
- 1 teaspoon of fresh lemon zest
- ½ teaspoon of ground cinnamon

Instructions:

1. In the food processor, add the raw almonds and cook until they are crumbly but not completely obliterated.

2. Add dried apricots, dates, coconut, flaxseed meal, new lemon zest, and cinnamon to taste.

3. Now filter it all together until it forms a ball or sticks to itself and is fully blended. You can need to use a spatula to force everything down a couple of times to even integrate anything.

4. Use a flat, shallow baking dish to line it with parchment paper to press the mixture into the bars, and then put the condensed mixture into the baking dish.

5. Press evenly into the dish with both hands; take care to keep it as fully lined and level as possible, so the bars would be cut from this mold.

6. To allow the bars to harden, put the mold in the fridge for around 20-30 minutes.

7. Lay the mold out on a cutting board once more solidified and slice lengthwise once in ½ and then again to create the actual bars-you should have around 12-14 bars.

3. I keep these, covered by parchment paper, stored in the fridge to keep them from sticking. In an airtight jar, they'll last for about a week.

Grilled Asparagus

(Ready in 18 Minutes, Serve 4, Difficulty: Easy)
Nutrition per Serving:

Calories 153, Protein 2.5 g, Carbohydrates 4.4 g, Fat 3.5 g, Cholesterol 0mg, Sodium 2.3mg.

Ingredients:

- 453 g of fresh asparagus spears, trimmed
- 1 tablespoon of olive oil
- Salt and pepper, to taste

Instructions:

1. Preheat grill at high heat.

2. Coat the spears of the asparagus lightly with olive oil. To taste, season with salt and pepper.

3. Grill for 2-3 minutes over high heat or to the perfect tenderness.

Fresh Strawberry Granita

(Ready in 2 Hours and 25 Minutes, Serve 8, and Difficulty: Easy)
Nutrition per Serving:

Calories 269, Protein 0.8 g, Carbohydrates 17.1 g, Fat 0.3 g, Cholesterol 0mg, Sodium 26.3mg.

Ingredients:

- 907 g of ripe strawberries, hulled and halved
- ⅓ cup of white sugar, or to taste
- 1 cup of water
- ½ teaspoon of lemon juice (Optional)
- ¼ teaspoon of balsamic vinegar (Optional)
- 1 tiny pinch of salt

Instructions:

1. Rinse and drain the strawberries with cold water. Remove the berries and add the sugar, water, lemon juice, balsamic vinegar, and salt to the blender.

2. To get the mixture going, pulse several times, then blend until smooth, or for around 1 minute. Pour into a large bakery dish. The purée in the dish can only be about 3/8 inches deep.

3. Put the uncovered dish in the freezer for about 45 minutes before the mixture starts to freeze around the edges. The mixture in the middle would also be slushy.

4. Using a fork, gently stir the crystals from the side of the Granita mixture into the middle and completely blend. Close the freezer and chill for another 30-40 minutes until the Granita is almost frozen. With a fork, blend gently as before, scratching the crystals free. Run 3-4 times with the fork to freeze and stir until the Granita is light, the crystals are separate, and the Granita appears dry and soft.

5. Place the Granita in small baking bowls for serving.

Strawberry Firecracker Banana Wobblers

(Ready in 2 Hours and 35 Minutes, Serve 3, and Difficulty: Normal)
Nutrition per Serving:

Calories 244, Protein 3.9 g, Carbohydrates 59.7 g, Fat 0.3 g, Cholesterol 0mg, Sodium 128.9mg.

Ingredients:

- 1(3 ounces) package of strawberry Jell-O® Mix
- 1 cup of boiling water
- ½ cup of cold water
- 3 empty (6-ounces) cans of juice
- 3 banana halves, cut crosswise
- 3(4 inches) pieces of red string licorice candy

Instructions:

1. In a cup, mix the strawberry gelatin with the hot water before the gelatin dissolves. Stir in cold water and refrigerate for about 15 minutes, until the gelatin is dense but not fully fixed.

2. At the bottom of each juice, you can put around 2-teaspoons of thickened gelatin. Center 1 ½ of the banana, cut side down, and spoon the remaining gelatin around the banana into the center of each juice container, filling the cans to the brim. Chill the cans for about 2 hours until the gelatin is solid.

3. To serve, to loosen the gelatin, dip each can in hot water up to the rim, invert cans on a serving tray, and puncture the bottom of the can to let air in. To imitate a fuse, raise the cans from the desserts and drop a red licorice string into the middle of each dessert.

Pretzel Turtles®

(Ready in 14 Minutes, Serve 20, Difficulty: Easy)

Nutrition per Serving:

Calories 182, Protein 1.7 g, Carbohydrates 14.1 g, Fat 2.2 g, Cholesterol 0.4mg, Sodium 262.9mg.

Ingredients:

* 20 small mini pretzels
* 20 chocolate-covered caramel candies
* 20 pecan halves

Instructions:

1. Preheat the oven to 300 degrees Fahrenheit (150 degrees Celsius).

2. Arrange the pretzels on a parchment-lined baking sheet in one single layer. On each pretzel, put one chocolate-covered caramel candy.

3. For 4 minutes, bake. Press ½ pecan onto each candy covered pretzel when the candy is soft. Cool absolutely in an airtight jar before storage.

Frozen Fruit and Soda Cups

(Ready in 35 Minutes, Serve 6, Difficulty: Easy)

Nutrition per Serving:

Calories 146, Protein 1.3 g, Carbohydrates 37.6 g, Fat 0.4 g, Cholesterol 0mg, Sodium 23mg

Ingredients:

* 1 cup of cubed cantaloupe
* ½ cup of cubed honeydew
* 2 cups of cubed watermelon
* ½ cup of diced apple
* 1 cup of sliced banana
* 1 cup of cubed fresh mango
* 3 cups of lemon-lime flavored carbonated beverage, chilled

Instructions:

1. Toss together the cantaloupe, honeydew, watermelon, apple, banana, and mango in a large bowl.

2. Divide the fruit into six paper cups.

3. Pour 1/2 cup of lemon-lime soda into each cup. Place in the freezer for 5 minutes, then serve.

"CranCrack" Cranberry Salad

(Ready in 55 Minutes, Serve 6, Difficulty: Normal)

Nutrition per Serving:

Calories 212, Protein 2.3 g, Carbohydrates 53.5 g, Fat 0.1 g, Cholesterol 0mg, Sodium 87.7mg.

Ingredients:

* 1(12 ounces) package of fresh cranberries
* 1 large orange, peeled

* 2 cups of boiling water
* 1 cup of white sugar
* 1(6 ounces) package of cherry-flavored gelatin mix, (such as Jell-O®)
* 1(14 ounces) can of crushed pineapple with juice

Instructions:

1. In a food processor, grind cranberries and oranges before finely crushed.

2. In a bowl, stir together the boiling water, sugar, and gelatin until the gelatin and sugar dissolve. Add the cranberry mixture and juice to the pineapple and stir. Pour into an 8-inch square serving bowl, cover the plastic wrap with the dish, and refrigerate for about 45 minutes until set.

Refried Beans without the Refry

(Ready in 8 Hours and 15 Minutes, Serve 15, and Difficulty: Normal)

Nutrition per Serving:

Calories139, Protein 8.5 g, Carbohydrates 25.4 g, Fat 0.5 g, Cholesterol 0mg, Sodium 784.7mg.

Ingredients:

* 1 onion, peeled and halved
* 3 cups of dry pinto beans, rinsed
* ½ fresh jalapeno pepper, seeded and chopped
* 2 tablespoons of minced garlic
* 5 teaspoons of salt
* 1 ¾ teaspoon of fresh ground black pepper
* ⅛ teaspoon of ground optional
* 9 cups of water

Instructions:

1. In a slow cooker, put the onion, rinsed beans, jalapeno, garlic, salt, pepper, and cumin together. To mix, pour in the water and stir. Cook for 8 hours on high flame, add more water as needed.

2. Strain the beans and conserve the oil. To achieve the desired consistency, mash the beans with a potato masher, by adding the water as needed.

Smoothie Pops

(Ready in 4 Hrs.10 Minutes, Serve 12, Difficulty: Normal)

Nutrition per Serving:

Calories 39, Protein 1.3 g, Carbohydrates 5 g, Fat 1.8 g, Cholesterol 3.8mg, Sodium 11.1mg.

Ingredients:

* 1 cup of hulled strawberries
* 1 cup of fresh blueberries
* 1 cup of fresh raspberries
* 1 cup of Greek yogurt

- 5(1 gram) packets of stevia powder
- ½ teaspoon of vanilla extract

Instructions:

1. In a blender, mix the strawberries, blueberries, raspberries, yogurt, stevia powder, and vanilla extract until tender.

2. In 12 ice pop molds, pour the mixture and place sticks or handles. Freeze until firm, approximately 4 hours.

Ice Cream Sandwich Cake

(Ready in 30 Minutes, Serve 12, Difficulty: Normal)

Nutrition per Serving:

Calories 278, Protein 6.5 g, Carbohydrates 85.4 g, Fat 24.8 g, Cholesterol 39.8mg, Sodium 260mg

Ingredients:

- 24 vanilla ice cream sandwiches, unwrapped
- 2(8 ounces) containers of whipped topping (such as Cool Whip®), thawed
- 1(12 ounces) jar of hot fudge ice cream topping, warmed
- 1(12 ounces) jar of caramel ice cream topping
- ¼ cup of chopped pecans, or to taste

Instructions:

1. Arrange a line of ice cream sandwiches on top of a layer of whipped topping, hot fudge topping, and caramel topping at the bottom of a 9x13-inch dish. Repeat layering, whipped topping, hot fudge topping, and caramel topping for the leftover ice cream sandwiches, finishing with a top layer of whipped topping.

2. Sprinkle pecans. Cover the dish with aluminum foil and freeze for a minimum of 30 minutes until set.

Tapioca Pudding (Oil Free)

(Ready in 28 Minutes, Serve 4-6, Difficulty: Normal)

Nutrition per Serving:

Calories 187, Protein 2.5 g, Carbohydrates 39.6 g, Fat 2.5 g, Fiber 1g.

Ingredients:

- 1 ¼ cups almond milk
- ½ cup water
- ⅓ Cup sugar
- ½ split vanilla bean
- ⅓ Cup seed tapioca pearls

Instructions:

1. Through your pressure cooker, pour 1 cup of water.

2. Rinse the pearls with tapioca.

3. Add tapioca, sugar, water, milk, and vanilla to a 4-bowl bowl (safe for a pressure cooker) and blend.

4. Lower it into a steamer basket and then into a cooker until the sugar has melted.

5. Click 'manual,' and cook for 8 minutes at high speed.

6. Hit "cancel" as time is up and wait for the weight to come down independently.

7. Wait 5 minutes before opening the lid when the pressure is lifted.

8. Yeah, stir.

9. Serve warm or cold for at least 3 hours in a refrigerator (covered with clinging wrap).

Jamie's Sweet and Easy Corn on the Cob

(Ready in 15 Minutes, Serve 6, Difficulty: Easy)

Nutrition per Serving:

Calories 194, Protein 2.9 g, Carbohydrates 21.5 g, Fat 1.1 g, Cholesterol 0mg, Sodium 13.5mg.

Ingredients:

- 2 tablespoons of white sugar
- 1 tablespoon of lemon juice
- 6 ears corn on the cob, husks, and silk removed

Instructions:

1. Fill about 3/4 of a large pot full of water and bring it to a boil. Dissolve the sugar and stir in the sugar and lemon juice.

2. Place the corn ears gently in the boiling water, cover the pot, turn off the heat and let the corn cook for about 10 minutes in hot water until tender.

Shudder uppers

(Ready in 1 hrs. 3 Minutes, Serve 20, and Difficulty: Easy)

Nutrition per Serving:

Calories 122, Protein 1.2 g, Carbohydrates 27 g, Fat 1.6 g, Cholesterol 1.4mg, Sodium 59.8mg.

Ingredients:

- 1(14 ounces) package of individually wrapped caramels, unwrapped
- 1(10.5 ounces) package of large marshmallows

Instructions:

1. Build a nice fire and let the wood burn down into coals. This takes about 1 hour.

2. Thread a marshmallow onto a stick, then thread a caramel candy onto the stick in front of the marshmallow. Roast over the coals from the fire until the marshmallow is the desired doneness, but not on fire. Pull the marshmallow up over the caramel so that it is inside. Let cool and enjoy!

Yummy Watermelon Pops

(Ready in 4 Hours and 15 Minutes, Serve 8, and Difficulty: Normal)

Nutrition per Serving:

Calories 143, Protein 0.4 g, Carbohydrates 10.9 g, Fat 0.1 g, Cholesterol 0mg, Sodium 0.5mg.

Ingredients:

* 2 ½ cups of cubed seeded watermelon
* 1 tablespoon of lemon juice
* ¼ cup of white sugar
* ½ cup of fresh raspberries

Instructions:

1. Place the watermelon, lemon juice, sugar, and raspberries into a blender, and blend on high speed until the sugar has dissolved and the mixture is smooth.

2. Pour the mixture into ice pop molds, and insert sticks or handles. Freeze until firm, several hours or overnight.

Cinnamon Pear Frozen Yogurt

(Ready in 30 Minutes, Serve 4, Difficulty: Easy)

Nutrition per Serving:

Calories 180, Protein 1.6 g, Carbohydrates 11.2 g, Fat 0.5 g, Cholesterol 0mg, Sodium 29.3mg.

Ingredients:

* 1(15 ounces) can of pear halves
* 2 cups of vanilla yogurt
* ⅓ cup of white sugar
* ½ teaspoon of ground cinnamon
* ¼ teaspoon of ground allspice

Instructions:

1. With 1/2 cup of juice reserved, rinse the pears. In a blender or food processor, mash the pears.

2. Combine the pears, reserved juice, yogurt, sugar, cinnamon, and allspice in an ice cream maker canister. Freeze according to manufacturers' instructions.

Cinnamon Gelatin Salad

(Ready in 3 hours and 5 Minutes, Serve 4, and Difficulty: Normal)

Nutrition per Serving:

Calories 165, Protein 2 g, Carbohydrates 40.5 g 1, Fat 0 g, Cholesterol 0mg, Sodium 85.3mg.

Ingredients:

* 1(3 ounces) package of raspberry-flavored Jell-O® Mix
* 1 cup of boiling water
* 1(2.25 ounces) package of cinnamon red-hot candies

* 1 cup of applesauce

Instructions:

1. Mix the gelatin and the hot water in a shallow serving bowl before the gelatin is fully dissolved. Stir in the cinnamon sweets until they are melted, then add in the applesauce. Chill until set, about 3 hours.

Strawberry Banana Oatmeal Greek Yogurt Waffles

(Ready in 15 Minutes, Serve 2, Difficulty: Easy)

Nutrition per Serving:

Calories 249, Protein 12.4 g, Carbohydrates 39.4 g, Fat 5.9 g, Saturated Fat 1.7 g, Fiber 5.5 g, Sugar 7.1 g.

Ingredients:

* 2 cups of old-fashioned oats, gluten-free if desired
* 1 tablespoon of baking powder
* 1/2 teaspoon of cinnamon
* ¼ teaspoon of salt
* 1 medium ripe banana
* ½ cup of 2% low-fat plain Greek yogurt
* ¼ cup of Almond Breeze® Unsweetened Vanilla Almond Milk
* 2 eggs
* 1 teaspoon of vanilla extract
* 1/2 cup of diced strawberries (from about 8 medium strawberries)

Instructions:

1. Preheat waffle iron and spray with non-stick cooking spray.

2. In a mixer, add all ingredients except strawberries and mix well until well blended and creamy.

3. Unplug the blender and carefully fold a spatula onto the strawberries.

4. You can pour half of the batter into the waffle iron if you use a Belgian waffle iron, and cook until the steam stops and the waffles are golden brown and slightly crispy on the outside.

5. The recipe consists of 2 major Belgian waffles. Serving size: ½ waffles from Belgium. Top with peanut butter, Greek yogurt, fruit, maple syrup, and/or chia seeds.

Applesauce Cinnamon Gelatin Salad

(Ready in 3 Hours and 10 Minutes, Serve 6, and Difficulty: Hard)

Nutrition per Serving:

Calories 124, Protein 1.4 g, Carbohydrates 30.6 g, Fat 0 g, Cholesterol 0mg, Sodium 82.1mg.

Ingredients:

* ⅓ cup of cinnamon red-hot candies

- 1 ½ cups of boiling water
- 1(3 ounces) package of lemon-flavored Jell-O® Mix
- 1 ½ cups of applesauce

Instructions:

1. In a large bowl, melt the candy in hot water.

2. Using gelatin and whisk until dissolved.

3. Stir in a couple of applesauce and ice cubes and chill for 3 hours or until set. And the ice cream, the cold serving.

Easy Apple Peanut Butter Energy Bites

(Ready in 5 Minutes, Serve 2, Difficulty: Easy)

Nutrition per Serving:

Calories 292, Sugar 23 g, Sodium 232mg, Fat 13 g

Ingredients:

- 1 apple, sliced (I used a Gala apple)
- 2 tablespoons of peanut butter
- 1/4 cup of raisins
- 1 teaspoon of chia seeds

Instructions:

1. Split an apple into 8-9 slices of the same kind.

2. Fill each bit of peanut butter, raisins, and chia seeds, in equal amounts.

3. Serve.

Applesauce Salad

(Ready in 1 Hour, 20 Minutes, Serve 8, Difficulty: Normal)

Nutrition per Serving:

Calories 155, Protein 2 g, Carbohydrates 38.2 g, Fat 0 g, Cholesterol 0mg, Sodium 103.5mg.

Ingredients:

- 2 cups of water
- ½ cup of cinnamon red-hot candies
- 1(6 ounces) package of cherry flavored Jell-O® Mix
- 2 cups of applesauce

Instructions:

1. Put it to a boil with water. Dissolve the red-hot sweets in the boiling water with the cinnamon.

2. Add in and heat the cherry-flavored gelatin.

3. Transfer to a medium tub. With a mix of applesauce. Freeze in the refrigerator for 4 hours or until completely gelled.

Mocha Oat Protein Shake

(Ready in 5 Minutes, Serve 1, Difficulty: Easy)

Nutrition per Serving:

Calories 299.4, Protein 13.8 g, Carbohydrates 49.3 g, Fat 5.4 g, Cholesterol 18.6mg, Sodium 173.7mg.

Ingredients:

- 1 packet of Carnation Breakfast Essentials® Rich Milk Chocolate High Protein Powder Drink Mix
- ¾ cup of cold 2% milk
- ½ cup of cold strong brewed coffee
- 8 each of ice cubes
- ¼ cup of oats

Instructions:

Place a blender pitcher of chocolate drink mix, ice cubes, milk, coffee, and oats. Run the blender for 20-30 seconds on a smoothie cycle or liquefy it.

Frozen Blueberry Yogurt Pops

(Ready in 2 Hours and 5 Minutes, Serve 8, and Difficulty: Easy)

Nutrition per Serving:

Calories 237, Protein 0.9 g, Carbohydrates 8.4 g, Fat 0 g, Cholesterol 0.5mg, Sodium 15.3mg.

Ingredients:

- 1 cup of Ocean Spray® Blueberry Juice Cocktail
- 1 cup of Ocean Spray® Fresh Blueberries, cleaned and rinsed
- 1(6 ounces) container of fat-free vanilla yogurt
- 8 wooden craft sticks

Instructions:

1. Combine the blender with all the ingredients. Cover and blend for 15-20 seconds at higher speed, or until smooth.

2. Pour in 8 pop molds that are frozen (2.5 ounces to 3 ounces each). Cover, insert art sticks, and freeze until fully firm or for 2 hours.

3. To serve, dip the exterior of the molds to loosen them in warm water.

Banana Nut Breakfast Parfait

(Ready in 20 Minutes, Serve 1, Difficulty: Easy)

Nutrition per Serving:

Calories 330.2, Protein 21.1 g, Carbohydrates 58.1 g, Fat 2.8 g, Fiber 4.6 g, Sugar 29.4 g, Sodium 86.3mg.

Ingredients:

- 1 cup of free-vanilla Greek yogurt
- 1 medium banana, sliced
- 2 tablespoons of chopped pecans
- 2 tablespoons of low-fat granola

Instructions:

Layer everything as you like and enjoy it instantly!

Almond Ice

(Ready in 4 Hours and 15 Minutes, Serve 12, and Difficulty: Normal)

Nutrition per Serving:

Calories 71, Protein 1.7 g, Carbohydrates 16 g, Fat 0.1 g, Cholesterol 0mg, Sodium 5mg.

Ingredients:

- 5(.25 ounces) envelopes of unflavored gelatin
- 2 ¼ cups of boiling water
- 4 teaspoons of almond extract
- 4 cups of cold water
- 1 ⅓ cup of white sugar
- 1 cup of fresh strawberries, halved
- 1 cup of seedless grapes
- 1 cup cubed cantaloupe

Instructions:

1. In 1 cup of cold water, soften the gelatin. Add 2 ¼ cups of boiling sugar and water. Stir until it dissolves thoroughly. Add 3 cups cold water and the almond extract. Mix thoroughly.

2. In a 9x13-inch pan, pour the gelatin blend and refrigerate for at least 4 hours. Cut into squares of 1 inch and serve with fruits in a bowl.

Protein Peach Surprise

(Ready in 4 Minutes, Serve 6, Difficulty: Easy)

Nutrition per Serving:

Calories 182 Protein 22 g, Carbohydrates 21 g, Fat 2 g.

Ingredients:

- 1 cup of peaches
- 1/4 cup of fat-free cheese cream
- 1/4 teaspoon of cinnamon
- 1/2 scoop of vanilla whey protein powder

Instructions:

1. Preheat the oven to 500 degrees (260 degree C).

2. Mix the cream cheese, cinnamon, and protein powder in a small bowl. Place the peaches on a baking sheet and bake them for 8-10 minutes. Cover the blend of cream cheese with baked peaches.

Banana in Caramel Sauce

(Ready in 20 Minutes, Serve 2, Difficulty: Normal)

Nutrition per Serving:

Calories 258, Protein 3.1 g, Carbohydrates 79 g, Fat 50.9 g, Cholesterol 162.9mg, Sodium 193.4mg.

Ingredients:

- ½ cup of butter
- 1 cup of superfine sugar
- 1 ¼ cup of heavy cream
- 4 medium (7" to 7-7/8" long) bananas, peeled and halved lengthwise

Instructions:

1. Melt butter over medium heat in a large, heavy skillet. Stir in the sugar and boil, stirring well until the sugar is molten and slightly brown. Gently stir in the milk (mixture will bubble up).

2. Let the mixture cook for 1 minute, then bring it to medium heat. Place the bananas in the pan and cook until hot, for around 2 minutes. Serve warm.

Quick Ice Cream

(Ready in 8 hours, Serve 8, Difficulty: Normal)

Nutrition per Serving:

Calories 73, Protein 0.6 g, Carbohydrates 15.1 g, Fat 0.1 g, Cholesterol 0.6mg.

Ingredients:

- ¾ cup of prepared fat-free vanilla pudding
- 1(8 ounces) container of fat-free frozen whipped topping, thawed

Instructions:

1. For the whipped icing, fold the pudding together.

2. Return to the whipped topping tub and freeze with a partially open lid for 8 hours or overnight.

Fizzy Gelatin Salad

(Ready in 5 Hours and 10 Minutes, Serve 6, and Difficulty: Normal)

Nutrition per Serving:

Calories 83, Protein 1.3 g, Carbohydrates 20.2 g, Fat 0 g, Cholesterol 0mg, Sodium 69.4mg.

Ingredients:

- 1 cup unsweetened applesauce
- 1(3 ounces) package of lime-flavored Jell-O® Mix
- 1 cup of ginger ale

Instructions:

1. In a small saucepan, pour the applesauce, and bring to a boil. Add gelatin when absorbed, then set aside for around 1 hour to cool.

2. Whisk gradually in the ginger ale until cooled. Until set, refrigerate for about 4 hours.

Virginia Apple Pudding

(Ready in 40 Minutes, Serve 6, Difficulty: Normal)

Nutrition per Serving:

Calories 384, Protein 3.8 g, Carbohydrates 57.5 g, Fat 16.4 g, Cholesterol 43.9mg, Sodium 343.3mg.

Ingredients:

- ½ cup of butter, melted
- 1 cup of white sugar
- 1 cup of all-purpose flour
- 2 teaspoons of baking powder
- ¼ teaspoon of salt
- 1 cup of milk
- 2 cups of chopped, peeled apple
- 1 teaspoon of ground cinnamon

Instructions:

1. Preheat the oven to 375 degrees Fahrenheit (190 degrees Celsius).

2. Combine the butter, sugar, flour, baking powder, salt, and milk in a shallow baking dish until smooth.

3. Combine the apples and cinnamon in a microwave-proof dish. Microwave, 2-5 minutes, until the apples are tender. Onto the middle of the batter, dump the apples.

4. Bake for 30 minutes, or until crispy, in a preheated oven.

Rice Cake with Almond Butter

(Ready in 5 Minutes, Serve 1, Difficulty: Easy)

Nutrition per Serving:

Calories 89, Protein 3.2 g, Carbohydrate 10.8 g, Fat 9.8 g, Sodium 31mg.

Ingredients:

- 1 rice cake or brown rice cake.
- 1 tablespoon of plain almond butter (or peanut or almond butter)

Instructions:

Spread the rice cake with almond butter and enjoy!

Apple Cheese Crackers

(Ready in 5 Minutes, Serve 6, Difficulty: Easy)

Nutrition per Serving:

Calories 170, Protein 7 g, Carbohydrate 14 g, Sugars 6 g.

Ingredients:

- Crackers®, Ritz®, or Club® (or any favorite cracker)
- cheese, we used cheddar and pepper jack
- apples, thinly sliced
- cinnamon plus sugar

Instructions:

1. Place a slice of cheese on top of the crackers.

2. Sprinkle with cinnamon plus sugar, then place an apple slice on top.

Hummus with Pita Bread

(Ready in 20 Minutes, Serve 4, Difficulty: Easy)

Nutrition per Serving:

Carbs 40 g, Protein 11 g, Fat 4 g.

Ingredients:

For Hummus:

- 2 cups of chickpeas (Kabuli Chana)
- 3-4 cloves of garlic, minced
- 3-4 tablespoons of olive oil
- 3 tablespoons of tahini (sesame seeds)
- 1 tablespoon of lemon juice
- 1 teaspoon of cumin powder(jeer)
- ½ teaspoon of pepper
- ½ teaspoon of red chili powder
- Salt, to taste
- Fresh parsley and coriander leaves
- Olives

For Pita Bread:

- 1 cup of refined flour (Maida)
- 3 tablespoon of yogurt (curd)
- 1 teaspoon of sugar
- ¼ teaspoon of salt
- ¼ teaspoon of baking powder
- 1/8 teaspoon of baking soda
- 2 tablespoon of olive oil

Instructions:

1. Roast the white sesame (tahini) seeds and then drop them into a blender.
 Soak the chickpea overnight. Drain and simmer with salted water until smooth.

2. Place the cooked chickpeas in the food processor or blender.

3. Add garlic, salt, cumin seeds, tahini (roasted sesame seeds powder), red chili powder, pepper, and salt. Add 2 tablespoons olive oil and blend. Add lemon juice and continue to blend till absolutely smooth.

4. Sprinkle some olive oil on it before serving. Sprinkle red chili powder.

5. Garnish on top with fresh olives, coriander, or pita bread. Serve.

For Pita Bread

1. Add processed flour, curd, sugar, salt, baking powder, and baking soda to the dish. Gradually combine warm water and knead until smooth.

2. On your hands, add a bit of olive oil and knead the dough. Cover the dough and give 3 hours to relax.

3. Once the dough rises, knead again for 5 minutes and make balls.

4. On the rolling sheet, sprinkle some flour. Take any ball of dough and flatten it softly with your hands. Now you can use a rolling pin to make sure the rolling dough is smooth on either side.

5. On a medium flame, heat a saucepan spray it with some olive oil. Place the rolled pita brown in a warm spring pot and cook until the bread is browned up and down

6. Two minutes longer, flip, and prepare.

7. In the kitchen towel, cover the pita bread.

8. Cut into the shapes you like and serve with hummus.

Blueberry Banana Protein Smoothie

(Ready in 10 Minutes, Serve 1, Difficulty: Easy)

Nutrition per Serving:

Calories 230, Protein 19.1 g, Fat 2.6 g, Saturated Fat 0.1 g, Sugars 21.9 g.

Ingredients:

- ½ cup (70 g) of frozen unsweetened blueberries
- ½ medium(70 g) banana, sliced and frozen
- ¾ cup(180 g) of plain non-fat Greek yogurt
- ¾ cup(180ml) of unsweetened vanilla almond milk
- 2 cups(260 g) of ice cubes

Instructions:

1. Transfer all of the ingredients to a blender and blend until smooth. Serve.

The Ultimate Toast Topping Combination

(Ready in 7 Minutes, Serve 1, Difficulty: Easy)

Nutrition per Serving:

Calories 273, Protein 23.4 g, Carbohydrates 47.9 g, Fat 33.4 g, Cholesterol 283.9mg, Sodium 618.7mg.

Ingredients:

- 2 slices of bread of choice
- peanut butter crunchy or creamy, whatever you like best
- 1/2 tablespoon of chia seeds
- 1 banana
- Honey

Instructions:

1. Start by toasting two bread slices.

2. Top with the desired amount of peanut butter on each piece of bread after toasting.

3. Drizzle with the desired amount of honey in zig zag gestures-more or less depending on how good you like your toast to be.

4. Then, sprinkle the Chia seeds on both pieces of toast.

5. Then cut a banana into 18 slices and put three rows of 3 pieces each on top of your toast.

Lean Green Smoothie

(Ready in 10 Minutes, Serve 4, Difficulty: Easy)

Nutrition per Serving:

Calories 186, Protein 1.6 g, Carbohydrates 21.2 g, Fat 0.5 g, Cholesterol 0mg, Sodium 29.3mg.

Ingredients:

- 3 cups of honeydew melon, peeled, seeded, and cubed
- 3 cups of ice cubes
- 1 cup of green grapes
- 1 cucumber, peeled and chopped
- ½ cup of broccoli florets (optional)
- 1 sprig of fresh mint

Instructions:

1. Place the honeydew melon, ice cubes, grapes, cucumber, broccoli, and mint into a blender. Cover, and puree until smooth.

Orange Mango Smoothie

(Ready in 7 Minutes, Serve 1, Difficulty: Easy)

Nutrition per Serving:

Calories: 321, Protein 24.2 g, Carbohydrate 52.2 g, Fat 4.7 g, Sodium 188mg, Sugars 35.3 g, Iron 5mg.

Ingredients:

- 1 cup of unsweetened almond milk or another plant milk of choice
- 1 scoop (30 g) of vegan vanilla protein powder
- 1 cup (140 g) of frozen mango chunks
- 1 peeled, quartered (200 g) of frozen navel orange
- 1/2 (60 g) frozen banana
- 1 teaspoon of pure vanilla extract
- 1 tablespoon of hemp seeds (12 g, optional)
- 1/2 teaspoon of turmeric (optional)

Instructions:

In a high-speed blender, combine all ingredients until smooth. Serve in a glass.

Lime Jell-O® Waldorf salad

(Ready in 4 Hours and 15 Minutes, Serve 12, and Difficulty: Easy)

Nutrition per Serving:

Calories 163, Protein 3.3 g, Carbohydrates 29.3 g, Fat 4.9 g, Cholesterol 0mg, Sodium 115.8mg.

Ingredients:

* 2(3 ounces) packages of lime-flavored gelatin mix (such as Jell-O®)
* 2 cups of boiling water
* 2 cups of cold water
* 4 red apples, chopped
* 4 stalks of celery, chopped
* ½ cup of chopped walnuts, or to taste (Optional)

Instructions:

1. In a bowl of hot water, melt the lime gelatin, and add the gelatin's cold water. Pour gelatin into a mold.

2. Mix the grapes, celery, and walnuts into the gelatin. Cool until it's firm, about four hours. Dip the mold in hot water to remove the salad, put a plate on top of the mold and invert it to release the molded salad.

Freezer Friendly Sandwiches

(Ready in 10 Minutes, Serve 6, Difficulty: Easy)

Nutrition per Serving:

Calories 225, Protein 14.1 g, Carbohydrates 17.0 g, Fat 11.3 g, Saturated 5.3 g, Fiber 1.6 g, Sugars 2.0 g, Sodium 303.0mg.

Ingredients:

* 12 eggs
* 2 tablespoons of milk
* 1 teaspoon of salt
* 1/2 teaspoon of freshly ground black pepper
* 12 slices of cooked bacon, sausage patties, ham, or Canadian bacon
* 12 English muffins
* 12 slices of cheddar cheese, or your favorite cheese

Instructions

1. Preheat the oven at 325 degrees F (165 degree Celsius). Generously oil a 9x13-inch pan.

2. Then mix the eggs, sugar, salt, and pepper.

3. Into the greased pan, pour the egg mixture and bake for 18-22 minutes, or only until the center is set. Don't get over-cooked.

4. Remove from the oven and allow to cool into 12 squares before cutting. 4. Top each English muffin with half of the egg, the cheese, the beef, and the muffin with the other ½. If you eat right now, heat the sandwiches for about 5 minutes at 350 degrees or before the cheese melts.

To Freeze:

1. Wrap each sandwich separately in tinfoil, wax paper, or parchment paper and put them in a resealable freezer-safe container. Freeze for a period of up to 1 month.

To Reheat:

1. Thaw overnight in the oven for best results. Cut the paper and wrap a paper towel around the sandwich. Microwave for 40 seconds-Defrost for 1 minute (or 50 percent power). Flip the sandwich over and microwave on high power for 10-30 seconds, until it has warmed through.

2. You can also reheat the sandwiches for around 10-15 minutes in the oven at 350 degrees or in the toaster oven.

Almond Coconut Mocha Protein Smoothie

(Ready in 10 Minutes, Serve 4, Difficulty: Easy)

Nutrition per Serving:

Calories 242.4, Protein 4 g, Carbohydrates 49 g, Fat 36.5 g, Cholesterol mg, Sodium 86.5mg.

Ingredients:

* 1/2 cup of unsweetened vanilla almond milk
* 1/2 cup up cold coffee
* 1 teaspoon of coconut extract
* 1 cup of ice
* 2 scoops of non-dairy/vegan vanilla protein powder (or your favorite brand)
* 1 teaspoon of instant coffee granules
* 2 tablespoon of cocoa powder
* 1/2 cup of shredded sweetened coconut
* 2 tablespoons of sugar
* Whipped cream for garnish (optional, of course)

Instructions:

1. Mix in the mixer and pulse until flat, with all ingredients. Serve.

Cranberry Apple Gelatin Mold

(Ready in 8 Hours 20 Minutes, Serve 12, Difficulty: Normal)

Nutrition per Serving:

Calories 180, Protein 3.4 g, Carbohydrates 36.7 g, Fat 3.3 g, Cholesterol 0.3mg, Sodium 121.7mg.

Ingredients:

* 1(16 ounces) can of whole cranberry sauce
* 1 cup of water
* 2(3 ounces) packages of raspberry-flavored Jell-O® Mix

- ¼ teaspoon of salt
- 2 apples, cored and diced with peel
- 2 oranges, peeled, sectioned, and chopped
- ½ cup of chopped walnuts
- 1 cup of lemon yogurt

Instructions:

1. Combine the cranberry sauce and water in a saucepan over medium heat. Heat the sauce until it melts. Stir gelatin until it dissolves. Remove from the heat. Apples, grapes, walnuts, and yogurt are blended in.

2. Pour the mixture into a fancy mold of gelatin or a nice bowl, and cool overnight. Dip briefly in hot water to serve, then invert onto a baking bowl.

5-Minute Protein Peanut Butter Energy Bites

(Ready in 5 Minutes, Serve 10, Difficulty: Easy)
Nutrition per Serving:

Calories: 150kcal, Fat: 8.8 g, Saturated Fat: 1.2 g, Carbohydrates: 14 g, Fiber: 3.2 g, Sugar: 7.7 g, Protein: 6.6 g.

Ingredients:

- ½ cup of natural drippy peanut butter (or sub almond butter)
- ¼ cup of honey (or date syrup or coconut syrup)
- 1 teaspoon of vanilla extract
- 1/3 cup of protein powder of choice*
- 1/3 cup of flaxseed meal
- ½ cup of rolled oats (gluten-free, if desired)
- 1/2 teaspoon of cinnamon
- 1 tablespoon of chia seeds
- 1 tablespoon of mini chocolate chips (vegan, if desired)
- ¼ cup of unsweetened shredded coconut (Optional)

Instructions:

1. Add the peanut butter, sugar, vanilla, protein powder, flax meal, and rice, cinnamon, and chia seeds to the food processor bowl. Until well paired, pulse together. Add the chocolate chips (and if using the coconut) and pump a few more times. Place a medium cookie scoop or your hands in an airtight jar to take the dough and roll it into ten balls.

2. To make without a food processor: add a medium bowl of wet ingredients and combine them. Put in the dried ingredients and blend until well mixed. Usually, I need to use my hands to mix the dough and work with it. You should be able to shape balls and stick them together at this stage. Since all peanut butter/nut butter consistencies are different, you may need to add more nut butter or sweetener to make the balls hold together, depending on what protein powder you use.

3. Store for up to 1 week in the fridge, or up to 2 months in the freezer. Enjoy!

Peanut Butter and Jelly Protein Pancakes

(Ready in 10 Minutes, Serve 2, Difficulty: Easy)
Nutrition per Serving:

Calories 303, Protein 23 g, Carbohydrates 29 g, Net Carbs 25 g, Fat 11 g, Fiber 4 g, Sodium 620mg, Cholesterol 5mg.

Ingredients:

For Pancakes

- 1 ½ scoop (45 g) of Peanut Butter Cookie Vegan Protein powder* (such as MacroChef®)
- 2 tablespoons (14 g) of coconut flour
- 6 tablespoons (96 g) of egg whites (or 2 egg whites)
- ½ cup (120ml) of unsweetened almond milk (or preferred milk)
- ½ teaspoon of baking powder
- Sweetener, to taste
- 1 pinch of salt

For PB Sauce:

- 2 tablespoons (16 g) of peanut flour
- 2 tablespoons (12 g) of Peanut Butter Cookie Vegan Protein Powder
- ¼ cup milk or water (enough to make it a smooth sauce consistency)
- Sweetener, to taste

For Strawberry Compote

- ¼ cup of strawberries
- 1 tablespoon (5 g) of chia seeds
- 2 tablespoons of sugar-free maple syrup

Instructions:

1. Preheat to medium/high heat on the pan or griddle. All the pancake ingredients are added to a bowl. Mix softly until it forms a smooth batter.

2. Spray pan with a cooking pan. To make 4 medium-sized pancakes, spoon the batter into the pan. Cook on each side for around 3 minutes or until golden brown.

3. When frying pancakes, mix the strawberry compote so that it can sit and thicken. Like a jam, the chia seeds can suck up moisture to make it thick.

4. In a separate bowl, combine the peanut butter sauce ingredients. Stack and drizzle the fried pancakes with strawberry compote and peanut butter sauce. Enjoy!

Banana Bites

(Ready in 60 Minutes, Serve 2, Difficulty: Normal)

Nutrition per Serving:

Calories: 76, Protein: 2.5 g, Carbohydrates: 23.6 g, Fat: 1.6 g, Fiber: 2.7 g.

Ingredients:

- 5 bananas
- 2ounces of vanilla Greek yogurt
- 1 tablespoon of all-natural peanut butter

Instructions:

1. Cover the waxed paper on a baking sheet.

2. Across each banana slice, spoon a thin layer of peanut butter on top. Into the banana, put a toothpick into the peanut butter sheet. On the prepared baking sheet, put banana bites; freeze for 30 minutes to overnight.

4. Melt chocolate and shorten it over simmering water at the top of a double boiler, stirring regularly and scraping down the sides with a rubber spatula to resist scorching.

5. Cover with waxed paper on another baking sheet.

6. Remove 2-4 banana bites from the freezer at a time; coat each bite with chocolate mixture. Place coated banana bites on the second baking sheet; sprinkle each with toffee bits. Repeat until all the bites are coated. Return banana bites to freezer until set, at least 1 hour. Allow bites to sit at room temperature for about 15 minutes before serving.

Chapter 10: 30 Days Meal Plan

In this chapter, we are going to give you a 30-day meal plan for a healthy lifestyle.

Day 1

Breakfast: 1 serving Avocado-Egg Toast

Afternoon Snack: 1 medium orange

Lunch: 1 serving Butternut Squash Soup with Avocado & Chickpeas

Evening Snack: 1 medium kiwi

Dinner: 1 serving Citrus Poached Salmon with Asparagus with 3/4 cup Cauliflower Rice.

Day 2

Breakfast: 1 serving Blueberry-Banana Overnight Oats

Afternoon Snack: 1 serving Apple Cider Vinegar Tonic

Lunch: 1 1/2 cups of Slow-Cooker Vegetable Soup with 1 slice Everything Bagel Avocado Toast

Evening Snack: 1/2 cup of edamame (in pods) sprinkled with a pinch of coarse sea salt

Dinner: 1 serving Vegan Coconut Chickpea Curry

Meal-Prep Tip: Prepare the Blueberry-Banana Overnight Oats, so it's ready to grab-and-go in the morning of Day 3.

Day 3

Breakfast: 1 1/2 cup of Blueberry-Banana Overnight Oats

Afternoon Snack: 1 medium orange

Lunch: 1 1/2 cup of Slow-Cooker Vegetable Soup with 1 slice Everything Bagel Avocado Toast

Evening Snack: 2 medium kiwis

Dinner: 1 serving Zucchini Noodles with Pesto & Chicken.

Day 4

Breakfast: 1 slice of Peanut Butter-Banana Cinnamon Toast

Afternoon Snack: 1 cup Apple Cider Vinegar Tonic with 1 cup of blueberries

Lunch: 1 serving Green Salad with Edamame & Beets

Evening Snack: 1 medium orange

Dinner: 1 serving Spicy Jerk Shrimp with 1/2 cup of Easy Brown Rice

Meal-Prep Tip: Freeze any leftover Easy Brown Rice in individual 1/2-cup of servings.

Day 5

Breakfast: 1 slice Peanut Butter-Banana Cinnamon Toast

Afternoon Snack: 1 kiwi

Lunch: 1 1/2 cups of Slow-Cooker Vegetable Soup with 3 Tbsp. hummus and 6 seeded crackers

Evening Snack: 1 kiwi

Dinner: 1 serving Taco Spaghetti Squash Boats.

Day 6

Breakfast: 1 cup of raspberries topped with 1 cup of non-Fat Greek yogurt, 1 tablespoon of Sliced almonds & 1 tsp. honey.

Afternoon Snack: 1 cup of Apple Cider Vinegar Tonic

Lunch: 1 serving Veggie & Hummus Sandwich

Evening Snack: 1/2 cup of edamame (in pods) sprinkled with a pinch of coarse sea salt

Dinner: 1 serving Sheet-Pan Chicken & Vegetables with Romesco Sauce.

Day 7

Breakfast: 1 serving Avocado-Egg Toast

Afternoon Snack: 3/4 cup of raspberries topped with 1/2 cup of non-Fat Greek yogurt & 1 tsp. honey

Lunch: 1 serving Green Salad with Edamame & Beets

Evening Snack: 1 medium orange

Dinner: 1 serving Salmon Tacos with Pineapple Salsa with Broiled Mango to enjoy after dinner.

Day 8

Breakfast: 2 Muffin-Tin Quiches with Smoked Cheddar & Potato and 1 cup Herbal Chamomile Health Tonic

Afternoon Snack: 1 cup of blueberries

Lunch: 1 serving Curried Chicken Apple Wraps with 1 medium pear

Evening Snack: 1 cup of raspberries topped with 1/2 cup of non-Fat plain Greek yogurt

Dinner: 1 1/2 cup of Slow-Cooker Curried Butternut Squash Soup and 1 serving Kale Salad with Beets & Wild Rice

Meal-Prep Tips: Refrigerate the other 3 servings of the Herbal Chamomile Health Tonic to have on days 9, 10, and 11.

Refrigerate one 1-cup serving and one 1 ½-cup serving of the Slow-Cooker Curried Butternut

Squash Soup to have for lunch on Days 9 and 11. Save 1 serving (2 ½ cups) of Kale Salad with Beets & Wild Rice to have lunch on Day 9. Store in leak-proof, air-tight containers.

Day 9

Breakfast: 1 cup raspberries topped with 1 cup of non-Fat Greek yogurt, 1 tablespoon of. Sliced almonds & 1 teaspoon of honey

Afternoon Snack: 1 cup of Herbal Chamomile Health Tonic and 1 cup of blueberries

Lunch: 1 cup Slow-Cooker Curried Butternut Squash Soup and 2 ½ cups Kale Salad with Beets & Wild Rice

Evening Snack: 1/2 cup of edamame (in pods) sprinkled with a pinch of coarse sea salt

Dinner: 1 serving Greek Roasted Fish with Vegetables.

Day 10

Breakfast: 2 Muffin-Tin Quiches with Smoked Cheddar & Potato and 1 medium orange

Afternoon Snack: 1 cup of Herbal Chamomile Health Tonic

Lunch: 1 serving Curried Chicken Apple Wraps with 1 medium pear

Evening Snack: 1 cup of raspberries topped with ½ cup of non-Fat plain Greek yogurt

Dinner: 1 serving Garlic-Lime Pork with Faro & Spinach with 1 cup of Tangy Broccoli with Almonds.

Day 11

Breakfast: 2 Muffin-Tin Quiches with Smoked Cheddar & Potato with 1 medium orange

Afternoon Snack: ½ cup of blueberries

Lunch: 1 1/2 cups Slow-Cooker Curried Butternut Squash Soup with 3 tablespoons of hummus and 5 seeded crackers

Evening Snack: 1 cup Herbal Chamomile Health Tonic

Dinner: 1 serving Crispy Oven-Fried Fish Tacos.

Day 12

Breakfast: 1 cup of raspberries topped with 1 cup non-fat Greek yogurt, 1 tablespoon of Sliced almonds & 1 teaspoon of honey

Afternoon Snack: 2 medium plums with 1 cup of green tea

Lunch: 1 serving No-Cook Black Bean Salad

Evening Snack: 1 medium apple

Dinner: 2 cups of Slow-Cooker Pasta e Fagioli Soup

Meal-Prep Tip: Save 2 cups of the No-Cook Black Bean Salad to have for lunch on Day 13. Refrigerate dressing separately and add just before serving.

Day 13

Breakfast: 2 Muffin-Tin Quiches with Smoked Cheddar & Potato and 1 medium orange

Afternoon Snack: 1 plum and 1 cup of green tea

Lunch: 2 cups No-Cook Black Bean Salad

Evening Snack: 3/4 cup of raspberries topped with 3 tablespoons of Non-Fat Greek yogurt and 1 tablespoon of slivered almonds

Dinner: 2 cups of Slow-Cooker Pasta e Fagioli Soup.

Day 14

Breakfast: 2 Blueberry-Pecan Pancakes topped with 2 tablespoons of Blueberries, and 2 tablespoons of Non-Fat Greek yogurt mixed with 1 teaspoon of maple syrup

Afternoon Snack: 1 cup green tea

Lunch: 1 serving Whole-Wheat Veggie Wrap

Evening Snack: 1/2 cup of edamame (in pods) sprinkled with a pinch of coarse sea salt

Dinner: 2 servings (5 cups) Indian-Spiced Cauliflower & Chickpea Salad

Meal-Prep Tip: Freeze leftover Blueberry-Pecan Pancakes to have for breakfast on Days 22 and 29.

Day 15

Breakfast: 1 serving Avocado-Egg Toast

Afternoon Snack: 1 cup of Apple Cider Vinegar Tonic with 1 plum

Lunch: 1 serving Veggie & Hummus Sandwich

Evening Snack: 1 cup of raspberries topped with 1/4 cup of non-Fat Greek yogurt & 1 teaspoon of honey

Dinner: 1 serving Hawaiian Pork with 1 cup of steamed broccoli tossed in 1 teaspoon each olive oil & lime juice and seasoned with a pinch each salt and pepper (435 calories)

Meal-Prep Tip: Prepare the Blueberry-Banana Overnight Oats, so it's ready to grab-and-go in the morning of Day 16.

Day 16

Breakfast: 1 1/2 cup of Blueberry-Banana Overnight Oats

Afternoon Snack: 1 cup of green tea

Lunch: 1 serving Spicy Slaw Bowls with Shrimp & Edamame

Evening Snack: 1/2 cup of diced cucumber and 1/4 cup of shelled edamame tossed in 1 teaspoon of lime juice and a pinch each of salt and pepper

Dinner: 1 serving Chickpea Curry with 1/2 cup of Easy Brown Rice and 1 serving Turmeric-Roasted Cauliflower

Meal-Prep Tip: Save any leftover Easy Brown Rice to use for dinner on later days. You could also plan to make a double batch and freeze it in individual portions to save time down the road.

Prepare the Blueberry-Banana Overnight Oats, so it's ready to grab-and-go in the morning of Day 17.

Day 17

Breakfast: 1 serving Blueberry-Banana Overnight Oats

Afternoon Snack: 1 cup of Apple Cider Vinegar Tonic

Lunch: 1 serving Spicy Slaw Bowls with Shrimp & Edamame

Evening Snack: 3/4 cup of raspberries

Dinner: 1 serving Spaghetti Squash & Chicken with Avocado Pesto.

Day 18

Breakfast: 1 slice Peanut Butter-Banana Cinnamon Toast

Afternoon Snack: 2 plums

Lunch: 1 serving Spicy Slaw Bowls with Shrimp & Edamame

Evening Snack: 1 cup of raspberries and 1 cup green tea

Dinner: 1 serving Roasted Salmon with Smoky Chickpeas & Greens.

Day 19

Breakfast: 1 slice Peanut Butter-Banana Cinnamon Toast

Afternoon Snack: 1 cup of green tea

Lunch: 1 serving Spicy Slaw Bowls with Shrimp & Edamame

Evening Snack: 1 medium orange

Dinner: 1 serving Butternut Squash Soup with Avocado & Chickpeas and 1 slice whole-wheat toast drizzled with 1 tsp. olive oil and seasoned with a pinch each of salt and pepper

Meal-Prep Tip: Transfer the 2 individual servings of the Slow-Cooker Vegetable Soup from the freezer to the refrigerator to defrost.

Day 20

Breakfast: 1 cup of raspberries topped with 1 cup of non-fat Greek yogurt, 1 tablespoon of Sliced almonds & 1 tsp. honey

Afternoon Snack: 1 medium orange and 1 cup of Apple Cider Vinegar Tonic

Lunch: 1 1/2 cup of Slow-Cooker Vegetable Soup with 1 slice Everything Bagel Avocado Toast

Evening Snack: ½ cup of diced cucumber and ¼ cup of shelled edamame tossed in 1 teaspoon of lime juice and a pinch each of salt and pepper

Dinner: 1 serving Jerk Chicken & Pineapple Slaw and 1 cup of Easy Brown Rice.

Day 21

Breakfast: 1 serving Avocado-Egg Toast

Afternoon Snack: 1 cup of raspberries topped with 2 tablespoons of non-fat Greek yogurt

Lunch: 1 ½ cups Slow-Cooker Vegetable Soup with ¼ cup of hummus and 6 seeded crackers

Evening Snack: ¼ cup of diced cucumber and ¼ cup of shelled edamame tossed in 1 teaspoon of lime juice and a pinch each of salt and pepper

Dinner: 1 serving Stetson Chopped Salad and ½ slice of whole-wheat toast drizzled with 1 teaspoon of olive oil and seasoned with a pinch each of salt and pepper

Meal-Prep Tip: Save 1 serving of the Stetson Chopped Salad to have for lunch on Day 22.

Day 22

Breakfast: 2 Blueberry-Pecan Pancakes topped with 2 tablespoons of non-fat Greek yogurt mixed with 1 teaspoon of maple syrup

Afternoon Snack: 1 1/4 cup of raspberries

Lunch: 1 serving Stetson Chopped Salad

Evening Snack: 1/3 cup of diced cucumber and 1/3 cup of shelled edamame tossed in 1 teaspoon of lime juice and a pinch each of salt and peppers.

Dinner: 1 serving Asian Beef Noodle Bowl and 1 kiwi

Meal-Prep Tip: Save 1 serving of the Asian Beef Noodle Bowl to have for lunch on Day 23.

Day 23

Breakfast: 2 Muffin-Tin Quiches with Smoked Cheddar & Potato and 1 medium orange

Afternoon Snack: 1 cup of raspberries

Lunch: 1 serving Asian Beef Noodle Bowl

Evening Snack: 1 cup of Herbal Chamomile Health Tonic with 2 kiwis

Dinner: 1 serving Eggs in Tomato Sauce with Chickpeas & Spinach with 1/2 (6-inch) whole-wheat pita bread

Meal-Prep Tip: Refrigerate the 3 remaining servings of the Herbal Chamomile Health Tonic to have on Days 24, 25, and 26.

Day 24

Breakfast: 2 Muffin-Tin Quiches with Smoked Cheddar & Potato and 1 cup of Herbal Chamomile Health Tonic

Afternoon Snack: 1 medium orange

Lunch: 1 serving Veggie & Hummus Sandwich

Evening Snack: ½ cup of diced cucumber and ½ cup of shelled edamame tossed in 1 teaspoon of lime juice and a pinch each of salt and pepper

Dinner: 1 serving (3 patties) Falafel with 2 cups of mixed greens, ½ cup of sliced cucumber and topped with 2 tablespoons of Tahini Sauce with Lemon & Garlic

Meal-Prep Tip: Refrigerate 2 Falafel patties to have for lunch on Day 25.

Day 25

Breakfast: 2 Muffin-Tin Quiches with Smoked Cheddar & Potato and 1 cup of Herbal Chamomile Health Tonic

Afternoon Snack: 1 medium orange

Lunch: ½ (6-inch) whole-wheat pita bread stuffed with 2 Falafel patties, 1 cup of mixed greens, ¼ cup of sliced cucumber, and 1 tablespoon of Tahini Sauce with Lemon & Garlic

Evening Snack: 1 cup of raspberries topped with ¼ cup of non-fat Greek yogurt & 1 teaspoon of honey

Dinner: 1 serving Roasted Chicken & Winter Squash over Mixed Greens.

Meal-Prep Tips: Plan to use any leftover chicken from tonight's dinner or cook extra so you have enough for the Curried Chicken Apple Wraps on Days 26 & 27 (you'll need 1 cup of shredded chicken Total).

Prep the Blueberry-Banana Overnight Oats, so it's ready to grab-and-go in the morning of Day 26.

Day 26

Breakfast: 1 ½ cup of Blueberry-Banana Overnight Oats

Afternoon Snack: 1 cup of Herbal Chamomile Health Tonic

Lunch: 1 serving Curried Chicken Apple Wraps with 1 medium pear

Evening Snack: 2 kiwis

Dinner: 1 serving Ginger Roasted Salmon & Broccoli and ½ cup of Cauliflower Rice.

Day 27

Breakfast: 2 Muffin-Tin Quiches with Smoked Cheddar & Potato and 1 medium orange

Afternoon Snack: ½ cup of blueberries and 1 cup of green tea

Lunch: 1 serving Curried Chicken Apple Wraps with 1 medium pear

Evening Snack: 2 tablespoons of hummus and ½ medium bell pepper, sliced

Dinner: 2 cups of White Turkey Chili

Meal-Prep Tip: Refrigerate two (1 ½-cup) servings of the White Turkey Chili to have for lunch on Days 28 and 29.

Day 28

Breakfast: 2 Muffin-Tin Quiches with Smoked Cheddar & Potato

Afternoon Snack: 1 cup of raspberries and 1 cup of green tea

Lunch: 1 ½ cups of White Turkey Chili

Evening Snack: 2 tablespoons of hummus and 1/2 medium bell pepper, sliced

Dinner: 1 serving Easy Kale Cheese with ½ cup of Easy Brown Rice.

Day 29

Breakfast: 2 Blueberry-Pecan Pancakes topped with 3 tablespoons of Blueberries, and 2 tablespoons of non-fat Greek yogurt mixed with 1 teaspoon of maple syrup

Afternoon Snack: 1 cup of raspberries and 1 cup of green tea

Lunch: 1 ½ cup of White Turkey Chili

Evening Snack: 1 medium orange

Dinner: 1 serving Cod with Tomato Cream Sauce with ½ cup of Easy Brown Rice and 2 cups of mixed greens dressed with 2 teaspoons of each olive oil and balsamic vinegar.

Day 30

Breakfast: 2 Muffin-Tin Quiches with Smoked Cheddar & Potato and 1 medium orange

Afternoon Snack: 3/4 cup of blueberries and 1 cup of green tea

Lunch: 2 cups of No-Cook Black Bean Salad

Evening Snack: 1/3 cup of diced cucumber and 1/3 cup of shelled edamame tossed in 1 teaspoon of lime juice and a pinch each of salt and pepper

Dinner: 1 serving Mexican Stuffed Acorn Squash with 3/4 cup Mexican Cauliflower Rice.

Conclusion

Lean & Green may be healthy for your heart, but no more than many other diets. Lean & Green states that its meals are lower in fat and cholesterol, and all contain ample high-quality soy protein to satisfy the Heart Health Claim of the Food and Drug Administration. You'll collaborate with Lean & Green coaches while on a diet and will become part of a group to help support your progress. When you hit your target weight, it is theoretically easier to move from the diet, and new ones replace your old habits.

"Lean & Green" meals, and one nutritious snack, such as a serving of fruit or sweet potato, for people looking for a much more versatile and higher-calorie diet. Lean & Green advises 30 minutes most days with a low-intensity workout that you like and can easily incorporate, such as walking. But don't go crazy, or you're going to run out of energy.